Politics, Policy, and Organizations

Politics, Policy, and Organizations

Frontiers in the Scientific Study of Bureaucracy

Edited by George A. Krause & Kenneth J. Meier

The University of Michigan Press
Ann Arbor

First paperback edition 2005
Copyright © by the University of Michigan 2003
All rights reserved
Published in the United States of America by
The University of Michigan Press
Manufactured in the United States of America
∞ Printed on acid-free paper

2008   2007   2006   2005   5   4   3   2

A CIP catalog record for this book is available from the British Library.

Library of Congress Cataloging-in-Publication Data

Politics, policy, and organizations : frontiers in the scientific study of bureaucracy /
edited by George A. Krause & Kenneth J. Meier.
p.   cm.
Original scholarly essays based on a workshop, The Scientific Study of Bureaucracy,
held at the fifth Public Management Conference, Texas A&M University, Dec. 3–4, 1999.
Includes bibliographical references and index.
ISBN 0-472-11317-8 (cloth : alk. paper)
1. Bureaucracy.   2. Public administration.   I. Krause, George A., 1965–
II. Meier, Kenneth J., 1950–

HD38.4.P65   2003
351—dc21   2003044772

ISBN 0-472-03114-7 (pbk. : alk. paper)

Contents

Preface   vii

The Scientific Study of Bureaucracy: An Overview
Kenneth J. Meier and George A. Krause   1

Part 1. Theory

Why Do Bureaucrats Delay? Lessons from a Stochastic
Optimal Stopping Model of Agency Timing, with
Applications to the FDA
Daniel P. Carpenter   23

Agency Risk Propensities Involving the Demand for
Bureaucratic Discretion
George A. Krause   41

Veto Points, Policy Preferences, and Bureaucratic
Autonomy in Democratic Systems
Thomas H. Hammond   73

The Benefits of Agency Policy-making:
Perspectives from Positive Theory
David B. Spence   104

Part 2. Methodological Technology

Donut Shops, Speed Traps, and Paperwork:
Supervision and the Allocation of Time to
Bureaucratic Tasks
John Brehm, Scott Gates, and Brad Gomez   133

Adapting Agencies: Competition, Imitation, and
Punishment in the Design of Bureaucratic Performance
  Andrew B. Whitford   160

Part 3. Empirical Studies

Consensual Rule Making and the Time It Takes to
Develop Rules
  Steven J. Balla and John R. Wright   187

Why It Matters Whether State Bureaucrats as Opposed to
Federal Bureaucrats Administer Federal Programs
  Lael R. Keiser   207

Structural Choice and Political Control of Bureaucracy:
Updating Federal Credit Programs
  Kevin Corder   233

Administrative Structure and Social Democratic Results:
The Case of Education
  Kevin B. Smith   259

Bureaucratic Discretion and Regulatory Success
without Enforcement
  Michael J. Licari   276

Conclusion: An Agenda for the Scientific Study
of Bureaucracy
  Kenneth J. Meier and George A. Krause   292

References   309

Contributors   341

Author Index   343

Subject Index   349

Preface

The genesis for this volume came from the organized workshop The Scientific Study of Bureaucracy held at the Fifth Public Management Conference, Texas A&M University, College Station, Texas, December 3–4, 1999. The contents of this volume represent original scholarly essays that enhance our understanding of how bureaucracies function as both organizational entities and also within a larger political system. The common denominator among these essays is a central interest in the functioning of public bureaucracies. This is distinct from research on new institutionalism in political science, whose primary emphasis is on democratic institutions (i.e., chief executive, legislature, and judiciary) and public administration's largely applied and prescriptive nature, which is oriented toward practitioners.

Besides this primary emphasis on bureaucratic organizations from a basic social scientific perspective, the essays are rather diverse in terms of the substantive questions and methodological approaches that are brought to bear by the volume's contributors. Topics ranging from bureaucratic decision making to administrative structure and institutional arrangements are covered by the essays contained in this volume. Methodological tools ranging from formal theory/rational choice deductive analyses to computational modeling and econometric testing of theoretical hypotheses are utilized by the contributors to analyze how public bureaucracies operate in a variety of tasks and settings. The purpose of this breadth is to provide generalizable insights into some of the most important issues confronting students of public bureaucracy within both political science and public administration. At the same time, however, the research questions posed by the contributors are not only timely but also have their roots in classic scholarship in public administration within political science.

First and foremost, we wish to thank the volume's contributors for providing us with some of their finest original research. We are also extremely grateful to Jeremy Shine and his colleagues at the University of Michigan Press, who have been very supportive of this project and have advocated the publishing of social scientific books and monographs on various political science topics for more than a decade. Professor Krause is ever grateful to his best friend and spouse—LeeAnne Krause—for her patience and support during the process of putting this edited volume together. Professor Meier would also like to thank LeeAnne Krause because she keeps George out of trouble most of the time. Finally, we would like to thank the numerous scholars studying public bureaucracy (both past and present) who have played a large role in developing the contours as to how we think about public bureaucracy. Without their valuable insights, this volume would never have come to fruition.

The Scientific Study of Bureaucracy: An Overview

Kenneth J. Meier and George A. Krause

The Foundations of the Scientific Study of Public Bureaucracy

The study of bureaucracy is the analysis of how administrative agencies function as organizations within a governmental system. The study includes interinstitutional relationships with democratic institutions such as chief executives, legislatures, or the judiciary as well as intrainstitutional activities concerned with explaining the organizational structure and behavior of administrative agencies. Scientific inquiry pertains to the development of systematic, generalizable explanations and subsequent empirical tests of the "what, how, and why" of bureaucratic agencies. This book contains essays that emphasize theory building and empirical testing of theories, theories of interest to students of public administration within political science. Our primary concern is how public bureaucracies operate in a democracy.

The study of bureaucracy within political science has an intellectual history that harkens back over a century. German sociologist Max Weber's (1947) notion that maintaining a "rational-legal authority" was the appropriate way to conduct the business of governance was both a normative and an empirical theory. He advocated the basis for *general* explanations regarding how bureaucratic institutions should be designed, including the need for a division of labor, career personnel with specialized training and expertise, hierarchical formal organizational structures that do not duplicate other administrative units, and explicit rules and procedures to ensure clear lines of authority and accountability within the organization. This work has had a profound impact on our theoretical understanding of how superior-subordinate relationships within such organizations actually play out (e.g., Barnard 1938; Brehm and Gates 1997; Crozier 1964; Cyert and March 1963; Downs 1967; March and Simon 1958; Miller 1992; Simon 1947; Tullock 1965).

Similarly, Woodrow Wilson's (1887) argument for an administrative apparatus that is devoid of politics and meddling arose from a normative concern of the era that American bureaucracy served as a bastion for political patronage (Nelson 1982; Skowronek 1982). Wilson's call for an independent administrative state not beholden to the particularistic interests of elected officials reflects issues of theoretical interest in understanding the role and functioning of bureaucracy within our American democracy that range from whether the bureaucracy responds to political control from electoral institutions (e.g., Moe 1982, 1985; Weingast and Moran 1983; Wood and Waterman 1994) to the importance of professional expertise in policy administration (Eisner 1991; Khademian 1992; Mosher 1968).

Goodnow, Taylor, and Gulick: The Progressive Era

The early American study of bureaucracy finds its roots in the work of Goodnow, Gulick, and Taylor rather than that of Weber and Wilson. The influence of both Weber and Wilson, substantial as it was, came late to scholars of administration. Weber was not translated into English until 1946 (Weber 1946, 1947) and therefore his work was relatively inaccessible. Similarly, Wilson's original essay disappeared from the literature until it was republished in 1941 (Van Riper 1983).

Goodnow (1900) also proposed a politics-administration dichotomy; he considered these to be two different functions but recognized that in practice politics was rarely separate from administration. This distinction became part of the progressive philosophy in public service training and was incorporated in the field's first textbook (White 1926). The functional division allowed progress on two dimensions. On the administrative side, efforts were made to study implementation and the processes of bureaucracy in a scientific manner. On the political side, the focus was on designing governmental institutions, that is, creating the institutions that would formulate, adopt, and implement policy. The latter was inherently prescriptive. This effort (known as the study of the separation of powers) continued to occupy the time of public administration scholars until the 1950s (Waldo 1984, chap. 7; Appleby 1949).[1]

On the administrative side, efforts were made to discover the principles of administration, the one best way to design a work process or structure an organization. Work process design is most closely associated with the work of Fredrick W. Taylor (1919), who used experiments to determine how jobs should be structured. Taylor advocated a division of tasks with management charged with designing the optimal work processes and individual workers charged with responding based on the incentives offered for production. Taylor's controversial motivation theory, the reliance on piecework and pure economic incentives, drew attention away from his scientific, albeit atheoretical, approach and generated skepticism (including a congressional investigation) about the contribution of Taylor (see Henry 1995, 55–56).

Taylor's experimental approach also generated the first empirical challenge to this type of inquiry with Western Electric's Hawthorne experiments. Those experiments demonstrated how human factors and relationships subverted material incentives (see Roethlisberger and Dickson 1939). Although scholars of public administration paid little attention to this work after the Hawthorne experiments, the fields of industrial engineering and operations research continue within the tradition of Taylor and the Hawthorne experiments.

A second stream of work went beyond production processes to examine how to structure organizations such as specialization, span of control, unity of command, and similar factors (Gulick and Urwick 1937; Fayole 1949). The method of analysis was observation rather than systematic data collection and analysis (for an early attempt at formal theory, see Stene 1940). Despite an impressive set of principles, Gulick (1937) himself lamented the lack of research supporting the principles and sketched out a research design to determine how one of them, span of control, could be systematically verified. That research agenda remained untouched, however. Simon's (1947) devastating critique of the "proverbs of administration" effectively ended this approach to the science of administration within public administration.[2]

The work of Progressive Era scholars arguing for a scientific approach to administration gave way to the behavioral revolution in the study of organizations. The intellectual roots of this revolution can be traced to Barnard's (1938) *The Functions of the Executive,* in which issues of authority relating to superior-subordinate relationships were analyzed. Central to Barnard's argument are joint issues: (1) what motivates bureaucrats to behave as they do? and (2) why are they willing to sacrifice their individual goals and belong to an organization? This line of inquiry sought to develop generalizable theoretical principles to facilitate our understanding of how administrative agencies make decisions rather than emphasizing normative descriptions as to how administrative agencies should function as entities in their own right and within a larger governmental system.

Simon's (1947) classic *Administrative Behavior* focused on individuals as the key unit of analysis in order to understand how organizations perform. The two major cornerstones of this work were an emphasis on (1) providing a theory of administration centered on efficiency and (2) analyzing the nature of information processing by bureaucratic organizations by asserting that individuals' cognitive limitations did not allow for rational-comprehensive decision making. The latter subject is developed in March and Simon's (1958) *Organizations,* in which the rational-comprehensive method is shown to be empirically unrealistic and theoretically ungrounded. This stream of work also emphasized how routines (standard operating procedures [SOPs]) could be employed to overcome uncertainty and individual cognitive limitations and allow individuals in organizations to behave in a more efficient manner (Cyert and March 1963). Within this intellectual stream, Cyert and March attack the foundations of the neoclassical theory of the firm by maintaining that organizations are not optimizers in the traditional sense of maximizing profits. Instead, organizations behave inefficiently in a strict microeconomic sense since they will accrue slack resources.

Constitutional Perspectives

As the administrative science side of public administration focused on management and organizational questions, a parallel movement grappled with the issue of how to fit bureaucracy into the Constitution. The key challenge was reconciling the policy-making discretion of nonelected bureaucrats with the imperatives of democracy. Scholars were well aware of bureaucracy's potential to subvert democratic ends; Herring's (1936) work on bureaucratic power documented the ability of bureaucracy to engage in politics and shape the direction of public policy.

This debate was effectively framed by an exchange between Carl Friedrich and Herman Finer. Friedrich (1940) challenged the notion that elected officials could control the bureaucracy. Foreshadowing future principal-agent concerns about information asymmetry, Friedrich focused on the influx of scientists in government and how the possession of technical knowledge made political control difficult. In such a situation, the potential for a bureaucrat to dress his or her policy preferences in the guise of expertise was high. Friedrich's solution was a fellowship of science whereby competing sets of scientists would serve as a check on each other and thus provide multiple viewpoints for politicians.

Finer (1941) responded critically to this proposal, arguing that democracy was the preeminent value, not one on a par with technical competence. Finer contended that democratic institutions had sufficient methods with which to control bureaucracy and therefore abrogating their political responsibility was not necessary. The Friedrich-Finer debate established two competing camps on the question of bureaucracy and democracy—the proponents of overhead democracy or control by political institutions (Finer 1941; see also Hyneman 1950; Key 1959; Redford 1969; and Wood and Waterman 1994)—and the proponents of the inner check or competition, ethics, participation, and so on (Friedrich 1940; see also Long 1952; Dahl 1970; Appleby 1952; and Frederickson 1997).

Significant for the development of public administration was the publication of Waldo's (1946, 1984) *Administrative State*. Waldo considered himself a normative theorist and generally eschewed empirical questions for normative ones. His approach provided a place for scholars not interested in the behavioral revolution but still concerned about the relationship between bureaucracy and democratic institutions.

Research questions in this area were not only concerned with how the bureaucracy fit into constitutional governance (e.g., Rohr 1986) but also with alternative views of the constitutional chain of command. The separation of powers in the United States made the establishment of clear lines of bureaucratic authority difficult (Appleby 1949), a topic later known as the multiple principals problem. Although most scholars accepted the notion of presidential hierarchy in terms of the bureaucracy, a sizable group of scholars defended the constitutional preeminence of Congress (Rosenbloom 2000; Hyneman 1950; Key 1959). Accepting a Congress-centered view of the Constitution with regard to bureaucracy has clear implications for how the bureaucracy should relate to other political institutions (see Rosenbloom 2000).

Of the inner check proposals, one, representative bureaucracy, is of particular interest because it developed and tested a systematic body of midrange empirical theory of public bureaucracy. Representative bureaucracy in a nutshell contends that a bureaucracy representative of the general public in demographic terms is likely to produce policies generally in accord with public preferences. The logic of the theory was first set forth by Long (1952), although he made no effort to test it. Critical tests and theoretical reformations came later (Meier and Nigro 1976; Rosenbloom and Featherstonhaugh 1977; Saltzstein 1979). A consistent body of empirical literature now indicates when and under what conditions passive representative (demographic similarity) might lead to active representation (policy congruence) in terms of race, ethnicity, and gender (Selden 1997; Meier 1993b).

Bureaucratic Pathologies and the Public Choice Approach to Administrative Organizations

Public choice approaches to the study of organizations focus on problems of control and responsiveness. Using economic tools of analysis, this brand of research analyzes the pathologies of the administrative state and their implications for organizational performance. Tullock's (1965) work on hierarchical distortion posited the pernicious effects of misinformation that can be channeled both horizontally and, even more critically, vertically through administrative organizations. According to Tullock, agency efforts to combat information flow problems within organizations are essentially futile since "authority leakages" are both inevitable and cumulative.

In his classic treatise *The Bureaucratic Phenomenon,* Crozier (1964) arrived at conclusions similar to Tullock's. Rather than focusing on information flows, Crozier viewed the crux of the problem confronting administrative agencies as being centered on the question, How is power allocated within bureaucratic organizations? Crozier argued that organizations reflect imperfect social compromises that arise in bargaining among individuals and groups. Specifically, the organizational design, structure, and operation are not randomly determined but reflect an equilibrium agreement among actors and stakeholders behaving in a purposeful manner.[3]

Both Tullock and Crozier separately conclude that bureaucratic agencies are sufficiently ossified that they require abolishment. This lack of responsiveness to constituency demands, whether it be from elected officials, citizens, or pressure groups, is attributable to bureaucratic inertia that occurs within the organizational setting. Subsequent work by Niskanen (1971) extended this work on the limitations of administrative governance. Niskanen's central claim is that bureaucracy is preoccupied with resource (budget) maximization and that its monopoly power over the distribution (administration) of the supply of public goods and services made it inefficient and unresponsive to both citizen and politician preferences.[4]

One notable departure from this malignant view of bureaucratic pathologies is Downs's *Inside Bureaucracy* (1967). He argues that individual bureaucrats have different preference structures, thus making effective coordination and policy-making difficult. He extends the behavioral tradition, describing different behaviors exhibited by zealots, advocates, statesmen, conservers, and climbers. The implication of these bureaucratic personality types is that communication channels in bureaucratic organizations will be muddled and will lead to performance distortions. Downs contends that bureaucratic pathologies can be corrected by finding the proper mix of agency personnel types, adopting extraorganizational means such as reorganization, obtaining feedback on its performance from outside sources, or creating overlapping administrative responsibilities to encourage competition and discourage subordinate collusion.[5]

The Modern Advent of the Scientific Study of Bureaucracy

Principal-Agent Theory

At the heart of much of the modern "scholarship" on administrative organizations is the application of the principal-agent model. According to Terry M. Moe,

> The principal-agent model is an analytic expression of the agency relationship, in which one party, the principal, considers entering into a contractual agreement with another, the agent, in the expectations that the agent will subsequently choose actions that produce outcomes desired by the principal. . . . [T]he principal's decision problem is far more involved than simply locating a qualified person—for there is no guarantee that the agent, once hired, will in effect choose to pursue the principal's best interests or to do so efficiently. The agent has his own interests at heart, and is induced to pursue the principal's objective only to the extent that the incentive structure imposed in the contract renders such behavior advantageous. (1984, 756)

Implicit in the notion of a principal-agent relationship for studying the bureaucracy is not only the issue of task delegation by a superordinate (principal) to a subordinate (agent) but also the existence of inherent goal conflict between the principal and agent (e.g., Mitnick 1980; Perrow 1972). This began as a means of investigating issues pertaining to incomplete information and uncertainty in microeconomic decision making (Mitnick 1980; Moe 1984; Jensen and Meckling 1976; Ross 1973). Incomplete information means that principals, who wish to delegate authority to perform tasks on their behalf, have neither full nor accurate information regarding agents' actions. Typically, agents possess specialized knowledge about the particular problem that the principal does not. Hidden information and actions are therefore embedded within these relations (Arrow 1985; Moe 1987, 480–82). Even in those rare instances in which the principal has specialized knowledge equivalent to that of the agent, he or she still experiences informational problems since the responsibility for task execution lies with the agent.

How do principals attempt to rein in the behavior of agents whose preference profiles are not in sync with their own? The dual cornerstones of the principal-agent model are its emphasis on the nature of incentives and the monitoring of behavior employed by the principal (superordinate) to ensure faithful action by an agent (subordinate). The principal, in theory, can structure incentives to get the agent to comply with the principal's wishes. For example, an elected official may provide greater slack resources to an agency that is faithfully executing the former's policy preferences (ex post incentive). He or she may also provide an agency possessing a credible organizational reputation with greater discretion vis-à-vis the rules and procedures issued through enactment legislation. Monitoring of agent behavior is a more intricate task than creating incentive structures, thus making the former more daunting for purposes of ensuring agent compliance. Intensive monitoring of bureaucratic performance initiated by congressional oversight committees akin to "police patrols" is a costly endeavor (McCubbins and Schwartz 1984; Ogul 1976; Scher 1963; but see Aberbach 1990). Similarly, presidents who invest heavily in "activist" monitoring devices, such as detailed budgetary and performance auditing via the Office of Management and Budget (OMB), also incur transaction costs (i.e., costs incurred in carrying out such oversight activity) as well as opportunity costs (i.e., time and resources that could be spent on policy activities that would yield greater marginal net benefits to the administration's policy agenda). The use of active monitoring, therefore, contains the stigma of punishment and generates displeasure among agents who receive close and frequent scrutiny of their task performances (Brehm and Gates 1997, 43).

The use of principal-agent theory in political science has generated conflicting models. Considerable work within this paradigm by scholars suggests that agencies' information asymmetries are sufficiently large to make it difficult for elected officials (principals) to monitor the behavior of administrative agencies (agents) (e.g., Banks and Weingast 1992; Bendor, Taylor, and Van Gaalen 1985, 1987; Niskanen 1971; Woolley 1993). Conversely, a larger body of work adopting the principal-agent perspective views incentive structures and monitoring activity employed by elected officials as being effective in reining in the behavior of administrative agencies (Breton and Wintrobe 1975; McCubbins and Schwartz 1984; McCubbins 1985; McCubbins, Noll, and Weingast 1989; Miller and Moe 1983). Specifically, these works are termed principal-agent models of political control over the bureaucracy since political institutions have various policy and administrative tools at their disposal to ensure bureaucratic compliance to their policy wishes. A voluminous body of empirical literature testing this theory in various manifestations over the past two decades has demonstrated strong support for the principal-agent model of political control over the bureaucracy (e.g., Carpenter 1996; Moe 1982, 1985, 1987; Rothenberg 1994; Scholz and Wei 1986; Scholz, Twombly, and Headrick 1991; Weingast and Moran 1983; Weingast 1984; Wood and Waterman 1994; but see Krause 1996a, 1999).

Principal-agent theory has both strengths and weaknesses as an analytic device for understanding public bureaucracies in a democratic system. One advantage of principal-agent theory is that it makes relationships between superordinates and subordinates tractable, which in turn can cull generalizable theoretical and empirical insights about how public bureaucracies function in a democracy. Also, while this paradigm at its elemental level is a static theoretical conceptualization, it has the flexibility to allow for the dynamic elements of principal-agent relationships (Carpenter 1996; Wood and Waterman 1993). Finally, not only can principal-agent theories be applied to study relationships external to the administrative organization that are commonplace, but this paradigm can also be adapted to investigate intraorganizational relations within bureaucratic agencies (Brehm and Gates 1997).

Inherent limitations associated with principal-agent theory do exist. The theory assumes goal conflict from the onset (Mitnick 1980; Perrow 1972). In numerous instances, however, agency-political relationships may typically reveal goal congruence (Meier, Wrinkle, and Polinard 1995; Waterman and Meier 1998). Second, the application of principal-agent relationships in numerous studies of public bureaucracy falsely views administrative agencies as being subservient agents of the principal(s) (see Brehm and Gates 1997 for an exception). In such studies, hierarchy is imposed, which assumes that principals serve as superordinates to the agent's subordinate relational position. This alternative view, however, is problematic since a contract is an agreement between equals; introducing hierarchy negates the ability to use standard economic principles that do not assume an ability to coerce agents into compliance.

Moreover, classical organizational theorists have long noted that agency-political as well as supervisor-subordinate relationships are predicated on a "zone of acceptance" where both parties have a stake and a voice in the agent's actions (Barnard 1938; Simon 1947). Finally, principal-agent models of bureaucracy are generally not flexible in how they handle the inherent complexity of structural relationships among relevant actors (Krause 1996a, 1999). For instance, the multiple levels containing multiple principals and agents that are common in bureaucratic organizations, and more broadly the administrative state, are difficult to fit into this framework. Relatedly, principal-agent models do not allow one to assess potentially vital relationships that fail to fit neatly within the confines of this theoretical paradigm. A principal, for example, can possess noncontractual authority over an agent whereby the former is not responsible for appointing or selecting individuals to represent his or her interests yet the latter perform this role anyway given both the positions that they hold within an organization and the resulting policymaking authority that it possesses (Krause 1994).

Transaction Cost Theory

Running parallel to the evolution of the principal-agent approach has been the increasing use of transaction cost economics. Transaction costs are distinguishable from production costs in that the former term refers to the costs incurred by operating in a complex environment where information and coordination problems exist while the latter pertains to the "nuts and bolts" of the production process found in neoclassical theory of the firm. Simply, the transaction is the unit of analysis for investigating institutions (Williamson 1985, 41). What matters according to this theory is not simply the production of outputs by the firm or administrative agency but rather the costs incurred in the contractual arrangements and production processes that go beyond conventional factors such as labor, capital, and land. Transaction cost theory places an emphasis on how interactions among individuals or institutions will invariably incur costs of information acquisition and task performance concerning either ex post or ex ante activities. Examples of the former include drafting, negotiating, and safeguarding an agreement, and cases of the latter are disequilibrium costs when transactions drift out of alignment, corrections to ex post misalignments, the start-up and operating costs corresponding to government institutions where disputes are typically handled, and those costs incurred in the process of obtaining commitments from other parties (18–19).

Information costs among institutions and actors are nonzero (or at least nontrivial). Knowledge about other actors' preferences and actions is costly because the value of items is not known with certainty and monitoring the behavior of others is expensive. Transaction costs will result in decisions that are allocatively inefficient (Coase 1937). While monitoring costs are considered in principal-agent models in matters of delegation, measurement costs usually are not. Transaction costs are thus simply the costs associated with planning, adapting, and monitoring task completion under alternative governance structures (Williamson 1985, 2). In this light, the underpinnings of this theory serve as a means of gauging the flow of information and subsequent behavior of relevant actors. Since human, organizational, and institutional relations are not frictionless, positive transaction costs will be incurred by these entities.

The transaction cost perspective of public organizations complements the research on public organizations that views public bureaucracies as experiencing information deficiencies (e.g., Downs 1967; March and Simon 1958; Simon 1947; Stinchcombe 1990; Wilson 1989; cf. Williamson 1985), failing to operate in a neatly ordered, authoritative hierarchical fashion (Alchian and Demsetz 1972; Barnard 1938; Simon 1947), and having structures and jurisdictions that play a notable role in defining the parameters of performance (Knott and Miller 1987; Moe 1989, 1990; North 1990; Williamson 1975, 1985). While this theory has been applied to studying how chief executives and legislatures bargain to determine whether or not the former wish to delegate administrative authority to the latter (Epstein and O'Halloran 1999; Huber and Shipan 2002), it has yet to be explored by political scientists with regard to specific questions of how public bureaucracies make decisions or how they behave in either a political setting or as organizations in macro- or microlevel terms (see Horn 1995 for some initial work). The analysis of public bureaucracies through a transaction cost lens makes sense since these types of costs can be viewed as the operating costs of a system (Arrow 1969). As a result, the application of transaction cost theory to the study of public bureaucracy could be quite useful for understanding how these entities operate in a larger political environment as well as within their organizational subunits and subfunctions.

Transaction cost approaches can also illustrate some advantages of organizations. If, for instance, one views public institutions, including bureaucracies, as having the potential to generate increasing returns to scale in the production of public goods and services, this can result in greatly reduced transaction costs (Pierson 2000).[6] Government, for example, has the ability to coerce, and thus it can eliminate some transaction costs by fiat (declaring standards for products [e.g., high-definition television] or processes [pollution control]). The ability to apply a uniform pattern of policy to all situations nationwide dramatically reduces the overall transaction costs of implementing a government policy.[7]

Organizational Theory Perspectives

Although political scientists rarely contribute to organizational theory, they frequently use it to guide their research. Four strains of work in organizational theory are relevant to our discussion here—the open systems approach of Thompson, the organizational behavior approach of Argyris and others, the empirical work on public versus private organizations, and the contributions of Herbert Kaufman. Each will be discussed in turn.

Interest in organizational structure per se (rather than in how external political institutions use structure) has roots in the work of Gulick (1937) but was brought back to respectability by Thompson (1967) and Perrow (1972). Thompson presented the classic theory of organizations as open systems; within this presentation, he provides a series of testable hypotheses about how organizations respond to environmental pressures and how structures influence what the organization does. Although Thompson's hypotheses have not been of interest to political scientists, his open systems approach can be found in the work of several scholarly works in political science (Rourke 1984; Keiser 1999; Meier 2000). Perrow's work, in turn, is a vigorous defense of organizational sociology and the importance of structure in studying organizations. It interprets the literature, stressing structural rather than "people" questions. Within sociology, the work of Perrow and Thompson is most fully developed in Mintzberg's (1979) research agenda on structural influences in organizations.

The organizational behavior approach traces its roots to the Hawthorne experiments, but the key work was McGregor's (1960) distinction between theory X and theory Y management. The influence of McGregor meant that devotees of organizational behavior was interested in internal management questions (rather than political ones) and how to generate greater performance in the organization. Management theories based on the organizational behavior literature proliferated, including those of Likert (1967) and Argyris (1972). The applied nature of the theory (e.g., in management) means that it has not spawned a significant body of empirical research among scholars of public administration. On a more theoretical level, Mosher (1968) linked many organizational behavior questions to the political side of bureaucracy and in the process presented a strong argument for the inner check on bureaucratic autonomy.

One active area of empirical scholarship is that of public versus private sector differences. This literature starts with March and Simon's (1958) notion of a generic theory of organizations. Subsequent work has found that the public sector attracts individuals with different values than does the private sector (Nalbandian and Edwards 1983; Edwards, Nalbandian, and Wedel 1981); public organizations are also likely to have more and conflicting goals (Rainey 1997), more restrictive procedures (Bozeman 1987), lower levels of turnover except at top levels of the organization (Rainey 1997), and different incentive structures (Perry and Wise 1990). These differences provide a fertile ground for hypotheses for scholars interested in external control over the bureaucracy and how public bureaucracy is likely to respond to efforts aimed at control.

The other notable stream of research is Herbert Kaufman's series of studies on public organizations. In *The Forest Ranger* (1960), Kaufman documented the ability of an organization to socialize its members by structuring personnel policies. In *Administrative Feedback* (1973), he found evidence that agency heads had sufficient tools to monitor subordinate behavior but did not necessarily use them. In *Red Tape* (1977), Kaufman analyzed both the functional and the dysfunctional aspects of procedural controls. In *Are Government Organizations Immortal?* (1976), he found empirical evidence that government organizations, once created, are difficult but not impossible to eliminate (Carpenter 2001; but see Lewis 2000a for a different perspective). Finally, in *Time, Chance, and Organizations,* Kaufman (1991) provocatively argues that government organizations survive not because they perform well but because they are blessed with favorable environments. Although Kaufman generally used case studies and qualitative methods, his systematic approach to key organizational questions and his willingness to probe inside the black box of organizations make his work a key forerunner of contemporary scientific studies of bureaucracy.

What We Have Learned; What Do We Still Have to Learn?

The preceding approaches have one ingredient in common—they have each assisted our systematic thinking on how bureaucratic organizations operate. For instance, the principal-agent approach has helped make the relationship within bureaucratic agencies, and in relation to their political superordinates, a tractable one in which one can deal with the moral hazard and adverse selection problems inherent in the delegation of authority.

The traditional public administration literature has demonstrated the importance of the values held by bureaucrats and the impact that these values have on both political control and public policy outputs (e.g., Eisner 1991; Khademian 1992). Additional research has demonstrated Downs's concerns about external control; specifically, attempts to impose rational budgeting systems (Program Planning Budgeting System [PPBS], Zero-Based Budgeting [ZBB], Management by Objectives [MBO]) have been altered and even subverted by bureaucrats in the implementation process (Wildavsky 1984). Open systems theories of bureaucracy have demonstrated their value in focusing research on how organizations cope with the political environment (Keiser 1999) and as a general framework for assessing political control (Meier 2000).

These approaches also have one common ingredient lacking for continued rapid progress—they apply theories of behavior from economics, sociology, or psychology to understand bureaucratic organizations. As a result, many key issues have been neither addressed nor resolved. Uniquely political science theories of the administrative state are uncommon, even given the notable advances made in this field of inquiry over the past two decades by political scientists.[8] This is not to imply that interdisciplinary approaches to the study of bureaucracy should be eschewed; instead it is meant to encourage the development of theories and methods that are appropriate for understanding administrative organizations as governmental institutions, not just externally but internally as well. For instance, how do conflicting policy preferences within an agency come about? How does this, in turn, affect its ability to execute its policy mission?

More recent research over the past twenty years has typically (though not always) been more preoccupied with external political forces than with what goes on inside the agency (cf. Brehm and Gates 1997, 2–3). As a result, our knowledge of how politicians structure rules, procedures, and incentives (e.g., McCubbins and Schwartz 1984; Moe 1984, 1989, 1990; McCubbins, Noll, and Weingast 1989); the tools that apply to elicit responsiveness from public bureaucracies (e.g., Carpenter 1996; Scholz and Wei 1986; Scholz, Twombly, and Headrick 1991; Wood and Waterman 1994); and the bargaining among electoral institutions that takes place in determining the fate of administrative agencies (e.g., Bawn 1995; Epstein and O'Halloran 1999) is well developed.

Unfortunately, the systematic, generalizable body of knowledge concerning what makes administrative agencies tick is still largely uncharted territory in need of theoretical and empirical investigation. We know little about how bureaucratic agencies make decisions in a political environment or how bureaucratic structures affect responsiveness and performance in a variety of settings. While we know that all public organizations deal with multiple and conflicting goals, we have little information about how they resolve goal conflict on a day-to-day basis. Similarly, we are just beginning to ask how external performance criteria affect bureaucracies and how they can shape responses in unexpected ways (Bohte and Meier 2000). Finally, we only have general ideas about how well organizations socialize their members (Downs 1967; Kaufman 1960) and have little empirical knowledge about how effective such methods are and whether or not they can be overcome by external political actors (see Carpenter 2001 for a notable exception).

This volume intends to shed light on several issues of considerable importance to understanding public bureaucracies as both governmental institutions and administrative organizations. One basic theme underlying these works is an emphasis on theory-ladeness, whether it involves mathematical/symbolic logic, statistical analysis, or verbal conceptualization. Another is a bureaucentric focus that places administrative agencies front and center in understanding how the administrative state functions. We feel that the original scholarly essays contained in this volume will stimulate ideas and research on topics that either have not been addressed or need to be reexamined in a distinct, fresh manner that will challenge our current way of thinking. While the vast majority of research on public administration within political science has focused on top-down accountability issues involving political control over the bureaucracy by democratic institutions, this volume is intended to redirect some of those energies toward administrative decision making and behavior.

The dual emphasis on systematic social scientific inquiry and a bureaucentric focus contained in this volume reflects a neoorganizational approach to studying administrative institutions. This general thematic approach parallels that of new institutionalism, which has risen to prominence within political science over the past two decades.

Daniel P. Carpenter's essay, "Why Do Bureaucrats Delay? Lessons from a Stochastic Optimal Stopping Model of Agency, Timing, with Applications to the FDA," advances a theoretical model of bureaucratic decision-making processes that allows us to gain insight into the *timing* of decisions. With theoretical roots linked to March and Simon (1958), Carpenter's approach can be refined and applied to other bureaucratic settings in which we wish to understand *when* agencies make policy decisions such as the timing of prosecution cases (Whitford 1998). George A. Krause's essay, "Agency Risk Propensities Involving the Demand for Bureaucratic Discretion," focuses attention on the demand side of this commodity, as opposed to the supply side commonly analyzed within political science. Krause derives comparative-static results concerning the risk-bearing nature of an administrative organization based on a simple model of agency demand for discretion under uncertainty derived from the separate impact of discretion and policy outcome (implementation) uncertainty. Thomas H. Hammond's essay, "Veto Points, Policy Preferences, and Bureaucratic Autonomy in Democratic Systems," provides us with an important theoretical window into the amount of bureaucratic autonomy agencies enjoy based on the preference configuration of elected officials in relation to potential veto points across different institutional designs. Hammond entices us to grapple with important cross-national differences in the design of electoral institutions and administrative governance that often get overlooked in the study of political control over the bureaucracy. David B. Spence's essay, "The Benefits of Agency Policy-making: Perspectives from Positive Theory," extends his recent line of research on a key point central to this volume—that bureaucracy matters in the delegation of authority. Spence argues that agencies enjoy expertise advantages in delivering public goods and services that enable them to serve citizens' needs better than elected officials can. These essays are contained in part 1 of this volume, "Theory," since each study employs a deductive-theoretical approach to analyzing issues germane to public bureaucracies.

Part 2 of the volume contains essays that advance cutting-edge methodological technologies for studying public bureaucracy. The essay by John Brehm, Scott Gates, and Brad Gomez, "Donut Shops, Speed Traps, and Paperwork: Supervision and the Allocation of Time to Bureaucratic Tasks," examines the allocation of time along a variety of work-related task subfunctions of a street-level bureaucrat. This is done by applying a rarely employed statistical distribution, the Dirichlet distribution, to deal with compositional data problems that involve the allocation of a fixed total amount of labor effort. Andrew B. Whitford's essay, "Adapting Agencies: Competition, Imitation, and Punishment in the Design of Bureaucratic Performance," employs numerically based computer simulation methods in order to analyze administrative agencies as a complex adaptive system. Whitford demonstrates that the design of bureaucratic organizations with respect to optimal performance entails difficult trade-offs involving predictability versus change, search versus outcomes, and stasis versus growth.

Part 3 contains a set of theoretically motivated empirical studies of bureaucratic institutions. Steven J. Balla and John R. Wright's essay, "Consensual Rule Making and the Time It Takes to Develop Rules," examines a regulatory reform/regulatory renegotiation. By structuring the regulatory process akin to a corporatist process, various parties that will be affected by a regulation are allowed to participate in the actual rule-making process. In theory, such processes should result in a faster process with fewer post-regulation disputes. Lael R. Keiser's essay, "Why It Matters Whether State

Bureaucrats as Opposed to Federal Bureaucrats Administer Federal Programs," poses the important question, Does it matter that state bureaucrats administer the social security disability program? Her study finds that state bureaucracies respond rationally to fiscal incentives and thus shape programs in ways not necessarily intended by the federal government.

Michael J. Licari's essay, "Bureaucratic Discretion and Regulatory Success without Enforcement," on indoor smoking policies, presents the interesting null case. At times, bureaucracies might be given too much credit for program results. Licari examines a policy with no bureaucratic enforcement and still finds a fair amount of compliance. This raises interesting questions about what one might expect without bureaucratic activities and whether this implies that we need to reformulate the null hypothesis. Kevin B. Smith's essay, "Administrative Structure and Social Democratic Results: The Case of Education," examines the relationship between institutional structure and bureaucratic goals. Using data on teachers, he compares how mission goals change in public, Catholic, other religious, and nonsectarian schools. How these goals vary and their relationship to liberal democratic values permit him to make inferences about the impact of major structural changes in the implementation of education such as school choice programs. Kevin Corder's essay on federal credit programs, "Structural Choice and Political Control of Bureaucracy: Updating Federal Credit Programs," examines an underresearched area of the federal bureaucracy. Corder finds that bureaucratic institutions are afforded considerable autonomy and that this does not come into conflict with legislative goals as much of the existing scholarly research on the topic would predict.

In presenting these studies, we showcase what we feel reflects the frontier of basic scholarly inquiry into the study of public bureaucracy within political science. This subfield is an interesting blend of rigorous theoretical reasoning and well-crafted, sophisticated empirical research. All the essays in this volume represent original scholarly inquiry. The work is both a showcase and a challenge, however. It raises many more interesting questions than it answers. Specifically, it highlights the potential of analyzing public bureaucracies from a bureaucentric as opposed to the common focus on elected officials. We hope that our readers take up these challenges, use the material presented here, and conduct their own research to further our knowledge about the role of bureaucracy in politics, policy, and governance.

Notes

1. This work is similar in approach to recent new institutionalism scholarly works on political structure (e.g., Calvert, McCubbins, and Weingast 1989; Knott and Miller 1987; McCubbins 1985; McCubbins, Noll, and Weingast 1989; Moe 1989, 1990). The early work in this vein was not characterized by the same methodological rigor but had a much broader substantive reach. Both literatures addressed the question, Who benefits from the design of a set of structures?

2. The approach remained viable in business administration and organizational sociology. Joan Woodward's (1965) classic study of the relationship between organizational structure and performance is one notable effort. Within organizational sociology, questions of structure have been addressed empirically by Blau (1968), by Meyer (1968), and theoretically by Perrow (1972). The journal *Administrative Science Quarterly* has continued to serve as an outlet for this work.

3. In this way, one can view Crozier's line of inquiry as being antecedent to the theory of the politics of institutional choice proposed over two decades later by both Knott and Miller (1987) and Moe (1989, 1990).

4. These authors never explain how an organization can be a closed system and still survive. This theoretical flaw perhaps explains the lack of empirical support for these models (Blais and Dion 1991).

5. Downs's work is unique among formal studies in that it builds on the extensive preexisting literature. Although he presents his work as axiomatic and deductive, he incorporates much of the empirical and theoretical work in the field at the time (e.g., his life cycle of bureaucracy is borrowed from the work of Bernstein [1955] and Huntington [1952]). This integration of prior work often went unnoticed because Downs rarely footnoted existing scholarship.

6. This interesting hypothesis is also derived from the institutional economics literature, but it has not yet been subjected to empirical research to the best of our knowledge.

7. Simon (1997), in the fourth edition of *Administrative Behavior*, sees transaction costs as half a step in the right direction away from what he feels is the misleading orientation of the theory of the firm. Simon is critical of the ability to interpret employee relations solely in terms of contracts.

8. One exception is Emmette Redford's "overhead theory of democracy," which serves as a precursor to the principal-agent literature developed in other disciplines (Jensen and Meckling 1976; Mitnick 1980; Ross 1973; Spence and Zeckhauser 1971).

Part 1. Theory

Why Do Bureaucrats Delay? Lessons from a Stochastic Optimal Stopping Model of Agency Timing, with Applications to the FDA

Daniel P. Carpenter

Why do bureaucratic agencies often exhibit a reluctance to make their decisions quickly?

Why do some agency decisions take longer than others, even when they are made under identical statutes, agency structure, and administrative procedures?

Despite two decades of illuminating research in bureaucratic politics, one of the fundamental powers of the government—*the power to wait,* to delay its response to the requests of citizens—has not been systematically studied. The popular adage that agencies are "slow," whether right or wrong, does not answer either of these questions. It simply restates the first query and cannot answer the crucial issue of variation in the second. The aim of this essay is to develop a modeling framework that will offer some generalizable answers to these questions. I will model the regulatory approval decision as the optimal stopping of a stochastic process, derive a set of predictions about the duration of regulatory review, and conduct tests of the model in duration analyses of drug review times by the U.S. Food and Drug Administration (FDA).

The duration of government decisions, in addition to their content, is one of the central issues of modern democracy. Government agencies display a high degree of variability in the time they take to grant permits, issue licenses, adopt new policies, take criminal and civil cases to trial, and approve new products.

Of these examples, there is no more controversial and seminal case than the approval of new pharmaceutical products by the FDA. The FDA exhibits wide variation in review times for new drug applications (NDAs). From 1993 to 1995, for instance, the FDA approved sixty-seven new chemical entities (NCEs), but the drug Flumadine (marketed by Forest Labs) spent eighty-two months in the NDA review stage, whereas Orlaam (BioDevelopment Corp.) was approved in less than a month (Kaitin and Manocchia 1997, 47). The speed of approval is important for patients and firms alike. As scholars and politicians have agreed, these are nontrivial differences. Drugs that are approved more quickly will be available to patients who need them. And firms that are able to get their drugs approved more quickly will gain important advantages over competitors in product recognition and physician prescribing practices (Olson 1997, 378).

All new drug applications are considered under *the same statute*—the Food, Drug, and Cosmetic Act of 1938, as amended—and *the same administrative procedures*. They are also approved by *the same agency*. The question is obvious, but it cannot be answered well by reference to procedures, structure, or statute: Why are some NDAs approved more quickly than others?

Political science research has until recently eschewed questions of the duration of agency operations. Beginning with the work of Simon (1947) and Bernstein (1955), scholars in institutional political science have studied extensively the behavior of bureaucratic agencies. In the main, this research has taken two forms. The first is the study of political control. During the past two decades, following largely the work of Arnold (1979, 1987), Moe (1982, 1985), Weingast (1983 [with Moran], 1984), and Wood (1988, 1991 [with Waterman]), a number of quantitative studies have concluded that political control of bureaucratic agencies by elected authorities (or "principals") does prevail (see also McFadden 1976; Magat, Krupnick, and Harrington 1986; Rothenberg 1994; Wood and Anderson 1993; Ringquist 1995; and Carpenter 1996; but see Krause 1996a). Moreover, scholars have identified a number of mechanisms by means of which elected authorities can influence agency behavior, including congressional committee oversight (Weingast and Moran 1983), presidential and multi-institutional control (Moe 1995; Hammond and Knott 1996), statute (Moe 1990; Huber and Shipan 2002), "fire alarm" oversight

(McCubbins and Schwartz 1984), interest group monitoring (Spiller 1990; Banks and Weingast 1992), direct citizen contact (Scholz, Twombly, and Headrick, 1991; Brehm and Gates 1997), administrative procedures (McCubbins, Noll, and Weingast 1987; Bawn 1995), appointments (Wood 1988; Ringquist 1995), and budgetary control (Yandle 1988; Carpenter 1996).

A closely related literature, grounded in organization theory, has attempted to analyze the internal behavior of agencies. These studies include analyses of agency adaptation (Bendor and Moe 1985), bureaucratic learning (Bendor 1995; Brehm and Gates 1997), conflict and decision making in hierarchies (Williamson 1975; Miller 1992), budgetary decision making under bounded rationality and hierarchy (Padgett 1980, 1981), and "parallel versus serial" information processing (Bendor 1985; Heimann 1993, 1997).

None of these studies has placed the duration of agency decisions at the center of analysis. It is as if political scientists have assumed that the timing of decisions has nothing to do with "politics" and that the proverbial slowness of government agencies is, for all intents and purposes, neutral or trivial. The aim of this essay is to redress these shortcomings of the bureaucratic politics literature by focusing directly upon the duration of agency decision processes.

The Benefits and Costs of Waiting

The theoretical core of this chapter may be expressed in two arguments. First, waiting is a way of gaining more information about an uncertain decision that the agency regards as irreversible (or reversible only at cost). In the case of drug approval, the FDA sees its approval decisions as reputationally irreversible even though drugs can be recalled; once a drug has done sufficient harm that it must be recalled, the damage done to the agency's reputation cannot be regained. (Indeed, recall as an agency admission of error may worsen the situation.)

Yet there are costs to waiting as well. Each potential drug has a *political demand* associated with it, a demand that rises in rough proportion to the number of potential citizens who need it (who have the diseases for which it is indicated), the degree of political organization of those citizens, the political power (or rents) of the pharmaceutical firm submitting the drug, and the degree of media and political attention given to the drug and the disease that it treats. Drugs may also have opponents to their approval, as in the case of the abortion-inducing "morning-after pill," RU–486. The degree to which the supporters of approval are unified, relative to any opposition, may be termed the *cohesion* of the political demand for the drug and may be considered an important part of the drug's political demand. The FDA's experience with AIDS drug approvals (see Epstein 1996) has forcefully demonstrated the political power of organized disease advocates.

The agency's response to these demands is a stochastic dynamic optimum that embodies the trade-off between the value of additional time and the political cost of delay. The model has several interesting and counterintuitive predictions and carries a specific distributional prediction about the form of the hazard to be used in duration analysis.

The essay thus has the advantage, I hope, of linking empirical estimation tightly to an underlying theory of choice, a theory that is "dynamic" in the sense of Bellman optimality.[1] The optimal stopping models considered here should serve as useful tools with which to analyze a range of bureaucratic behaviors as well as to structure duration analyses of bureaucratic and regulatory decision making. In previous uses of duration models in bureaucratic research, these models have not flowed explicitly from an underlying formal model (e.g., Whitford 1998; Balla and Knight 2002; though for a more intuitively based attempt to premise duration models upon an underlying theory, see Gordon 1999).

A central reason to analyze the duration of agency decisions is to redress an unfortunate theoretical and empirical imbalance in the bureaucratic politics literature. Most analyses in bureaucratic politics are either time-series analyses of agency enforcement aggregates (Moe 1982, 1985; Wood 1988; Ringquist 1995; Carpenter 1996; Krause 1996a; Olson 1995, 1997) or discrete choice analyses of agency behavior (McFadden 1976; Arnold 1979; Weingast and Moran 1983). While extensive insight has been generated by these studies, they all but ignore the critical question of the *timing* and *rapidity* of bureaucratic decisions. The speed with which agencies make decisions is an instrument of power over private sector actors and a source of immense agency discretion. Most new drug applications that pass the clinical trial stage are approved by the FDA. The critical question in FDA drug approvals is not *if* but *when*. This is the core issue in FDA reform debates.

Two Caveats: Other Explanations for Delay and
the Role of Political Intuition

Before proceeding with the theoretical and empirical analyses, it merits remarking that other mechanisms can generate delay in bureaucratic decision making. An agency may have too many tasks assigned to it by Congress. Delay may be equivalent to procrastination. Delay may be an attempt to pass the buck or dump an unpleasant task upon a successor. Or a certain procedure may simply take more time than another.

While some level of delay in organizational decision making occurs in all contexts, thinking of delay as overload, procrastination, buck passing, or procedural complexity has its limits. For one thing, it would be difficult to model any of these four phenomena in a way that would generate predicted variation in the delay time. If we observe the FDA taking more time with one drug than another, it surely cannot be due to buck passing or procrastination (the FDA will eventually have to decide upon the drug). If overload and the procedural complexity of the drug decision explain drug approval delay, then how can drugs considered by the same organization at the same time and under the same procedures receive different review times? Undoubtedly, all four of these factors are at work, but none of them can be the decisive component of variation.

A second caveat worth remarking here is that some of the hypotheses predicted by the model are relatively intuitive and are not derived entirely from the optimal stopping model itself. These include the hypothesis that a drug's approval time is decreasing with the political clout of the firm submitting it; the hypothesis that approval time is decreasing with the organization of sufferers of the disease for which the drug is intended; and the hypothesis that expected FDA approval time is increasing in the disease-specific order in which the drug enters the market. Still, the stochastic optimal stopping model is useful here because it shows that commonsense observations about FDA drug approval are consistent with dynamic optimality and bureaucratic learning.

The chapter is organized as follows. In the section that follows, I outline the formal model that I will use to model an approval decision. In the next section, I will offer hypotheses and suggest measurements, and I will briefly test one of the model's predictions.

An Optimal Stopping Model of the Approval Decision

The approval of a product or license presents the regulator with a learning problem. The agency must study a new product application (with accompanying "data") and decide when the apparent benefits of the application—whether a product, a proposal, or a permit for new economic activity such as grazing or construction—outweigh the costs or risks associated with its use.

Learning in Continuous Time

The model here is tailored toward the bureaucratic review of a new product application, specifically a new drug application. The framework is, however, generalizable to learning about the guilt or innocence of a suspect (Whitford and Helland forthcoming; Gordon 1999) or the eventual environmental damage of a construction or grazing permit or energy-generating license. For the present, the model imagines product review as a process of page turning through a product application. One by one, the agency observes a series of experiments (in the case of FDA drug approval, clinical trials) in which a drug either harms or does not harm the person taking it. The sequence of binary outcomes—"harm" or "not harm"—becomes the data for the agency's decision. I model the evolution of these observations as a continuous-time Wiener process, more commonly known as "Brownian motion."[2]

Let all drugs be indexed by i, diseases by j, and firms by k. All drugs in the model are characterized by two parameters.[3] First, let $\gamma_{ij}(0 \leq \gamma_{ij} \leq 1)$ be the *curing probability* of the drug (which can be interpreted as the fraction of people with disease j that drug i will cure). I assume that γ_{ij} is fixed and known with certainty throughout the agency's decision process.

Second, let μ_i be the *danger* of the drug, which can be thought of as the expected number of people who will be harmed or killed by the drug over a given interval of time. Normalizing the interval to unity, μ_i may be thought of as the *rate* of harming consumers. The greater the danger of the drug the more its approval will harm the agency's reputation for protecting public safety. I assume throughout that a drug's danger is independent of its curing power, which implies $\text{cov}(\mu_i, \gamma_i) = 0$.

Observed harm in regulatory review evolves according to a Wiener process $X_{it} = X(t)$, a linear function of underlying danger (μ) plus a random component, as follows:

$$X(t) = \mu t + \sigma z(t), \tag{1}$$

where μ and σ are constants and $\sigma > 0$ and where $z(t)$ is a standard normal variable with mean zero and variance t. A more "dangerous" drug—one with higher μ—will yield more harm, but harm will also be affected by the random term $z(t)$. A higher σ will yield a more volatile review—namely, a series of clinical results from which the agency will find it harder to learn what μ is.[4]

Observed harm is therefore a Markov process with independent increments, and the agency learns about μ in a simple Bayesian fashion based upon the stochastic history of $X(t)$. Letting $X(t)$ start arbitrarily at 0, then it is normally distributed with mean μt and variance $\sigma^2 t$. We assume that σ is the same across drugs but that μ differs across them, according to a normal distribution with mean m and variance s.[5] For any drug review of length t and accumulated harm $X(t) = x$, all relevant information for the agency's decision is captured in a pair of "sufficient statistics" (x and t). Bayesian estimates of μ are

$$\text{Posterior Mean} \equiv E_{xt}(\mu) = \hat{\mu} = \frac{m/s + x/\sigma^2}{1/s + t/\sigma^2}, \tag{2a}$$

$$\text{Posterior Variance} \equiv S(t) = \frac{1}{1/s + t/\sigma^2}, \tag{2b}$$

where m is the mean danger for the average drug in the population—or the expected danger of any drug, before the agency knows anything about it—and s is the "prior" (or preexperimental) variance of this danger. Notice that

$$\lim_{t \to \infty} \hat{\mu} = \frac{x}{t} = \mu \quad \text{and} \quad \lim_{t \to \infty} S(t) = 0. \tag{3}$$

The posterior variance $S(t)$ is a crucial parameter. Simply put, $S(t)$ is the best estimate of the agency's uncertainty about the true value of μ. For this reason, at any time *the value of waiting for another moment is an increasing function of $S(t)$.*

Reputation and the Value of Waiting to Approve

The fundamental assumption of the model is that the regulator guards its reputation for protecting citizen welfare (here "safety"). Students of the 1962 Kefauver Amendments argue that the FDA's decision not to approve the drug thalidomide played a crucial role in the expanded discretion that the agency received under the new laws (Quirk 1980). This reputation is an important political asset—it can be used to generate public support, to achieve delegated authority and discretion from politicians, to protect the agency from political attack, and to recruit and retain valued employees (Carpenter 2000b, 2001).

Yet, although waiting to approve always has *some* value, there is not always a *net benefit* to waiting. In other words, in many cases it is *not* optimal to wait forever. As with most inference problems in politics, the marginal return to more information is decreasing. Voters may not need ten debates or twenty polls to help them sort out the differences between two candidates; often two or three of each will do. A similar logic prevails in regulatory product approval: *the value of waiting declines over time, as more is learned about the drug.*

The Approval Payoff as the Cost of Information

There is another reason why waiting is not always optimal. Put simply, waiting is costly. Patients want a drug for their diseases, and firms that profit from drug sales want entry into potentially lucrative markets. To delay the approval of a drug is to impose costs upon these interests, and when these interests are organized or well publicized they can make it costly for the agency to delay. The case of AIDS offers a lucid example. When ACT-UP (AIDS Coalition to Unleash Power) protestors, dismayed that the FDA might delay approval of lifesaving therapies, demonstrated at agency headquarters in 1988, they embarrassed the agency and prompted a sharp change in policy on AIDS drugs (Epstein 1996).

In short, the information obtained while waiting, though valuable, is not free. To approve a drug is to please the patients who need it and the firms that will profit from its sales. I assume that the approval payoff A for any drug is strictly positive and is a combinatorial and strictly decreasing function of the number of drugs that have already been approved for disease j, as follows:

$$A = \theta(\psi_j, L_j, N_j, \omega_k) = (1 + \lambda_k)\psi_j\gamma_{ij}L_j \prod_{i=0}^{N_{i-1,j}} (1 - \gamma_{ij}), \qquad (4)$$

where L_j is disease j's *prevalence*, or the number of persons with disease j, and ψ_j is the *political multiplier* of disease j, a positive parameter.[6] We can interpret ψ_j as the expected number of citizens, for every citizen afflicted by disease j, who will apply pressure upon the agency or the politicians governing it. The term N_j is the number of marketed drugs that already treat disease j; and λ_k is the political clout of the submitting firm, also strictly positive.

Since the approval payoff is a multiplicative function of its components, it is possible to collapse the different terms of the approval payoff in equation (4) into a single-index parameter. In this case, the function θ can represent the entire payoff.

The Agency's Optimal Policy

The problem facing the agency can be described as the optimal stopping of the process $\hat{\mu}_t$ (see eq. 2), consistent with the following objective:

$$\max Ee^{-\delta(t_{app})}[A - E_{\hat{\mu},t}\int_t^\infty e^{-\delta(y-t)}\alpha\mu^*(y,\omega)dy]$$

$$= Ee^{-\delta(t_{app})}[A - \delta^{-1}\alpha\mu^*(t_{app},\omega)], \qquad (5)$$

where δ is the discount factor, t_{app} is a given approval time, μ^* is the agency's estimate of danger at the optimal stopping time (as given in eq. 2), ω denotes an elementary event in the probability space Ω, and y is a variable of integration (a variable that has the same dimensions as time and functions purely as an index in the optimization problem). The parameter α represents the agency's aversion to danger, or its "preferences" with respect to the relative weight it puts upon danger versus the clinical benefits of drugs.[7] In all respects, the agency can be modeled as stopping the process $\alpha\hat{\mu}_t$.

The political cost of approval, then, is simply the reputational loss that accrues to the agency from the observable danger of the drug. Upon the approval of the drug, the agency therefore "pays" the parameter $\alpha\mu$, which can be learned only through preapproval review of the product.

The problem facing the agency, then, is the problem of "stopping" the review only when the payoff of approval exceeds both the utility losses associated with the danger of the drug *and* the value of waiting for more information. In other words, the rational agency does *not* simply approve the drug when its apparent danger is less than the payoff of approval. This is the aspect of the agency's decision that differentiates product approval from standard problems of administrative choice.

It is shown elsewhere (DeGroot 1970) that for sequential decision problems upon Markov processes of this sort the optimal policy entails the division of the space of possible outcomes $[\hat{\mu}_t, t]$ into two regions— a *continuation region,* where observed values of $\hat{\mu}_t$ suggest waiting, and a *stopping region,* where values of $\hat{\mu}_t$ suggest termination of the review process and approval of the drug. Figure 1 offers a sample division of the space, where $\hat{\mu}_t$ has been replaced by W_t. The policy can be described by a unique partitioning of $[\hat{\mu}_t, t]$ by a "barrier" $\eta(t)$ such that the first departure from the continuation region involves the process $\hat{\mu}_t$ "hitting" the barrier $\eta(t)$ for the first time.

For purposes of the present discussion, I assume the existence of an optimum for the agency's problem. Elsewhere (Carpenter 2000c) I prove the existence of an optimum for this problem, and existence theorems for related problems appear in Jovanovic 1979 and, most important, Miroschnichenko 1963.

The solution to (5) is complex and must satisfy three conditions. First, the agency's policy must be *dynamically optimal.* It must be the case that whatever the agency's initial decision its subsequent choices constitute an optimal policy with respect the subproblem starting at the state that results from the initial actions (Dixit and Pindyck 1994, 100). Second, the optimal barrier $\eta^*(t)$ must satisfy a *value-matching condition* such that the agency is indifferent between taking the approval payoff A and losing the capitalized value of the drug's danger. The value-matching condition says simply that the barrier represents indifference between the matched value of two options. Finally, the optimal stopping of Wiener processes must satisfy a third condition known as the *smooth-pasting* condition (Dixit 1993). The smooth-pasting condition is difficult to explain simply, but it requires that along the approval barrier the time derivative of the approval payoff and the time derivative of the danger losses are equivalent. At the point of indifference between waiting and approving, the time path of the approval payoff cannot differ from the time-path of the danger loss or the agency would be better off either to have approved the drug earlier or to wait.

PROPOSITION 1. *The optimal barrier is*

$$\eta(t) = \delta A - \frac{S(t)^2}{2\sigma^2} \, F_{\hat{\mu}\hat{\mu}}[\eta(t), t]. \tag{6}$$

PROOF. *Carpenter 2002.*

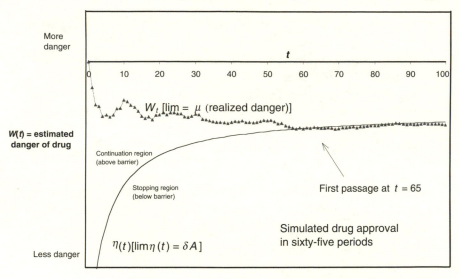

Fig. 1. Simulated first passage of the danger process $W(\mu, t)$ through the agency's approval barrier $\eta(t)$

Here the term $F_{\hat{\mu}\hat{\mu}}$ represents the second derivative of the function F with respect to the estimate $\hat{\mu}$. By equation (3), the limit of $\eta(t)$ is δA, which $\hat{\mu}_t$ approaches from above. In the asymptote, the agency can learn nothing more about the drug because uncertainty about its danger (the posterior variance of μ) is at zero. The benefits of approval (which have remained constant throughout the decision but are fully capitalized in the limit) are equal to δA. Meanwhile, the costs of approval are $(\alpha)\mu$. In the limit, the estimated danger converges to the true danger, so that the drug is approved asymptotically if $\alpha\mu < \delta A$, or $\mu < \delta A$ if we set α to one as we have done above. In finite time, of course, the agency cannot make the decision in such terms. *There is always a value to waiting for more information, regardless of the agency's risk aversion.*

Risk-Neutral Delay and Other Characteristics of the Approval Distribution

The optimal rule for waiting has now been derived. Let $G^*(t)$ be the approval distribution, or the probability of approval under the optimal policy. Then an approximation to $G^*(t)$ can be retrieved from the class of first-passage-time distributions:

$$\Pr[\alpha\hat{\mu}_t < \eta^*(t)] = 2\left\{1 - \Phi\left[\frac{(m - \delta A)}{\sqrt{r(t)}}\right]\right\} = 2\Phi\left[\frac{(\delta A - m)}{\sqrt{r(t)}}\right], \qquad (7)$$

where $\Phi(\cdot)$ is the cumulative standard normal integral and $r(t)$ is the posterior *precision* of the Wiener process, or $r(t) = s - S(t)$. $G^*(t)$ and its density $g^*(t)$ then comprise an *inverse Gaussian* or *Wald variate* (for a derivation see Harrison 1985). Notice that a greater approval payoff increases the approval probability.

The following propositions note interesting properties of the approval distribution.

PROPOSITION 2: DE FACTO REJECTION WITHOUT A REJECTION OPTION. *In expectation, a nonzero fraction of drugs will never receive the agency's approval, as $\lim_{t \to \infty} G^*(t) < 1$.*

SKETCH OF PROOF. *The proof comes from examination of $G^*(t)$ in (7). Because $\lim_{t \to \infty} r(t) = s < \infty$ (eq. 3), the term in brackets in $G^*(t)$ never reaches unity.*

Proposition 2 implies that the probability of an endless review is strictly positive. Statistically, proposition 2 is sufficient to identify $G^*(t)$ as a defective distribution.

In two ways, proposition 1 coheres with the FDA's actual behavior. It is trivially consistent, of course, with the fact that not all drug submissions are approved. Yet it is also consistent with the fact that *the FDA never formally rejects a drug*. It simply deems a drug "not approvable," and nothing prevents the producing company from submitting more data about the drug if it seeks approval at a later date (GAO 1995).

A central result of the model is that drug approval should be least likely precisely when some firms and patients most desire it: when a drug has completed early clinical testing and is submitted for review.

PROPOSITION 3: THE SCARCITY OF QUICK APPROVAL. *For any drug i [$t_{app}(i) < \infty$] such that an optimal approval time exists, the approval hazard $\theta(t) = g^*(t)/[1 - G^*(t)]$ has the following two properties:*

(1) $\theta(t = 0) = 0$,
(2) $\forall t, t < (A - \delta\mu)^2$, $\lim_{t \to 0} \theta(t) = 0$.

PROOF. *Result (1) obtains by the property of $g^*(t)$ such that $g^*(0) = 0$. Result (2) follows from the unique mode of $g^*(t)$ at $(A - \delta\mu)^2$, below which $g^*(t)$ tends to zero faster than $G^*(t)$.*

PROPOSITION 4: NONMONOTONICITY OF THE APPROVAL HAZARD. *The hazard* $\theta(t) = g(t)/[1 - G(t)]$ *is nonmonotonic.*

SKETCH OF PROOF. *By proposition 3, result (1),* $\theta(t = 0) = 0$. *By proposition 2,* $\theta(t)$ *must return to zero in the asymptote.*

Propositions 2 through 4 have important theoretical and empirical implications. First, we now have a generalizable explanation for agency delay, one derived under the assumption of risk neutrality and without assuming anything about the "slowness" of the agency. The reason for bureaucratic delay, the model suggests, is not sloth or slack but uncertainty reduction: *the information to be gained by waiting is most valuable at the beginning of a decision problem.* Even when A is large, the hazard of approval will be near zero at the beginning of bureaucratic review.

Second, the model shows that waiting can be a de facto form of rejection. Even where no formal rejection option exists, long-term waiting increasingly implies a zero probability of eventual approval under the optimum policy.

Finally, the model offers some important lessons for hazard estimation. The likelihood employed should be inverse Gaussian, and, more significantly, the hazard function should be nonmonotonic. This rules out the simple exponential distribution as a hazard specification, but it *also rules out the most commonly used parametric distribution of political science duration analysis: the Weibull distribution.*

Hypotheses

With the characterization of a dynamic stochastic optimum in proposition 1 and the theoretical results in propositions 2 through 4, the following hypotheses can be posed.

H1: Below a unique mode, the approval hazard $\theta(t)$ tends to zero.

H2: $\theta(t)$ is an increasing function of the prevalence L_j of the disease j treated by the drug i.

H3: $\theta(t)$ is an increasing function of the political influence and publicity of the patients with the disease treated by the drug, or ψ_j.

H4: $\theta(t)$ is an increasing function of the political clout ω_k of the firm k.

H5: If the agency's preferences over danger versus availability are affected by elected authorities (as captured in α), then $\theta(t)$ is decreasing in α.

The hypotheses advanced here can be tested using a maximum likelihood duration model. Specifically, the model predicts that the duration of product approval for an agency faced with the problem in (5) will approve products according to an *inverse-Gaussian distribution*. The present framework therefore offers a more theoretically driven approach to the estimation of duration models in political science than is customarily the case (Carpenter 2002). From a strictly scientific point of view, an important advantage of stochastic process models is that they allow the functional form of statistical tests to be derived directly from the underlying model of behavior (Padgett 1980; Carpenter 1996, 2002).

A Nonparametric Test of H1

The first hypothesis can be tested using nonparametric statistics calculated from duration data that are unaccompanied by covariates. Before doing so, it will be useful to describe the FDA approval process and the approval time data that result from it.

Drug review by the FDA occurs only after a drug completes phase I clinical trials (testing for information on drug safety), phase II trials (testing for effectiveness and safety), and phase III trials (verification of safety and effectiveness and testing for adverse effects). On average, these trials consume six years of drug development. This is more than half of the time required to bring a new drug to market (Dranove and Meltzer 1994). After completion of phase III clinical trials,[8] the sponsoring company submits a new drug application to the FDA. The FDA's Center for Drug Evaluation and Research (CDER) then reviews the NDA by assigning it to a review team composed of doctors, pharmacologists, chemists, statisticians, microbiologists, and regulatory affairs experts. The most novel of these drugs, and the drugs that occasion the greatest controversy over approval and delay, are called new chemical entities. The dependent variable in the following analyses is the length of the NDA review stage (in months) for an NCE.

I have consciously restricted the sample in two ways. First, I analyze only NCEs, while the FDA screens hundreds of other drugs annually. These include both "generic drugs" (simple copies of drugs whose patent protection has expired) and "supplemental" applications, which occur when a company seeks to market its drug for a disease other than the one for which it was originally submitted. Because the review process is very different for these applications, I leave them to another study. Second, the data (and the model) ignore the clinical trial stage of drug development. I have chosen not to analyze it here because the length of the clinical trial stage depends heavily upon the speed of the company and its clinical testing regime.[9]

Figure 2 displays a plot of the estimated hazard function along with a "confidence function" plot (the dotted line), which represents the value of two standard errors of the hazard estimate from zero. The hazard function is estimated using the nonparametric Kaplan-Meier method. In other words, when the estimated hazard function crosses the dotted line in figure 2, we can say as statisticians that the expected hazard differs from zero at a statistical significance level of $p < 0.05$.

Figure 2 shows that the expected hazard cannot be judged to be statistically distinguishable from zero until ln (review time) equals 1.7, or somewhere between seven and nine months into the review process. This is an interesting result because the 1962 Kefauver Amendments to the Food, Drug, and Cosmetic Act state that the FDA shall approve all drugs within six months of their submission. In other words, figure 2 suggests that for the entire period of legal review, plus one to three months, the expected instantaneous likelihood of approval for a drug is zero.

Yet the model also offers some logic as to why this is the case. The pattern in figure 2 is the result not of bureaucratic sloth nor of mismanagement of the review process. The most compelling theoretical explanation is that the value of waiting for information is greatest at the outset of a product approval process. Because the value of waiting is so high, there is a rational scarcity of quick approval. It is important to note, again, that this result is derived under risk neutrality—the agency neither prefers nor avoids gambles between high- and low-variance drugs—though the agency is always danger averse.

It is also worth noting that figure 2 essentially supports proposition 4 of the model, which predicted the nonmonotonicity of the hazard. Since almost one-half of submitted drugs are not approved (GAO 1995; this is an empirical fact that does not require a statistical test), the empirical hazard function must eventually fall to zero. All that is required for a demonstration of nonmonotonicity, then, is evidence that the hazard starts at zero in addition to ending at zero, which figure 2 shows. (Note that inclusion of nonapproved drugs in the sample would not change this result since the hazard can rise only if a drug is approved.)

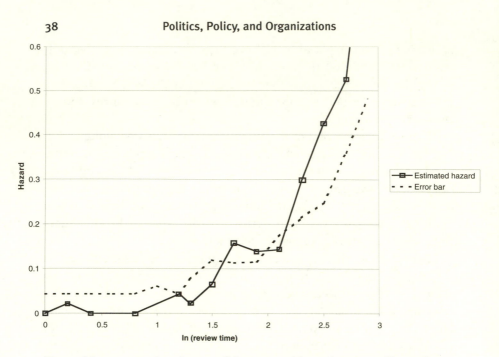

Fig. 2. Nonparametric estimates of the approval hazard, 1985–95 (first eighteen months of NDA review)

Conclusion

While instructive, the theoretical and empirical analyses presented here could doubtless be improved and extended in fascinating ways. Theoretically, it would be interesting to incorporate a budget into the model and allow the agency to bestow resources explicitly upon drugs. A more interesting issue, to my mind, concerns the organizational factors that affect information processing. The FDA has long been hampered by high turnover, particularly when talented reviewers leave for the lucrative pharmaceutical sector. What happens if the agency loses information over time? What happens if agency decision makers are forgetful or, as is more likely the case, that organizational turnover results in a loss of "institutional memory"? Work is currently under way in this direction (Mullainathan 1998; Carpenter 2000d).

Empirically, an obvious shortcoming of the hazard rate analysis is the absence of drug applications that are rejected or withdrawn. As I have noted, the proprietary character of rejected drug applications renders this problem far more difficult than one of simply collecting more data. Efforts are currently under way to collect a partial sample of rejected or withdrawn applications, though I note that only a partial sample will be possible and that theoretically substantive and interesting results can be drawn from analyzing approvals themselves. Review times conditioned upon approval, again, lie at the center of the political controversy over FDA regulation.

As a concluding note, I call attention to the fact that optimal stopping offers a different way of thinking about the dynamic behavior of bureaucracies. Most research on bureaucratic dynamics has been associated with the time-series tradition, which includes models of autoregressive and adaptive behavior (Moe 1982, 1985; Wood 1988; Wood and Waterman 1991; Wood and Anderson 1993; Carpenter 1996; Krause 1996b). These models have demonstrated the dynamics of bureaucratic behavior for aggregated decisions made over time. The contribution of the present study, I hope, is that it instructs students of public bureaucracy about the dynamics of *single decisions* in which time itself has value and is an object of choice.

Notes

An earlier version of this essay was presented at National Public Management meetings, December 3, 1999, Texas A&M University. For helpful comments on earlier and different versions, I thank Greg Adams, Frank Baumgartner, John Brehm, Michael Chernew, Scott Gates, Rick Hall, Thomas Hammond, William Keech, George Krause, Ken Meier, Mary Olson, Ken Shotts, Michael Ting, and Andrew Whitford.

1. Under Bellman optimality (or dynamic optimality), it must be the case that the choices at a given period t (or for a given infinitesimal dt) must maximize the agent's utility function for this increment of time and the (assumed) optimal path of all future decisions. Put in more crude and intuitive terms, dynamically optimal actors ignore sunk costs and care only about an optimal (step-by-step) sequence of choices in the future.

2. As Dixit (1993) shows, the Wiener process representation can also be derived by taking limits toward zero on the discrete walk of the binary outcomes harm and not harm. Thus, a discrete time process becomes, in the limit,

a continuous time process; accordingly, all of the results described in this essay may be replicated in a discrete time framework. I use continuous time for its greater mathematical generality and its convenience in the Brownian motion case.

3. I assume an exogenous industry production process in which the agency expects drugs to be submitted at a constant rate over time. Drugs are assumed to treat one disease and one disease only. See the conclusion for planned extensions of the model in which these assumptions will be relaxed.

4. Equivalently, infinitesimal movements in X are given by $dX = \mu dt + \sigma dz$, where z is a standardized Weiner variable whose increment dz has zero mean and variance dt (Harrison 1985).

5. I make the assumption of constant variance only to simplify the exposition of the model.

6. The parameter can exceed unity because citizens other than those directly afflicted by a disease may lobby for drug approval. Those afflicted may have relatives, friends, or other allies in organized patient associations and the media who wish to see the drug approved.

7. Although it does not affect the mathematics of the model, I assume that the agency's utility is linear in danger (μ) and not harm [$X(t)$]. Other functional forms are possible. If the agency's reputation has the character of a durable asset subject to erosion, then perhaps the regulator's utility is dependent not upon μ but upon $\exp(\mu)$. This would render the stochastic process a "geometric" Brownian motion (Dixit 1993). In much of the discussion that follows, I set α to unity without loss of generality. The model sidesteps the question of political control. One can assume that α is a function purely of the preferences of the agency's enacting coalition, or one can assume that the agency's preferences are independent. The model's predictions are the same under either regime.

8. This is a highly cursory summary of the drug approval process. See <www.fda.gov/cder> for more information. Drugs with an "accelerated approval" or "fast-track" status may be submitted for NDA approval before phase II trials are fully completed.

9. Dranove and Meltzer (1994) observe that the length of the Investigational New Drug (IND) stage is positive correlated with the length of NDA review. The speed of NDA review, while doubtless affected by drug firms, is more easily represented as a decision variable. I am currently working on a formal model of product approval with strategic firm submissions (see Carpenter and Ting 2001).

Agency Risk Propensities Involving the Demand for Bureaucratic Discretion

George A. Krause

> Motivation to exercise discretion is another matter and poses serious problems for all types of complex organizations. . . . Nevertheless, we will work with a very simple assumption—*that individuals exercise discretion whenever they believe it is their advantage to do so and seek to evade discretion on other occasions.*
>
> —James D. Thompson

In the study of public bureaucracy, an inherent tension arises concerning the balance of policy-making authority between politicians and administrative agencies. Administrative agencies enjoy some degree of discretion over policy-making via implementation via agency enforcement and rulemaking activities (e.g., Bryner 1987; Meier 1993a; Rourke 1984; Wilson 1989). Important theoretical breakthroughs emanating from the positive theory of bureaucratic discretion (PTBD) have generally focused on the supply side of this commodity. This strand of research treats the level of agency discretion as being determined by political choice, whether it pertains to the "hardwiring" of administrative agencies[1] (e.g., Calvert, McCubbins, and Weingast 1989; McCubbins 1985; McCubbins and Page 1987; McCubbins, Noll, and Weingast 1987, 1989) or a trade-off that exists between political control and agency expertise (Bawn 1995; Epstein and O'Halloran 1994, 1996, 1999; Martin 1997).[2] While these works provide valuable insights into the supply of bureaucratic discretion that is produced from bargaining between political institutions, they fail to enhance our knowledge concerning the (agency) demand for this good.[3] In other words, if the putative assumption noted in the opening quote by James D. Thompson is valid then it suggests that our present understanding of bureaucratic discretion is noticeably underdeveloped from the agency's perspective.

The purpose of this essay is to undertake a new organizations theoretical approach to explain agency demand for bureaucratic discretion under conditions of uncertainty. The focus lies solely on the agency's choice as to how much discretion it wishes to obtain (demand) in relation to the amount of policy outcome uncertainty that it experiences. In doing so, different types of risk-bearing behavior and contextual conditions that shape agency preferences for discretion can be theoretically examined. Particular emphasis on agency decision making under uncertainty reflects the imperfect and incomplete information that agencies possess on how policy implementation will turn out (e.g., Pressman and Wildavsky 1973). This, in turn, allows for an opportunity to assess the range of risk propensities that bureaucratic agencies will engage in an uncertain world. Bureaucratic discretion does not simply entail the level of slack provided by political principals from a well-defined (ideal) point noted in public choice models (e.g., Niskanen 1971; Tullock 1965). Rather, bureaucratic discretion more broadly refers to a range of parameters by means of which administrative agencies operate. This analysis departs from past research on bureaucratic discretion in political science since it does not focus on the decision making of political institutions but rather on how administrative agencies arrive at such decisions.

The layout of this essay is as follows. First, agency choice is shown to be a vital aspect in understanding administrative discretion. Second, it is demonstrated that the context in which agencies seek to obtain discretion will affect their decision-making calculus. Third, a positive theoretic analysis of an agency's demand for discretion is examined in order to provide insight into the risk propensities for this commodity. Based on deriving the agency's demand for bureaucratic discretion given a fixed level of agency utility, the comparative-static results demonstrate the following: (1) both risk-averse and risk-seeking agencies will exhibit an inverse relationship between bureaucratic discretion and policy (implementation) outcome uncertainty, (2) the bureaucratic discretion–policy outcome uncertainty relationship will be the same for a risk-averse agency operating under a negative discretionary context as it will be for a risk-seeking agency operating under a positive discretionary context, and (3) a risk-averse agency operating under a positive discretionary context will behave the same as a risk-seeking agency operating under a negative discretionary context with regard to this relationship, and (4) a risk-neutral agency's preference for bureaucratic discretion will be insensitive to changes in policy outcome uncertainty. Finally, the implications of these theoretical results as well as the limitations of this study are discussed.

The Importance of Understanding Agency Choice in Obtaining Bureaucratic Discretion

Bureaucratic policy implementation necessarily involves administrative discretion (Meier 1993a, 57). Discretion refers to the ability of an administrator to choose among alternatives and to decide how the policies of government should be implemented in specific instances (Rourke 1984, 36). Discretion is an important commodity for successful policy-making and is woven into the fabric of the Constitution as a means of diffusing both power and conflict among interests (Bryner 1987). According to Martin Shapiro (1988), administrative agencies are "supplementary lawmakers" functioning akin to courts with the purpose of expanding legislative intent via their own decisions and interpretation of statutes. Discretion is obviously part and parcel of the administrative process, and sufficient discretion is essential for an agency to perform its tasks. However, the question remains: how is discretion determined within the venue of institutional politics?

Existing scholarship on the PTBD assumes that politicians determine the level of discretion agencies enjoy. Administrative agencies are generally treated as being exogenous to the decision of how much discretion politicians will bestow upon them (for a notable exception, see Volden 2002). Simply, agencies are treated as if they do not play an explicit role in determining the amount of discretion that they obtain from political principals. This is a very reasonable perspective if one takes a strict hierarchical view of public bureaucracy in a democracy. After all, elected officials have the appointment (e.g., Moe 1985; Wood and Waterman 1994), resources (e.g., Carpenter 1996; Wood and Anderson 1993; Wood 1990), oversight (e.g., Aberbach 1990; Fiorina 1982), and procedural means (McCubbins 1985; McCubbins, Noll, and Weingast 1987, 1989) to play a substantial role in shaping administrative behavior. Omitting agency choice from the analysis of bureaucratic discretion is problematic if one wishes to obtain a full understanding of this phenomenon. Relations between elected officials and bureaucratic agencies are a "two-way street" in matters involving policy administration (Krause 1996a, 1999). This argument is grounded in the existence of a certain level of agreement occurring between political (superordinate) and bureaucratic (subordinate) institutions, which yields a zone of acceptable behavior for the latter when administering public policy (Barnard 1938; Simon 1976). This, in turn, requires that students of bureaucratic politics must learn more about an agency's demand for discretion before students of institutional politics can construct valid general equilibrium models of bureaucratic discretion that treat both the demand and supply for this commodity in an explicit fashion.

The omission of the demand side of the bureaucratic discretion equation in existing positive political science research is noteworthy for several reasons. First, the policy-making power derived from discretionary authority that accrues to administrative agencies is vast (Rourke 1984, 39). Administrative agencies typically serve as the last line of defense in policy administration within a governmental system. This is because politicians are in a position to shirk responsibility for problems that may arise during policy implementation. Thus, a rational agency will find its interests best served by articulating its demands concerning discretion to politicians by actively lobbying in favor of legislation that it supports while trying to defeat the proposals it opposes (Rieselbach 1995, 212–14). This, in turn, suggests that variations in agencies' demand for discretion can shape the actual amount that they obtain from political superiors. Agencies are also engaged in other activities and stages of the policy process (Meier 1993a, 57), thereby further accentuating the proactive role played by these entities in the realm of policy implementation. An agency can also circumvent electoral institutions by using clientele groups to support its policy mission (Carpenter 2001; Quirk 1981; Rourke 1984; Wilson 1989), thus helping to assist it in conveying the demand for bureaucratic discretion. These activities enable bureaucratic institutions to help shape the level of discretion that they obtain from political superiors as opposed to merely allowing political institutions to make such unabridged choices on their behalf.

In addition, administrative agencies enjoy information advantages with respect to politicians. These asymmetries generate a broader range of policy options or activities in which administrative agencies can engage. As a result, any "discretion equilibrium" between politicians and agencies that exists must take into account the level of discretion the agency desires to obtain for policy implementation purposes. Administrative agencies regularly provide information to legislators and the White House in the formulation of policies that, in turn, often affect the degree of bureaucratic discretion obtained by the agency. Both politicians and agencies possess a strong incentive to ensure that policy administration is successful. Thus, politicians' realization that they do not have the time, expertise, or interest to implement policy on their own will often lead them to consider an agency's preference regarding the amount of bureaucratic discretion that it desires.

Bureaucratic discretion has been treated as being a purely political choice (supply side) and not an agency choice (demand side). Since previous approaches typically ignore the demand-side equation of bureaucratic discretion, the focus of this essay is centered solely on agency choice in obtaining this commodity. The next section focuses on how discrete differences in the discretionary context under which an agency performs are critical for understanding an agency's willingness to acquire discretion.

The Dilemma of Agency Choice: Positive versus Negative Contexts for Bureaucratic Discretion

In order to understand agency choice in determining the amount of discretion that agencies seek to obtain in response to uncertainty over policy (implementation) outcomes, one first must consider that they will possess differential views of this commodity based on whether the circumstances make it relatively more desirable (positive context) or less desirable (negative context). Francis Rourke (1984, 41–42) asserts that discretion is a variable commodity that can be either embraced or spurned by administrators depending upon the nature of its use. James Q. Wilson (1989, 179–81) maintains that bureaucratic autonomy sought by the agency may lead it to expand or cut back the scope of its activities in response to congressional demands. These statements indicate that an agency's discretion can also be viewed as being partly determined by its own choices and decisions, not just those made by politicians. In addition, risk-bearing behavior by administrative agencies will not be fixed but instead depends upon the context in which bureaucratic choices or decisions are made (March 1999, 229).

Likewise, agency utility from bureaucratic discretion can be viewed as varying depending upon the context in which public policies are to be implemented. The nature of the balance of marginal benefits and costs associated with bureaucratic discretion is what distinguishes between the positive and negative contexts confronting the agency. A positive discretionary context occurs when the agency's marginal benefits associated with bureaucratic discretion exceeds its marginal costs ($dB/dD > dC/dD$), while the opposite is true in a negative discretionary context ($dB/dD < dC/dD$).[4] In this analysis, the relative balance of marginal benefits and costs of bureaucratic discretion determines the shape or curvature of such functional relationships. When the balance of marginal benefits and costs associated with discretion are equal ($dB/dD = dC/dD$), then the discretionary context facing the agency will be neutral since they will find it neither more or less favorable to use this commodity.

Therefore, ceteris paribus, positive circumstances lead the agency to view discretion as a relatively more desirable commodity since they deem their environmental and organizational conditions favorable. In this case, the agency can mitigate blame directed toward the organization if policies go awry and/or feel confident that additional discretion will enable it to more effectively tackle the problem. Specifically, an agency operating in a positive discretionary context will be relatively more active in seeking this commodity since it is perceived as being vital to the agency's interests. Conversely, an agency operating in a negative discretionary context will feel that it has much to lose and/or too little to gain in policy implementation, and thus it will seek relatively less of this commodity. In such instances, marginal increases in delegated authority by elected officials to the bureaucracy are viewed negatively by the agency since it does not wish to be made a scapegoat if a favorable policy outcome fails to be obtained. Thus, if a task at hand is very easy or controllable by the agency, little is to be gained from seeking additional discretion. The agency has much to lose if policy outcomes do not turn out well and has little to gain if the policy is successfully implemented. An agency within this context will be less inclined to seek additional discretion.

So what constitutes positive versus negative discretionary contexts confronting an agency on a substantive level? Four possible characteristics can allow one to demarcate between these contexts. The first two are environmental in nature and thus completely beyond the control of the agency. The presence of *divided versus unified government* will have meaningful ramifications in determining whether bureaucratic discretion is viewed favorably or unfavorably by bureaucratic agencies. This distinction reflects discrete differences in the amount of political consensus that exists within electoral institutions.[5] An administrative agency will have a more difficult time making coherent policies under divided government vis-à-vis unified government since it has both less policy-making flexibility (Epstein and O'Halloran 1999, 78) and less institutional stability given the fragmented nature of its political environment. This makes bureaucratic discretion a potentially more harmful commodity in the former era compared to the latter. As a result, during times of divided government administrative agencies will feel less compelled to seek bureaucratic discretion than under an era of unified government since they might not receive the political unity and support that is required for effective policy implementation.[6] *Issue salience* is also important in determining the context in which agency preferences concerning discretion are formed. When issue salience is high for policy under the agency's jurisdiction, an agency will view bureaucratic discretion less favorably, ceteris paribus, because agencies involved in highly salient issues will be easy targets for blame by elected officials and the media. If issue salience is low, however, then the agency will be relatively more willing to seek additional discretion since it does not have to worry about being under the glare of intense scrutiny for its efforts at implementing policy.

Two organizational factors also delineate an agency as operating in a positive or negative discretionary context. When *task complexity* facing an agency is high, it will confront a negative discretionary context since it is more difficult for it to solve public policy problems in a successful fashion. Conversely, when task complexity is low, agencies will experience a positive discretionary context since it is easier for them to handle this particular class of public policy problems. Therefore, agencies will have less to gain from exercising discretion for policy problems of a complex nature (e.g., drug control policy) than when simpler tasks are sufficient for administering public policies (e.g., implementing agricultural subsidy programs). The existence of *agency stability* also plays a vital role in determining whether an agency will function in a positive or negative discretionary context. This concept refers to the overall or general stability of the bureaucratic organization, which comprises agency personnel turnover, workload volatility, the frequency with which rules and procedures for the agency are altered, and the like.

Agencies that are more stable are more apt to benefit from this commodity in relative terms than those that are more volatile. Simply, stable agencies will be more capable of handling discretion than unstable ones. Holding all else constant, agencies that are stable are better equipped to handle a relatively greater amount of discretion whereas agencies that are unstable are better off with relatively less discretion since a higher probability exists that it will be misused. Thus, stable agencies will view discretion in a positive manner while unstable agencies will regard this commodity in a negative light.

Agency Demand for Discretion and Policy Outcome Uncertainty: A Comparative-Static Theoretical Analysis

The aim of this study is to assess the amount of discretion that an agency will "demand" from elected officials in relation to the amount of uncertainty relating to policy implementation outcomes, conditional on the discretionary context. The purpose of this modeling exercise is not to find the level of discretion that maximizes agency utility. Rather, the focus is on agency preference for *more, less,* or the *same* level of discretion in response to a change in policy outcome uncertainty at a given (fixed) level of agency utility. This emphasis on analyzing risk propensities can inform our understanding of how agencies make choices under uncertainty.[7] This is an important avenue of inquiry given that agencies operate in an uncertain environment when implementing public policies (Barnard 1938; Crozier 1964; Downs 1967; Gormley 1989; March 1999; March and Olsen 1976; March and Simon 1958; Simon 1976b; Stinchcombe 1990; Thompson 1967; Wilson 1989). Thus, it is critical to analyze the nature of agency risk-bearing behavior since it is merely assumed a priori for these classes of utility maximization problems under conditions of uncertainty.[8]

The causal path of the theoretical model is portrayed in pictorial terms in figure 1. This diagram shows that the discretionary context has a conditioning effect on how agencies deal with policy outcome uncertainty when determining how much discretion they seek. Assumptions about the direction and curvature of the relationship between (1) agency utility and bureaucratic discretion and (2) agency utility and uncertainty initially must be set forth. The discretionary contexts are reflected in the curvature or shape of these relationships. Positive discretionary contexts will always

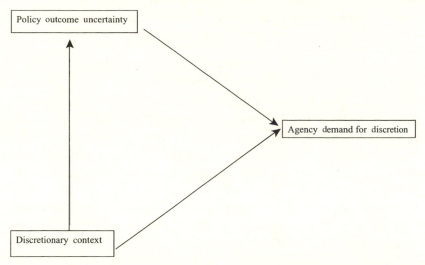

Fig. 1. A theoretical model of bureaucratic discretion as agency choice under uncertainty

exhibit a *convex* agency utility function with respect to bureaucratic discretion and policy outcome uncertainty. Intuitively, for a risk-averse (risk-seeking) agency, a positive discretionary context indicates that each successive drop (rise) in discretion and uncertainty will result in an increasingly smaller (larger) than proportional reduction (increase) in agency utility. In a negative discretionary context, the agency will possess a *concave* utility function with respect to discretion and uncertainty. Therefore, each successive drop (rise) in discretion and uncertainty will result in an increasingly larger (smaller) than proportional reduction (increase) in agency utility under conditions of risk aversion (risk seeking). When a curve is neither convex nor concave (i.e., linear), the positive and negative discretionary contexts are not distinguishable by definition. In instances in which an agency exhibits a mixed discretionary context, whereby discretion is viewed in a positive and uncertainty in a negative context and vice versa, the slope of the rate of change involving the relationship between agency demand for bureaucratic discretion and policy outcome uncertainty will be ambiguous. In addition, the next three subsections analyze the implications of these various risk-bearing behaviors and discretionary contexts in order to understand agency demand for bureaucratic discretion under conditions of uncertainty.

Risk-Bearing Behavior and Discretionary Context:
Case 1—Risk Aversion

One might suppose that a risk-averse agency will be one that wishes to have less bureaucratic discretion as uncertainty rises since they will have the desire to take as little responsibility for the consequences of policy implementation as possible. This means that such an agency will delegate this responsibility to politicians by asking for as little discretion as possible, ceteris paribus. After all, administrative agencies may wish to cut back on the amount of discretion that they desire under certain conditions (Rourke 1984, 41–42; Wilson 1989, 179–181). This proposition can be assessed through a deductive comparative-static analysis.

I assume that an agency's utility function can be expressed in the following general terms.

$$U(D,\sigma) = f(D) + g(\sigma), \tag{1}$$

where agency utility is an additive function of bureaucratic discretion (D) and policy (implementation) outcome uncertainty (σ).[9] For simplicity, I also assume that a risk-averse agency's utility function can be redefined as a power function of the following form.

$$U = c - D^\alpha - \sigma^\beta, \tag{2}$$

where c is a positive constant and utility is declining with respect to bureaucratic discretion and policy outcome uncertainty at the rate of α and β ($\alpha, \beta > 0$), respectively. Furthermore, I assume that the agency's demand for bureaucratic discretion and the uncertainty that it experiences is positive by definition ($D > 0$, $\sigma > 0$), which implies that an agency will desire at least a modicum of discretion and experience at least some minimal amount of policy outcome uncertainty. There are reasonable assumptions given that (1) tightly written laws will typically afford bureaucratic agencies some amount of leeway in interpreting these statutes when implementing public policy, and (2) an agency will not know with certainty the consequences of a policy decision or choice.

The risk-averse agency is assumed to receive negative marginal utility from bureaucratic discretion since it does not wish to obtain considerable leeway, all else being equal. In other words, a risk-averse agency is presumed to exhibit a tendency to spurn additional units of bureaucratic discretion, all else being equal. This assumption differs from much of the PTBD research on this topic, which implicitly views the agency as wishing to maximize its power via discretion in a monotonic fashion. Instead, agencies can prefer either more or less bureaucratic discretion, which varies by the nature of their risk-bearing behavior. Likewise, this type of risk-bearing agency will also obtain negative marginal utility from policy outcome uncertainty regarding the policy that it wishes to implement. Applying the power function rule of differential calculus to solve the partial derivatives of agency utility with respect to bureaucratic discretion and policy outcome uncertainty yields

$$\frac{\partial U}{\partial D} = -\alpha D^{\alpha-1} < 0, \quad \text{and} \tag{3a}$$

$$\frac{\partial U}{\partial \sigma} = -\beta \sigma^{\beta-1} < 0, \tag{3b}$$

where a risk-averse agency must have decreasing utility with respect to both bureaucratic discretion (D) and policy outcome uncertainty (σ). An agency that is risk averse with respect to bureaucratic discretion and policy implementation outcome uncertainty is one that receives disutility from each phenomenon. Simply, a risk-averse agency will prefer less bureaucratic discretion, ceteris paribus. This is because a risk-averse agency, all else being equal, will not wish to have the responsibility associated with additional units of bureaucratic discretion that allows it (instead of politicians) to bear the onus of blame if policy implementation goes awry. Moreover, the risk-averse agency will prefer less policy outcome uncertainty, ceteris paribus. Thus, one can presume that a risk-averse agency will seek less discretion as policy outcome uncertainty rises since it will not wish to have greater responsibility attributed to it by politicians, among others, if policy implementation is deemed unsuccessful. In order to determine whether this proposition is true, I employ the standard power utility function in (2) to examine the manner in which bureaucratic discretion will respond to variations in policy outcome uncertainty.

This requires solving for bureaucratic discretion (D) in (2) and setting agency utility constant, equal to a fixed value, ($U = \bar{U}$), which produces

$$D = (c - \bar{U} - \sigma^\beta)^{1/\alpha}, \tag{4}$$

where $0 < \bar{U} < c$. Thus c serves as a supremum for $\bar{U}$ since $D > 0$ by assumption. Next, the *direction* of this relationship is solved by taking the derivative of (4) with respect to σ. This leads to

$$\frac{dD}{d\sigma} = \frac{1}{\alpha} (c - \bar{U} - \sigma^\beta)^{(1/\alpha)-1} \cdot -\beta\sigma^{\beta-1} < 0 \tag{5}$$

$$= \frac{-\beta}{\alpha} \sigma^{\beta-1} (c - \bar{U} - \sigma^\beta)^{(1/\alpha)-1} < 0,$$

where a risk-averse agency will seek less (more) bureaucratic discretion in response to an increase (decline) in policy outcome uncertainty, ceteris paribus. In simpler terms, a risk-averse agency that enjoys neither bureaucratic discretion nor policy outcome uncertainty will want less bureaucratic discretion when policy outcome uncertainty rises because it will fear the political retribution that it might receive from an unsuccessful policy implementation outcome more than the burden of having to handle a greater amount of bureaucratic discretion. Thus, a risk-averse agency that obtains disutility from both discretion and uncertainty will have an incentive to seek less bureaucratic discretion as a means of coping with the policy outcome uncertainty that it confronts as an organization.

Introducing discretionary context into this model involves allowing the curvature of the relationships involving agency utility with respect to bureaucratic discretion and policy outcome uncertainty to vary accordingly. The rate of change (or slope) parameters associated with these posited relationships will be greater than unity by definition ($\alpha, \beta > 1$) for risk aversion in a negative discretionary context.[10] Solving for the second-order conditions of agency utility with respect to bureaucratic discretion (D) and policy outcome uncertainty (σ) requires taking the partial derivatives of (3a) and (3b), respectively, yielding

$$\frac{\partial^2 U}{\partial D^2} = -(\alpha^2 - \alpha)D^{\alpha-2} < 0 \quad \text{and} \tag{6a}$$

$$\frac{\partial^2 U}{\partial \sigma^2} = -(\beta^2 - \beta)\sigma^{\beta-2} < 0. \tag{6b}$$

A risk-averse agency functioning in a negative discretionary context will exhibit decreasing marginal utility with respect to bureaucratic discretion as well as policy outcome uncertainty. Solving for the second-order derivative associated with (4) will indicate the nature of the curvature of the relationship between agency demand for bureaucratic discretion in relation to policy outcome uncertainty:

$$\frac{d^2D}{d\sigma^2} = \frac{-(\beta^2 - \beta)}{\alpha} \cdot \sigma^{\beta-2} \cdot (c - \bar{U} - \sigma^\beta)^{\frac{1}{\alpha}-1} + \left(\frac{\beta^2}{\alpha^2} - \frac{\beta^2}{\alpha}\right)$$

$$\cdot \sigma^{2\beta-2} \cdot (c - \bar{U} - \sigma^\beta)^{\frac{1}{\alpha}-2} < 0. \tag{7}$$

This comparative-static result reveals that an agency whose marginal disutility from bureaucratic discretion and policy outcome uncertainty is rising at an increasing rate will prefer successively lower amounts of this commodity as uncertainty grows, holding all else constant. Therefore, a risk-averse agency operating under a negative discretionary context will seek larger than proportional reductions in bureaucratic discretion as a rational response to rising uncertainty concerning the policy that it must implement, ceteris paribus.

In the positive discretionary context, the risk-averse agency will also experience an inverse relationship between its utility with respect to bureaucratic discretion and policy outcome uncertainty (i.e., $\partial U/\partial D < 0$; $\partial U/\partial \sigma < 0$). What differs in the positive vis-à-vis the negative context is that the rate of change of this inverse relationship differs. Specifically, the rate of change (or slope) parameters associated with these relationships will lie in the interval between zero and positive unity ($0 < \alpha, \beta < 1$). Taking the partial derivatives of agency utility with respect to bureaucratic discretion (D) and policy outcome uncertainty (σ) in (3a) and (3b) produces

$$\frac{\partial^2 U}{\partial D^2} = -(\alpha^2 - \alpha)D^{\alpha-2} > 0 \quad \text{and} \tag{8a}$$

$$\frac{\partial^2 U}{\partial \sigma^2} = -(\beta^2 - \beta)\sigma^{\beta-2} > 0. \tag{8b}$$

Thus, a risk-averse agency confronting a positive discretionary context will exhibit increasing marginal utility with respect to bureaucratic discretion as well as policy outcome uncertainty. Taking the second-order derivative of (5) with respect to σ determines the curvature of the relationship between agency demand for bureaucratic discretion in relation to policy outcome uncertainty.

$$\frac{d^2D}{d\sigma^2} = \frac{-(\beta^2 - \beta)}{\alpha} \cdot \sigma^{\beta-2} \cdot (c - \bar{U} - \sigma^\beta)^{\frac{1}{\alpha}-1} + \left(\frac{\beta^2}{\alpha^2} - \frac{\beta^2}{\alpha}\right)$$

$$\cdot \sigma^{2\beta-2} \cdot (c - \bar{U} - \sigma^\beta)^{\frac{1}{\alpha}-2} > 0. \tag{9}$$

This comparative-static result reveals that an agency whose marginal disutility from bureaucratic discretion and policy outcome uncertainty is increasing at a declining rate will prefer successively smaller cuts in this commodity as uncertainty grows, holding all else constant. Therefore, a risk-averse agency operating in a positive discretionary context will seek smaller than proportional reductions in bureaucratic discretion as a rational response to rising uncertainty concerning the policy that it must implement, ceteris paribus.

There are two intermediate situations in which the agency might be facing a positive context with respect to discretion and a negative context with respect to uncertainty. Under these circumstances, rate of change (or slope) parameters associated with these relationships will lie in the interval between zero and positive unity for the discretion parameter ($0 < \alpha < 1$) and will be greater than positive unity for the uncertainty parameter ($\beta > 1$). This will lead to the following result involving the curvature of the relationship between agency demand for bureaucratic discretion in relation to policy outcome uncertainty based on (9).

$$\frac{d^2D}{d\sigma^2} > 0 \quad \text{if } \Gamma < \Pi; \frac{d^2D}{d\sigma^2} = 0 \quad \text{if } \Gamma = \Pi; \qquad \text{and}$$

$$\frac{d^2D}{d\sigma^2} < 0 \quad \text{if } \Gamma > \Pi, \tag{10}$$

where $\Gamma = -(\beta^2 - \beta)/\alpha \cdot \sigma^{\beta-2} \cdot (c - \bar{U} - \sigma^\beta)^{(1/\alpha)-1}$ and $\Pi = (\beta^2/\alpha^2 - \beta^2/\alpha) \cdot \sigma^{2\beta-2} \cdot (c - \bar{U} - \sigma^\beta)^{(1/\alpha)-2}$. Conversely, when the mixture of a negative context for discretion and a positive context for uncertainty exists the risk-averse agency will possess a discretion parameter that is greater than positive unity ($\alpha > 1$) and an uncertainty parameter that lies between zero and positive unity ($0 < \beta < 1$). As before, the curvature of the relationship between agency demand for bureaucratic discretion in relation to policy outcome uncertainty based on (9) will be ambiguous so that it is a mirror image of (10).

$$\frac{d^2D}{d\sigma^2} > 0 \quad \text{if } \Gamma > \Pi; \frac{d^2D}{d\sigma^2} = 0 \quad \text{if } \Gamma = \Pi; \quad \text{and}$$

$$\frac{d^2D}{d\sigma^2} < 0 \quad \text{if } \Gamma < \Pi. \tag{11}$$

If discretionary context does not matter for risk-averse agencies, they will exhibit constant diminishing marginal utility (i.e., a negative linear relationship) with respect to bureaucratic discretion and policy outcome uncertainty ($\alpha, \beta = 1$). Thus, risk-averse agencies experiencing neither favorable nor unfavorable discretionary conditions will prefer proportional reductions in bureaucratic discretion in response to policy outcome uncertainty, ceteris paribus. Simply, a risk-averse agency whose marginal benefits associated with discretion equal its marginal costs, $dB/dD = dC/dD$, will have a downward-sloping linear relationship with policy outcome uncertainty, $dD/d\sigma < 0$, $d^2D/d\sigma^2 = 0$. In other words, the risk-averse agency's demand for bureaucratic discretion will be negative with respect to policy outcome uncertainty; however, it will not display a proclivity for additional marginal gains or reductions in this commodity. This makes logical sense when one considers that if the marginal benefits and costs of bureaucratic discretion are equal then discretionary context is neutral and hence the agency will not have any incentive to acquire successively greater or smaller reductions in bureaucratic discretion in response to changes in policy outcome uncertainty.

Risk-Bearing Behavior and Discretionary Context: Case II—Risk Neutrality

In the risk-neutral case, it must necessarily be true that agency utility is unrelated to policy outcome uncertainty by definition (i.e., $\partial U/\partial \sigma = 0$). Although one cannot as confidently state the sign of the relationship associated with agency utility and bureaucratic discretion, it is sure to be small in magnitude relative to the risk-averse and risk-seeking cases $|\partial U_{RN}/\partial D_{RN}| < |\partial U_{RA,RS}/\partial D_{RA,RS}|$. This is because these latter types of agencies will derive greater (or less) utility from additional units of bureaucratic discretion.[11] Moreover, one can deduce that the following pattern will hold.

$$\frac{\partial U_{RA}}{\partial D_{RA}} < \frac{\partial U_{RN}}{\partial D_{RN}} < \frac{\partial U_{RS}}{\partial D_{RS}}, \tag{12}$$

where the slope for the risk-neutral agency falls somewhere between those of the risk-averse and risk-seeking agencies yet is assumed to be nonzero by definition. Then, if $\partial U/\partial \sigma = 0$ and $\partial U/\partial D \neq 0$, it must follow that $dD/d\sigma = 0$. In other words, a risk-neutral agency will not seek additional increases or reductions in bureaucratic discretion in response to policy outcome uncertainty, ceteris paribus.[12] Thus, an agency exhibiting risk neutrality in its demand for bureaucratic discretion is insensitive to policy outcome uncertainty. If this is the case, then it naturally follows that discretionary context cannot affect the bureaucratic discretion–policy outcome uncertainty relationship since $d^2D/d\sigma^2 = 0$ by definition.

Risk-Bearing Behavior and Discretionary Context: Case III—Risk Seeking

An agency that is risk-seeking will have the following utility function.

$$U = c + D^\alpha + \sigma^\beta, \tag{13}$$

which is the same form as (2) except that utility is assumed to be increasing with respect to bureaucratic discretion and policy outcome uncertainty at the rate of α and β ($\alpha, \beta > 0$), respectively. In other words, a risk-seeking agency will accrue positive marginal utility from both bureaucratic discretion and policy outcome uncertainty. This is because a risk-seeking agency will prefer both the greater responsibility associated with increases in discretion and the increased uncertainty surrounding policy implementation outcomes, ceteris paribus. Thus, a risk-seeking agency is viewed as willing to take on the dual pressure of more freedom or leeway in implementing policies as well as facing a more uncertain policy environment. Solving the partial derivatives of agency utility with respect to bureaucratic discretion and policy outcome uncertainty demonstrates this to be the case.

$$\frac{\partial U}{\partial D} = \alpha D^{\alpha-1} > 0 \quad \text{and} \tag{14a}$$

$$\frac{\partial U}{\partial \sigma} = \beta \sigma^{\beta-1} > 0, \tag{14b}$$

where a risk-seeking agency must have increasing utility with respect to both bureaucratic discretion (D) and policy outcome uncertainty (σ).

Solving for D in (13) and setting agency utility constant equal to a fixed value, $(U = \bar{U})$, yields

$$D = (\bar{U} - c - \sigma^\beta)^{1/\alpha}, \tag{15}$$

where $0 < c < \bar{U}$. Thus $\bar{U}$ serves as a supremum for c since $D > 0$ by assumption. Next, one can solve for the *direction* of this relationship by taking the first-order derivative of (15) with respect to σ in order to obtain

$$\frac{dD}{d\sigma} = \frac{1}{\alpha}(\bar{U} - c - \sigma^\beta)^{\frac{1}{\alpha}-1} \cdot -\beta\sigma^{\beta-1} < 0$$

$$= \frac{-\beta}{\alpha}\sigma^{\beta-1}(\bar{U} - c - \sigma^\beta)^{\frac{1}{\alpha}-1} < 0, \tag{16}$$

where a risk-seeking agency, just as the case with a risk-averse agency, will seek less (more) bureaucratic discretion in response to increases (decreases) in policy outcome uncertainty. Therefore, a risk-seeking agency that obtains increasing utility from both greater bureaucratic discretion and policy outcome uncertainty will seek less (more) of the former commodity as the latter rises (declines). This counterintuitive relationship suggests that a risk-seeking agency may treat bureaucratic discretion in relation to policy outcome uncertainty as a double-edged sword whereby increases in uncertainty provide it with an incentive to reduce its demand for this commodity.

Consistent with the risk-averse scenario, if discretionary context matters then the discretion-uncertainty relationship cannot be a linear one—that is, $d^2D/d\sigma^2 \neq 0$. In the negative discretionary context, the rate of change parameters lies in the interval between zero and positive unity ($0 < \alpha, \beta < 1$). The subsequent second-order partial derivatives of agency utility with respect to bureaucratic discretion and policy outcome uncertainty must be negative by definition.

$$\frac{\partial^2 U}{\partial D^2} = (\alpha^2 - \alpha)D^{\alpha-2} < 0 \quad \text{and} \tag{17a}$$

$$\frac{\partial^2 U}{\partial \sigma^2} = (\beta^2 - \beta)\sigma^{\beta-2} < 0. \tag{17b}$$

Put simply, risk-seeking agencies operating under a negative discretionary context obtain diminishing marginal utility from bureaucratic discretion and policy outcome uncertainty. Therefore, agencies operating under these conditions will demand smaller than proportional reductions (increases) in bureaucratic discretion relative to increases (decreases) in policy outcome uncertainty—that is, $d^2D/d\sigma^2 > 0$. Thus, a risk-averse agency operating in a positive discretionary context will behave in the same manner as a risk-seeking agency functioning under a negative discretionary context according to these comparative-static results.

Conversely, risk-seeking agencies functioning in a positive discretionary context will exhibit increasing marginal utility from bureaucratic discretion and policy outcome uncertainty ($\alpha, \beta > 1$) so that each relationship is convex: $\partial^2 U/\partial D^2 > 0$; $\partial^2 U/\partial \sigma^2 > 0$. This implies that this type of risk-seeking agency will prefer larger than proportional reductions (increases) in bureaucratic discretion relative to increases (decreases) in policy outcome uncertainty—that is, $d^2D/d\sigma^2 < 0$. A risk-seeking agency in a positive discretionary context behaving in such a manner is suggestive of an organization that wishes to reduce the level of this commodity when uncertainty rises. Surprisingly, this is the same behavior one can expect from a risk-averse agency dealing with a negative discretionary context. In the case in which discretionary context does not matter (i.e., is neither positive or negative), the negative relationship between bureaucratic discretion and policy outcome uncertainty will be linear—that is, $d^2D/d\sigma^2 = 0$.

In the case of a mixture context, whereby discretion is consistent with a positive context while uncertainty transpires under a negative context ($\alpha > 1, 0 < \beta < 1$), the comparative-static results are a function of the relative magnitude of the Γ and Π expressions noted earlier.[13] Specifically,

$$\frac{d^2D}{d\sigma^2} > 0 \quad \text{if } \Gamma > \Pi; \frac{d^2D}{d\sigma^2} = 0 \quad \text{if } \Gamma = \Pi; \text{ and } \frac{d^2D}{d\sigma^2} < 0 \quad \text{if } \Gamma < \Pi.$$

In the opposite case, in which discretion is a negative and uncertainty a positive context for the risk-seeking agency ($0 < \alpha < 1, \beta > 1$), the comparative-static results are as follows.

$$\frac{d^2D}{d\sigma^2} > 0 \quad \text{if } \Gamma < \Pi; \frac{d^2D}{d\sigma^2} = 0 \quad \text{if } \Gamma = \Pi; \text{ and } \frac{d^2D}{d\sigma^2} < 0 \quad \text{if } \Gamma > \Pi.$$

Table 1 presents a summary of the theoretical predictions derived from this simple comparative-static analysis of agency demand for bureaucratic discretion under conditions of (policy outcome) uncertainty. These theoretical results indicate that risk-averse agency behavior will resemble that

TABLE 1. Summary of Theoretical Predictions of Bureaucratic Discretion as Agency Choice under Uncertainty (power functional form and corresponding set of assumptions)

	Positive Discretionary Context	Mixed Discretionary Context		Neutral Discretionary Context	Negative Discretionary Context
		Discretion, Positive Uncertainty, Negative	Discretion, Negative Uncertainty, Positive		
Type of agency risk-bearing behavior	$\frac{dB}{dD} > \frac{dC}{dD}$	D: $\frac{dB}{dD} > \frac{dC}{dD}$ σ: $\frac{dB}{dD} > \frac{dC}{dD}$	D: $\frac{dB}{dD} < \frac{dC}{dD}$ σ: $\frac{dB}{dD} > \frac{dC}{dD}$	$\frac{dB}{dD} = \frac{dC}{dD}$	$\frac{dB}{dD} < \frac{dC}{dD}$
Discretionary risk aversion	$\frac{dD}{d\sigma} < 0$ $\frac{d^2D}{d\sigma^2} > 0$	$\frac{dD}{d\sigma} < 0$ $\frac{d^2D}{d\sigma^2} > 0$ if $\Gamma < \Pi$ $\frac{d^2D}{d\sigma^2} = 0$ if $\Gamma = \Pi$ $\frac{d^2D}{d\sigma^2} < 0$ if $\Gamma > \Pi$	$\frac{dD}{d\sigma} < 0$ $\frac{d^2D}{d\sigma^2} > 0$ if $\Gamma > \Pi$ $\frac{d^2D}{d\sigma^2} = 0$ if $\Gamma = \Pi$ $\frac{d^2D}{d\sigma^2} < 0$ if $\Gamma < \Pi$	$\frac{dD}{d\sigma} < 0$ $\frac{d^2D}{d\sigma^2} = 0$	$\frac{dD}{d\sigma} < 0$ $\frac{d^2D}{d\sigma^2} < 0$
Discretionary risk neutral	$\frac{dD}{d\sigma} = 0;\ \frac{d^2D}{d\sigma^2} = 0$	$\frac{dD}{d\sigma} = 0;\ \frac{d^2D}{d\sigma^2} = 0$	$\frac{dD}{d\sigma} = 0;\ \frac{d^2D}{d\sigma^2} = 0$	$\frac{dD}{d\sigma} = 0;\ \frac{d^2D}{d\sigma^2} = 0$	$\frac{dD}{d\sigma} = 0;\ \frac{d^2D}{d\sigma^2} = 0$
Discretionary risk seeking	$\frac{dD}{d\sigma} < 0$ $\frac{d^2D}{d\sigma^2} < 0$	$\frac{dD}{d\sigma} < 0$ $\frac{d^2D}{d\sigma^2} > 0$ if $\Gamma > \Pi$ $\frac{d^2D}{d\sigma^2} = 0$ if $\Gamma = \Pi$ $\frac{d^2D}{d\sigma^2} < 0$ if $\Gamma < \Pi$	$\frac{dD}{d\sigma} < 0$ $\frac{d^2D}{d\sigma^2} > 0$ if $\Gamma < \Pi$ $\frac{d^2D}{d\sigma^2} = 0$ if $\Gamma = \Pi$ $\frac{d^2D}{d\sigma^2} < 0$ if $\Gamma > \Pi$	$\frac{dD}{d\sigma} < 0$ $\frac{d^2D}{d\sigma^2} > 0$	$\frac{dD}{d\sigma} < 0$ $\frac{d^2D}{d\sigma^2} > 0$

of a risk-seeking agency given that in both cases an agency will seek less bureaucratic discretion in response to rising policy outcome uncertainty. Furthermore, they also show that a risk-averse (-seeking) agency operating in a negative (positive) discretionary context will behave the same as a risk-seeking (averse) agency facing a positive (negative) discretionary context. The theoretical predictions become ambiguous when one considers a mixture of contexts in which bureaucratic discretion is sought by administrative agencies under conditions of uncertainty.

Even so, this model predicts that under no circumstances will an agency seek greater bureaucratic discretion in response to rising uncertainty. Underlying this result is the assumption made earlier that risk-averse agencies will receive disutility from additional units of bureaucratic discretion and policy outcome uncertainty while risk-seeking agencies will garner positive utility from additional units of each commodity. Moreover, the rate at which bureaucratic discretion and policy outcome uncertainty separately contribute to agency utility is assumed to lie in the same parameter interval range for those instances in which a discretionary context is neither neutral nor a mixture process.

Substantive Hypotheses Involving Discretionary Contexts Implied from the Theoretical Model

Underlying this theory is the presumption that bureaucratic discretion is a tool of policy influence that administrative agencies can either embrace or spurn (Rourke 1984, 41–42; Wilson 1989, 179–81). This section presents specific theoretical predictions of this model within the context of both environmental and organizational characteristics. In turn, these characteristics determine whether the agency is operating under positive or negative conditions, and thus affects the context by which they seek discretion. For purposes of brevity, this discussion is limited to this qualitative distinction and does not explore the mixture contexts considered in the comparative-static analysis presented earlier. This latter task is best left for subsequent research on this topic.

Hypothesis 1: Divided versus Unified Government

The existence or absence of unified partisan control of the executive and legislative branches will be important in understanding the discretionary context in which administrative agencies operate as decision makers. For reasons discussed earlier in this essay, divided government will constitute a negative discretionary context for the agency, while unified government will provide a positive discretionary context. Therefore, a risk-averse agency operating under divided government will have the same inverse discretionary response to uncertainty as a risk-seeking agency under unified government. In both instances, an agency will prefer a larger rather than a proportional inverse change in bureaucratic discretion relative to policy outcome uncertainty. It will also prefer successively less bureaucratic discretion as policy outcome uncertainty rises, even though its posited risk-bearing behavior (via its demand for discretion and policy outcome uncertainty's separate impact on utility) and discretionary context could not be more different. Conversely, a risk-averse (-seeking) agency operating under unified (divided) government will prefer a *smaller* than proportional inverse change in bureaucratic discretion in response to a unit change in policy outcome uncertainty. In these latter instances, discretionary context offsets risk-bearing behavior so that the positive context of the risk-averse agency under a unified government leads it to behave in a substantively identical manner to the risk-seeking agency under divided government. Finally, the distinction involving divided versus unified government has no substantive bearing on the agency's demand for discretion under conditions of risk neutrality since it is indifferent to uncertainty by definition.

Hypothesis 2: Issue Salience

Issue salience is also important in determining how agencies view bureaucratic discretion. If issue salience is high for the policy under the agency's jurisdiction, then the agency will view discretion as providing a negative discretionary context. However, if issue salience is low for the policy under the agency's jurisdiction, then the agency will operate in a positive discretionary context. Therefore, low issue salience will lead a risk-averse agency to seek a smaller than proportional decline in bureaucratic discretion in response to a rise involving policy outcome uncertainty, while a risk-seeking agency will seek a larger than proportional reduction in this commodity. Conversely, high issue salience will make a risk-averse agency seek a larger than proportional decline in bureaucratic discretion in response to a rise involving policy outcome uncertainty, while a risk-seeking agency will desire a smaller than proportional reduction in this commodity. Issue salience will not have an effect on the amount of discretion that the agency wishes to obtain when it behaves in a risk-neutral manner.

Hypothesis 3: Task Complexity

The technical complexity of policy tasks (referred to as *task complexity*) performed by the implementing agency will also be important in determining whether bureaucratic discretion is viewed in a positive or negative light on behalf of the agency. As discussed earlier, from the agency's perspective low task complexity is conducive to bureaucratic discretion (positive discretionary context) while high task complexity is not (negative discretionary context). The comparative-static results suggest that a risk-averse agency confronting low task complexity will demand successively smaller reductions in bureaucratic discretion as policy outcome uncertainty rises, whereas a risk-seeking agency facing the same type of complexity will prefer successively larger decreases of this commodity. In the case of high task complexity, the risk-averse agency will demand successively larger reductions in this commodity in response to rising policy outcome uncertainty. The risk-seeking agency facing the same situation will prefer successively smaller reductions in bureaucratic discretion as policy outcome uncertainty increases. Task complexity will have no effect on the relationship between agency demand for discretion and the policy outcome uncertainty that agencies experience in the case of risk neutrality.

Hypothesis 4: Agency Stability

Agency stability will also be essential in determining whether the pursuit of discretion under uncertainty results in a particular type of risk-bearing agency behavior. For reasons discussed earlier, stable agencies will possess a positive discretionary context, ceteris paribus, since they will be better equipped to handle bureaucratic discretion. Unstable agencies will be operating under a negative discretionary context, ceteris paribus, since greater discretion translates into a higher likelihood of bungling policy implementation. According to the theoretical model, a risk-averse agency in a stable (unstable) organizational setting will seek successively smaller (greater) reductions in bureaucratic discretion as policy outcome uncertainty increases. However, a risk-seeking agency that is stable (unstable) will seek larger (smaller) than proportional decreases in this commodity as policy outcome uncertainty rises. In the risk-neutrality scenario, whether the agency is stable or unstable will make no difference in how the agency's demand for bureaucratic discretion responds to policy outcome uncertainty.

Discussion

Existing positive theories of bureaucratic discretion (PTBD) typically view this commodity as being solely determined in a top-down fashion by either legislators' decision-making calculus (e.g., Bawn 1995; Fiorina 1986; McCubbins 1985; McCubbins, Noll, and Weingast 1987, 1989; see Huber and Shipan 2002 for an excellent overview of this literature) or as a separation of powers struggle between the legislature and chief executive (Epstein and O'Halloran 1994, 1996, 1999; Huber and Shipan 2000, 2002). This body of research constitutes an extremely significant contribution to our basic understanding as to when and why administrative agencies receive discretion from political superiors based on the latter's willingness to supply this commodity.

In these studies, however, the degree of agency independence (i.e., discretion) is a choice not left to administrative organizations; instead, it is purely a function of political institutions' choice (but see Volden 2002). Thus, one obtains a well-developed portrait of the supply side of bureaucratic discretion that captures what the producers of this good (politicians) are willing to supply to their consumers (administrative agencies). Unfortunately, the other half of the story, the agency's demand (or desire) for discretion, has gone unexplored in these accounts. This is an important omission for those wishing to understand agency-political equilibrium outcomes concerning both the demand and supply of this commodity. The rise of bureaucratic discretion over the past century has provided agencies with considerable policy-making power in the modern administrative state (Lowi 1969). This has provided bureaucratic institutions with a voice of their own in shaping the contents of legislation by lobbying for legislation that they support and in trying to defeat the proposals they oppose (Rieselbach 1995, 212–14). As James Q. Wilson (1989, 251) aptly notes in his discussion of agency response to legislative control, "The bureaucracy is hardly the passive agent of its congressional overseers; like the wily manservant in *The Marriage of Figaro,* it is constantly working to manipulate its master so as to achieve mutually profitable arrangements." Therefore, considering the demand side of bureaucratic discretion is essential if one wishes to obtain an equilibrium-based understanding of this commodity that is explicitly determined by agency-political interactions.

The basic theoretical motivation underlying the comparative-static analysis conducted in this study is straightforward. Understanding an agency's pursuit of discretion in an uncertain environment requires scholars to consider the discretionary context reflected by the balance of marginal costs and benefits associated with this commodity. This is consistent with theoretical research on organizations that emphasizes context-dependent considerations affecting bureaucratic choice under uncertainty (March 1999, 244–45; Thompson 1967, 118–21). Further, the nature of risk-taking behavior observed in administrative organizations is not only affected by expected risk calculations akin to a risk-neutral decision maker but also by the propensities of these organizations to either seek or avoid a particular level of expected risk (March 1999, 20).

The analytical results of this study demonstrate that an agency demanding less bureaucratic discretion in response to higher policy outcome uncertainty may paradoxically reflect either risk-averse or risk-seeking behavior regardless of the discretionary context, yet the rate at which this inverse relationship varies will depend upon whether agencies are confronting a positive or negative discretionary context. In a positive discretionary context, the comparative-static results reveal that risk-averse agencies will seek decreasing marginal declines in bureaucratic discretion as policy outcome uncertainty rises, whereas a risk-seeking agency will exhibit increasing marginal reductions in this commodity. In a negative discretionary context, the comparative-static results indicate that a risk-averse agency will prefer larger rather than proportional inverse changes in bureaucratic discretion with respect to policy outcome uncertainty, while a risk-seeking agency will prefer a smaller rather than proportional inverse change involving this same relationship. When the discretionary context is mixed, the theoretical predictions that flow from this comparative-static analysis are ambiguous and depend partly upon the extent to which a positive discretionary context, on one hand, is offset by a negative discretionary context. In the case in which discretionary context is neutral, one can neither theoretically nor empirically discriminate between risk-averse and risk-seeking agency behavior since each will possess constant marginal declines in bureaucratic discretion in relation to policy outcome uncertainty. In the special case of risk neutrality, the agency's discretionary context will have no conditional bearing on determining its risk-bearing behavior since its demand for bureaucratic discretion is completely divorced from policy outcome uncertainty. The theoretical predictions generated from this analytical exercise are empirically testable and also directly relevant to administrative agencies' desire to have variable levels of discretion at their disposal for policy administration purposes (Rourke 1984, Thompson 1967, Wilson 1989).

This study has important implications for advancing our understanding of how bureaucratic agencies operate within a political environment on a systemic level. The theoretical argument contained in this essay is suggestive of the considerable importance associated with agency response to uncertainty being conditioned by the context that they experience on a given dimension at a single point in time. Specifically, if the goal is to understand the risk-bearing behavior of bureaucratic agencies in seeking discretion, then one must consider the context that these administrative organizations are confronting. In this particular analysis, agency decision making is a function of context and uncertainty, where the former refers to the known environment that they observe ex post and the latter pertains to uncertainty concerning ex ante successful policy implementation. On a more fundamental level, the motivation underlying this study attempts to convey the important point that administrative agencies do not passively serve as the pawns of electoral institutions in a representative democracy, as is portrayed in a considerable portion of the existing research on bureaucratic organizations within political science. Instead, these entities exhibit proactive behavior and thus can directly shape both the political and policy environments in which they operate (Brehm and Gates 1997; Carpenter 2001; Krause 1996a, 1999).

In the parlance of consumer theory in microeconomics, the concept of equilibrium typically refers to the relationship between supply and demand of a commodity. If one views bureaucratic discretion as a commodity that is supplied by electoral institutions and demanded by administrative agencies, then one cannot accurately characterize agency-political equilibrium relationships involving policy administration without explicit consideration of both components. David Spence (1997a) correctly notes that existing positive theories of bureaucratic discretion emphasize the goals and decision making of politicians in shaping administrative behavior yet fail to provide commensurate attention to agency goals and policy choice. While this study does not provide a general equilibrium framework for understanding the issue of agency-political equilibrium relations, it does take an initial step in this direction by investigating the nature of agency demand for bureaucratic discretion.

Much scholarly effort is needed in exploring both the theoretical explication and the systematic empirical testing of the demand side of bureaucratic discretion before knowledge can be acquired that can appropriately complement the increasingly well developed literature on the supply side of how political institutions choose to allocate (delegate) this commodity to bureaucratic organizations. The ultimate goal of a political-agency general equilibrium theory of bureaucratic discretion can only be attained when our understanding involving the supply and demand of this commodity are each sufficiently well developed. While this essay has set forth an analytical framework for studying the risk propensities of bureaucratic agency decision making, considerably more work remains to be done on this fertile topic for both students of institutional politics and administrative organizations to explore.

Appendix: General Solution to Agency Risk Propensities and Demand for Bureaucratic Discretion

The general solution that demonstrates the comparative-statics hold for the bureaucratic discretion policy outcome and uncertainty relationship, irrespective of the functional form adopted for purposes of analysis, is straightforward. If one begins with the generic agency utility function involving agencies' demand for bureaucratic discretion under conditions of uncertainty, as in (2)—dropping constant terms—the following remains.

$$U(D,\sigma) = f(D) + g(\sigma),$$ (A1)

where agency utility is an additive function of bureaucratic discretion (D) and policy (implementation) outcome uncertainty (σ). The partial derivatives of (A1) are such that

$$f'(D) = \frac{\partial U}{\partial D}; \qquad g'(\sigma) = \frac{\partial U}{\partial \sigma}.$$ (A2)

In order to solve for $dD/d\sigma$ and $d^2D/d\sigma^2$, respectively, agency utility must be fixed so that $U = \bar{U}$. Rewriting (A1) based on a positive level of fixed utility gives us

$$\bar{U} = f(D) + g(\sigma).$$ (A3)

Differentiating (A3) with respect to σ yields

$$0 = f'(D) \frac{dD}{d\sigma} + g'(\sigma), \tag{A4}$$

and solving (A4) in terms of $dD/d\sigma$ gives us the following expression for the general first-order condition of this problem.

$$\frac{dD}{d\sigma} = \frac{-g'(\sigma)}{f'(D)}. \tag{A5}$$

Since I assume that agency utility has the same directional relationship with respect to D and σ separately in the risk-averse and risk-seeking conditions, $dD/d\sigma < 0$ by definition. In the risk-neutral case, $dD/d\sigma = 0$ by definition because $g'(\sigma) = 0$ and $f'(D) \neq 0$ by assumption. Solving for the second-order conditions involves differentiating (A5) via the quotient rule and yields the following general solution.

$$\frac{d^2 D}{d\sigma^2} = \frac{-f'(D) \cdot g''(\sigma) + g'(\sigma) \cdot f''(D) \cdot \frac{dD}{d\sigma}}{[f'(D)]^2}, \tag{A6a}$$

and substituting the equivalent $-g'(\sigma)/f'(D)$ for $dD/d\sigma$ gives us

$$= \frac{-f'(D) \cdot g''(\sigma) + g'(\sigma) \cdot f''(D) \cdot \frac{-g'(\sigma)}{f'(D)}}{[f'(D)]^2}. \tag{A6b}$$

Multiplying both sides by $f'(D)$ and combining some terms yields the general solution for discretionary context:

$$= \frac{-[f'(D)]^2 \cdot g''(\sigma) - [g'(\sigma)]^2 \cdot f''(D)}{[f'(D)]^3}. \tag{A6c}$$

The sign of the function associated with the general solution to the second-order conditions will depend upon the sign of $f'(D)$ as well as for both $f''(D)$ and $g''(\sigma)$. There are eight possible combinations covering risk aversion and risk-seeking agency behavior under nonneutral (positive or negative) discretionary contexts. They are summarized here.

Agency Risk Aversion

Case I (Positive):

If $f'(D) < 0$ and $f''(D) \cdot g''(\sigma) > 0$, then $\frac{d^2 D}{d\sigma^2} > 0.$ $\tag{A7}$

Case II (Mixed) (D, Positive; σ, Negative):

If $f'(D) < 0$ and $f''(D) > 0$, $g''(\sigma) < 0$, then $\tag{A8}$

$$\frac{d^2D}{d\sigma^2} > 0 \quad \text{when } |[f'(D)]^2 \cdot g''(\sigma)| < |[g'(\sigma)]^2 \cdot f''(D)|,$$

$$\frac{d^2D}{d\sigma^2} = 0 \quad \text{when } |[f'(D)]^2 \cdot g''(\sigma)| = |[g'(\sigma)]^2 \cdot f''(D)|,$$

$$\frac{d^2D}{d\sigma^2} < 0 \quad \text{when } |[f'(D)]^2 \cdot g''(\sigma)| > |[g'(\sigma)]^2 \cdot f''(D)|.$$

Case III (Mixed) (D, Negative; σ, Positive):

If $f'(D) < 0$ and $f''(D) < 0$, $g''(\sigma) > 0$, then   (A9)

$$\frac{d^2D}{d\sigma^2} > 0 \quad \text{when } |[f'(D)]^2 \cdot g''(\sigma)| > |[g'(\sigma)]^2 \cdot f''(D)|,$$

$$\frac{d^2D}{d\sigma^2} = 0 \quad \text{when } |[f'(D)]^2 \cdot g''(\sigma)| = |[g'(\sigma)]^2 \cdot f''(D)|,$$

$$\frac{d^2D}{d\sigma^2} < 0 \quad \text{when } |[f'(D)]^2 \cdot g''(\sigma)| < |[g'(\sigma)]^2 \cdot f''(D)|.$$

Case IV (Negative):

If $f'(D) < 0$ and $f''(D)$, $g''(\sigma) < 0$, then $\dfrac{d^2D}{d\sigma^2} < 0.$ (A10)

Agency Risk Seeking

Case V (Positive):

If $f'(D) > 0$ and $f''(D)$, $g''(\sigma) > 0$, then $\dfrac{d^2D}{d\sigma^2} < 0.$ (A11)

Case VI (Mixed) (D, Positive; σ, Negative):

If $f'(D) > 0$ and $f''(D) > 0$, $g''(\sigma) < 0$, then   (A12)

$$\frac{d^2D}{d\sigma^2} > 0 \quad \text{when } |[f'(D)]^2 \cdot g''(\sigma)| > |[g'(\sigma)]^2 \cdot f''(D)|,$$

$$\frac{d^2D}{d\sigma^2} = 0 \quad \text{when } |[f'(D)]^2 \cdot g''(\sigma)| = |[g'(\sigma)]^2 \cdot f''(D)|,$$

$$\frac{d^2D}{d\sigma^2} < 0 \quad \text{when } |[f'(D)]^2 \cdot g''(\sigma)| < |[g'(\sigma)]^2 \cdot f''(D)|.$$

Case VII (Mixed) (D, Negative; σ, Positive):

If $f'(D) > 0$ and $f''(D) < 0$, $g''(\sigma) > 0$, then   (A13)

$$\frac{d^2D}{d\sigma^2} > 0 \quad \text{when } |[f'(D)]^2 \cdot g''(\sigma)| < |[g'(\sigma)]^2 \cdot f''(D)|,$$

$$\frac{d^2D}{d\sigma^2} = 0 \quad \text{when } |[f'(D)]^2 \cdot g''(\sigma)| = |[g'(\sigma)]^2 \cdot f''(D)|,$$

$$\frac{d^2D}{d\sigma^2} < 0 \quad \text{when } |[f'(D)]^2 \cdot g''(\sigma)| > |[g'(\sigma)]^2 \cdot f''(D)|.$$

Case VIII (Negative):

$$\text{If } f'(D) > 0 \text{ and } f''(D), g''(\sigma) < 0, \text{ then } \frac{d^2D}{d\sigma^2} > 0. \tag{A14}$$

In the preceding eight cases, the discretionary context is presumed to be non-neutral (i.e., a positive or negative discretionary context). In instances in which discretionary context is neutral, the second-order conditions must equal zero. If this is to be true, then the following must hold: $f'(D) \neq 0$; $f''(D)$, $g''(\sigma) = 0$. This occurs for both risk-averse and risk-seeking agencies when the marginal benefits and costs associated with bureaucratic discretion are equal (i.e., $dB/dD = dC/dD$) and also under the condition of risk neutrality (i.e., $dD/d\sigma = 0$).

Notes

An earlier version of this essay was prepared for delivery at the Fifth National Public Management Conference. The George Bush School of Government and Public Service. Texas A&M University. College Station, Texas, December 3–4, 1999. The current version has greatly benefited from the thoughtful insights of Dan Carpenter, Stephen Dilworth, Brad Gomez, Ken Meier, Matt Potoski, Dale Thomas, Andy Whitford, LeeAnne Krause, and two anonymous referees. None of the aforementioned individuals bear responsibility for any shortcomings associated with this essay.

The quotation that appears at the beginning of this essay is from Thompson 1967 (118).

1. The most sanguine empirical evidence to date shows limited support for the hardwiring proposition in diverse policy areas such as Medicare payments (Balla 1998), state air pollution (Potoski 1999), and federal hydroelectric licensing programs (Spence 1999b). Research on hazardous waste implementation reveals that informal rules are successfully substituted by an agency in place of formal rules when politicians constrain agency decision making by reducing the agency's discretion (Hamilton and Schroeder 1994; Hamilton 1996).

2. Furthermore, the salience of a policy will also have an impact on discretion (Epstein and O'Halloran 1999). As a policy becomes more attractive, the amount of discretion given to the agency will decline. In addition, another trade-off exists between the additional information obtained by politicians and the distributive losses felt by the agency since the latter cannot efficiently use its expertise in implementing policies.

3. The omission of bureaucratic demands for discretion makes it practically impossible to arrive at a true general agency–political equilibrium perspective that captures the full nuances of such relationships. Simply, a general equilibrium theory can be ascertained regarding the bargaining over the supply of discretion between political institutions, as recent research over the past decade has done an impressive job of demonstrating. This approach, however, does not allow one to ascertain the nature of agency preferences and hence ignores their role in shaping political supply and bureaucratic demand based equilibrium outcomes involving this commodity.

4. These contexts must be defined in terms of marginal costs and benefits since the agency must necessarily prefer or receive, in absolute terms, a nonnegative level of discretion by assumption.

5. This discrete distinction simplifies the analysis and is consistent with existing research on this topic (e.g., Epstein and O'Halloran 1999). Alternatively, one can view the degree of political consensus in terms of the continuous differences that exist within electoral institutions.

6. The view taken here runs counter in two ways to what a traditional power accrual story would predict since a coalition of politicians will have a harder time thwarting an agency's policies (e.g., Bryner 1987; Dahl and Lindblom 1953; Hammond and Knott 1996). First, I presume that agencies care not so much about playing political principals against each other to accrue power as an end as these accounts infer; rather, the context in which they wish to exercise policymaking authority is related to its consequences for policy outcomes. This is especially important given that the purpose of this study is to analyze the risk-bearing behavior of administrative agencies. Second, one can view the power accrual account as an increase in the *supply* of bureaucratic discretion (i.e., a downward shift in supply schedule) made available to administrative agencies attributable to comparative-static changes in political institutions and thus results in a higher equilibrium level of discretion when holding agency demand for discretion fixed. The agency response will result in a shift toward less demand for bureaucratic discretion in these instances for the reasons noted earlier. In agency-political equilibrium terms, the relative magnitude of these changes to the supply and demand schedules will subsequently determine the net effect on the actual level of bureaucratic discretion. It is important to note, however,

that in the present study the focus is exclusively on agency choice under uncertainty and thus on an agency's incentive for desiring additional power in the face of policy outcomes that are uncertain.

7. The isolation of this relationship for a given level of utility was motivated by seminal research on portfolio choice under uncertainty (Tobin 1958).

8. This perspective conceptually departs from the traditional PTBD view that politicians bargain and subsequently allocate a certain amount of bureaucratic discretion and thus their demand cannot exceed their supply over the long run. This presumes that an agency cannot effectively seek more discretion than is being supplied by political institutions at a given point in time. This line of reasoning is problematic unless one treats agencies as being passive entities that cannot affect the (political market) equilibrium level of discretion that they actually obtain. For reasons noted earlier in this essay, if one views agencies as proactive policy actors then it is plausible to suggest that politicians may shift their supply of discretion in response to a shift in agency demand for this commodity so as to reach a new equilibrium quantity. Moreover, agencies can also seek as much discretion as they deem fit, although this does not necessarily mean that they will obtain what they request. Given that the focus of this study is on agency preferences for bureaucratic discretion under conditions of uncertainty, this potential criticism is moot for the purposes of the present study.

9. The mathematical proof of the general solution, independent of the type of functional form utilized, can be found in the appendix to this essay.

10. The comparative-static analysis throughout this essay assumes that the α and β lie in the same range of values for the clear-cut positive and negative discretionary contexts, while they differ for the mixed discretionary contexts. The former assumption is based on the view that the agency's utility obtained from discretion must be consistent with its relationship with uncertainty for a given type of risk-bearing behavior and discretionary context. Relaxing this assumption obviously affects the curvature of these functions by allowing for a mixed discretionary context, whereby the sign associated with the second-order derivative is based upon the relative amount that α deviates from unity vis-à-vis β in the opposite direction. Furthermore, it is also possible for risk-averse and risk-seeking behavior under a neutral discretionary context to be observationally equivalent in the special case when $1 + \alpha = 1 + \beta$ since the curvature of the function will be linearized by definition due to symmetry around unity.

11. This discussion presumes that agency utility must not be completely inelastic to variations in bureaucratic discretion—that is, $\partial U / \partial D \neq 0$. This is not an untenable simplifying assumption given that an agency is likely to receive at least a modicum of utility (or disutility) from changes in this commodity.

12. Besides deducing this from the power function expression in (4) where $\alpha \neq 0$ and $\beta = 0$, this can also be shown to generally hold by applying the chain rule via implicit differentiation to the utility function and setting it equal to zero: $\partial U/\partial D \cdot dD/d\sigma + \partial U/\partial \sigma = 0$. Solving for $dD/d\sigma$ yields $dD/d\sigma = (-\partial U/\partial \sigma)/(\partial U/\partial D) = 0$.

13. Please recall from equations (4) and (5) (risk-averse case) as well as (15) and (16) (risk-seeking case) that one notable difference between these expressions is that they possess different supremum. The interpretation of the Γ and Π expressions take this fact into account.

Veto Points, Policy Preferences, and Bureaucratic Autonomy in Democratic Systems

Thomas H. Hammond

In the development of democratic systems over the past two centuries, a major thrust has been to remove policy-making power from the hands of autocrats and their bureaucrats and place it in the hands of elected political leaders. Hence, it is an irony of twentieth-century governance that, as the social and economic responsibilities placed on democratic governments have increased, their elected political leaders have responded by delegating increasing amounts of policy-making authority back to unelected officials—in particular, back to the bureaucrats.

While the expansion of the modern welfare state has occasionally stimulated claims that modern bureaucrats have become our new rulers, it would be a gross exaggeration to say that the bureaucrats in democracies are generally able to operate independently from elected officials. Nonetheless, these bureaucrats often have at least some independent policy-making power, whether explicitly delegated to them or not. Hence, it is important to determine the conditions under which bureaucrats in democracies have more independent policy-making power and when they have less.

There is some evidence that bureaucrats—both within and across democracies—do vary in the extent to which they are controlled by elected officials. Regarding evidence for differences within democracies, for example, there is general agreement that the Federal Reserve System in the United States is able to operate more independently from the president and Congress as it makes monetary policy than are, say, the Department of Agriculture and the Agency for International Development as they make agricultural and international aid policies. Evidence for these kinds of differences across democratic systems can be found in studies such as Aberbach, Putnam, and Rockman 1981 and Weaver and Rockman 1993.

These varying degrees of bureaucratic autonomy can have important consequences for the policies that emerge. The reason is that the policy preferences of the bureaucrats are not always representative of the policy preferences of their elected overseers (see Aberbach and Rockman 2000 for the United States and Aberbach, Putnam, and Rockman 1981 for additional democracies). To the extent that the bureaucrats have policy preferences that differ from those of the elected officials, and to the extent that the bureaucrats also have some independent policy-making capability, then to that extent their policy choices will differ from those of the elected officials.

There are two major reasons why the bureaucrats might develop an independent policy-making capability. One reason, which follows the tradition established by Weber, is that the bureaucrats may know more than the elected officials about what needs to be done and how to do it. Even if elected officials do not explicitly delegate policy-making authority to the bureaucrats, the bureaucrats' greater information, theoretical understanding, and operating expertise may give them scope for independent action.

The other reason why bureaucrats may develop a capability for independent action is related to an age-old strategy for victory in both warfare and politics: "Divide and conquer!" If the elected officials are divided among themselves (i.e., if they have differing preferences over what they want the bureaucrats to do), then the bureaucrats may be able to conquer (in the sense of maintaining some scope for independent action). But if the elected officials are unified in what they want the bureaucrats to do, the bureaucrats may have to do what they are told.

Most discussions of bureaucratic autonomy have focused on the autonomy that stems from the asymmetries in information, understanding, and expertise; less attention has been paid to the bureaucratic autonomy that may result from divisions among the elected officials. However, recent work—see, for example, Hammond and Knott 1996, 1999, 2000, which build on Hammond and Miller 1987—has begun to explore the extent to which divisions among the elected officials in the United States can also allow bureaucrats some autonomy. This essay further examines the extent to which divisions among elected officials may generate autonomy for bureaucrats, both within and across democracies.

There are two different kinds of divisions among politicians that might affect bureaucratic autonomy. One involves the political *veto points* that can reject proposals for policy change. For example, in analyzing why different kinds of political systems respond in different ways to social and economic challenges, Weaver and Rockman (1993) discuss why two-party unicameral parliamentary systems (the "Westminster" systems) might respond more quickly than presidential systems (the separation of powers systems, as in the United States). The basic argument is that because presidential systems are characterized by multiple veto points (e.g., a House, Senate, and president) whose members are able to block attempts at policy change, the systems' responses to social and economic challenges are often problematic. In contrast, the existence of only a single veto point—the majority party—in Westminster systems enables these systems to respond to challenges more readily.

However, Weaver and Rockman (1993) find that this institutional explanation is insufficient to account for the patterns of policy change that they empirically observe. Instead, a second kind of division among politicians also seems important, focusing on the *extent of policy disagreements* among the elected officials within and among the veto points. When policy disagreements across institutions are modest, a system's capacity for responding quickly to social and economic challenges may seem to be greater than when policy disagreements among the institutions are more substantial.

These insights have been formalized in Tsebelis 1995 and Tsebelis and Money 1997, which advance two general arguments. First, holding constant the extent of policy disagreements, an increase in the number of veto points will not decrease policy stability and may increase it. The logic here is straightforward: the more veto points there are the more difficult it is to gain approval for a policy change. Second, holding constant the number of veto points, an increase in the extent of policy disagreements among the actors will not decrease policy stability and may increase it. Empirical research by Tsebelis (1999) and Bawn (1999) provides support for this general line of argument.

However, Hammond and Butler (2003) caution that both variables must be considered in evaluating the extent of policy stability in any particular kind of system: just by itself, the number of veto points may not distinguish policy stability in presidential systems from policy stability in parliamentary systems. Instead, differences in policy stability between two different kinds of systems depend on the *interaction* between the number of veto points and the distribution of preferences (what may be called the *preference profile*) of the elected officials populating the veto points in the two kinds of systems. In fact, it was demonstrated that for some preference profiles presidential and parliamentary systems should be expected to select similar policies and exhibit similar patterns of policy change, despite the systems' institutional differences.[1]

In this essay, we utilize these two variables—the number of institutional veto points in a system and the extent of policy disagreements among the elected officials in these veto institutions—to develop an answer to a central question: Are different kinds of democratic political systems necessarily characterized by different degrees of bureaucratic autonomy?

Policy Equilibria and Bureaucratic Autonomy

To answer this question, we begin by observing that multiple veto points in a system may enable the bureaucracy to adopt new policies unilaterally. The reason is that the multiple veto points may create a set of policies that are in equilibrium; policies in equilibrium cannot be upset by any possible decisive coalition of the elected officials (given their individual policy preferences).[2] The existence of a set of equilibrium policies means that the bureaucracy could adopt any one of the equilibrium policies, and change from one equilibrium policy to another, without fear that its chosen policy will be upset by any decisive coalition of elected officials. If the set of equilibrium policies is large, then the bureaucracy will have substantial room for unilateral policy change (and thus might be considered relatively autonomous), whereas if the set of equilibrium policies is small the bureaucracy will have little room for unilateral policy change (and thus the bureaucracy might be considered to have relatively little autonomy).

These arguments lead to a clearer and more specific definition of *bureaucratic autonomy.* Earlier definitions referred to the general ability of a bureaucracy to do what it wants, but the definitions did not embed the bureaucracy in any particular political context. This left it unclear as to whether the bureaucracy could adopt any policy it wanted or just some policies, and if just some policies were feasible the definition did nothing to specify what particular policies were feasible and why.

The definition advanced here links bureaucratic autonomy to the policy preferences of the elected leaders and resulting equilibrium policies. This definition of bureaucratic autonomy makes it clear that a bureaucracy can be more or less autonomous, depending on the size of the set of equilibrium policies. Moreover, by relating the extent of bureaucratic autonomy to the size of a set of equilibrium policies, there is always a boundary to the set. This boundary sets limits on what the bureaucracy can and cannot do: it can move from policy to policy within this equilibrium set, but it cannot sustain a policy that lies outside this equilibrium set. While this definition makes it clear that the preferences of the elected officials will always collectively constrain the range of bureaucratic choices, it also suggests that as long as the bureaucracy selects some new policy from inside the boundary the disagreements among the politicians will keep them from upsetting the bureaucracy's choice and imposing some other policy.

The possibility that presidential and parliamentary systems may have sets of equilibrium policies that differ in size has been examined by Hammond and Butler (2003). However, while an increase in the number of veto points *can* increase the size of the set of equilibrium policies, it remains to be determined whether we should *necessarily* expect to find systematic differences in the size of the set, and thus in the extent of bureaucratic autonomy, across democratic systems. The problem is that the preference profile will almost invariably differ from country to country, even for countries with the same number of veto points. Determining what, if anything, should thus be expected from the relationships among veto points, preference profiles, equilibrium policies, and bureaucratic autonomy is the general problem we must consider in the rest of this essay. As we will demonstrate, variation in both key variables makes it difficult to develop logically valid expectations, for hypothesis-testing purposes, about how much bureaucratic autonomy we should find in the different kinds of systems.

Policy Equilibria in Democratic Systems

To assess the size of the sets of equilibrium policies, and thus the extent of bureaucratic autonomy, in different kinds of democratic political systems, we construct several unidimensional spatial models of policymaking. A *political system* is defined here as a set of rules used to aggregate the preferences of the individuals in the system into the choice of a policy. Two political systems are thus different if their policy-making rules are different. Understanding policy choice thus requires understanding both the nature of the policy-making rules and the nature of the individual preferences to be aggregated. Because the argument explored here is that bureaucratic autonomy stems from the existence of a set of equilibrium policies, how the policy-making rules interact with the individual preferences to produce different-sized sets of equilibrium policies will be our focus.

Six models are developed. Four are models of unicameral parliamentary systems: two kinds of majority party systems (one with majority party discipline, one lacking majority party discipline) and two kinds of multiparty systems (one with coalition party discipline and one lacking coalition party discipline). The last two are a model of a bicameral system with two legislative chambers but no parties and a model of a presidential system with two legislative chambers and a president but no parties.

For each of these six systems, our central purpose is to determine what set of equilibrium policies is created. In particular, we identify the policies that are in the *core*, that is, the policies that no decisive coalition of elected officials could replace with some alternative policy, given their preferences and their system's policy-making rules. If a policy is in the core, it is in equilibrium and cannot be upset. A large core thus indicates a large amount of bureaucratic autonomy, while a small core indicates a small amount.

We assume that each individual—for example, a member of Parliament, a president, a representative, or a senator—has a most-preferred position on a unidimensional issue space. This most-preferred position maximizes the individual's utility and so is called his or her "ideal point." The farther some policy is from the individual's ideal point (either to the left or to the right), the less utility it provides; the individual's utility functions are thus single peaked.

We assume that each individual knows the location of the ideal point of each other individual. And we assume that there is no disjunction between a formal policy choice by some authoritative actor or set of actors (i.e., by the bureaucracy, a winning coalition in a parliament, or a winning coalition of the president, House, and Senate in a presidential system) and what policy is actually implemented. That is, I am developing complete-information models.

To illustrate these concepts, in figure 1A we assume that a member of

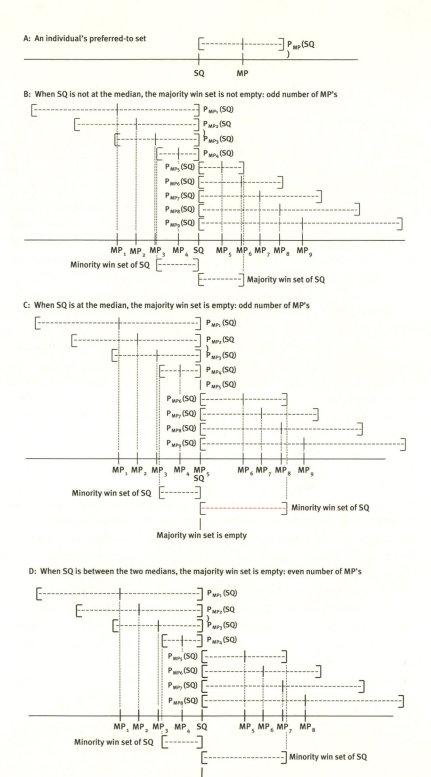

Fig. 1. Preferred-to sets and win sets

parliament (MP) has an ideal point at MP and that the status quo (SQ) policy is at SQ. The dashed line with the brackets at each end encompasses the set of points that the member prefers to SQ; every point within the brackets is closer to MP than is SQ, but the member is indifferent between SQ and a policy at the right-hand bracket. The set of points that the member prefers to SQ is labeled $P_{MP}(SQ)$; it is this member of parliament's "preferred-to" set of SQ.

Assume that some nine-member unicameral parliament chooses policies via majority rule, as in figure 1B. With SQ lying between MP_4 and MP_5, four members—MP_1 through MP_4—wish to move policy to the left, and they could agree on some point to the left of SQ in the region where their preferred-to sets overlap; this region is labeled the "minority win set of SQ" in the figure.[3] However, their four votes do not comprise a majority of the parliament, so they would not succeed in moving policy leftward. In contrast, the other five members—MP_5 through MP_9—do comprise a majority, and they all wish to move policy to the right. In particular, they could all agree on some point in the region where their preferred-to sets overlap; this region is labeled the "majority win set of SQ" in the figure. They could thus succeed in moving policy rightward.

Next consider an SQ at the ideal point of the median member, MP_5, as in figure 1C. In this case, no mutual improvement is possible for any majority-sized coalition: members MP_1 through MP_4 wish to move policy leftward from MP_5 into the region where their preferred-to sets overlap (into the left-hand minority win set of SQ), member MP_5 wants policy to stay at the MP_5 location (i.e., at his or her own ideal point), and members MP_6 through MP_9 wish to move policy rightward from MP_5. Since there is no region where a majority—at least five—of the preferred-to sets overlap (i.e., the majority win set of SQ is empty here), the SQ at MP_5 cannot be upset. In fact, with an odd number of MPs the only equilibrium policy lies at the median member's ideal point.

When there is an even number of members, there is no unique median member. Instead, there are two median members and a set of equilibrium policies that *spans* the ideal points of the two median members; the set of equilibrium policies is the region between (and including) the ideal points of the two median members. (We assume that the two median members do not have identical ideal points here.) In figure 1D, for example, there are eight members—MP_1 through MP_8—and MP_4 and MP_5 are the median members. Because SQ lies in the MP_4 to MP_5 space, it cannot be upset, for there is no region where at least five of the pre-ferred-to sets overlap.

We can now develop our six models. There are several variables whose values collectively define each system. Phrased as questions, these variables are as follows.

1. Does the system have one institutional veto point (as in uni-cameralism), two institutional veto points (as in bicameralism), or three institutional veto points (as in a presidential system with a bicameral legislature)?

2. Within each institutional veto point, is there one party, two parties, or three parties?

3. Does the governing party or coalition have monopoly agenda authority (i.e., it alone can present motions on the floor) or can the opposition party or parties propose a motion on the floor?

4. Will a governing party or a coalition send a proposal to the floor only if it is sure to be approved on a floor vote or will such a pro-posal be made even if it could be defeated on a floor vote?

5. Do any parties in the system exhibit perfect party discipline (i.e., each party member always votes for some official party position on a floor vote) or are party members free to vote for or against any official position their party adopts?

6. Do the members of any opposition party automatically vote against a proposal by some governing party or coalition or do the members of the opposition consider voting for such a proposal?

Our six models represent just some of the many possible combinations. Nonetheless, these models demonstrate that the size of a system's set of equilibrium policies, and thus the extent of its bureaucratic autonomy, are very sensitive to the details of these procedures and practices.

A Two-Party Unicameral Parliament with Perfect Majority Party Discipline

Our first model involves a unicameral parliament in which the majority party has perfect party discipline. In particular, we assume that the ma-jority party adopts its most preferred policy via majority rule within the party and once this party position is adopted *all* party members will sup-port it in a vote against SQ. We further assume that the majority party has monopoly control over the legislative agenda (i.e., the minority party cannot propose its own motion). Next, we assume that minority party members automatically vote against the majority party motion; the majority party cannot count on help from minority party members to pass its bills. Finally, we assume that the majority party will propose a motion to the floor only if that motion will defeat the status quo policy.

To illustrate, assume there are nine members of parliament who are partitioned into the Labor and Conservative parties. As indicated in figure 2A, we assume that the Conservative Party has five members, C_1 through C_5, and that the Labor Party has four members, L_1 through L_4. As the majority, the Conservative Party's most-preferred policy position lies at its party median at C_3. Because the Conservative Party has a majority and because of its party discipline, any SQ will be replaced by the official party policy at C_3. Because this policy at C_3 cannot be upset, it is the Majority Party Unicameral Core.

If an election is held and Conservative Party member C_1 is replaced with Labor Party member L_5 (and everyone else remains the same), then the Labor Party has the majority. The ideal point of its median member, L_3, would then become its most-preferred policy position, which would thus become the Core (see fig. 2B).

If the majority party has an odd number of members, as in figures 2A and 2B, then the Majority Party Unicameral Core will be the single policy at the ideal point of the median party member. If the majority party has an even number of members, then the size of the Core depends on how far apart are the ideal points of the party's median members. For example, if the two median members of a six-member Conservative Party have identical ideal points, as in figure 2C, then the Core will include just their common ideal point. If their ideal points are far apart (e.g., when the party is divided into two distinct factions), the Core would be rather large, spanning the set of policies between the median members' ideal points. In figure 2D, for example, the Conservative Party has two distinct three-member factions; hence, the Core spans the region between the two median party members, C_3 and C_4.

A Two-Party Unicameral Parliament without Perfect Majority Party Discipline

Assume now that the majority party's discipline is not perfect: any member may vote against any proposal of his or her own party if the member prefers the status quo. Assume that minority party members continue to

A. The Conservative Party has a majority

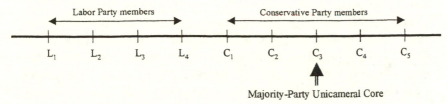

B. The Labor Party has a majority

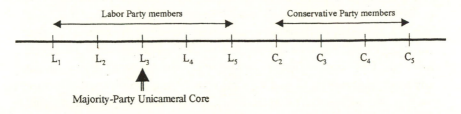

C. The Conservative Party has an even number of members, with medians at the same ideal point

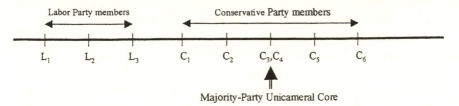

D. The Conservative Party has an even number of members, with two dissimilar factions

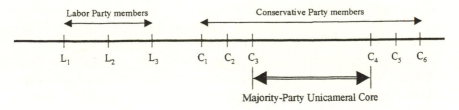

Fig. 2. A two-party unicameral parliament with perfect majority party discipline

vote automatically against any majority party proposal. If enough majority party members vote against their party's own proposal, their votes when combined with the minority party votes could defeat this proposal. With its monopoly agenda control, the majority party could avoid such defeats by not proposing changes to any status quo policy that would risk this kind of defection. The result can be a Majority Party Unicameral Core that is substantially larger than the party median alone (or than what is spanned by the party medians).

For example, in figure $3A$ the Conservative Party has a bare majority in parliament (five of the nine members) and its median member is C_3. For any SQ to the left of C_1, there exists a policy at or to the right of C_1 that would upset the SQ with the support of all five Conservative members; hence the Core cannot include any points to the left of C_1. However, for any SQ lying between C_1 and C_3 a proposal to move policy rightward toward C_3 would be rejected, at least by C_1, because he or she would prefer SQ; lacking the vote of C_1, at most only four Conservative Party members (C_3, C_4, C_5, and perhaps C_2) would support the proposal, and these three or four members do not constitute a majority of parliament. Thus, the proposal would fail (since the Labor Party members would all vote against it as well). Hence, the Core must include the policies from C_1 to C_3. Similar arguments hold for policies lying on the right side of the Conservative Party, and so the Core would also include the policies from C_3 to C_5.

Overall, then, the Core here would be the set of policies from C_1 to C_5; that is, this Core spans the ideal points of *all* Conservative Party members. Since the Core with perfect party discipline was just the policy at C_3 (see fig. $2A$), the prospect of defection by majority party members can thus increase the size of the Core.[4]

For another example, consider figure $3B$. The Conservative Party here has seven members (two more than a bare majority of the nine-member parliament), so policy change requires the votes of only five of the seven Conservative Party members. In this case, the Majority Party Unicameral Core need not include the ideal points of all the members of the Conservative Party. For example, for any SQ to the left of C_3 there exists some policy at or to the right of C_3 that would gain both a party and a parliamentary majority against SQ: five members—C_3, C_4, C_5, C_6, and C_7, who collectively comprise both a party and a parliamentary majority—could agree on some policy at or to the right of C_3 that would upset this SQ. Hence, the Core cannot include any points

A. The Conservative Party has a bare (five-member) majority

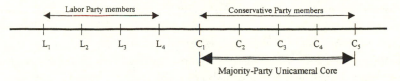

B. The Conservative Party has a seven-member majority

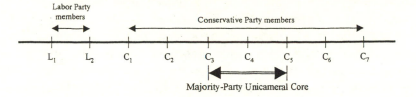

C. The Conservative Party has a nine-member majority

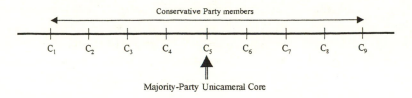

Fig. 3. A two-party unicameral parliament without perfect majority party discipline

to the left of C_3. Similarly, for any SQ to the right of C_5 there exists some policy at or to the left of C_5 that would gain both a party and a parliamentary majority against SQ: seven members—C_1, C_2, C_3, C_4, and C_5, who collectively comprise both a party and a parliamentary majority, plus L_1 and L_2—could agree on some policy at or to the left of C_5 that would upset this SQ. Hence, the Core cannot include any points to the right of C_5.

However, for any SQ lying between C_3 and C_5 a proposal to move policy rightward would be rejected at least by C_1, C_2, and C_3 (and possibly C_4, depending on the location of SQ), leaving at most only four Conservative members—C_1, C_2, C_3, and possibly C_4, depending on the location of SQ—to vote for the move, and they are not a majority in parliament. Similarly, for any SQ lying between C_3 and C_5, a proposal to move policy leftward would be rejected at least by C_5, C_6, and C_7 (and possibly C_4 as well, depending on the location of SQ), again leaving at most only four Conservative members (C_1, C_2, C_3, and possibly C_4) to vote for the move, and they are not a majority in parliament. (Again, recall that we are assuming that the minority party automatically votes against any majority party motion.) In sum, if the majority party members are not perfectly disciplined, the core will span the policies from C_3 to C_5.[5]

For a third example, in figure 3C, if the majority party includes every member of parliament the Core will include just the party median, which is the chamber's overall median as well.

When the majority party lacks perfect discipline (but retains monopoly proposal authority) and the members of the minority party automatically vote against any majority party proposal, the size of the Core is an inverse function of the size of the majority party. For example, as the size of the majority party *increases* from a bare majority toward the whole chamber in size (figs. 3A through 3C), the size of the Core will *decrease* toward the median of the entire parliament. If the majority party has just a bare majority, the Core spans the ideal points of all the party's members, as from C_1 to C_5 in figure 3A. If the size of the majority party increases to seven, as in figure 3B, the Core shrinks to the region spanned by C_3 and C_5. And if the majority party includes every member of parliament, as in figure 3C, the Core includes just the party median, which is the chamber's overall median as well. This pattern occurs because as the majority party increases in size a decreasing proportion of its membership is necessary for a proposal to be approved by an overall parliamentary majority; hence, the Core is smaller, and as the party grows in size its own median converges on the median of the overall chamber. Thus, when the majority party reaches its maximum size (i.e., when it includes the entire chamber), the Core becomes the overall medium.

A Three-Party Unicameral Parliament with Perfect Coalition Party Discipline

When a unicameral parliament has three or more parties, none of which has a majority, a coalition government may have to be constructed. Consider a case in which the nine members of parliament are partitioned into the Labor, Green, and Conservative parties, each with three members, and with the ideal points of the Green Party MPs lying between those of the Labor and Conservative MPs. Assume that a coalition government forms between the Labor and Green parties, that the parties in coalition have joint monopoly control of the agenda (i.e., the Conservative Party cannot make a proposal), and that a coalition proposal must be adopted by a majority vote of each party in the coalition before the coalition's proposal can be presented in a floor motion. Assume further that the parties in the coalition have perfect discipline, so that all the members of each party vote for any policy proposal made on the floor by the coalition. And assume, finally, that the opposition party automatically votes against any motion made by the governing coalition. What is the set of equilibrium policies in this system?

For example, in figure 4A any policy to the left of L_2 could be upset by some coalition proposal at or to the right of L_2: L_2 and L_3 (who comprise a majority of the Labor Party) would vote for such a proposal, as would G_1, G_2, and G_3 (all the members of the Green Party), and these five members collectively comprise a parliamentary majority. Similarly, any policy lying to the right of G_2 would be upset by some coalition proposal lying at or to the left of G_2: G_2 and G_1 would vote for such a proposal, as would L_1, L_2, and L_3, and these five members comprise a parliamentary majority. But no policy in the region spanned by L_2 and G_2 could be upset. For instance, an SQ at L_2 could not be upset by any proposal to its right because L_1 and L_2 would vote against it (i.e., a majority of the Labor Party would oppose the move), and an SQ at G_2 could not be upset by any proposal to its left because G_2 and G_3 would vote against it (i.e., a majority of the Green Party would not support the move). Hence, the set of equilibrium policies is defined by the region spanned by the ideal points of the median members of the two parties—by L_2 and G_2—in the governing coalition; these policies comprise the Party Coalition Unicameral Core.

An alternative coalition would be for the Green Party to unite with the Conservative Party (see fig. 4B). In this case, the Core would shift rightward and would span the ideal points of G_2 and C_2.

To determine the Core, we need only determine the median member of each of the outermost parties in the governing coalition. In figure 4A, for example, these median members are L_2 and G_2; the Core here is thus the set of points spanning the ideal points of L_2 and G_2. In figure 4B, the outermost median members are G_2 and C_2 and the Core here is the set of points spanning the ideal points of G_2 and C_2. In each case, the ideal points of no other members need be depicted.

As long as neither party of the coalition has a parliamentary majority,

A. A governing coalition of the Labor and Green Parties

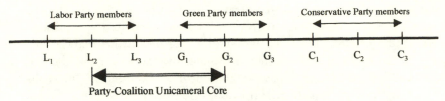

B. A governing coalition of the Green and Conservative Parties

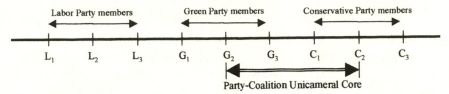

C. A small core with a Labor-Green governing coalition

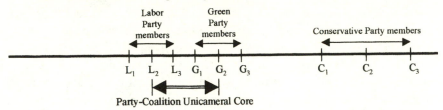

D. A single-point core with a Labor-Green governing coalition

E. A large core with a Labor-Green governing coalition

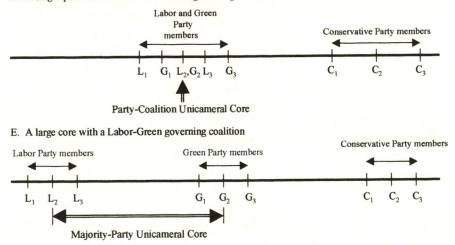

Fig. 4. A party coalition unicameral parliament with perfect coalition party discipline

the Core will span the ideal points of the median members of the outermost parties in the coalition. Thus, the size of this Core will be a function of the distance between the median members of these two outermost parties in the coalition. For example, if L_2 and G_2 are close together, as in figure 4C, the Core will be small; indeed, if L_2 and G_2 have the same ideal point the Core will be a single policy, as in figure 4D. But if L_2 and G_2 are far apart, the resulting Core will be large, as in figure 4E.

A Three-Party Unicameral Parliament without Perfect Coalition Party Discipline

If the coalition parties' discipline is imperfect, some party members may vote against their coalition's own proposal to replace SQ; if enough members of the coalition parties defect in this manner, the coalition's motion could be defeated. We continue to assume that the majority coalition has monopoly agenda control authority and that the opposition party members automatically vote against the coalition parties' proposal. To avoid defeat, the coalition's leaders would propose no amendments to SQ that would risk this kind of defection. What impact would this lack of party discipline have on the size of the Party Coalition Unicameral Core?

For an answer, consider figure 5A, in which the Labor Party has three members and the Green Party has only two; their coalition now has only five members, which is a bare majority in the parliament. Since defection is possible by members of the parties in the coalition, defection of any of either party's members would result in the defeat of any coalition proposal. For any SQ to the left of L_1, there exists some proposal at or to the right of L_1 that would defeat this SQ with the support of all five coalition members. Similarly, for any SQ to the right of G_2 there exists some proposal at or to the left of G_2 that would defeat it with the support of all five coalition members. But for any SQ lying at or to the right of L_1 and at or to the left of G_2 there exists no proposal that could defeat it with the support of all five coalition members. Whereas the Core without perfect party discipline would span just the ideal points of L_2 and G_2 (the coalition parties' median members), the possibility of defection increases the size of the Core to span the ideal points of L_1 and G_2.

However, the possibility of defection does not necessarily increase the size of the Core. Consider figure 5B, in which the Labor-Green coalition has six members. Even allowing for the possible defection of members of

A. A Labor-Green governing coalition with a bare (five-member) majority

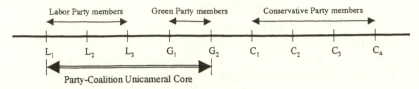

B. A Labor-Green governing coalition with six members

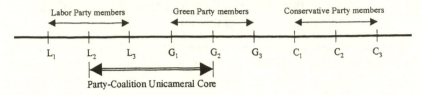

C. A Labor-Green governing coalition with eight members

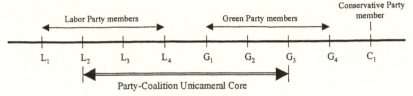

D. A single-point core with a Labor-Green governing coalition with six members

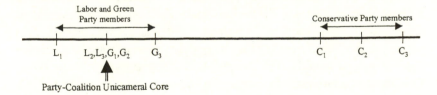

Fig. 5. A party coalition unicameral parliament without perfect coalition party discipline

either coalition party, the Core would still span just the ideal points from L_2 to G_2: there exist proposals that could upset an SQ lying to the left of L_2 with the support of L_2, L_3, and G_1, G_2, and G_3 (these five members comprise a parliamentary majority); similarly, there exist proposals that could upset an SQ lying to the right of G_2 with the support of L_1, L_2, L_3, and G_1 and G_2 (who comprise a parliamentary majority). So the possibility of defection could still produce a Core that is the same size as when defection is not possible (compare the identical Core in fig. 4A).[6]

If the governing coalition includes only a bare majority of the chamber's members, as in figure 5A, the resulting Core will span the ideal points of all the members of all the parties in the coalition. In this case, the size of the Core will depend on the distance between the "outermost" members of the two "outermost" parties in the coalition: the farther apart are these outermost members the larger the Core. In figure 5A, for example, the size of the Core hinges on the distance between L_1 and G_2.

At the other extreme, if the coalition includes almost all the members of the entire chamber, then the size of the Core might span only the ideal points of the median members of the two outermost parties in the coalition. In figure 5C, for example, the governing coalition includes eight of the nine members of the parliament. The Core here spans the ideal points of L_2 and G_3, the relevant (e.g., outside) median members of the two outermost parties. While these first three examples show Cores of substantial size, if the ideal points of these two parties were to overlap sufficiently a single-point Core could be produced, as in figure 5D.

Overall, then, if the parties in the coalition lack perfect discipline the Core will span at least the ideal points of the median members of the two outermost parties in the coalition and the Core may grow larger as the size of the coalition decreases. And, of course, the size of the Core will depend on the distance between the relevant members of the two outermost parties in the coalition: the closer together their ideal points the smaller the Core.

A Party-Free Bicameral Parliament

Next we consider a bicameral parliament consisting of two chambers, to be called the House and Senate. In this system, some status quo policy can be upset whenever a majority of the House and a majority of the Senate can agree on some other policy; each chamber has authority to block efforts by the other to change policy. Our goal is to determine the set of equilibrium policies in this bicameral system. We assume there are no parties. Since there are no parties, questions of party discipline, monopoly agenda control authority, and so forth are moot.

We begin with the same nine actors used previously, constructing a model of a bicameral parliament in which the nine individuals are partitioned into a four-member Senate and a five-member House (see fig. 6A).

A. A Party-Free Bicameral Core

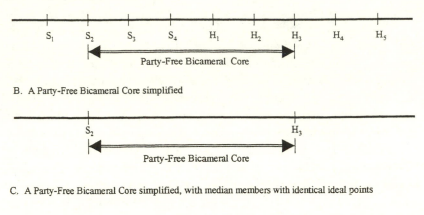

B. A Party-Free Bicameral Core simplified

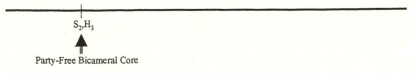

C. A Party-Free Bicameral Core simplified, with median members with identical ideal points

S$_2$,H$_3$

Party-Free Bicameral Core

Fig. 6. A party-free bicameral system

Note that three senators constitute a bare majority of the four-member Senate and three representatives constitute a bare majority of the five-member House.

Finding the equilibrium policies in a bicameral parliament is similar to what occurs when there are two parties in a coalition in a unicameral parliament. First, for each SQ lying to the left of S$_2$ in figure 6A there exists some proposal to upset this SQ, which would gain the support of three of the four Senate members (S$_2$, S$_3$, and S$_4$, who comprise a Senate majority) and all five House members. But now consider an SQ lying between S$_2$ and S$_3$: there exists a proposal to replace this SQ with a policy on or to the right of S$_2$, which would be supported by S$_3$ and S$_4$ *and by all the House members,* but S$_1$ and S$_2$ would reject this proposal. Since this proposal would not be supported by a majority of the Senate (three votes are needed for this), the proposal would fail. The same logic holds for status quo policies lying to the right of H$_3$. Hence, the proposal would fail for lack of a House majority. The result is that the points spanned by the line from S$_2$ to H$_3$ are in equilibrium; hence, all these points from S$_2$ to H$_3$ comprise the Party-Free Bicameral Core.

The size of this Core is simply a function of how far apart the House and Senate median members are. If they are relatively far apart (as with S_2 and H_3 in fig. 6B), the Core is relatively large; if they are close together (in fig. 6C, these two medians are identical), the Core is small.

A Party-Free Presidential System

Finally, consider a presidential system lacking disciplined parties: there is a bicameral legislature consisting of a House and Senate, plus a president. In this system, each of these three institutional actors has authority to block efforts by the others to change policy; the status quo policy can be upset only when a House majority plus a Senate majority plus the president can agree on some other policy. Our goal is to determine the set of equilibrium policies in this system. We assume there is no veto override.[7]

For example, in figure 7A the president is at P, and the set of equilibrium policies thus spans the ideal points of P and H_3; that is, the Party-Free Bicameral Executive Veto Core is the set of points from P to H_3. The reason is that an SQ to the left of P could be upset since there exists a policy at or to the right of P that the president, all senators, and all representatives prefer to the SQ. Similarly, an SQ to the right of H_3 could be upset since there exists a policy at or to the left of H_3 that the president, all three senators, and a majority of House members (H_1, H_2, and H_3) would prefer to the SQ. But no SQ lying in the P to H_3 region could be upset; for example, an SQ at H_1 could not be upset by any proposal to its left because all the House members (including H_1) would vote against it, and this SQ at H_1 could not be upset by some proposal to its right because the president and all senators (and H_1 as well) would vote against it.

If the president is more centrally located, we can get a different Core. For example, with the president as shown in figure 7B a somewhat smaller Core is produced. Note in figure 7B that the ideal point of the president could be moved anywhere in between S_2 and H_3 (i.e., within the bicameral core, ignoring the president) without changing the size or location of this Core at all.

Depiction of the Party-Free Bicameral Executive Veto Core can be simplified considerably. First identify the relative locations of the ideal points of the president, the median House member, and the median Senate member; for instance, figure 7A can be reduced without any loss of

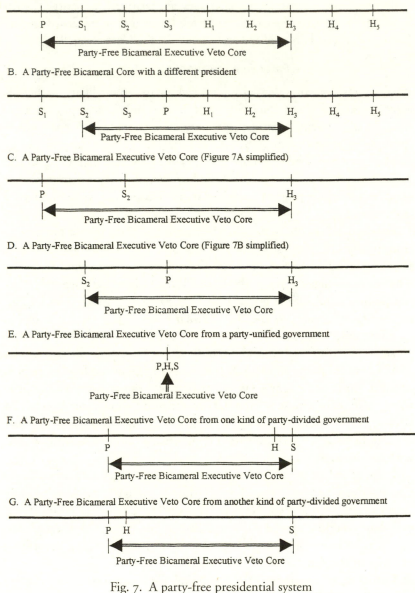

A. A Party-Free Bicameral Executive Veto Core

P S_1 S_2 S_3 H_1 H_2 H_3 H_4 H_5

Party-Free Bicameral Executive Veto Core

B. A Party-Free Bicameral Core with a different president

S_1 S_2 S_3 P H_1 H_2 H_3 H_4 H_5

Party-Free Bicameral Executive Veto Core

C. A Party-Free Bicameral Executive Veto Core (Figure 7A simplified)

P S_2 H_3

Party-Free Bicameral Executive Veto Core

D. A Party-Free Bicameral Executive Veto Core (Figure 7B simplified)

S_2 P H_3

Party-Free Bicameral Executive Veto Core

E. A Party-Free Bicameral Executive Veto Core from a party-unified government

P,H,S

Party-Free Bicameral Executive Veto Core

F. A Party-Free Bicameral Executive Veto Core from one kind of party-divided government

P H S

Party-Free Bicameral Executive Veto Core

G. A Party-Free Bicameral Executive Veto Core from another kind of party-divided government

P H S

Party-Free Bicameral Executive Veto Core

Fig. 7. A party-free presidential system

information to what is shown in diagram C, and figure $7B$ can be reduced without any loss of information to what is shown in figures $7C$ and $7D$. The Core is simply the set of policies spanning the median ideal points of the two "outside" actors. (From this perspective, we are considering the ideal point of the president to be his institution's own "median.") Thus, in figure $7C$ the outside actors are P and H_3, and so the Core spans these points; in figure $7D$, the outside actors are S_2 and H, and so the Core spans these two points.

The size of this Core depends on the extent of preference differences among the "outside" pair of actors in the simplified representation (as in figs. $7C$ and $7D$). If the outermost two actors have similar median ideal points, the Core will be relatively small. In figure $7E$, for example, the president, median House member, and median Senate member have identical ideal points, thereby producing a single-point Core; this depicts what may be characteristic of an extreme case of "unified party" government. But if the outermost pair of actors have rather different median ideal points, the Core will be relatively large, as in figures $7F$ and $7G$; these are two possible types of "divided party" government.

Summary

While we have presented results for just six of the many possible systems, some important generalizations can be drawn from these systems that I think are representative of all possible democratic systems. In the next section, I discuss these generalizations.

Are There System-Related Differences in Core Sizes?

The core for each of our six democratic systems has now been identified. For any pair of systems, if one system always has a core that is larger than the core of the other system, we could then conclude that a bureaucracy in the first system will always have more autonomy than a bureaucracy in the second system. We could even arrange our six systems in decreasing order of bureaucratic autonomy (the smaller the cores the less the autonomy), and we could then base an empirical investigation on this expected (i.e., hypothesized) rank ordering of systems.

However, if for any pair of systems it is *not* the case that one system always has a core that is larger than the core of the other system, then we may be unable to draw any general conclusions about which system's bureaucracy will have more autonomy. That is, it may be that, for one pair of preference profiles, one system's bureaucracy will have more autonomy than the second system's, while for some other pair of preference profiles the second system's bureaucracy will have more autonomy than the first. This would mean that we cannot rank the six systems in decreasing order of bureaucratic autonomy. Hence, it would not be clear, for hypothesis-testing purposes, what our theoretical expectations should be.

So the question is: To which of these two conclusions do our models lead? To answer this question, we will make three different kinds of comparisons.

Variations in the Size of Each System's Core

Observe in figures 2 through 7 that the core of each system can take on a wide range of sizes. In particular, the core of each system can contain either a single policy or multiple policies.

1. The *Majority Party Unicameral Core* (with perfect discipline) can contain either a single policy (figs. 2A, 2B, and 2C) or multiple policies (fig. 2D).
2. The *Majority Party Unicameral Core* (without perfect discipline) can contain either a single policy (fig. 3C) or multiple policies (figs. 3A and 3B).
3. The *Party Coalition Unicameral Core* (with perfect discipline) can contain either a single policy (fig. 4D) or multiple policies (figs. 4A, 4B, 4C, and 4E).
4. The *Party Coalition Unicameral Core* (without perfect discipline) can contain either a single policy (fig. 5D) or multiple policies (figs. 5A, 5B, and 5C).
5. The *Party-Free Bicameral Core* can contain either a single policy (fig. 6C) or multiple policies (figs. 6A and 6B).
6. The *Party-Free Bicameral Executive Veto Core* can contain either a single policy (fig. 7E) or multiple policies (figs. 7A through 7G).

For each system, then, the core can vary in size from a single policy to a range of policies.

Empirically, this has two implications. First, since the policy preferences of the elected officials in a system may vary from issue area to issue area, the size of the system's core may vary from issue area to issue area. This suggests that bureaucratic autonomy in this system can thus be expected to vary from agency to agency. Second, since the policy preferences of the elected officials in a system may vary over time (which could happen for a variety of reasons) the size of the system's core may vary over time as well. Hence, bureaucratic autonomy in the system can also be expected to vary over time.

Comparing the Sizes of the Cores for Any Two Systems

The possible variation in size for each system's core has direct implications for what we might expect from comparisons of bureaucratic autonomy across pairs of systems.

With six systems, one can make a total of $\binom{6}{2} = 15$ pairwise comparisons of the sizes of two systems' cores. Fortunately, it is not necessary for our purposes to make all fifteen comparisons. The reason stems from the fact, noted earlier, that every system can have a core with just a single policy or a core with multiple policies. Thus, to compare system i (for $i = 1, 2, \ldots, 6$) with system j (for $j = 1, 2, \ldots, 6$) we need only consider *four* possible situations (for $i \neq j$).

1. If the core of system i contains a single policy and the core of system j contains multiple policies, then the core of system i will be smaller than the core of system j.
2. If the core of system i contains a single policy and the core of system j contains a single policy, then the core of system i will be the same size as the core of system j.
3. If the core of system i contains multiple policies and the core of system j contains a single policy, then the core of system i will be larger than the core of system j.
4. If the core of system i and the core of system j both contain multiple policies, the core of system i can be smaller than, the same size, or larger than the core of system j.

Because each system could have a single policy or multiple policies in its core (as noted in the previous section), it follows that virtually *anything* could emerge from a comparison of any pair of systems: the core of system i could be smaller than the core of system j, or the core of system i could be the same size as the core of system j, or the core of system i could be larger than the core of system j. In other words, the two sets of rules defining any pair of systems do not necessarily lead to systematic differences in the extent of bureaucratic autonomy.

Rank Ordering the Core Sizes for All Six Systems

This "anything can happen" result has a further implication. If we are conducting an empirical study of bureaucratic autonomy in all six systems, we might wish to develop some prior theoretical expectations, for hypothesis-testing purposes, about how to rank these six systems in terms of their bureaucratic autonomy. With six different systems in our study, there are 6! = 720 possible rank orderings of the sizes of their cores (ignoring the possibility of ties).

However, since for any pair of systems one system can have a larger core than the second system, and the second system can have a larger core than the first, it follows that each of these 720 possible rankings could possibly occur. That is, there is no logically necessary rank ordering of bureaucratic autonomy across our six systems.

Discussion

These three sets of results—on the possible size of any one core, on the pairwise comparison of the sizes of any two systems' cores, and on the rank ordering of the sizes of the cores of all six systems—suggest that there does not exist a logically necessary relationship between the policy-making rules defining a particular system and the size of the system's core. This means that knowing just the systems' policy-making rules does not allow us to develop any logically valid expectations about which systems will have bureaucracies with more autonomy and which will have bureaucracies with less. And if it is not clear what the expectations should be it is not clear what testable hypotheses can be derived. Hence, it is not clear what could be learned from the empirical research. If anything could happen theoretically, then empirical research that focuses only on the impact of the systems' policy-making rules on bureaucratic autonomy will not be theoretically informative.

The key implication is that we cannot rely *just* on the institutional variables—that is, on the number and variety of veto points and the other policy-making rules—to structure and inform our cross-national research on bureaucratic autonomy. Because results from any empirical study will always be due to the *interaction* among veto points and preference profiles, if the preference profile variable is omitted from the empirical analysis these empirical results will be ascribed, erroneously, to just the impact of the institutional variables.

Of course, an identical argument can be made about the hazards of relying just on the beliefs and preferences of the elected politicians—that is, on the characteristics of the preference profile—to structure and inform our empirical research. Note that some comparative politics research uses results from public opinion surveys as indicators of various kinds of national cultures and then attempts to explain trends in national policy-making on the basis of these changes in cultures (see, e.g., Inglehart 1990). However, such studies rarely integrate their preference profile data with any institutional variables. Unfortunately, if the institutional variables are omitted from an empirical analysis of policy trends any results that are due to the *interaction* among the veto points and the preference profiles will be ascribed, erroneously, just to the preference profile variable.

So if we wish to empirically examine bureaucratic autonomy in a comparative perspective it is imperative that measures of *both* the institutional *and* preference profile variables be included. Unfortunately, this will greatly complicate cross-system empirical research. It is a difficult though manageable task to gather cross-system data on the institutional variables. However, gathering data on each system's preference profile is likely to be much more difficult (as well as time consuming and expensive). For this reason, it will be difficult to conduct meaningful cross-national empirical research on bureaucratic autonomy.

Possible Criticisms

A number of criticisms might be aimed at the approach from which these conclusions have been derived. In reviewing these criticisms, what must be considered is whether the two broad conclusions—the "anything can happen" results and the necessity of including both preference profile and institutional variables in our theoretical and empirical research—would have to be modified if any one criticism is valid. In general, even where there is some basis for the criticisms it is not apparent that either of the two central conclusions is significantly undermined.

More Complex Sets of Rules for Each System

The set of rules characterizing each of our six systems is undoubtedly far simpler than the full set of rules actually characterizing any real world country. Inclusion of a wider range of institutional variables could be expected to change the size, shape, and location of each system's core.

For example, committees with gatekeeping authority could be included (especially in presidential systems) along with a veto override, the nomination and confirmation process for bureaucratic leaders, procedures for their dismissal or removal, and the courts (see Hammond and Knott 1996 for details on how these all might be included in a spatial model of bureaucratic autonomy in a presidential system). Agency budgets and the appropriations process could be included as well. For coalition governments in parliamentary systems, how cabinet seats are allocated to various parties might affect the extent of autonomy for the bureaucracies involved. And if bureaucratic autonomy also stems from informational asymmetries between the bureaucrats and the elected officials, as Weber hypothesized, then these asymmetries could also be included.

Changes in any of these factors may well change the size, shape, and location of the resulting cores, given some preference profile. However, it is unclear what the *net* impact of these additional factors would be: inclusion of some variables might increase the size of a system's core (e.g., if more veto points are added, as with legislative committees or multiparty coalition governments), whereas the inclusion of other variables (e.g., the appropriations process and the chief executive's ability to dismiss the agency head) would seem likely to decrease the size of the system's core. Moreover, it could be argued that some aspects of our models, such as the number of political parties, should be endogenized and treated as a product of the systems' electoral rules (which would also have to be included in our models).

Nonetheless, the key issue is not whether these models are sufficiently descriptive of real world countries but whether our central conclusions would change if more complete rules were developed for each system. In part because it is not clear what the net effect of including all these additional variables would be, it is not clear that these conclusions would be undermined.

The Unidimensionality Assumption

It could be asserted, with some plausibility, that policy-making in many political systems is usually multidimensional and not unidimensional. Nonetheless, even with a multidimensional representation of policy-making in each of our systems it seems likely that the anything can happen results would emerge from a theoretical multidimensional analysis. The reason is that, even in a multidimensional setting, for each pair of systems there probably exist pairs of preference profiles that would produce sets of equilibrium policies that vary greatly in size, thereby reproducing the anything can happen result.

Of course, for any one system preference profiles that produce any cores at all may be less common in higher dimensional issue spaces than in lower dimensional spaces. The implication is that bureaucratic autonomy would be less likely in multidimensional settings: for any policy the bureaucracy might adopt, the absence of a core means that there exists some other policy that some decisive coalition of elected officials would prefer. Hence, the bureaucracy would not be in a position to play a "divide and conquer" game with these officials.

However, Humphreys (2001) presents formal and simulation results indicating that cores are not completely improbable in higher dimensional spaces. Moreover, a different line of work—see, for example, Baron and Ferejohn 1989—indicates that even in multidimensional spatial settings policy stability may exist if elected officials find the unending decision making implied by policy disequilibrium to be costly. In either case, policy equilibrium may be maintained, with the result that some bureaucratic autonomy may still be possible.

The Empirical Improbability of Particular Preference Profiles

Several of the core sizes generated by our models stem from preference profiles that may seem empirically improbable. If these empirically improbable profiles are eliminated from consideration, this might place at least some constraints on what we should expect theoretically when comparing two or more systems.

Nonetheless, while it may be possible to rule out some preference profiles as empirically improbable for particular systems it remains unclear whether as a result any one system, given the restricted range of profiles, will necessarily produce a core that is always larger than, or always smaller than, the core of some other system. Hence, it is unclear that these restrictions would undermine our central conclusions.

Conclusion

The major conclusions thus remain the same. First, even with all the modifications just proposed, different preference profiles can still be expected to change the size of a system's core, holding constant whatever set of policy-making rules is attributed to this system. And, second, this means that any effort to empirically investigate the impact of policy-making rules on bureaucratic autonomy (either within or across systems) should incorporate the preference profiles as a variable. As a general rule, then, policy choices by a system must be seen as the product of an interaction between the policy-making rules and the preferences of the actors in the system. Hence, empirical efforts to explain variations in the extent of bureaucratic autonomy within and across democratic systems must take both sets of factors into account.

Notes

1. Tsebelis (1995) does explicitly talk about the impact of the preference profile on policy stability (see, e.g., his proposition 2, p. 298, and also pp. 308–11), and his empirical work (see, e.g., Tsebelis 1999) takes into account the ideological range of governing coalitions. However, the general nature of the interaction between the number of veto points and the preference profiles in various kinds of systems remains underexplored.

2. A "decisive coalition" is one that, by the system's policy-making rules, is empowered to select some new policy. Thus, in the United States there are two possible decisive coalitions in the policy-making process: (1) a coalition of the president, a House majority, and a Senate majority; and (2) a coalition of two-thirds of the House and two-thirds of the Senate. In a unicameral parliament, a decisive coalition would be simply a majority of the single chamber.

3. This is slightly nonstandard terminology, for if some legislators comprise a minority they cannot generate a win set. Instead, I am using the term *win set* to indicate the area where several preferred-to sets overlap and then modifying the term to indicate whether it is generated by a minority or a majority.

4. If the minority party does not automatically vote against the proposal of the majority party but each of its members instead simply votes in terms of whether the majority party's proposal is better or worse for him or her than the status quo, then the Majority Party Unicameral Core could again be different. To illustrate, consider a case in which SQ lies just to the right of C_3 in figure 3A. A majority party proposal to replace this SQ with a policy at C_3 would be rejected by C_4 and C_5 but would be supported by the other party members—C_1, C_2, and C_3—as well as all four Labor Party members. Hence, points to the right of C_3 are not in equilibrium. However, if SQ lies between C_1 and C_3 a majority party proposal to replace it with a policy at C_3 would be supported at most only

by C_3, C_4, and C_5 (and possibly C_2, depending on the location of SQ); it would be rejected at least by C_1 and all four Labor Party members, who collectively comprise a parliamentary majority. Hence, the Core would span the ideal points from C_1 to C_3.

5. If the minority party members here do not automatically vote against the majority party proposal but instead vote on the basis of the utility of the proposal to them, then the Majority Party Unicameral Core here spans just the C_3 and C_4 ideal points. Consider a case in which SQ lies to the right of C_4. A party proposal to replace this SQ with a policy at C_4 would be approved by four Conservative Party members— C_1, C_2, C_3, and C_4—as well as L_1 and L_2, for a total of six votes; these six votes comprise a parliamentary majority. Hence, status quo policies to the right of C_4 cannot be in equilibrium. Similarly, SQ policies to the left of C_3 are not in equilibrium. However, if SQ lies between C_3 and C_4 any proposal to replace this SQ with a policy to its left would be opposed by C_4, C_5, C_6, and C_7, who comprise a majority of the Conservative Party. While a majority of the parliament would support this proposal (i.e., C_1, C_2, C_3, L_1, and L_2), since a majority of the majority party (the Conservative Party) opposes the proposal it would never be sent to the floor. And if SQ lies between C_3 and C_4 any proposal to replace this SQ with a policy to its right would be opposed by C_1, C_2, and C_3 as well as L_1 and L_2. Hence, the Core here spans just the C_3 to C_4 interval.

6. If the members of the opposition party vote simply on the basis of their own individual valuation of SQ and the policy proposal, the Core here will also span just the ideal points of the median members of the coalition.

7. The creation of a veto override will never increase the size of the core but can decrease it.

The Benefits of Agency Policy-making: Perspectives from Positive Theory

David B. Spence

Why would people prefer to have the federal agency resolve this problem rather than their own elected officials?

—John Nalbandian

The question posed by John Nalbandian is as old as the administrative state and as pressing today as it ever was. If politicians have a very limited ability to exert control over most of the policy choices made by un-elected bureaucrats, does this pose a problem for the democratic legitimacy of the administrative state? Many positive theorists seem to think so. Unlike most public administration, administrative law, and bureaucratic politics scholars, positive theorists seem never to have gotten comfortable with the notion of agency autonomy. Some would attribute that discomfort to ideology, based on the supposition that positive theory analyses of law and politics lead inexorably to politically conservative conclusions (Lowi 1992; Mikva 1988; Hirshman 1989; Spann 1995; Brest 1988; Rubin 1991). Certainly, some aspects of the neoclassical economic model—particularly the assumption of self-interested behavior—do ignore elements of human motivation that make government work better, such as altruism, law abidingness, and cooperation. It is also true that seminal early works on positive theory, including early positive theory analyses of the administrative state, were at once penetrating positive analyses and powerful normative critiques of democratic decision making, implying that less government might be better government[1] (Arrow 1951; Olson 1971; Niskanen 1971; Stigler 1971; Peltzman 1976). While later positive theorists were more optimistic about agency policy-making, that optimism tended to hinge on the contention that politicians could control agency discretion.[2]

However, positive theory scholarship need not be hostile to agency autonomy. Indeed, the normative argument in favor of the administrative state can easily be expressed in positive theory terms. The first step in that process is acknowledging that positive theory is more of a "how" than a "what." It is an analytical method, one that employs the tools of economic analysis to analyze politics and law. With its emphasis on methodological individualism, the assumption that individuals are goal maximizers, and deductive logic, positive theory illustrates nicely the Madisonian argument for deliberative decision making in government and, I will argue, the modern administrative state. Thus, the analysis to follow echoes an older literature on "representative bureaucracy" and nonpositive theory defenses of administrative agencies as loci of deliberation (Meier 1993b; Rohr 1986; Seidenfeld 1992) and does not predicate the legitimacy of agency autonomy on the ability of elected politicians—Congress or the president—to control most agency policy choices. Rather, I contend that agency policy-making is legitimate because (1) it fulfills voters' wishes irrespective of the ability of elected politicians to control what agencies do, and (2) it is consistent with our constitutional design.

Madisonian Liberalism, Positive Theory, and the Administrative State

It is certainly true that positive theory shares several important characteristics with Madisonian constitutional theory (Grofman and Wittman 1989). Both begin with the assumption that individuals are rational and self-interested, that an individual, when presented with a choice, will choose the alternative that maximizes his or her utility. Like Madison's analysis of constitution building, positive theorists study the ways institutions might be designed to harness this ongoing process of individual goal maximization so as to produce the best possible collective outcome. Positive theoretical models of government tend to be Madisonian in another sense as well: they model the relationship between voters and their government from the classic Madisonian liberal perspective. All begin with the notion that rational voters participate in democracy primarily through the election of their representatives (see, e.g., Mayhew 1974; Fenno 1978; Fiorina 1981; Arnold 1990; and Bianco 1994). This is, of course, the model of the voter associated with the seminal work of Anthony Downs (1957) and other positive theorists who have followed in his footsteps.

For that reason, it is fair to associate positive theory scholarship with one kind of conservatism—not political conservatism in the modern sense but rather the philosophically conservative view of citizen participation that is associated with the classical liberalism of Madison and Locke. Stated differently, it is difficult to envision a positive theoretical analysis of participatory democracy of the kind associated with Rousseau or Jefferson, one that is based on the notion of a reciprocal causal relationship between participation and civic virtue.[3] By focusing on individual, purposive behavior and conceiving of voters as mere delegators of power to government, positive theorists seem to define away inspirational notions of virtue and of humans as social beings that we associate with Rousseau, Jefferson, and a more populist strain of democratic theory. Because positive theoretical models usually assume that individuals' preferences are fixed and endogenous, they have difficulty accommodating (or at least accommodating *well*) the idea that participation transforms the individual voter, producing civic virtue in the process. Indeed, this may be one reason why William Riker's positive theoretical analysis of these competing democratic theories offers such a forceful defense of classical liberalism, which is generally seen as the more conservative philosophy (1982).

Positive theory fits the Madisonian vision nicely, but does that imply a poor fit with the administrative state? Positive theoretical models of government have had little to say *directly* about the wisdom or desirability of the delegation of policy-making discretion to administrative agencies. As a rule, most disclaim any normative component and purport merely to analyze the relationship, without any explicit argument that particular kinds of power arrangements are "good" or "bad" in any sense. The so-called economic theories of regulation come closest to a self-conscious normative critique in their explanations of how rent-seeking interest groups secure agency-enabling legislation that provides those groups with private benefits while allocating the costs (costs that often exceed the benefits) to the general public (Stigler 1971; Peltzman 1976). But most positive theory analyses of administrative agencies are only indirectly critical of agency autonomy. William Niskanen, for example, merely explains the growth of the administrative state as the product of budget-maximizing behavior by rational bureaucrats, given certain informational and other advantages agencies enjoy over their political overseers (1971). Likewise, proponents of capture theories use logic to argue that private sector rent seekers use their competitive advantages in the policy process to "capture" or undermine regulation in the long run.[4] Yet another strain of the literature uses standard principal-agent models to demonstrate how politicians can control agencies (McCubbins, Noll, and Weingast 1987; Epstein and O'Halloran 1999; Bawn 1994, 1995).

However, while most positive theorists disclaim any normative agenda, it is easy to view these analyses of administrative agencies as indictments of the administrative state. Niskanen's budget-maximizing bureaucrat, for example, shirks his duties and pads his own pocket. Capture seems to be an equally insidious notion, one that offers a ready justification for discrediting agencies and their actions. I have suggested elsewhere that this dim view of agency independence is due in part to a combination of (1) the methodological imperatives of positive theory scholarship and (2) social scientists' desire to avoid normative issues (Spence 1997a, 1997b.) Economists value parsimony in model building, which helps keep problems tractable, particularly in the context of formal analyses. For that reason, most of the formal analyses of the delegation of policy-making authority use principal-agent models that posit elected politicians as the principals to whose wishes agencies may be more or less obedient. Given our existing constitutional design, in which voters have only an indirect relationship with agencies, any formal *descriptive* model of that relationship must posit a two-stage principal-agent problem. That added complexity may provide a powerful disincentive to analysis of the voter-agency relationship, leaving us with separate models of the two steps of that relationship that seem not to capture fully the value of delegation to voters.[5]

A Model of Voter Choice

Goal, Definitions, Assumptions

The question with which we began—of why voters might prefer decisions to be made by unelected bureaucrats rather than elected politicians—puts aside the two-stage delegation problem in order to focus on its normative dimensions. Returning to that normative question, I will begin by positing the following goal of government policy choice, adapted from Lupia and McCubbins 1994a.

> Goal: Voters want government to do what they would have done (e.g., what the median voter would have done) if they had the time and resources to devote to the problem.

By stating the goal in this way, I am posing the problem differently than in much of the delegation literature, particularly those analyses of the delegation of authority by voters to elected politicians that tend to view the problem as one of predicting outcomes. Voters are thought to have preferences over outcomes, not over policy choices; because voters cannot foresee outcomes, they must choose (to delegate policy choices to a particular candidate) based on some sort of decision rule that maps voter preferences over outcomes to the (candidate's presumed) policy choice.[6] By contrast, this analysis assumes a more self-conscious version of voter uncertainty. Voters are not merely uncertain over how policy choices will be translated into outcomes. Rather, voters know that: (1) they lack the information necessary to make fully informed choices in the first place, and (2) their uninformed preferences over policy alternatives are in part a function of that missing information. Thus, this analysis assumes the relative desirability of deliberative policy-making over government by public opinion poll.

Recognizing that voters do not have the power to make direct choices about who makes policy—that their only direct recourse is against elected politicians—the analysis will examine the question of how voters *would* choose if they could. Assume, then, three sets of actors: *voters, elected politicians* (a unicameral legislature),[7] and an *agency*.[8] Assume further that individual voters and elected politicians have single-peaked preferences[9] over a single dimension of policy choice. Let O_i represent any person's preferred policy choice, such that

O_A = ideal point of the agency on a policy dimension,

O_V = ideal point of the median voter on a policy dimension,

O_P = ideal point of the median elected politician on a policy dimension.

Assume further that each actor's ideal point (O) is a function of (1) the amount of accurate information that actor possesses (I) about the policy choice, and (2) a vector or combination of that actor's values (V), representing the other internal influences on each actor's opinion.[10] That is,

$$O = f\{I, V\}.$$

Therefore,[11] if

I_A = the amount of accurate information held by the agency,

I_V = the amount of accurate information held by the median voter,

I_P = the amount of accurate information held by the median elected politician,

V_A = vector or combination of values held by the agency,

V_V = vector or combination of values held by median voter,

V_P = vector or combination of values held by median elected politician,

and if

$$I_A = I_V = I_P \quad \text{and} \quad V_A = V_V = V_P,$$

then

$$O_A = O_V = O_P.$$

In other words, differences in opinion over policy choices are a function of, and are only a function of, differences in (1) the amount of accurate information the actors hold and/or (2) their values.

Argument

Decision Rule

Consistent with Downs, we can conceive of voters as rationally ignorant. For the vast majority of policy problems, busy voters choose not to devote the time or resources necessary to make a fully informed choice.[12] Policy choices may not be salient to voters and may escape their notice. Voters may be aware of the issues but have difficulty sorting through the information they are given by interest groups and others. In either case, voters do not acquire the information necessary to make a fully informed choice. Elected politicians have more time to devote to policy-making and are therefore more informed/less ignorant about policy choices than voters are. However, because elected politicians are generalists within the field of policy-making, they too are rationally less informed/more ignorant than administrative agencies about policy matters within the agencies' jurisdiction. Not only do agency bureaucrats have more time to devote to specific policy matters, but they often bring more specialized expertise to the problem as well. Hence, we can construct a hierarchy of rational ignorance, such that for the usual policy choice $I_V < I_P < I_A$.[13]

Of course, I_V, I_P, and I_A are not static. Voters, elected politicians, and agencies are constantly gathering information and evaluating its accuracy. Indeed, voters in particular must face a barrage of information designed to persuade them and to change the location of O_V. Assuming that these actors are capable of separating good from bad information in the long run, we can infer that over the very long run the distance between I_V, I_P, and I_A will diminish or in some instances that voters will eventually acquire enough information to pass the threshold required to make an informed choice.[14] That is, we might imagine the existence of a threshold of information beyond which additional information will have no effect on voters' preferences. For some issues, voters may acquire this threshold level of information over the long run. For many less salient policy choices, however, this hierarchy will continue, even over the very long run, such that most voters will never acquire the expertise necessary to make a fully informed choice. More importantly, this ignorance hierarchy is always present in the short run, extending from the time agencies first become aware of a policy issue through the early phases of its appearance on the larger public agenda.

Voters may understand this hierarchy of ignorance and may have a sense of the current ideal points (O) of the other actors. In other words, while voters may have opinions about some policy choices, they may also know that (1) there are other policy choices about which they are unaware or otherwise have no opinion and (2) some of the opinions they hold may be both relatively uninformed and information elastic.[15] Thus, if differences in information accounted fully for differences of opinion across the three sets of actors, voters would always prefer to have agencies make policy choices. In that case, administrative agencies ought to be able to do the best job of choosing the policy voters would have chosen but for their information deficit, since agencies have more information than politicians do. However, voters know that each actor's ideal point is also a function of its values (V), and voters cannot tell exactly what determines the difference between O_A, O_V, and O_P in any given case, because voters do not know precisely how their own values differ from those of politicians or agencies. This formulation of the problem, then, suggests the following decision rule.[16]

> Decision Rule: If $|V_A - V_V| \leq |V_P - V_V|$, then voters prefer to leave the decision to the agency.
>
> If $|V_A - V_V| > |V_P - V_V|$, then the result is indeterminate.

That is, if the agency's values are no more dissimilar to the median voter's values than are the median elected politician's values, then the median voter prefers that the agency make the policy choice, since the agency has access to the largest amount of accurate information. However, if the agency's values are more dissimilar, the decision depends upon how the opinion function translates information and values into preferences. Stated differently,

> if $I_V = I_A$ would $O_A - O_V$ be $<$ or $> O_P - O_V$?

The answer depends upon how much V_P and V_A influence O_P and O_A, respectively. Figure 1 depicts this problem. If voters had as much information as agencies do, would the median voter's ideal point (O_V) move (along the x-axis) toward the agency's ideal point (O_A) or toward the median politician's ideal point (O_P)? Because values are hidden, voters cannot know the answer to that question with any certainty.

This is, of course, a problem to which James Madison devoted considerable attention. That is, Madison's political theory gave central importance to the factors that guide policy choice, particularly the role of self-interest as a determinant of an actor's policy preferences. To Madison, even the best-intentioned public official could succumb to the problem of faction because one's view of the public interest is always colored by self-interest (Federalist 10). Thus, to Madison the problem of faction was not simply a problem of rent seeking. Rather, it concerned ways in which private interests could contaminate the pursuit of the public interest unintentionally or unconsciously as well. Madison suggested that voters can use information about actors' interests to inform political

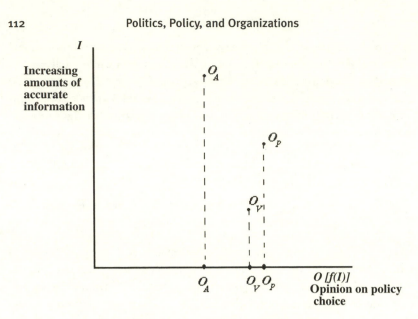

Fig. 1. Opinion as a function of information

decision making.[17] Indeed, one of the major arguments in favor of vesting policy-making authority in elected politicians as against unelected agencies rests on this very notion. That argument states that the electoral connection between voters and politicians implies that $|V_A - V_V| > |V_P - V_V|$. I turn to that argument now.

The Electoral Connection Argument

Much of the hostility toward agency autonomy, both within positive theory literature and without, is predicated on the notion that since elected politicians are electorally accountable to voters and agency experts are not voters' values correspond more closely to those of their elected politicians than to those of the agency. The political science literature addressing the motives of elected politicians is large and rich. From that literature, we can distinguish (1) instances in which the policy choice is determined by an assessment of its electoral consequences from (2) instances in which the choice is made without concern for its electoral consequences. Some political scientists contend that most politicians' choices are motivated, first and foremost, by concern for their electoral consequences, or that this is at least the most useful working assumption (Mayhew 1974). Others emphasize "trust" as the key to an elected politician's ability to make choices irrespective of their electoral consequences, noting that trust is itself a function of the electoral connection (Fenno 1978; Bianco 1994). Politicians build up trust by attending to the electoral consequences of their actions; that trust acts as a leeway account from which the politician can draw in the future to make policy choices that might displease constituents. If the key to election or reelection is securing voters' trust, it seems clear that one way politicians try to do this is by convincing voters that they share their values. Likewise, if the best way for a candidate to secure election or reelection is to convince voters that he or she will make wise policy choices, one way to get that message across in an uncertain multidimensional world is through this same sort of appeal to shared values. If we assume that voters are able to select candidates whose personal values reflect their own, in a world of divided government the median politician's values ought to be similar to those of the median voter.

Not only does electoral accountability suggest that $|V_P - V_V|$ is small, the positive theory literature suggests at least three different (and partly inconsistent) ways in which agency values are likely to differ systematically from voters' and politicians' values. The first of these involves *agency self-interest:* concepts like shirking, budget-maximizing bureaucrats, and the like are examples of ways in which agency self-interest undermines agencies' pursuit of the public interest. We can certainly imagine situations in which this is true. Agencies' self-interest is indeed implicated in budgeting decisions, and we infer therefore that in that context $|V_A - V_V| > |V_P - V_V|$. This might also be the case for agency decisions involving the expansion or retraction of agency jurisdiction or authority. For example, when an agency is charged with interpreting its own enforcement powers under a statute it may have every incentive to interpret the statute so as to maximize its enforcement leverage.[18] Adopting an expansive interpretation of its own enforcement authority is one way the agency can ease the performance of its mission and tasks. Likewise, when agencies must make decisions about the reach of their own jurisdiction, self-interest propels them toward ever more expansive interpretations of the law.[19] In these cases, we might expect the agency's values to differ from voters' and elected politicians' values in systematic ways.

Capture theory suggests a second set of systematic differences between agencies, on the one hand, and voters and elected politicians on the other—differences that implicate both values and information as determinants of preferences. One variant of capture theory focuses on information, and suggests that industry captures an agency by virtue of the pervasive presence of industry, and *industry information,* in agency policy-making proceedings over the long term. After the initial interest in regulation surrounding the creation of the agency and the definition of its original mission has subsided, the proponents of the regulatory scheme lose interest in the problem and turn their attention elsewhere. The result is that the agency is presented with a skewed sample of information, leading to its capture by the very industry it was designed to regulate. Another variety of capture involves the complicity of congressional committees. According to this view, congressional committees populated by *ideological outliers* exert influence over the agency they oversee for the benefit of powerful industry constituents (e.g., Weingast and Marshall 1988). Over the long haul, the committee exerts influence over the agency's values, moving them toward its own and away from the median elected politician's and the median voter's.[20]

Another strain of positive theory scholarship suggests yet a third way in which agencies' values are different and stands in partial conflict with capture theory. This literature focuses on the agency's "structure" as a determinant of its values, raising the danger of "legislative drift" or, more accurately, the *locking in of agency values* (McCubbins, Noll, and Weingast 1987; Horn and Shepsle 1989). That is, we can expect agency bureaucrats to have values that are consistent with the agency's mission; otherwise, the bureaucrats would not be attracted to work in the agency in the first place. Some positive theorists suggest that politicians are fully aware of this tendency when they design the agency and (re)define its mission (McCubbins, Noll, and Weingast 1987). Therefore, the agency's values will be consistent with the values of the winning legislative coalition that defined the agency's mission in the first place. Horn and Shepsle (1989) suggest that this poses a problem because V_A and V_P are likely to drift apart over time.[21] While the statutory mission locks in agency values over time, voters' values are subject to no such stickiness. As time passes, then, agencies may come to be populated by an unrepresentative sample of the population—a sample that is more dedicated to the agency's mission than the population as a whole.

Rejoinders to Electoral Connection Argument(s)

There are several important reasons why the electoral connection argument does not adequately capture all of the important elements of the decision calculus. First, the argument overstates the value differences between agencies, on the one hand, and politicians and voters on the other. Indeed, there are good reasons to believe that in many choice situations there are no systematic differences between the agency's values (V_A) and those of the median voter (V_V). Second, the argument leaves unexamined the relative magnitudes of $|V_P - V_A|$ and $|V_A - V_V|$ or it simply assumes that $|V_P - V_V| \leq |V_A - V_V|$. Finally, this argument sidesteps our decision rule by ignoring the relative importance of information (I) versus values (V) in determining preferences (O). That is, the decision rule states that even if $|V_A - V_V| > |V_P - V_V|$ the result is indeterminate; in that case, voters might still prefer agencies to make policy choices in those situations.

Rejoinder 1: Agency Values. Of course, positive theory analyses of the administrative state that stress the role of self-interest in agency decision making stand in stark contrast to a long, rich, public administration literature emphasizing very different values in agency decision making (Wilson 1887; Goodnow 1900; Weber 1946). In fact, many of the policy choices agencies make do not implicate the agency's self-interest. Rather, they involve statutory interpretations and decisions in which agency bureaucrats have no personal interest at stake—questions such as (1) Is this drug safe? (2) Under what conditions should polluting facilities receive permits? and (3) Should this anticompetitive activity be outlawed? For most of these kinds of commonplace policy choices, agency bureaucrats' values are not likely to be contaminated by self-interest. Stated differently, one can concede (1) that agencies care first and foremost about preserving their own existence, protecting their turf, and the like; and (2) that these considerations affect a large number of agency policy choices, without conceding that *most* agency policy choices are driven by self-interest. To the contrary, the great majority of policy choices are driven by other kinds of values.

Likewise, capture models paint an equally unrealistic picture of agency values. No family of positive theoretical models seems more irrelevant yet is more widely cited than capture models. Legal scholars and economists, in particular, seem enamoured of capture theory, much more so than political scientists. Regardless of its continued influence, the picture of agency decision making dominated by special interests, "iron triangles," and impenetrable "subgovernments" bears little relation to agency policy-making in the era of procedural openness and media hyperscrutiny. While it remains true that industry enjoys enormous resource advantages over others in the struggle to influence policy-making in Congress and at the agency level, those resource advantages have simply not led to the kind of outlier-dominated policy process capture models describe. Part of this may be due to capture theorists' inability to foresee the rise of sophisticated, litigious, public interest organizations, open meetings laws, sunset legislation, and the like. In any case, few would argue that the Food and Drug Administration, the EPA, and the Federal Trade Commission act at the behest of industry (either directly or indirectly) when they decide whether drugs are safe, permits should be issued, or anticompetitive activities should be outlawed, respectively, or that industry's relative over-representation in the agency decision-making process has skewed the process in that way.[22] The weakness of the tools of congressional oversight, the constraints imposed by judicial review, and the ossification of the administrative decision-making process all conspire with a more attentive public to impede capture.

That is not to say, however, that agencies' values are identical to those of voters. To the contrary, the argument that agencies are systematically more loyal to their basic mission seems persuasive, even obvious. People who are sympathetic to that mission *are* more likely to be attracted to work at the agency, and to the extent that the mission is articulated in the agency's enabling legislation interest groups and courts may try to hold the agency to that mission. All of this increases the potential for voter drift, described earlier. However, the problem of voter drift is minimized by the relative stability of values. That is, unlike opinions, values tend to be relatively stable over time. Certainly, people's values evolve; they are not static. Nor are they subject to rapid fluctuation. For example, we might hypothesize that one's attitude toward trade policy is a function of both ideology (liberal vs. conservative) and one's familiarity with neoclassical economic theory, which offers a powerful critique of protective trade barriers. Conservatives with low levels of economic expertise may be more favorably disposed toward free trade than liberals with low levels of economic expertise. As liberals gain familiarity with economic theory, some portion of them may come to view free trade more favorably. It does not follow from this that they are no longer liberals. Rather, their opinions are simply more information elastic than their values. In other words, while voter drift seems likely to occur, it also seems likely that voters' values drift apart (that $|V_V - V_A|$ grows) very slowly. Therefore, to the extent that agency values reflect those of the median voter at the time the agency's mission was established, there is a reasonably good possibility that $|V_A - V_V|$ remains relatively small except in those choice situations in which V_A is contaminated by the agency's self-interest.[23]

Rejoinder 2: Politicians' Values. What about politicians' values? It is true that elected politicians have no defined mission that prevents their values from drifting along with voters' values.[24] That argument notwithstanding, there are good reasons to suspect that self-interest contaminates the policy choices of elected politicians at least as often as it does those of agencies and that it does so in ways that do not contaminate subsequent agency choices. Even if voters do choose politicians who share their personal values, politicians' policy choices are not always driven by those personal values. Rather, the relative immediacy and complexity of the electoral connection for politicians offers a great deal of opportunity for values that differ from those of the median voter to influence the policy choices of elected politicians. Of course, positive theory offers a variety of reasons why legislative policy choices may not reflect the preferences (O_P) of the median elected politician. Outliers may be able to manipulate process so as to produce policy choices to their liking. Gatekeeping committees can facilitate this kind of capture of the process; indeed, some have suggested that Congress is organized precisely to produce this kind of result, citing a long history of logrolling that decreases social welfare. However, there are other reasons for believing that for any given policy choice the distance between V_V and V_P may be great, reasons that are based upon the complex forces that compete for influence over politicians' policy choices, even those of the median elected politician.

When an elected politician makes a policy choice so as to minimize the adverse electoral consequences of that choice at the next election, that decision may reflect a variety of values that are different from those that would have guided the median voter under those same circumstances. For example, elected politicians may be able to maximize the probability of reelection by attending to the interests of particular constituencies, such as those that make up the politician's core supporters, important campaign contributors, and the like. In addition, particular issues may be more salient to some groups than others, such that the politician can maximize the probability of reelection by making a policy choice that differs significantly from the choice the median voter would have made. Indeed, as many others have noted, there ought to be a direct relationship between issue salience and the degree to which the politician's policy choice reflects the median constituent's preferences. In this way, elected politicians' self-interest—the desire for reelection—can contaminate the policy choice. Given the importance political scientists ascribe to reelection concerns in the decision calculus of elected politicians, it seems reasonable to conclude that this kind of self-interest contamination of preferences occurs at least as often for elected politicians as it does for agencies. While voters may try to elect representatives whose values match their own, voters may also suspect that many of the policy choices elected politicians make are not based primarily on those personally held values. This is indeed ironic. The reason why voters vote for the politician that is most "like me" is so that politician will make the policy choices "I would make if I were in that position." However, the process of convincing a heterogeneous constituency that he or she is worthy of that trust leads the politician to make policy choices using a very different set of values. Hence, it may often be true that $|V_P - V_V| > |V_A - V_V|$.

However, if the agency is loyal to its mission, and the agency's mission is defined by Congress, one might ask why $|V_A - V_V|$ will ever be less than $|V_P - V_V|$. The answer is that Congress is more likely to be expressing the will of the median voter when it passes major enabling legislation defining the agency's mission than when it makes other, lower-salience decisions that might otherwise be delegated to agencies. This is the so-called republican moment explanation for major regulatory legislation (Schroeder 1998), one that echoes Anthony Downs's description of the "issue attention cycle" (1972) in the context of environmental law. When an issue captures the public's imagination, legislators face greater electoral risk and have a strong disincentive to deviate from the median voters' wishes.

Rejoinder 3: The Role of Information. When we reintroduce information into the decision process, we strengthen the relative attractiveness of agency policy choice. Recall that even if $|V_A - V_V| > |V_P - V_V|$ that does not imply that voters would prefer that elected politicians make the policy choice. This is because the agency always has more information than the median politician and politicians cannot (in the short run at least) acquire sufficient information such that $I_A = I_P$. Voters know this. Thus, even when $|V_A - V_V| > |V_P - V_V|$, voters have no clear preference under our decision rule. In this situation, voters cannot tell which actor would

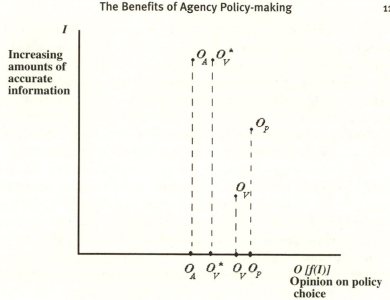

Fig. 2. Hypothetical voter opinion with information

make the "better" decision because they cannot know how each actor's opinion translates values and information into preferences. For that reason, voters will discount the relative proximity of O_P and O_V in any given instance. In figure 2, voters know that when $|O_P - O_V| < |O_A - O_V|$ it is also true that $I_V < I_P < I_A$, and voters have no way of knowing whether the proximity of O_P and O_V is due merely to the distribution of information or to values. If O_V^* represents the median voter's hypothetical ideal point when $I_A = I_V$, voters want government to be loyal to O_V^*, not to O_V. The problem, of course, is that while voters know that $I_A > I_P > I_V$ they cannot know with certainty the locations of V_A and V_P;[25] nor can they ever calculate $|O_V^* - O_P|$ or $|O_V^* - O_A|$.

Why, then, might voters prefer delegation of decision-making authority to the agency given this uncertainty? There are at least two good reasons. One might be that voters' believe they have a sense of the location of V_A and that $|V_A - V_V|$ is small. Voters may get a sense of the location of V_A from their knowledge of the agency's mission. For example, if the median voter values environmental protection and knows that the EPA was created to protect the environment, the voter might prefer delegation of authority to the EPA even if he or she doesn't know the location of V_P

or O_V^*. A second reason why voters might prefer that a particular policy choice be made by an agency is their belief that information differences are accountable for differences in preferences over policy alternatives in the given choice situation. Voters may suspect that study and deliberation will produce something close to consensus, or at least suggest a clear majority-preferred alternative. In that instance, voters ought to prefer to vest decision-making authority in the administrative agency, where the decision will be relatively more insulated from direct interest group pressure.

There is no shortage of evidence to support this view of decision making. We can get some insight into the information elasticity of opinion by looking at the results of recent experiments in deliberative polling by James Fishkin and others. Fishkin's work involves panels of representatives of citizens whose preferences are measured before and after they deliberate on a particular public policy topic. The deliberation process involves not only the gathering and digesting of information but discussion among participants. In several different deliberative polling experiments covering a variety of subjects and respondents, Fishkin found that opinions change significantly as the result of deliberation and that run of the mill (nondeliberative) polling *misrepresents* informed (deliberative) public opinion. For example, one of Fishkin's deliberative polls sampled British public opinion on crime issues. Fishkin reported that after the deliberation process, "respondents showed an increased sense of the limitation of prisons as a tool for fighting crime" and "an increased willingness to support alternatives to prison" (1996). Of course, because most opinion polls are not deliberative, informed opinions are hidden. Elected politicians cannot respond to informed opinion; they can and do respond to less informed opinions about crime and punishment. As Fishkin notes, British participants in one of his deliberative polls seemed, after their deliberation, to be unrepresentative of British public opinion but "representative of the views the entire country would come to if . . . they actually had a better opportunity to think about the issues" (137). Likewise, because Congress and the president can never know the location of O_V^*, politicians who are responsive to electoral pressures do not necessarily choose the policies the voters want them to.[26]

This same phenomenon is illustrated by the large literature on the perception of risks. A 1987 EPA study showed that there are vast differences between the way these two groups of people prioritize risks. For example, experts rank indoor air pollution as among the most serious risks and hazardous waste disposal sites as among the least serious; laypeople reverse that ordering (EPA 1987). Some scholars attribute these differences to value differences between laypeople and experts and to other contextual factors that mediate lay perceptions of risks but not those of experts (Graham and Wiener 1995). There is a growing body of evidence, however, showing that when laypeople can overcome the information deficits they face their preferences over risk reduction priorities tend to look much more like those of experts. For example, a 1991 comparative risk project undertaken by the state of Vermont and the EPA enlisted laypeople to study and deliberate before prioritizing environmental, health, and safety risks. The result was a ranking that was typical of experts' risk rankings (State of Vermont 1991). Thus, if (1) voters' preferences are highly information elastic, (2) voters know this, and (3) there are many policy choice situations in which voters' values tend not to differ significantly from those of agency experts, then it makes sense that voters might often prefer to vest decision-making authority in administrative agencies rather than their elected representatives.[27]

Accountability and the Risk of Error

However, despite the fact that voters might prefer to have agencies make certain policy decisions, might there still be good reasons to prohibit agency policy-making? That is, even if there are good reasons to suspect that agencies will do a better job than politicians of choosing policies at or near O_V^*, one might ask whether that suspicion is wrong. What is the risk associated with placing authority in the wrong hands? The electoral connection argument suggests that if politicians choose poorly at least voters can correct that error through the discipline of the ballot box. This is not so with administrative agencies. Agencies are not directly electorally accountable, and political control of agencies is difficult and costly (Spence 1999a). Therefore, there is a danger—a greater downside risk—associated with agency autonomy. However, that danger is overstated *even if* political control is difficult and costly. The reason is because in the long run political control is more likely and more effective when the agency has chosen poorly—that is, when it has deviated greatly from O_V^*—and less likely and less effective when the agency has chosen well by choosing a policy that is close to O_V^*.

Why? Recall that the distance between O_V^* and O_V increases as I_V increases. As voters acquire more and more accurate information, they are increasingly able to judge for themselves whether O_A is a good or poor approximation of O_V^*. In the usual case, voters do not acquire enough information to make that judgment. However, when the agency chooses a policy that lies a great distance from O_V^* interest groups and political entrepreneurs who oppose the choice will mobilize. If they suspect that $|O_V^* - O_A|$ is large, those groups and politicians have a strong incentive to supply voters with more information; they will try to increase the salience of the issue among voters because it is to their advantage to do so. (By the same token, it is to their advantage not to try to increase the salience of agency policy choices they favor if they suspect that those choices deviate significantly from O_V^*.) Indeed, in a world of scarce resources it would be irrational for an interest group opposed to an agency policy to engage in a sustained lobbying effort against the agency choice if it suspects that $|O_V^* - O_A|$ is small. Of course, this is not to suggest that those agency policy choices are not the subject of lobbying efforts. Interest groups are constantly flooding voters with information designed to move O_V in a favored direction, and voters are constantly filtering, ignoring, and using that information. The important point is that in the midst of all that noise interest groups, strategic politicians, and other information providers (such as the news media) have a systematic incentive to devote more effort to educating voters about agency policy choices that deviate significantly from O_V^*.

Because of this relationship between O_V^* and the agency's policy choice, voters should acquire more information and develop more expertise over time with respect to policy choices that deviate greatly from O_V^*. If, as I_V increases, voters discover that $|O_V^* - O_A|$ is great, political momentum to reverse that choice legislatively will grow as political entrepreneurs in Congress or the presidency see electoral benefits to be gained from championing the issue. Similarly, a rational agency will also be more likely to resist change when $|O_V^* - O_A|$ is small (and less likely to do so when $|O_V^* - O_A|$ is large), reasoning that that resistance will tend to lead to increases in I_V. That, in turn should provide a disincentive to elected politicians to continue the fight when $|O_V^* - O_A|$ is small. This is a commonly observed dynamic. During the first Reagan administration, environmental interests and their congressional allies successfully opposed the policies advanced by new EPA administrator Anne Burford, despite the president's electoral margin, perceived deregulation mandate, and personal popularity. Environmental groups suspected (correctly, it turned out) that the Burford EPA was pursuing policies that deviated greatly from O_V^*. By contrast, more recent efforts by business groups and conservative Republicans to reverse or roll back EPA policy choices have been short-lived, and have failed, in part because moderate Republicans have correctly surmised that the EPA policy choices lie closer to O_V^* than the Republican-sponsored alternatives. Thus, in the long run indirect electoral discipline is likely to bring O_V^* closer to O_A over time.

Of course, the long run can be a long time. What about agency policies that deviate from O_V^* in the short run? Can we rely on courts to police this short-run deviation problem? That depends. Sometimes the agency's policy choice deviates from O_V^* because it reflects the agency's relatively greater loyalty to its mission (reflecting a large distance between V_V and V_A). In that case, courts will usually let agency choice stand. While judicial review is based upon the notion that the agency decision should, first and foremost, be faithful to the statutory mandate, agencies are given wide discretion in interpreting that mandate. However, sometimes the agency's policy choice deviates from O_V^* because it is contaminated by the agency's self-interest, for example, by financial gain or through increased jurisdiction or increased enforcement leverage over regulated parties. Then the case for according the agency great deference is less compelling because the decision may be based on factors other than those traditionally used by the courts to justify agency autonomy. Courts accord the agency discretion because agencies have expertise or because agencies seek the president's or their own ideological goals. Courts do not justify autonomy based upon the agency's self-interest.

Irrespective of whether agencies tend to choose well (i.e., whether they often approximate O_V^*), and whether their poor choices can be corrected in the long run, one might ask whether broad delegations of authority to agencies are consistent with constitutional theory. Perhaps the nondelegation doctrine reflects a constitutional preference for policy-making by elected politicians, one meant to prevent not only poor policy choices but the making of those choices in the first place. In other words, delegation allows government to produce *too much law*. This argument, however, is misplaced.

First, as others have noted, while the argument I have made here seems to be superficially inconsistent with Madison's (and the other founders') design, it is entirely consistent with their concept of democratic theory. The founders sought to create a system in which government could produce decisions that were *imperfectly* responsive to majority opinion. The Federalist Papers are replete with distinctions between immediate and permanent preferences and admonitions against government attending too readily to the former and not readily enough to the latter. Madison warned not only of ideologically narrow or geographic factions but also of factions based upon passions.[28] In Federalist 63, Madison makes it clear that government ought to be designed to prevent "temporary errors and delusions" from dominating the decision process and that the "cool and deliberate sense of the community" ought to be reflected in policy choices (Federalist 63).[29] By insulating Senate decision makers from direct electoral pressure (through indirect election and six-year terms) the founders sought to create an environment conducive to deliberation and the development of expertise. In Madison's words, the electoral accountability of members of the House of Representatives made that body prone to "temporary errors" in which the house might lose sight of its "true interests."[30] Senators, by contrast, would be able to acquire "a competent knowledge of the public interests," resist "fickleness and passion,"[31] and have "sufficient permanency" to provide for such objects as require a continued attention" (Federalist 63).

Of course, the Senate is no longer insulated from direct electoral pressure in this way. Administrative agencies are. Indeed, many of the traditional justifications for delegating responsibility to administrative agencies echo the concerns of Federalist 63—the need for a decision-making environment in which individuals can devote long-term attention to complex problems. John Rohr has made a careful and persuasive argument that administrative agencies serve the deliberative function that the Senate once did (1986). When voters express a preference for vesting decision-making authority in administrative agencies, they echo the arguments of the founders. In the twenty-first century, only agencies have the opportunity to make fully informed decisions; if it is true that direct electoral pressures promote factionalism and interfere with deliberation, then agency policy-making seems relatively consistent with the view of democratic decision making advanced by Madison and Hamilton.

On the other hand, it is one thing to conclude that agency policy-making is "like" the kind of decision process the founders envisioned for the Senate; it is another to conclude that it serves exactly that same constitutional function. The Senate represents one part of a tripartite constitutional system for producing laws. In the constitutional scheme, each of those bodies must agree to produce legislation: either the House, the Senate, or (absent a legislative override) the president can veto legislation. When they agree not to make a policy choice, but rather to delegate it to an agency, they circumvent that constitutional process, or so the argument goes. However, the fact that politicians cannot agree on all of the specifics of a policy choice does not undermine their conclusion that some change, within very general boundaries, is desirable (Mashaw 1998). The argument against agency autonomy seems to suggest that Congress ought not to have that option available to it and to promote form over substance. Agency policy-making is efficient in that it offers the opportunity for flexibility and adaptation in policy-making that would not be available were politicians forced to make each and every specific policy choice. Further, the executive power implies delegation. That is, public administration and public management scholars have long viewed as ridiculous the notion that there is some sort of bright line distinction between making and implementing the law. Implementation implies policy choice (Lipsky 1980; Brehm and Gates 1997; Mashaw 1998). These are the reasons we have traditionally offered to explain the creation of the administrative state.

Conclusion

I have attempted to demonstrate that positive theory need not be hostile to the administrative state. On the contrary, it offers a new and precise way to articulate one of the principal rationales for agency autonomy: the notion that expert agencies can sometimes do a better job of giving voters what they want than politicians can. The technology of positive theory offers a useful way of breaking down the choice process and of thinking about the role of information in that process. In so doing, it helps us to understand why policy-making by unelected agencies is consistent with democracy and our constitutional design.

Notes

The author would like to acknowledge the helpful comments of the editors and the participants in the Fifth Annual Public Management Conference, College Station, Texas, December 3–4, 1999.

The John Nalbandian quotation that appears at the beginning of the essay is from a personal communication with the author (1996). Nalbandian, mayor of

Lawrence, Kansas, at that time, was commenting on public attitudes toward a controversial development proposal in Lawrence.

1. Some economists and legal scholars have gone further, suggesting that legislation should be thought of as nothing more than interest group deals and that much of it is designed to provide rents (private benefits) to powerful organized interests. As a consequence, most legislation reduces social welfare (Easterbrook 1983).

2. There were some exceptions to this rule (see Hammond and Knott 1996; Bendor 1995; Bendor and Moe 1985, 1986; and Miller 2000). Other exceptions are found in the literatures on central bank independence (Hassapis 1996; de Haan 1997; Eijffinger and de Haan 1996; and Eijffinger, Hoeberichts, and Schaling 1996) and transaction cost explanations of bureaucratic organization (Williamson 1990, 1991; Moe 1997).

3. Of course, Arrow's theorem is sometimes interpreted as proving the impossibility of such an analysis.

4. There are at least two different varieties of capture theory. Under one version, capture takes place with the complicity of congressional committees via iron triangles, subgovernments, and the like. Another version argues that after an initial burst of interest in regulation the general public eventually loses interest in agency policy-making, leaving only regulated interest groups to participate in the process. Eventually, the agency is persuaded to adopt the policy preferences of the regulated industry, based in part upon the skewed information set with which the agency is presented (Kolko 1966; Ferejohn 1987).

5. See Krause 1996a for another critique of principal-agent models of this relationship.

6. For example, Douglas Arnold's model of voter delegation works this way. Voters evaluate the probability that a particular candidate will choose a policy that produces the outcomes voters want based upon an evaluation of the candidate's past record.

7. This conflates all elected politicians into one decision-making body and assumes that the median voter within that body, the "median elected politician," controls the outcome of decisions made by that hypothetical body. Of course, that is not how decisions are actually made, though in an era of divided government it might be a fair approximation in that ideological moderates usually must be satisfied in order to produce a government decision.

8. Of course, this assumption sidesteps questions about how agencies decide by treating the agency as a unitary actor. This is not to imply that I think agencies are unitary actors, nor is that assumption crucial to this analysis. For reasons outlined subsequently, I assume that agencies can be said to have preferences that are reflected in the decisions agencies produce, regardless of how individual bureaucrats' preferences are translated into agency preferences.

9. That is, the distribution of individual preferences is single peaked such that individual utility over choices falls (at the same rate in each direction) as the distance between the individual's ideal point and the selected policy choice grows. Of course, collective (voter or politician) preferences need not be single peaked in order for the collective to make a policy choice.

10. Think of values (V) as a representation of all the internal forces that determine how an individual translates information into preferences. This is, therefore, a broader use of the term than the dictionary definition.

11. One might argue that this conception of the determinants of preferences is another way in which this model differs from models of participatory democracy, in which external forces (social relations) exert powerful influences on opinion. On the other hand, we can think of values (V) as representing both internal and external forces that influence public opinion, in which case notions like "civic virtue" might be included within V.

12. This is not to suggest that voter choice is meaningless or that democracy fails as a consequence of voter ignorance. Rather, I mean only to begin with the proposition that voters are relatively ignorant about policy choices—and systematically so—compared to elected politicians and agencies.

13. This description of the information hierarchy implies a deterministic (rather than stochastic) view of the information variable. That is, while I do not assume that information levels are constant, nor is information a random variable. I do assume the continued existence of this information hierarchy, and the conclusions drawn in the "Rejoinders to Electoral Connection Argument(s)" subsection depend upon that assumption.

14. An example of the former type of policy choice might be abortion policy. Policy choices that require technical expertise—like many of those within the jurisdiction of regulatory agencies—are more likely to fall into the latter category.

15. As Lupia and McCubbins (1998) argue, voters can gather information about policy choices from media, interest groups, and other sources. But consistent with Downs (1957), it is irrational for voters to overcome their information deficits for most policy choices. That is, voters remain relatively ignorant deliberately and rationally and are conscious of the fact that their opinions are conditioned on this relative ignorance.

16. It suggests this decision rule if we can conceive of V as quantifiable or as a point on an ordered dimension.

17. This is the core insight in Lupia and McCubbins's model as well. They argue that voters can assess the trustworthiness of government actors by examining the context in which they speak. For example, if the government actor's position entails "costly effort," indeed, they contend that delegators of authority can design institutions that facilitate reasoned choice by making it costly for agents to lie (1998, 70–76).

18. For example, the Environmental Protection Agency (EPA) has adopted an expansive interpretation of its own authority to enforce the federal Superfund Law, an interpretation that serves the agency's interests (Spence 1999c).

19. For example, during the latter part of the twentieth century the Army Corp of Engineers, the Federal Energy Regulatory Commission, and the EPA benefited from a series of court decisions that expanded their regulatory jurisdiction by expanding the definition of the term *navigable waters* under the Rivers and Harper's Act of 1899, the Federal Power Act of 1935, and the Clean Water Act of 1972, respectively.

20. This view depends upon several strong premises. First, it assumes that oversight committees are ideological outliers. Second, it assumes that committees, not the congressional majority, control the tangible ways in which elected politicians influence agencies' budgets, legislative mandates, and so on. Third, this view assumes that ex post control by committees is effective.

21. McCubbins, Noll, and Weingast (1987) suggest that legislators can minimize the problem of agency drift by clearly defining the agency's mission and otherwise structuring the agency to adhere to that mission. Indeed, this is one logical ex ante response to the problem of capture, that is, specifying the agency's mission, coupled with the opportunity for interest groups to hold the agency to that mission using litigation, is one way for legislators to try to guard against capture. There is ample evidence in support of the notion that agencies do a good job of adhering to the original mission and that their values tend to reflect that mission (Spence 1999a).

22. For example, Cary Coglianese has examined interest group participation in rule-making proceedings at the EPA, finding that industry participation dwarfs participation by environmental groups. Yet that overrepresentation does not seem to be translated into influence in the process. ("Challenging the Rules," 47–51, manuscript on file with author).

23. Of course, the agency's mission is not static, and so neither are its values. Politicians can and do redefine the agency's mission. We might expect that redefinition to provoke subsequent changes in the agency's values. This possibility further minimizes the expected amount of voter drift in any given situation.

24. Indeed, the electoral connection argument maintains that elections redefine the politician's mission over time.

25. One could argue that the agency's specialized mission gives voters a clearer picture of V_A than they can get of V_P.

26. Some (but not all) of Fishkin's deliberative polls show that differences of opinion become moderated as a result of the deliberation process. In another deliberative poll conducted in Austin, Texas, he found that, while respondents were split on their support for foreign aid, after deliberation support for foreign aid solidified and they tended to agree with one another more than they had at

the outset. If information deliberation produces more agreement, or with less widely dispersed preferences, we might infer that information and deliberation can produce better decisions.

27. It should be noted that Fishkin advocates the use of deliberative polling to increase citizen participation in politics and to enhance the quality of representation by elected officials. His is not an argument for delegation by the uninformed to the better informed.

28. See Federalist 49, in which Madison argues that "it is the reason, alone, of the public that ought to control and regulate the government. The passions ought to be controlled and regulated by the government."

29. See also Hamilton's arguments in Federalist 6, in which he distinguishes momentary impulses from more permanent interests of the community.

30. Speech of James Madison, June 26, 1787, in Max Farrand, the records of the federal convention of 1787, 1937.

31. Ibid. These same concerns are reflected in Federalist 62 ("the necessity of a Senate is not less indicated by the propensity of all single and numerous assemblies to yield to the impulse of a sudden and violent passion, and to be seduced by factious leaders into intemperate and pernicious resolutions").

Part 2. Methodological Technology

Donut Shops, Speed Traps, and Paperwork: Supervision and the Allocation of Time to Bureaucratic Tasks

John Brehm, Scott Gates, and Brad Gomez

Supervisory Roles and Subordinate Compliance

Principal-agent models of hierarchical control (e.g., Alchian and Demsetz 1972; Holmström 1982) emphasize the coercive elements of supervision as the means of inducing subordinate compliance. In this view, supervisors extract work from subordinates by rewarding good workers, that is, those who comply with the supervisor's preferences, and punishing inadequate performers (Kadushin 1992). The principal's job is to anticipate the rational responses of agents and to design a set of incentives such that the agents find it in their own interest (given the incentive system) to take the best possible set of actions (from the principal's perspective). These models assume that the principal's ability to induce compliance is constrained by asymmetric information regarding the agent's effort (moral hazard) or ability (adverse selection).

As we have previously found (Brehm and Gates 1997), the coercive abilities of supervisors are limited by more than informational asymmetry. We have found that the coercive capacity of most supervisors is much less important as an influence over subordinate compliance than the subordinates' preferences, the selection process, intersubordinate learning, and contacts with clients (Brehm and Gates 1993, 1997). The demonstrated weakness of supervisory coercion leads us to reexamine the nature of the supervisor-subordinate relationship. If we dispense with the coercive capacities of supervisors, does this leave other supervisory functions as potential levers on subordinate compliance?

Organization theorists writing about hierarchical control have long suggested that the supervisor's role in inducing compliance is not limited to coercion. Chester Barnard (1938) suggested that supervision is a combination of potential functions. Supervisors provide a system of communications, promote the securing of essential efforts, and formulate and define purpose (217). The coercive aspect of supervision is only one means of achieving these functions. Supervisors may act as "teachers" in helping subordinates to identify more efficient ways to accomplish what is in both of their interests. In exhorting subordinates to identify with the mission of the organization, a supervisor may take on the role of "preacher" (an elaboration of Kreps [1984] 1990). A supervisor is a "recruiter" when he or she hires subordinates who share his or her preferences for work (Carpenter 1997; Johnson and Libecap 1994). A "participant" supervisor is also a contributor to work. Supervisors also provide "support," providing political cover so that subordinates can work. Finally, supervisors must execute the role of "coordinator," applying sanctions and rewards to encourage greater work on more productive tasks. Obviously, this list of supervisory roles is not complete and some are potentially contradictory. However, we believe these roles point to an expanded view of supervisors, their tasks, and their ability to persuade subordinates.

The principal contribution of this essay is to examine the supervisor as coordinator within a public bureaucracy, a role that is consistent with both principal-agency approaches and organizational theory. In this role, the supervisor must define and allocate tasks across subordinates (Wilson 1989). Tasks define what it is that bureaucrats, and hence bureaucracies, do. The challenge for the supervisor as coordinator is to match the right subordinates with the right tasks. This requires that subordinates be given tasks that they prefer. However, a perfect match is doubtful, since a subordinate is likely to receive a bundle of tasks, some of which are preferred and some not. What is the capacity of supervisors to coordinate subordinate work across a variety of tasks?

The change in our approach from the simple working/shirking dichotomy to a range of tasks offers many advantages. One advantage is that by looking at specific tasks rather than cumulative time spent in "working" we can permit a much more nuanced understanding of what it is that public bureaucrats do. Our previous analysis of working and shirking by police officers required that we collapse together all tasks that lead toward production when there is obviously considerable variation in the form of those tasks. It is of considerable interest to the supervisor to know whether his or her subordinates are devoting the majority of their time to mobile dispatches at the expense of time spent on paperwork. Further, the notion of "tasks" as the unit of bureaucratic effort squares much more cleanly with organizational theory on routines (e.g., Steinbruner 1974) and bureaucratic politics literature (e.g., Wilson 1989). Finally, by switching to an analysis of time spent among different forms of working, we reduce the sensitivity of our results to the potential for effects of the observer upon the performance of the subordinate. That is, while the amount of time spent working probably increases when the subordinate is being observed, the amount of time allocated to any particular form of work is probably less sensitive to observation.

We expand upon the working/shirking dichotomy by examining the compliance of public bureaucrats across multiple tasks, and we choose police officers as the bureaucrats to study. By examining the amount of time a police officer allocates to specific tasks, we have an opportunity to evaluate the supervisor's role in both maintaining subordinate compliance and coordinating work effort. Based upon our previous models of supervision, we believe that subordinate work across tasks will be a function of supervisory coercion, subordinate preferences, and the solidary attachments of subordinates. Although the findings here relate specifically to police work, we believe that they are generalizable to the behavior of bureaucrats in other contexts. In our previous analyses (Brehm and Gates 1997), we found strong similarities across a wide variety of bureaucrats, from police officers to social workers to federal civil servants.

We proceed in three parts. We begin with an explication of propositions derived from two of our previously published models that attempt to explain why subordinate bureaucrats behave the way they do and who influences them. The first of these models, the enhanced principal-agent (EPA) model, recasts agents' efforts toward the production of output by assuming that the utility of work for individual agents varies across tasks. This model assumes that agents' behavior is influenced by a broader set of incentives than simply the flow of residuals. A second model, an imitative model, draws on social psychological theories of organizational compliance in order to develop a model of intersubordinate learning.

Next we present our data set and explicate a statistical model for the analysis of time allocation across tasks. We then present the findings from the estimation of our model of supervision. Finally, we discuss the implications of our results for understanding both the analysis of time allocation and, most importantly, the theory of bureaucratic supervision.

Supervisors as Agency Coordinators

James Q. Wilson writes that "People matter, but organization matters also, and tasks matter most of all" (1989, 173). However, we know little about how tasks are allocated in an organization. What role do supervisors play in this allocation? In what capacity do supervisors serve as coordinators and facilitators of subordinates' work on different tasks? The traditional principal-agent model features agents' decision to work or shirk. (In Brehm and Gates 1997, we expanded the options available to subordinates to include sabotage, the act of producing negative output.) In this essay, we consider variation among the tasks available to subordinates, where the tasks vary in desirability to both the supervisor and to the subordinate. The key question is similar to that posed in our prior analysis: what accounts for the amount of time that subordinates devote to each task? We study the role of supervisors as coordinators by looking through the lenses of our two models, the enhanced principal-agent game and the imitative model, which are summarized here and presented elsewhere in greater detail (Brehm and Gates 1994, 1997).

The EPA Game

The EPA game models the strategic interactions between a supervisor and subordinates in order to provide greater insights into the problem of supervision and compliance in a bureaucratic setting. In terms of task allocation, the game begins with a supervisor deciding which subordinates should work on what policies. Every subordinate is given several assignments to maximize the supervisor's production goals. To do this, the supervisor attempts to match the "best" person to each task. In turn, each subordinate decides how he or she will allocate his or her time across these assigned tasks. Supervisors then must determine how and whom to supervise, given limited supervisory resources and the fact that some subordinates respond to supervision and some do not. The next time a supervisor decides who will do what, he or she takes into account how subordinates allocated their time and how responsive they were to supervision. A more formal overview of the EPA game is presented in our book (Brehm and Gates 1997, chap. 2).

One of the central assumptions of the EPA model is that the marginal effect of supervision on subordinate work inputs is a function of how amenable a subordinate is to supervision and the difference between the amount of work input by the subordinate toward a particular task and the amount of work input desired by the supervisor. (We assume that supervisors desire at least as much work from their subordinates as a subordinate would provide if left unsupervised.) Amenability is assumed to vary from subordinate to subordinate, but since we are not modeling responsiveness to supervision dynamically, we treat amenability to be given for an individual.[1]

To identify the equilibria for the EPA game, we explore the two main cases evident in the game. The first case arises when the difference between work desired by the supervisor and work provided without supervision is less than the marginal cost of supervision. This situation arises whenever the subordinate and the supervisor agree as to how much time to invest in a particular task, whether a great or little amount. This equilibria is pooling on type (meaning that there is no way to differentiate responsive from unresponsive subordinates).

The second case arises under the opposite condition, namely, when the difference between work desired and unsupervised work is greater than the marginal cost of supervision. If this condition holds, we can identify separating equilibria on type. Supervisors are able to identify responsive and unresponsive subordinates. If the subordinate is sufficiently unresponsive, no supervisory time is allocated. In other words, a supervisor will not waste time supervising an "insubordinate" subordinate, since the marginal costs exceed the marginal benefits associated with bureaucratic outputs.[2] Responsive subordinates, on the other hand, are supervised. Given that the marginal benefits of bureaucratic output are greater than the marginal costs, it is in a supervisor's interest to supervise a responsive subordinate.

From these equilibria generated by the EPA model we are able to derive the following testable propositions regarding subordinate work across tasks.

- If subordinates are indifferent between tasks (forms of work) and are homogeneously responsive to supervision (across tasks), then subordinates allocate greater work to tasks that receive greater supervision.

- If subordinates are not indifferent between tasks and are homogeneously responsive to supervision, subordinates allocate time to preferred activities, (largely) independent of supervision.
- If subordinates are indifferent between tasks but are heterogeneously responsive to supervision, subordinates allocate time to tasks for which they are more amenable to supervision.
- If subordinates are not indifferent between tasks and are heterogeneously responsive to supervision, subordinates will separate according to type. Nonresponsive subordinates will allocate time to preferred activities, and responsive subordinates will allocate time to activities for which they receive supervision.

The Imitative Model

The imitative model traces its origins to social psychological models of compliance and persuasion. Two central concepts are emphasized, social proof and consistency. Both concepts come into practice whenever a subordinate faces a request from a supervisor. In terms of consistency, the subordinate bureaucrat will ask "what have I done in the past?" As for social proof, the subordinate asks "what are others like myself doing?" If the subordinate is facing an uncertain or ambiguous situation, imitation serves as a simple and direct information shortcut.[3] These two central concepts are used to model how subordinates learn to respond to supervision by imitating one another.

Several factors influence the final distribution of work allocations by subordinates after many iterations of the simulated model. The adaptation of the bureaucrats is nonlinear and contingent on four discrete sets: the available set of responses to a policy, responses at first iteration, disposition toward a policy, and connections among bureaucrats and supervisors. We also consider supervisory tolerance for noncompliance and the level of sanction he or she applies to shape subordinate performance.

The imitative model simulation offers several conclusions for understanding task assignment and the role of a supervisor as coordinator. The central finding is that the more individual subordinates look to fellow subordinates for information about how to respond to a rule the greater the degree of conformity between subordinates. In turn, several factors influence the degree to which subordinates imitate one another, including the observability of subordinate actions, the level of uncertainty subordinates face, the frequency of contact between subordinates, the policy predispositions of subordinates (both the mean and variance), and the utility subordinates derive from working on a particular task. From these relationships, we are able to derive several propositions regarding the allocation of subordinate time across tasks.

- As the observability between subordinates increases, conformity of allocation of time across tasks increases (due to either information search or coercion by subordinates).
- As supervisors are better able to observe subordinate activity, subordinates allocate greater time to supervisors' preferred tasks (but see the "Data" section, which follows).
- Subordinates are more responsive to functional and solidary preferences than they are to supervisory coercion.
- As the number of tasks increases, uncertainty increases, and subordinates increasingly conform.

Data

The specific data at hand come from the 1977 Police Services Study, conducted by Elinor Ostrom, Roger Parks, and Gordon Whittaker in three cities (Rochester, St. Louis, and St. Petersburg). The study combined multiple methods, including observations of police officers' behavior during their shifts. The observational data provide an excellent opportunity to test our propositions about the allocation of time across tasks.[4] At the conclusion of each shift, the observer recorded the amount of time officers spent on a total of eleven tasks (the italicized phrase or word denotes our label in subsequent graphs).

1. Time spent on administrative duties (*Adm*)
2. Time spent on report writing (*Rept*)
3. Time spent out of car for foot patrol (not on an encounter or dispatched run) (*Foot Pat*)
4. Time spent on routine mobile patrol (*Mob Pat*)
5. Time spent at or en route to an encounter or dispatched run (*Run*)
6. Time spent on mobile traffic work (radar, vascar, etc.) (*Mob Traf*)
7. Time spent on stationary traffic work (radar, etc.) (*Stat Traf*)

8. Time spent on meals and other 10–7 breaks (*Meal*)
9. Time spent on mobile personal business (*Mob Pers*)
10. Time spent on stationary personal business (*Stat Pers*)
11. Time spent on other stationary police work (surveillance, stake-out, etc.) (*Other*)

We apply two different means for examining the amount of time an officer devotes to different tasks. The first of these, the "ternary" diagram, is most useful when one collapses the distribution of time across tasks into three categories. Here we consider time spent on personal business (meals and stationary and mobile personal business), time spent completing paperwork (administration, reports), and time spent policing (mobile and stationary traffic, runs, mobile and foot patrol, and other). The collapsing of time into three tasks corresponds nicely with a division into a police officer's principal responsibilities (policing and paperwork) plus a category denoting time not devoted to responsibilities. In our previous analysis (Brehm and Gates 1993, 1997), we facetiously referred to these as "donut shops" (shirking, here measured as time spent on personal business) and "speed traps" (working). In the present analysis, we divide time spent working between the categories of policing (speed traps) and paperwork.

If the amount of time spent on tasks is transformed into percentages of total time and total time is constrained to sum to 1, then the data are arranged on what is known as a simplex. One could produce a three-dimensional scatterplot of the data across the three dimensions of tasks, but all of the points would fall on the triangular plane intersecting the three axes at 1.0 (fig. 1). Instead, we focus solely on the triangular plane displayed in figure 2.[5]

The figure makes it quite clear that the majority of these officers' time is devoted to policing. The mode of the distribution is quite close to the extreme lower right corner, although there is a fair amount of dispersion throughout the lower right trident of the ternary diagram. Only five officers spent a plurality of their time on personal business, running counter to stereotypes about police behavior. Eight officers devoted a plurality of their time to paperwork, including one officer who spent the entire shift on paperwork. There are also some interesting edge conditions—officers who divided their time between either policing and paperwork or policing and personal business.

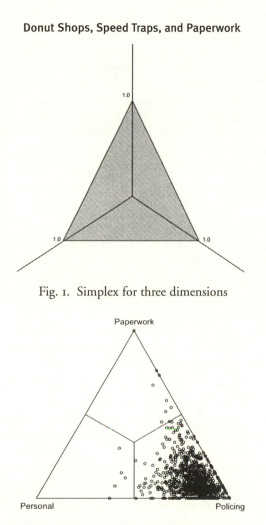

Fig. 1. Simplex for three dimensions

Fig. 2. Actual distribution of time on simplex, 1977 police data

The second graphical display (fig. 3) involves use of a novel technique called the checkerboard plot. Each officer is displayed as a vertical column of rectangles (here, quite thin—nearly lines—since we need to display more than nine hundred officers' shifts). Each row of rectangles corresponds to one of the eleven tasks (e.g., mobile patrol or meals). We shade each rectangle with a percentage of gray to denote the amount of time devoted by the officer to that task: rectangles that are completely

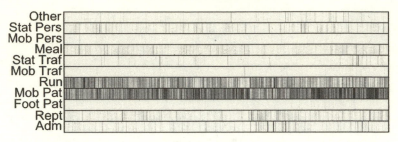

Fig. 3. Checkerboard plot of actual distribution of time spent on simplex, 1977 police data

white denote those tasks on which an officer spent zero time; rectangles that are completely black denote those tasks to which the officer devoted his or her entire shift; and those that are gray denote those tasks on which the officer spent some middling fraction of time. The darker the gray the more time was devoted to the task.

As is readily apparent from the checkerboard plot, police officers spend the majority of their days confined to two tasks: mobile patrol and on route to an encounter. Officers spend the least amount of their time on foot patrol and mobile and stationary traffic. Officers spend middling amounts completing reports or performing other administrative duties as well as on meals or stationary personal business. (The meals category is in third place, on average, although it is distantly behind runs and mobile patrol).

As is also apparent, these patterns are strikingly homogeneous across the more than nine hundred police officers in the three different cities. Although one can identify individuals who devote a plurality of time to administration and reports (the dark lines in those sections of the plot), as well as those who spend nearly twice as much time at meals than other officers, the general pattern here is one of uniformity, not variation.

This pattern of results is consistent with several of the conditions of the EPA and imitative models. The strong pooling equilibrium at work in the three cities (convergence on runs or mobile patrol) could be produced under the first and third hypotheses of the EPA model: it could be that the subordinates are either largely indifferent between tasks or fairly responsive to supervision. The mean behavior is also consistent with the logic of the imitative model, which generates a high degree of conformity as a result of intersubordinate contact and high solidary preferences.

To test the propositions of the EPA and imitative models, we require the following measures as explanatory variables. We need measures of the amount of supervision supplied. Here we use the number of contacts with the supervisor as the measure. Although we do not know how the supervisor is spending his or her time with the subordinate, the amount of contact is an excellent proxy for the amount of time available for supervision. (The EPA model explicitly treats supervisory time as a constrained budget, while the imitative model does not.) Note also that our use of the measure of the frequency of contact does not explicitly capture the duration of contact. One could reasonably suppose that the least responsive bureaucrats receive not only more frequent but longer periods of contact with their supervisors than more responsive bureaucrats do.

In addition, we include a dummy variable for radio contact to denote how observable the officer is to the supervisor. The imitative model explicitly models the supervisor's ability to observe subordinate output (although it predicts that observability is only weakly related to increased effort). We also need measures of the subordinates' preferences for work. Both the EPA and imitative models argue that subordinate preferences directly affect the amount of time spent on work. Here we use whether the subordinate expressed "functional" likes or dislikes (specifically commenting in the positive or negative about the responsibilities of officers). The imitative model argues that intersubordinate contacts influence performance. We employ a count of the number of contacts with fellow officers and whether the officer expressed a "solidary" like or dislike.

Inferential Methods for Analysis of Time Allocation

Suppose that one has a record for each bureaucrat i of the proportion of total time that the bureaucrat spends on each task j, denoted y_{ij}. Suppose further that the list of tasks $1 \ldots J$ are mutually exclusive and exhaustive and that a minimum amount of time is spent on each task. By definition, then, both of the following hold.

$$y_{ij} > 0, \qquad \forall j = 1 \ldots J \tag{1}$$

$$\sum_{j=1}^{J} y_{ij} = 1. \tag{2}$$

These two features mean that the allocation of time across tasks y_{ij} constitutes a simplex. Mathematical features of a simplex will mean that the distributions of the y_{ij} are not fully independent. For example, if one knows the values of y_{i1} up through $y_{i(J-1)}$, then one knows the value of y_j. In the simplest case, let y_{i1} describe the amount of time spent working; if "shirking" constitutes any time that is not spent working, then $y_{i2} = 1 - y_{i1}$. When the number of tasks increases beyond 2, the relationship is no longer as immediately straightforward—increased time spent on task 1 means less time for the remaining tasks but not necessarily any one particular remaining task—but it is still constrained. Similar problems are evident in any situation in which a variable is characterized by multiple outcomes that sum to unity for each observation.[6] Problems in this general class are referred to as "compositional data analysis" (Aitchison and Shen 1980; Aitchison 1986; Katz and King 1999). We consider one main variant of compositional data analytic strategies, the Dirichlet.

One relatively simple solution begins from an assumption that each stream of tasks is produced by an independent process. Suppose y_{ij}^* represents the hours in a week devoted by bureaucrat i to task j and that y_{ij}^* is distributed as J independent gamma random variates with shape parameters $v_1 \ldots v_J$. The probability density function for the gamma distribution is

$$y_{ij}^* = f_\gamma\left(Y_{ij}^* | v_j\right) \tag{3}$$

$$= y_{ij}^{v_j-1} \frac{\exp(-y_{ij})}{\Gamma(v_j)}. \tag{4}$$

The mean and variance for the gamma pdf are both v_j, and when the shape parameters are integer the distribution is also known as the Erlang distribution.

The total hours in the week is $T_i = \Sigma y_{ij}^*$. The proportion of time devoted to each task is then $y_{ij} = y_{ij}^* / T_i$. The proportion of time devoted to each task is distributed according to a Dirichlet distribution.

$$(y_1 \ldots y_J) = f_D(Y_1 \ldots Y_J | v_1 \ldots v_J) \tag{5}$$

$$= \frac{\Gamma(\Sigma_{k=0}^{J} v_k)}{\Pi_{k=0}^{J} \Gamma(v_k)} \prod_{k=1}^{J} y_k^{v_k-1}, \tag{6}$$

where

$$v_j > 0, \quad \forall j = 1 \ldots J.$$

One can reparameterize the v_j in terms of explanatory variables and coefficients with simple exponentiation.

$$v_j = \exp(X\beta_j),$$

where the effect parameters (β_j) vary by task and the X may or may not be the same set of explanatory variables (identification for the system is accomplished through covariance restrictions, detailed later, and through functional form). If one assumes that the observations are distributed identically and independently, then the log-likelihood for the reparameterized Dirichlet is

$$\ln L(\beta|X,y) = \sum_{i=1}^{N}\left[\ln\Gamma\left(\sum_{j=1}^{J}e^{X\beta_j}\right) + \sum_{j=1}^{J}e^{X\beta_j}\ln y_j - \sum_{j=1}^{J}\ln\Gamma\left(e^{X\beta_j}\right)\right].$$

(Note that we assume that intersubordinate influence is entirely captured by the intersubordinate contact and solidary preference measures in order to sustain the independence part of the ΠD assumptions). This log likelihood is easily optimized with a statistical package such as Gauss.

Several features of the Dirichlet lend themselves to some desirable properties for purposes of interpretation. The Dirichlet is a multivariate generalization of the Beta distribution (which we use extensively in our analysis of the allocation of time across two "tasks" (working and shirking) in Brehm and Gates 1997. As such, it is a highly flexible distribution permitting multiple modes and asymmetry. Further, the moments are easily found. Let $v^* = \Sigma_{k=1}^{j}v_k$. The mean of the amount of time spent on task j is

$$\mu_j = \frac{v_j}{v^*}. \tag{7}$$

The variance of time spent on task j is

$$\text{var}(y_j) = \frac{v_j(v^* - v_j)}{v^{*2}(v^* + 1)}, \tag{8}$$

and the covariance of time spent on tasks k and m is

$$\text{cov}(y_k,y_m) = \frac{-v_k v_m}{v^{*2}(v^* + 1)}. \tag{9}$$

Since all the v_j are positive, this means that the covariance of time spent on any pair of tasks k and m is negative or that any increase (decrease) in time spent on one task necessitates a decrease (increase) in time spent on *every other* task.

This property of the Dirichlet distribution is the first sign that there are hidden assumptions in the Dirichlet that may warrant another selection of distributional assumptions. Aitchison (1986) writes:

> It is thus clear that every Dirichlet composition has a very strong implied independence structure and so the Dirichlet class is unlikely to be of any great use for describing compositions whose components have even weak forms of dependence. . . . This independence property, which holds for every partition of every Dirichlet composition, is again extremely strong, and unlikely to be possessed by many compositions in practice. For example, one implication of it is that each ratio x_i/x_j of two components is independent of any other ratio x_k/x_l formed from two other components. (60)

What remains to be seen, however, is just how sensitive the analysis of composite data is to this particular "strong" independence of irrelevant alternatives (IIA) assumption. As we will demonstrate, the Dirichlet estimates turn out to be quite adequate for general prediction of the amount of time the officers in this sample devote to the different tasks.

The irony is that the Dirichlet distribution, like the Beta distribution, is capable of considerable variation in potential distributions of allocation of the compositions. Figures 4–7 demonstrate simulated Dirichlet distributions for varying selections of the parameters. It is possible to generate, among other forms, Dirichlet distributions that are uniformly dispersed (fig. 4), unimodal and centered (fig. 5), unimodal and off center (fig. 6), or multimodal and skewed (fig. 7).

Our selection of the Dirichlet is motivated by two distinct rationales. One is that the flexibility of the Dirichlet and relatively easy optimization (even for many equation systems) allow us to explore the task allocation problem at a high degree of disaggregation. In this sense, we chose the Dirichlet because of its tractability and good fit to the data. The second motivation is that the Dirichlet can be thought of as an outcome of some k gamma processes. In a separate work, we document that one can view the task allocation problem as a cooperative game where the supervisor encourages subordinates to work on the basis of the allocation of

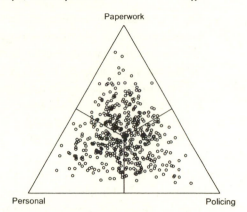

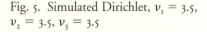

Fig. 4. Simulated Dirichlet, $v_1 = 1$, $v_2 = 1$, $v_3 = 1$

Fig. 5. Simulated Dirichlet, $v_1 = 3.5$, $v_2 = 3.5$, $v_3 = 3.5$

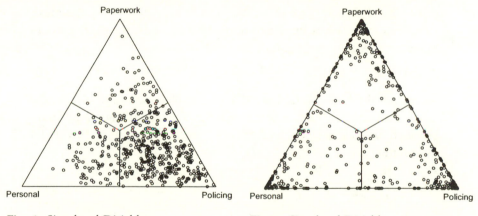

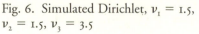

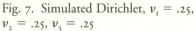

Fig. 6. Simulated Dirichlet, $v_1 = 1.5$, $v_2 = 1.5$, $v_3 = 3.5$

Fig. 7. Simulated Dirichlet, $v_1 = .25$, $v_2 = .25$, $v_3 = .25$

perks, represented as integer units (Brehm and Gates 1999). This stream of integer allocations would constitute a gamma process.

Results

Tables 1 and 2 display the maximum likelihood estimates for the Dirichlet distributions of the collapsed three-category and expanded eleven-category models, respectively. Positive signs on the coefficients indicate that an increase in the variable corresponds to an increase in the level of work. Frankly, more nuanced direct interpretation of the coefficients across even the simpler three-category model is cumbersome and across the eleven-category model even more so. Still, one should note that most of the variables are statistically significant for most of the equations, clearly so for the equations for "reporting" and "mobile patrol." Most of the time, the likes and dislikes are oppositely signed, which is sensible, although for the reporting equation all of the likes and dislikes are positive.

Because of the difficulties of providing more qualitative interpretation of the coefficients, our principal method for displaying the results of the Dirichlet analyses of time allocation is a form of computer simulation. We feature the Dirichlet analysis in this section. The process first requires that we generate estimates of the relevant parameters for each distribution based upon our estimated coefficients and selected values for the regressors and then generating vectors of random numbers drawn from the correct distributions with those parameters.

For the Dirichlet, the method works as follows (here using the mean values of the regressors for illustration). First compute the parameters v_j^* for each task j from the equation

$$v_j^* = \exp(\hat{\beta}_{0j} + \hat{\beta}_{1j}\bar{x}_{1j} + \cdots + \hat{\beta}_{kj}\bar{x}_{kj}) \tag{10}$$

for each of the k regressors. Then draw 1,000 observations of y_j^* from the gamma distribution with shape parameter v_j^*. Each of the y_j^* are independent. To scale the gamma variates to the simplex, simply divide by their sum.

$$y_j = y_j^* \Big/ \sum_{i=1}^{J} y_j^*. \tag{11}$$

TABLE 1.   Dirichlet Estimates for Allocation of Time Devoted to Tasks (collapsed), 1977 Police Data

Variable	Paperwork	Policing	Personal
Constant	.51*	2.37*	.86*
Patrol contacts	.01	.02*	.02*
Supervisor contacts	.04*	−.00	−.02
Radio contact	.00	.02*	.01
Functional likes	−.22*	−.18*	.02
Functional dislikes	.03*	.09*	.02
Solidary likes	.02	.06*	.05*
Solidary dislikes	.05*	.16*	.14*

$N = 944$.
*indicates coefficient statistically significant at $p < .05$.

TABLE 2. Dirichlet Estimates for Allocation of Time Devoted to Tasks (expanded), 1977 Police Data

Variable	Adm	Stat Traf	Rept	Meal	Run	Other	Foot Pat	Mob Pat	Stat Pers	Mob Traf	Mob Pers
Constant	−0.49*	−1.06*	0.41*	−0.97*	−1.06*	−0.93*	−0.02	1.38*	−0.24*	0.87*	−0.36*
Patrol contacts	0.01	0.00	0.06*	0.00	0.04*	0.01	0.00	0.04*	0.03*	0.00	0.01
Supervisor contacts	0.02*	−0.01	0.08*	−0.01	−0.01	0.00	0.04	−0.04*	−0.07*	−0.02	−0.01
Radio contacts	0.01	0.03*	0.08*	0.03	0.02	0.02	0.01	0.09*	0.10*	0.03*	0.07*
Functional likes	−0.16*	−0.07*	0.20*	0.00	0.01	−0.06*	−0.25*	−0.11*	−0.01	−0.01	0.15*
Functional dislikes	0.02	0.05*	0.13*	0.02	0.03*	0.03	0.03	0.00	−0.07*	0.01	0.12*
Solidary likes	0.01	0.00	0.07*	0.02	0.00	−0.02	0.00	0.07*	−0.01	0.02	0.04*
Solidary dislikes	0.03*	0.03	0.08*	0.05*	0.03	0.05*	−0.02	−0.05*	0.05*	−0.01	0.06*

$N = 944$.
*indicates coefficient statistically significant at $p < .05$.

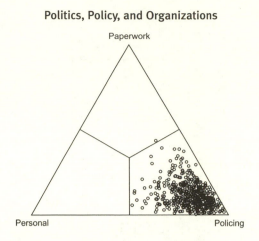

Fig. 8. Simulated Dirichlet at mean estimates

Figure 8 displays a simulated draw from the Dirichlet for the parameters computed at the mean. Clearly, this simulated distribution of time allocation comes quite close to the actual distribution (fig. 2). The mode of the simulated distribution falls approximately at the same location as the mode of the actual distribution (i.e., significantly skewed toward policing). The spread of the estimated distribution mimics the spread of the actual distribution, covering most of the lower-right trident. At the same time, the simulated distribution is missing some of the more striking features of the actual distribution. The simulated distribution does not capture the edge cases, neither the extreme outlier for time on paperwork, nor any of the cases that fall strictly between two tasks (either paperwork and policing or policing and personal business). Still, one would have to regard the Dirichlet distribution as one that replicates the actual distribution to a high degree.

Figure 9 presents the checkerboard plot of the simulated Dirichlet results, evaluated at the mean. While the ternary diagram leads one to conclude that officers spend the majority of their time policing, the checkerboard plot makes clear how officers spend time in the division of tasks within the category of policing.

As is consistent with the actual distribution of police officers' time-at-task, the simulation based on the mean values predicts that officers will spend the vast majority of their time on either runs or mobile patrol. Other forms of policing fall significantly behind. Unlike the actual distribution of time-at-task, the simulation based on means overpredicts the

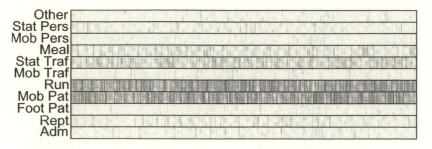

Fig. 9. Checkerboard plot of simulated Dirichlet at mean

amount of time that officers spend on static traffic duty. The Dirichlet estimates slightly underpredict the amount of time that officers spend on reports or administration, although it has the correct balance between the two forms of paperwork (i.e., more time is spent on reports). The model correctly predicts the amount of time that officers spend on meals, although it slightly overpredicts the amount of time spent on static personal business. Clearly, the Dirichlet estimates reproduce the actual distribution of time across the eleven tasks with great faithfulness.

The most interesting results will appear when we generate new simulations based upon selected values of the independent variables. Although we are not able to provide direct tests for the propositions developed here, we are able to examine the importance of supervisor observability (a key feature of principal-agency models is the extent to which action is hidden), subordinate observability (consistent with the ideas of the imitation model), and subordinate functional and solidary preferences. In the ternary plots of the simulated Dirichlets, we will show what happens at the maximum levels of the variables in question. With the checkerboard plots, we can simulate *increasing* levels of the variables, moving from left to right in the graphs.

What happens when the subordinate police officers are maximally observable to their supervisors? This situation ensues when the subordinates are in radio contact and when they have had the maximum number of contacts with the supervisor (twenty-one in this sample). (Note that we cannot ascertain the nature of the contact with the supervisor. This contact could have included specific requests for specific tasks to be completed, such as paperwork or policing; may have led to the imposition of formal or informal sanctions; or could have been strictly incidental.) Figures 10 and 14 display the simulated effect of being maximally observable.

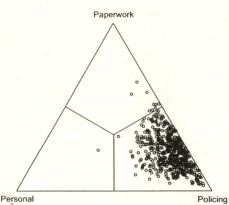

Fig. 10. Simulated Dirichlet when officers are most observable to supervisors

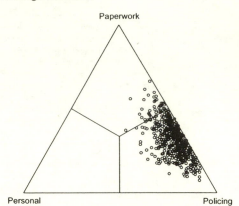

Fig. 11. Simulated Dirichlet when officers are most observable to subordinates

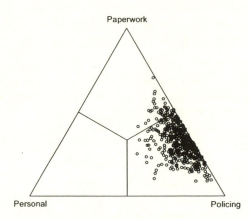

Fig. 12. Simulated Dirichlet when officers are most satisfied with squad

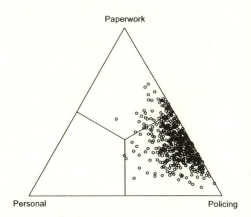

Fig. 13. Simulated Dirichlet when officers are most satisfied with job

The results of being under supervisory observation are hardly surprising. The variance of the distribution clusters away from time on personal business, suggesting a significant effect of supervisors on deterring shirking. Furthermore, the distribution of working tasks shifts away from policing and toward both paperwork and stationary traffic duty. Supervisors clearly have an influence on how subordinates allocate their time across policing and administration. Furthermore, as illustrated by the checkerboard plot, the greatest effect of increased supervision is upon in-

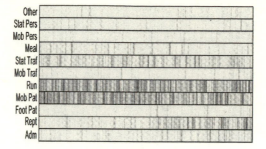

Fig. 14. Simulated Dirichlet when officers are most observable to supervisors

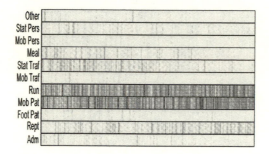

Fig. 15. Simulated Dirichlet when officers are most observable to subordinates

creased time spent completing reports, not on administration, and a significant reduction of the amount of time spent on personal business, meals especially.

The more complicated checkerboard plot reveals that supervisors have a significant role in encouraging subordinates to distribute time over a wide variety of tasks. In contrast to the simple work-shirk split, the supervisors exercise a high degree of influence over the subordinates' choices among different forms of work.

A similar figure may be produced to display the effect of being observable to fellow subordinates (figs. 11 and 15). In the present analysis, this entails raising the number of contacts with fellow officers to its maximum (thirty-one). As with the figure for officers maximally observable to supervisors, there is a pronounced shift toward increased time spent on paperwork. In fact, not only is there a greater increase in the amount of time spent on paperwork, but the dispersion of the distribution is

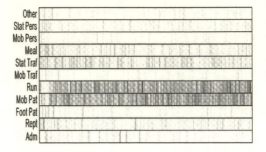

Fig. 16. Simulated Dirichlet when officers are most satisfied with squad

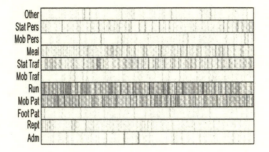

Fig. 17. Simulated Dirichlet when officers are most satisfied with job

noticeably more concentrated. This concentration is especially apparent in the checkerboard plot (fig. 15). There is an additional concentration that was somewhat obscured in the ternary plot: subordinates who have a great deal of contact with each other are much less likely to spend time on meals, which one would have to classify as a form of shirking.

Why would we see such strong effects? We think there are two classes of explanation. One follows from the first proposition, derived from the imitative model: under greater subordinate observability (presuming conditions of uncertainty about appropriate time allocation), subordinates are more likely to conform in their behavior. This explanation could account for the lesser dispersion but not the shift of the mean, however. The second explanation depends on a variety of the collective goods problem. Ask any bureaucrat, and he or she will tell you that the least desirable part of his or her job is completing paperwork. The police officers' condition not only requires completing reports on each meaningful activity during the day but that the task be completed for each partnership of officers. If an officer fails to complete the report, then the task falls to that officer's partner. What we believe we are demonstrating is that greater contact with fellow subordinates encourages officers to devote more time to the completion of mutually disliked tasks.

The other side of our propositions revolved around subordinate preferences. Although the present data collection permits only a modest evaluation of the effect of preferences, there is supporting evidence. During the shift, if the officer mentioned that he or she was satisfied (or unsatisfied) with the squad, we recorded this as a "solidary like" (or dislike). Similarly, if the officer mentioned that he or she was satisfied (or unsatisfied) with various functional aspects of the job (preventative checks at houses and businesses, maintaining visibility for residents, and satisfaction with the beat), we recorded this as a "functional like" (or dislike).

Figures 12 and 15 demonstrate the effect of strong solidary preferences on the allocation of work. As with the other figures, the officers spend the majority of their time on runs or mobile patrol. There is a very slight increase in the amount of time spent on paperwork and a very slight decrease in the amount of time spent on meals. What this implies is that intersubordinate contact exercises a different effect from solidary preferences—seeing one's fellow officers frequently is quite different from developing strong positive relations with them. The difference between the two plots also supports the idea that intersubordinate contact is a way for officers to resolve the collective production problem instead of copying the behavior of people with whom one has a positive relationship.

Similarly, figures 12 and 16 display the effect on the simulated distribution of time across tasks when officers are most satisfied with their jobs. Like the previous three, there is a marked increase in the amount of time spent on paperwork. In this simulation, however, there is also evidence of an increase in the amount of time that officers spend on personal business: the distribution is more dispersed, and there are even two (simulated) officers who devote a plurality of their time to personal business. There are also a greater number of officers who devote a greater fraction of their time to paperwork. The checkerboard plot (fig. 16) is the most evenly gray of all the plots, indicating a roughly equal allocation of time across many tasks. In other words, heterogeneous preferences lead to heterogeneous performance.

Given the structure of each of the propositions associated with the

EPA model, we first need to assess whether or not subordinates are indifferent between tasks and then determine whether subordinates are homogeneously or heterogeneously responsive to supervision. Figure 12 shows that police officers are not indifferent between tasks and heterogeneously responsive to supervision. While we do not find a clear differentiation of task allocation, we do see a good degree of differentiation when controlling for various other factors. These conditions indicate that we should be evaluating the fourth proposition derived from the EPA model: *if subordinates are not indifferent between tasks, and are heterogeneously responsive to supervision, subordinates will separate according to type. Nonresponsive subordinates will allocate time to preferred activities, and responsive subordinates will allocate time to activities for which they receive supervision.*

The EPA model, and this proposition in particular, make predictions about conditions for pooling and separating equilibria, which follow through in the four checkerboard plots. Two of the conditions generated pooling equilibria: both the high intersubordinate contact and high solidary preference plots were reduced to a small subset of the tasks. This is consistent with officers with relatively homogeneous preferences and responsiveness. Two of the conditions generated separating equilibria: both the high supervision and high functional preferences plots yielded a more diverse set of activities, especially for the high supervision plot. This is consistent with the surmise that officers have heterogeneous preferences and especially are heterogeneously responsive to supervision. Indeed, the EPA model emphasizes that those subordinates who are responsive to supervision will be the ones who are supervised. Those unresponsive to supervision will be left alone.

We are able to more directly evaluate one of the propositions derived from the imitative model. As noted earlier, we find very strong support for the first of these propositions: *as the observability between subordinates increases, conformity of allocation of time across tasks increases (due to either information search or coercion by subordinates).* Figures 11 and 15 show clear shifts in allocation of time by police officers when they are most observable to fellow officers.

Discussion

In our *Working, Shirking, and Sabotage* (Brehm and Gates 1997), we asked the question: Who, or what, controls the policy choices of bureaucrats? We have further explored this question in this essay by examining how subordinate police officers allocate their time across a variety of tasks. By further differentiating how officers devote their time, either across three dimensions (personal activities, administrative paperwork, or policing) or even more finely across eleven dimensions, we gain some understanding of the factors that shape subordinates' decisions as to how they spend their time.

Our analysis reveals that supervisory contact results in a shift in subordinate activities away from personal business and toward administrative paperwork. Contact with other subordinates results in an even more pronounced shift toward paperwork and a considerably more concentrated dispersion of time allocations. Satisfaction with the other members of the police squad also leads to shifts in work toward paperwork. Those officers most satisfied with their jobs tend to have the greatest dispersion of time allocation, with a shift away from policing toward personal business and administrative duties. We find relatively strong support for propositions derived from the imitative model. Frequency of contact and solidary between subordinates play a large role in shaping subordinates' decisions.

These results demonstrate how strongly fellow officers affect police behavior. The importance of solidary norms with respect to an officer's squad relates to this result as well, demonstrating that the imitative model offers powerful insights for understanding police bureaucracy. Our results also suggests that supervisors play an important role in shaping how police officers do their jobs.

What are the policy implications of this research? First and foremost, this research indicates that there is no homogeneous solution to the problem of monitoring task allocations in public bureaucracies, if only because some bureaucracies will prefer that bureaucrats concentrate on a narrow range of tasks, while others would prefer that bureaucrats complete a broad repertoire of tasks. Under Wilson's (1989) typology, "production organizations" (in which both outputs and outcomes are visible) such as the Social Security Administration (in the processing of checks) or the Postal Service (in the sorting of mail) may have a very limited set of tasks for bureaucrats to complete. Under these conditions, the paramount problem is selection of subordinates with the right mix of functional preferences or to design contracts and remuneration schemes that sufficiently reward the bureaucrat for completing tasks for which he or she does not have a preference. In contrast, "craft organizations" (in which neither outputs nor outcomes are visible) such as police forces or social work agencies may prefer that their bureaucrats complete a diverse set of tasks. Under these conditions, selection is also important but perhaps with an emphasis on recruiting bureaucrats who, as a group, have heterogeneous preferences in order to encourage separating equilibrium. Contact with the supervisor, especially for amenable subordinates, can further increase the diversity of task allocations. Restraining lateral contact with other subordinates may also be necessary to encourage production of a large number of tasks.

Since our main finding concerns subordinate preferences and observability, these characteristics can also be used to make comparisons across bureaucracies. Bureaucrats working in dispersed settings with relatively little contact with other subordinates, or with supervisors, should be expected to have more heterogeneous distributions of time allocations. A prototypical example of such a dispersed, low-connection bureaucrat would be the forest ranger. As Kaufman's 1960 classic detailed, forest rangers exhibited a relatively uniform level of effort, although they were quite heterogeneous in how they divided their efforts among such tasks as conservation, constituency relations, resource management, and (increasingly) policing. Bureaucrats who work in settings where intersubordinate contacts are quite high but contacts with supervisors are quite low should be expected to parallel the results obtained here for police officers. A second prototypical example would be the social worker.

We also think that there is general utility for the underlying logic of our models outside of the bureaucratic setting. Learning under uncertainty is a condition in which most humans find themselves most of the time. To the extent that multiple and competing demands create a range of necessary tasks for social actors, the diversity of tasks adds to the conditions of uncertainty. Our pooling equilibrium result confirms the power of imitation and social proof in such conditions of uncertainty.

We could not concur more with James Q. Wilson's aphorism about tasks ("People matter, but organization matters also, and tasks matter most of all" [1989, 173]). Tasks define what it is that bureaucrats, and hence bureaucracies, do. But instead of treating tasks as immutable routines or SOPs, our approach allows us to recognize the critical interactions between people, organizations, and tasks. The preferences that bureaucrats have and the degree to which they are seen by both their supervisors and fellow bureaucrats fundamentally alter the amount of time that officers devote to the range of tasks that they face.

Notes

An earlier version of this work was prepared for presentation at the annual meeting of the Midwest Political Science Association, Chicago, IL, April 23–25, 1998. Thanks to Frank Baumgartner, Tom Hammond, and Ken Meier for comments, to Jonathan Katz and Gary King for consultation, and to Jeff Gill for the idea of using checkerboard plots.

1. We do not attempt to model the psychology behind amenability. Obviously, amenability is affected by the relationship between a subordinate and a supervisor, which will change as the relationship changes, but such an analysis has been beyond the scope of our work.

2. We note in Brehm and Gates 1997 that in a dynamic environment it may be in the supervisor's interest to punish or even fire a recalcitrant subordinate.

3. Note that imitation follows much more closely with the social psychological literature of a dual-path model of persuasion, in which some are persuaded by low cognition heuristics like imitation, than it follows such game theoretic treatments as Lupia and McCubbins 1998 purporting to explain persuasion. The Lupia and McCubbins explanation explicitly regards the level of attention as a prerequisite for persuasion in a mass democratic context, a highly saturated information environment. That said, imitation can also be modeled as a problem of informational cascades (Bikhchandani, Hirshleifer, and Welch 1992) or in replicator dynamics (Friedman 1991), in which imitation can be shown to be a Nash equilibrium solution.

4. With such a data-gathering technique, a potential Hawthorne effect is possible. Presumably such an effect would lead to a bias against spending time on leisure activities. Yet our data demonstrate no significant compunction on the part of the police officers to refrain from such activities.

5. Our data do not provide detailed information regarding the allocation of overtime work. Such information would be valuable in assessing the effect of overtime on time allocation. Lacking such information, we must presume similar and uniform exogenous budgetary constraints for all individuals.

6. An example involves multiparty voting data (Katz and King 1999). In the United Kingdom, for example, the proportion of the vote can be seen to be divided across three parties, Labour, Tory, and Alliance. In turn, the vote total sums to unity.

Adapting Agencies: Competition, Imitation, and Punishment in the Design of Bureaucratic Performance

Andrew B. Whitford

The U.S. Department of Veterans Affairs (VA) serves millions of veterans across the world on a daily basis. It is the single largest governmental direct provider of medical care in the United States, serving 4.2 million patients per year; it also provides compensation to over 2.7 million veterans and their survivors yearly and oversees 2.1 million insurance policies. Not surprisingly, a primary concern is the rapid provision of benefits and settlement of claims. As its Departmental Performance Plan for fiscal year (FY) 2000 notes, the problem is to refine its goals, objectives, and strategies; measure its performance; and critically evaluate its programs.

For benefits provision, the VA uses a mixture of scorecards, measurement strategies, and information management technologies to meet quality and timeliness standards such as the rapidity of the treatment of cases. One component is the enhanced managerial review of over fifty regional offices through better cost accounting, regional comparisons, and benchmarking (1997 Strategic Plan for Fiscal Years 1998–2003).

Many have analyzed the 1993 Government Performance and Results Act (GPRA), some laudatory and some not (National Academy of Public Administration 1999). The VA's experiences show a concern greater than just performance measurement and analysis. The ongoing experiments focus on organizational change, comparison, and redirection. They recognize that agencies adapt, that they can be compared and compete with one another, and that they can learn from their and others' experiences.

This essay investigates the design of bureaucratic performance through comparison, competition, imitation, and redirection. Studies of bureaucratic politics, organizational change, and policy implementation regularly assume that agencies respond to external and internal circumstances and that organizations can be redirected. Agencies adapt when they choose actions or use information based on past experiences. They may adapt when they compete with other agencies over resources, constituencies, or policy areas, perhaps causing them to perform differently than they would absent competition. They may perform differently because an interested overseer compares agencies and uses those comparisons to reward or punish. Just as states can serve as policy laboratories, agencies may also perform differently because their counterparts offer opportunities for imitation when they compare how their own actions and performances and others' relate. In fact, comparison is often how the media, consultants, and academics learn about agencies' performance and productivity.

The central assumption in this essay is that agencies adapt to their surroundings in an imprecise way. This assumption is strongly related to an older but continuing theme in the study of organizations. Herbert Simon's bounded rationality—and the corresponding idea of incremental decision making—has served as a motivating force in numerous studies of decision makers, organizations, and even public decision processes (e.g., Bendor 1995; Cyert and March 1963; Lindblom 1959; Newell and Simon 1972; Simon 1947, 1957, 1976b).

In this context, I concentrate on three levers of redirection: comparison, punishment, and imitation. I begin by creating a simulation model of a baseline agency with measurable attributes of performance, goals, and technology. The agency can take only one action: it can search for technology, or a means of implementing policies, by means of procedures, information services, human knowledge, or even mechanical methods. In this model, the agency establishes goals or performance targets, observes its performance, adopts a technology, and sets new goals.

This model agency provides a baseline for the comparison of three specific structural features. In the first extension, I introduce the comparison and punishment of agencies, or simple competition. In the second, I allow for the differential punishment of agencies in a competitive system. Third, I allow agencies to imitate one another; "learning by others' doing" is often the purpose of experiments, pilots, and laboratories.

In the last extension, I replace these deterministic systems with a naive stochastic alternative: random punishment.

These extensions illuminate the difficult trade-offs encountered in designing agencies: predictability versus change, search versus outcomes, stasis versus growth. These represent competing "goods" in attempts to alter agency direction. By encouraging change, we upset prediction; by encouraging innovation, we do not guarantee outcomes. Additionally, the exercise showcases a flexible and powerful modeling strategy for the evaluation of specific design combinations discussed throughout political science and public administration.

This essay proceeds as follows. In the next section, I review basic literatures on adaptation and competition in bureaucracy. I then offer a simple model of adaptive agencies to establish a baseline against which to compare the specific structural features of comparison, imitation, and random punishment. Last, I conclude with thoughts on this modeling strategy, the results, and directions for future research.

Adaptation and Competition in Bureaucracies

This essay combines two major initiatives in the study of public agencies as organizations: the modeling of agencies as adaptive systems and the normative value of competition as a structure for pressing agency performance. In this section, I first review adaptation in public bureaucracies and technological search as basic ways of visualizing agency actions. Then I discuss issues of comparison, competition, and information revelation in bureaucracies.

The models I build here have attributes of complex adaptive systems, a descendant of cybernetics (Ashby 1957). This approach allows the creation of realistic models of organizational behavior in which the emphasis is on process, benchmarking, and flexibility. Studies of adaptive public bureaucracies date in Lindblom's work on incrementalism in policy (1959; see also Bendor 1995) and Simon's studies of individual decision making, bounded rationality, and incrementalism in public agencies (Newell and Simon 1972; Simon 1957, 1976b). Many have offered dynamic models of adaptive behavior in the behavioral tradition (Axelrod 1976, 1997; Bendor and Moe 1985; Cohen 1981, 1984; Cohen and Axelrod 1984; Cohen, March, and Olsen 1972; Crecine 1969; Cyert and March 1963; Kollman, Miller, and Page 1992; March and Simon 1958; Padgett 1980; Simon 1947). Adaptive models have grown in popularity with the massive growth in computing power, as in computational organizational theory (Burton and Obel 1995; Carley and Prietula 1994). In economic history, adaptation is a feature of and a solution to problems in large, modern organizations. With the coevolution of technology and business institutions, new forms are chosen because they solve organizational problems (Chandler 1990). Technology and efficiency intertwine as mechanisms of adaptation and selection. As Arthur (1989) and David (1985) show, the technology in place at a point in time is truly cumulative technology; today's technical advances build from and improve upon status quo technologies.

The baseline model here is an agency searching for technology in order to change its performance. Search is a way to change the relationship between performance and action, but it is fraught with error. Technology is a technical method; it is how the agency applies knowledge for practical purposes. Public agencies make constant investments in finding and implementing new technologies. As an example, the VA has made massive investments in integrating information technologies. One "soft" technological search in which agencies invest is selecting and training personnel.

Like all agencies, this adaptive agency resides in a larger social system that is concerned about social efficiency, the output of government, and political responsiveness. Political overseers shape public agencies and what they do. Over the past four decades, competition has been offered as a way to fuse the public goods provision with the efficiency of markets (Tullock 1965; Downs 1967; Niskanen 1971). Essentially, the competition movement is an exercise in the politics of bureaucratic structure, shaping the incentives of agencies to redirect their behavior to new ends.

Niskanen argues that competition allows the comparison of relative prices of competing bureaus and so shifts power from bureaucrats to politicians. As Boyne (1998) notes, these models' core hypotheses are that under competition total spending on services will fall and technical efficiency will increase; they make no specific prediction about allocative efficiency under competition. Direct descendents are "contracting out" and compulsory competitive tendering (Niskanen 1968; Boyne 1998; Kettl 1993).

Refinements of Niskanen argue that the model inaccurately characterizes the interaction between bureaucrats and legislators (e.g., Blais and Dion 1991). Migue and Belanger (1974) note that bureaucrats may maximize goals other than the supply of public services. Conybeare (1984) reveals an implicit assumption of perfect price discrimination (see also Bendor, Taylor, and Van Gaalen 1985; and Breton and Wintrobe 1975). Miller and Moe (1983) show that modeling the legislature alters predictions about the power of privatization and competition. Empirically, there are mixed findings at best on competition and agency costs and output (Boyne 1998; Conybeare 1984; Higgins, Shughart, and Tollison 1987). Conybeare (1984) notes that even if multiple, competitive bureaus are competing for funding rather than producing equivalent goods (as in McGuire, Coiner, and Spancake 1979) there may be negative side effects such as high monitoring costs.

What, then, is the value of competition? Miller and Moe (1983) show that competition for the public supply of a good is valuable when it reveals information about actual supply costs and thus places monitors in better decisional positions and enhances their power. The advantage of competition is how it reveals information by allowing comparison. Another reason for multiple and comparable agencies is the value of redundancy or parallelism so as to reduce system-level performance errors (Bendor 1985; Landau 1969; Heimann 1993).

Agencies will respond to comparison, competition, and information revelation because of the real world implications of failure. While bankruptcy is not possible in the public sector, there is agency deletion (e.g., the Interstate Commerce Commission), reductions in budgets (e.g., the Reagan era Environmental Protection Agency), media coverage (e.g., the Bureau of Alcohol, Tobacco, and Firearms), external options for agency heads (e.g., the Department of the Treasury), the simple incentive just to do well in the organization (Edwards, Nalbandian, and Wedel 1981), and other nonmonetary incentives (Crewson 1995).

Five Models of Adaptive Agencies

Basic Agency Adaptation

I start with Levinthal and March's (1981) model of adaptive organizational search. In this model, organizations change through their adaptive search for new technology. The model shows that an organization's behavior and performance reflect the consequences of simple adaptation in an ambiguous environment. The approach is a generalized search model from an organizational learning perspective. In this essay, this model serves as a baseline against which to examine the cases of competition, imitation, and random punishment among competitors (327).

The basic assumption is that organizations change their performance and goal attainment behavior by searching across possible implementation technologies. Agencies search by innovating (Radner 1975; Knight 1967; Nelson and Winter 1978). The technology an agency discovers is exogenous, but the search process depends on its past performance, goals, and search investments.

Agencies perform, have goals (that may be attained), and make expenditures to determine the best way to implement policies. To start, the agency sets a performance goal based on its past experience. The agency has only one way to attain that goal: to search for a new implementation technology. When it begins the search process, the agency examines its past performance and expenditures to assess the effectiveness of different types of technology search. Doing so helps determine the agency's propensity to search, its search efficiency, and the amount of resources it allocates to searching.

The key is how many times the agency will undertake a refinement or innovation search. Refinement involves only a local search; innovation is far ranging (but not global). The agency compares the search processes' results and its status quo technology. Once implemented, the agency experiences a new performance level based on its technology, expenditures, and environmental variation. The agency then adapts its goals based on this performance experience and starts the process again.

Specifically, performance in a given time period, P_t, is a function of the technology it implements (T_t), search costs, and an exogenous and varying environmental variable (a_t). The agency makes expenditures for two types of search: refinement (R_t) and (I_t).

$$P_t = (1 + a_t) T_t - R_t - I_t.$$

At the beginning of the period, the agency sets a performance target or goal (G_t) before experiencing performance. It modifies that target given performance as

$$G_t = b_1 P_{t-1} + (1 - b_1) G_{t-1}.$$

The term P_{t-1} is organizational performance in time $t - 1$.[1] Performance, goals, and technology are simple indices (or complex combinations that comprise complex phenomena) (Jones 2001). Organizations may pursue multiple goals simultaneously; this can affect search behavior in an organization and may even enhance organizational performance (Cohen 1984).

Technology largely determines the agency's performance, and the search process is what the agency controls. The agency never forgets its past technology, which forms a baseline against which all new technologies are compared. Technological search proceeds by means of refinement and innovation. The agency chooses the best of three technologies: that obtained from refinement (T_r) search, that obtained from innovation (T_i) search, or its technology from the past period.[2]

$$T_t = \max \left(T_r, \, T_i, \, T_{t-1} \right).$$

The key decision is for the agency to decide which resources it will commit to the search for a new technology. The agency compares its performance and the search resources it committed in the past period. The agency determines whether it met its goal: if it is met, it deems "successful" the type of search in which it engaged (innovation or refinement). Meeting a goal is the message the agency receives about the appropriateness of its past behavior. It is interested only in whether it meets its goal, not in how much it is exceeded.

The agency also assesses the value of engaging in any search at all. This *general propensity* for search ($S_{s,t}$) depends on whether search resources were made available and the agency met its performance target or goal ($Q_{s,t-1}$):

$$S_{s,t} = Q_{s,t-1} b_2 + S_{s,t-1}(1 - b_2).$$

Here $Q_{s,t-1}$ is a test that takes the value 1 in two cases: if search resources were expended and the performance goal was met or if search resources were not expended and the performance goal was not met. The term b_2 determines whether this propensity has memory; it would limit the agency's ability to make sudden changes, failure would not easily translate into lower search investments, and success would not necessarily cause more searching.

Second, the agency's propensity to undergo a particular kind of search ($S_{i,t}$ or $S_{r,t}$) depends on a test relating the size of the type of expenditure and past performance: innovation ($Q_{r,t-1}$) or refinement ($Q_{i,t-1}$).

$$S_{r,t} = Q_{r,t-1} b_3 + S_{r,t-1}(1 - b_3),$$

$$S_{i,t} = Q_{i,t-1}b_4 + S_{i,t-1}(1 - b_4).$$

The terms $S_{r,t}$ and $S_{i,t}$ do not necessarily sum to one because an agency may not search at all; their sum may exceed one given the differential allocation of resources between the two types.

While this model allows testing the differential effects of learning rates, I assume that $b_2 = b_3 = b_4 = 1$ so that the search propensities are functions of the past period's performance only. These specific learning rates make the change for a search propensity incremental in goal attainment; this is a restrictive assumption, but it is consistent with past work on learning, organizations, and policy formation (Lindblom 1959).

These search propensities drive both the amount of sampling and the search space through which agencies learn about alternate technologies. The agency's search resources in a time period are limited, and the amounts allocated for refinement and innovation search can differ. First, the agency determines the total amount of resources it can dedicate to search ($U_{s,t}$) given $S_{s,t}$.

$$U_{s,t} = S_{s,t}(P_{t-1} + R_{t-1} + I_{t-1}).$$

The restrictive assumption here is that the agency is not limited in search, performance, or goal attainment by a lack of resources.

Second, this total is allocated to the competing types. For public agencies, it is likely that the resources available for refinement are greater in lean times and that innovation resources are greater when the organization attains goals. If the performance goal was achieved, the refinement resources are greater than those for innovation.

$$U_{i,t} = U_{s,t},$$

$$U_{r,t} = (U_{s,t})^{1/h_r}.$$

Here h_r, the refinement slack coefficient, controls the shift from one type of search to another given performance achievement. If the performance goal was not achieved,

$$U_{i,t} = (U_{s,t})^{1/h_i},$$

$$U_{r,t} = U_{s,t},$$

where h_i is the innovation slack investment coefficient.

Not all available resources must be expended in this model. The resources expended on a search type depend on the propensity to undertake a kind of search and the amount of search resources available for that type. On one hand, agencies with limited resources may expend them all. On the other, agencies meeting performance goals may not expend any available resources when they reach a balanced state of performance and goal achievement.

The search propensities and resources available determine the innovation (I_t) and refinement (R_t) search resources expended.

$$I_t = S_{i,t}U_{i,t},$$

$$R_t = S_{r,t}U_{r,t}.$$

These search resources help determine the agency's sampling efforts for refinement ($K_{r,t}$) and innovation ($K_{i,t}$).

$$K_{r,t} = k_r R_t E_{r,t},$$

$$K_{i,t} = k_i I_t E_{i,t}.$$

The terms $E_{r,t}$ and $E_{i,t}$ are search efficiencies that reflect efficiency increases with increasing search but at a decreasing rate (Levinthal and March 1981, 313).

$$E_{r,t} = (E_{r,t-1} + K_{r,t-1})^{1/w_r},$$

$$E_{i,t} = (E_{i,t-1} + K_{i,t-1})^{1/w_i}.$$

Altogether, the agency has four interlocking constraints on its ability to generate changes in the technology it implements. It is limited by the existence of resources to commit to the search. Its propensity to search, regardless of resources, is limited by its past performance and expenditure experience. The agency's search efficiency is determined by its past search experience. Last, it is constrained by the weight applied to control the shift from one search type to the other. Most importantly, these are constraints on how the agency searches for technology—not on how it discovers it.

The technology an agency implements depends on the number of technologies it samples, the underlying distribution of possible (or undiscovered) technology, and its current technology. The returns to the search agencies undertake depend on their expenditures, the efficiency of the search, and the current opportunities for development. The likelihood of finding an appropriate change depends on the number of opportunities sampled.

Given $K_{r,t}$ and $K_{i,t}$, the search is drawn from distributions based on the technology implemented in the past time period. For refinement, in each time period, let $n = K_{r,t}$. A drawn procedure is a change from T_{t-1}, where

$$T_{r,n} \sim N(0, V_{r,t,n}),$$

$$V_{r,t,n} = c_1 T_{t-1} \quad \text{for } n = 1,$$

$$V_{r,t,n} = c_2 V_{r,t,n-1} \quad \text{for } n > 1.$$

In a time period, if search resources are great enough, the agency may make a number of draws from this distribution. As it does, the variance of the distribution falls over multiple draws. The term c_1 means that the variance in refinement depends on the past technology; c_2 means that that variance falls in the time period when an agency makes multiple refinement searches. The space of possible refinements becomes smaller over multiple searches.

For innovation, a drawn procedure is a change from T_{t-1}, where

$$T_i \sim LN(0, V_i),$$

$$V_i = c_3 T_{t-1}.$$

The term c_3 plays the same role as c_1.

It is possible to learn *not* to search due to estimation errors.

$$EE_{r,t} \sim N(0, V_{e,r,t}),$$

$$EE_{i,t} \sim N(0, V_{e,i,t}).$$

The term $V_{e,i,t}$ is initially greater than $V_{e,r,t}$, but each declines with the implementation of a given type of change in procedure.

The value of either a refinement or an innovation is known with certainty once it is implemented. It is known only with error when it is not implemented. Once drawn, T_r, T_i, and T_{t-1} are compared in each time period and the largest value is selected and implemented. The term $V_{e,i,t}$ shrinks if innovation is the final technology; $V_{e,r,t}$ shrinks if refinement is successful.

In this model, the agency chooses a technology, experiences performance, compares that level with its goal, and starts the search process

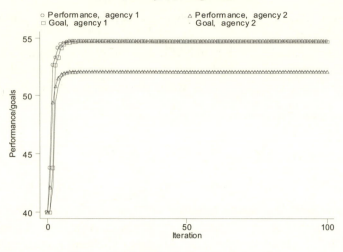

Fig. 1. Baseline: Performance and goals

again. I simulate this baseline model of simple adaptation for two agencies given the initial conditions and parameters in the appendix at the
end of this essay.[3]

Figure 1 shows the performance and goal paths for two agencies
where each agency evolves over one hundred time periods. Both agencies
quickly settle down to equilibrium levels of performance. Under these
initial conditions, agency performance and goals are in a steady state. By
giving the agency a "shock" in the first time period (forcing it to make
three technological searches), changes in technology spur changes in performance and goals. Both agencies explore new technologies and alter
their performance and goal attainment; for each, the result is a higher
performance level.

Figure 2 shows the time paths of one agency's propensities to undertake search for technology (general, innovation, and refinement); only
one agency's results are shown because of their similar experiences. The
general and innovation propensities track one another (due to the aver-
aging process) and settle down over time. As this clearly shows, the equilibrium performance level occurs because the agency becomes unlikely to
search after a period of time. As expected, refinement dominates innovation because this type of search is most closely related to an adaptive theory of organizational behavior. In fact, the adaptive model specified here
should produce this result.

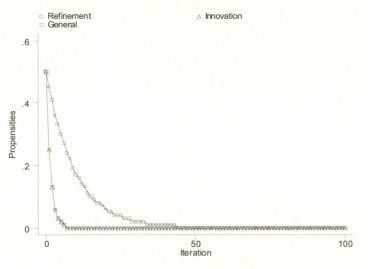

Fig. 2. Baseline: Propensities

Figure 3 shows the outcome of a search, or the likelihood of choosing an innovation, choosing a refinement, or retaining the status quo. On this scale, the agency is choosing innovations when the score is close to two, refinements when the score is close to one, and the status quo when the score is close to zero. The agency chooses innovation in the first period and then quickly rejects the search outcomes in favor of the status quo. This also shows that the likelihood of success (of performance exceeding or matching goals) goes to one as the likelihood of retaining the status quo goes to zero. Figure 4 shows how the number of searches approaches zero rapidly.

This baseline model demonstrates three basic propositions about agency learning and change. First, technology search, as defined here, produces changes in performance and goals, subject to constraints on search. It is the central mechanism by which the organization changes its operating behavior. Second, this system reaches a steady state of performance, goal attainment, and acceptance of the status quo technology. Without disturbances, the agency is unlikely to alter its technology, its goals, or its search for new technologies. Third, multiple indicators of agency activity are useful for examining how agencies use the search mechanism to change their performances. Here indicators go beyond simple performance attainment to include search propensities, success, and outcomes.

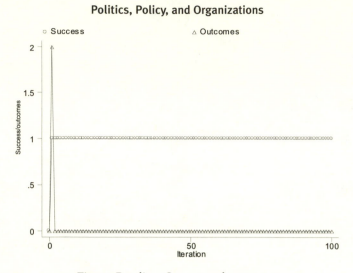

Fig. 3. Baseline: Success and outcomes

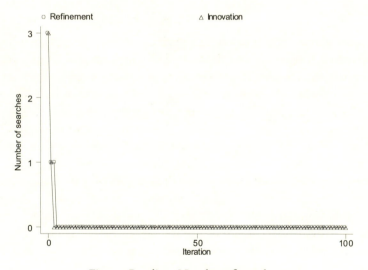

Fig. 4. Baseline: Number of searches

Competition among Adaptive Agencies

In the second model, two adaptive agencies compete on the basis of performance. The losing agency is punished, and agencies adapt their goals
given their realized performances. A fundamental reason for competition
is that comparison reveals information about what is possible for agency
performance. The baseline model provides a point of comparison with

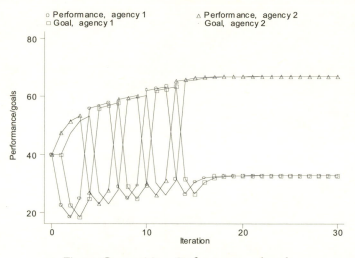

Fig. 5. Competition: Performance and goals

this second, institutional layer. This is competition over neither finite resources nor a pool of customers through price competition or rivalry.
Perhaps the best metaphor is athletes competing in time trials.

Specifically, the agencies have independent search processes but their
performances are compared at the end of each period. The lower-per-
forming agency is punished and given only partial credit. Its observed performance is recalculated, and the losing agency's new goal now depends
on this partial credit. In this application, two agencies are compared to
one another. "Thin" competition allows me to isolate the effects of competition and may be realistic for public agencies.[4]

In the first model, the losing agency's performance measure is halved
and punishment is symmetric (agencies are not distinguished). Figure 5
shows the time path for original initial conditions, where the model now
includes a competition step. The paths in this figure are substantially different from those in Figure 1. Both display greater variation in their performances over the iterative process; the goal path of each agency tracks
its performance path. The strong oscillation in the agencies' performance
and goal paths is linked. Essentially, the "meeting-separating" pattern is a
core result of this competitive process, as over time the aggressive movement of one agency to increase its performance leads to lagged increases
in the other's performance. Eventually, both agencies settle into separate
performance equilibria.

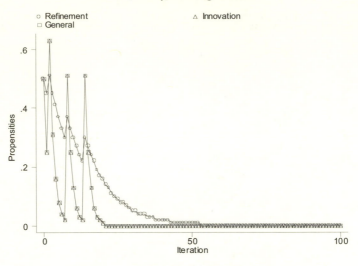

Fig. 6. Competition: Propensities

As noted earlier, the propensities help gauge how an agency's performance and goal find equilibrium. Figure 6 shows the time path for one agency for the three propensities. In contrast to figure 2, the search propensities do not settle down quickly. Moreover, innovation spikes follow punishment phases and refinement spikes follow innovation spikes: punishment induces innovation and local search follows innovation. Figure 7 visually confirms punishment's role in driving the agency's internal search process. The amount of search switches for the first periods of the simulation, but the number of searches falls over time.

When an agency is docked for underperformance, its key indicator is whether its credited performance does not meet its internal goal. This disparity generates any internal changes that the agency makes in response to competition and punishment. Specifically, these signals knock the agency off the performance-goal achievement steady state it naturally obtains in the underlying adaptive model. In this model, the central effect of competition and comparison is that agencies can find new levels of performance because performance inequities motivate their enhanced search for new technologies.

Competition with Differential Punishment

An alternate case is one in which competing agencies are punished differentially. In this case, the simulation involves a "90/10" punishment

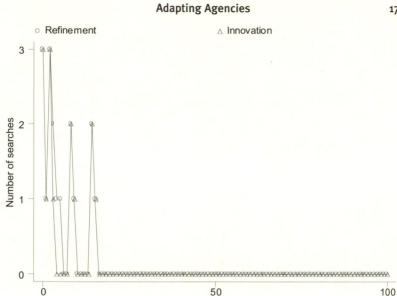

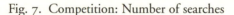

Fig. 7. Competition: Number of searches

scenario.[5] In this exercise, one underperforming agency receives 90 percent credit for its performance; the second receives 10 percent credit if it has a lower performance. The logic of this experiment is to uncover the potential differential impact of punishment on agency performance. Are lower punishments reflected in smaller agency increases in search, expenditures, and performance achievement? Figure 8 shows the paths for the performance and goals of the two agencies in one simulation.

This simulation highlights the differential responsiveness of an agency given the two punishment scenarios. The shallow valleys shown for agency 2 reflect the 90 percent credit rule; the deep valleys for agency 1 reflect the 10 percent rule. Note that agency 1—even given the strict 10 percent rule—finds a way to recover to globally higher performance levels. At a point in the model's evolution, agencies 1 and 2 diverge to different equilibrium performance levels.

What should we make of agency 1's higher equilibrium performance level given the strict 10 percent rule? Figure 9 shows pairs of equilibrium performance values for 100 simulations. For two agencies, 60 percent of the "10 percent" agency's equilibrium values are higher than that for the "90 percent" agency. However, the situation separates: for the other 40 percent, the 10 percent agency's values are substantially lower and the 90

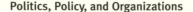

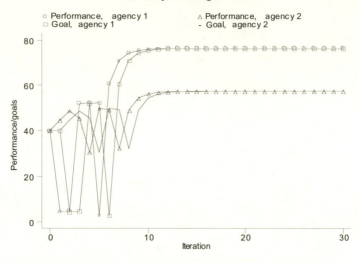

Fig. 8. Asymmetric competition: Performance and goals

percent agency's mean value is significantly higher. This difference is visually confirmed in figure 10 and is also confirmed statistically (unpaired t-test with an assumption of unequal variances; $t = 4.7902$; Satterthwaite's degrees of freedom, df, = 108.345; difference significant at better than $p = 0.0001$).

The reason for this separation is in how the agencies search for technology. Punishment means a lower credited performance, making necessary the enhanced search for innovation, but one that is sustainable only for a short period of time. If the payoff to search is slow in coming, search stops and an agency falls into a position of lethargy, with low performance and no innovation.

Essentially, a valuable indicator is how punishments are implemented. The core test within the agency for determining propensities remains whether performance fails to meet expectations (given punishments). Within this model, systematic significant punishments can spur greater global performance than light punishments (the punishment magnitude affects only $U_{s,t}$).

An agency switches to a refinement search when its performance exceeds its goals. If it is in refinement mode and a significant punishment occurs, the agency's propensity for refinement falls. While the punishment may reduce $U_{s,t}$, it encourages innovation by discouraging refine-

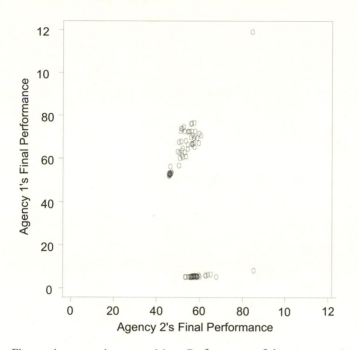

Fig. 9. Asymmetric competition: Performance of the two agencies

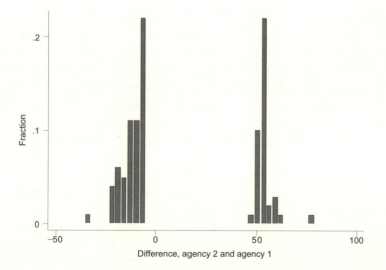

Fig. 10. Asymmetric competition: Relative performance

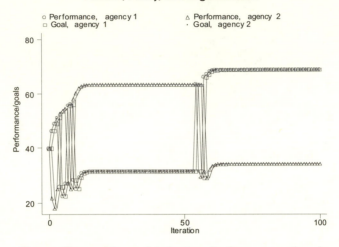

Fig. 11. Competition and imitation: Performance and goals

ment. Performance increases come from small levels of available funds because of the disjunction between credited performance and internal goals. The central result in this exercise is a counterintuitive one: on average, agencies that receive relatively heavy punishment (less credit for their performances) produce higher performance levels in the long run.

Imitation among Adaptive Agencies

Altering an agency's credited performance is just one way to alter its goals and search behavior. Instead, competing, adaptive agencies may imitate one another. Specifically, a losing agency may imperfectly imitate a dominant agency's technology. After it searches for a technology, experiences a level of performance, and competes with a counterpart, the losing agency imperfectly imitates a dominant agency's technology. Its technology is now a simple average of the two technologies in the system at that point in time.

Figure 11 shows the time path for the same initial conditions as in the adaptive system, except that the agencies now compete (with symmetric punishments set at 50 percent credit) and losing agencies imitate. The simulation initially proceeds similar to that under simple competition: initial oscillation is followed by a period of stability.

However, imitation produces a third dynamic. Here, a long period of stability is interrupted, as one agency's performance jumps once its tech-

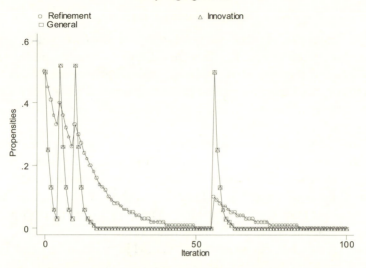

Fig. 12. Competition and imitation: Propensities for agency 1

nology evolves to a point where real performance changes occur. At that point, the formerly dominant agency is punished and responds with a short period of innovation. Notably, in this case the agencies actually switch positions and the dominant agency is replaced with the imitating one. As figure 12 shows, the dominant agency's search propensities signal the subordinate agency's intrusion in the last innovation spike. Agency 2 shows a similar propensity to search, generating increased search and causing a reversal of position.

In this model, imitation plays a peculiar role: it provides a basis for displacing dominant agencies with agencies that have been punished through competition. Competition creates the opportunity for the first agency to dominate. Yet imitation actually produces a globally higher level of performance *in the system* when it reaches equilibrium.

For agencies, the benefits of competition may be short-term benefits for the first agency. Under competition, imitation may produce a second set of benefits when the second agency matches and then replaces the first. Even so, imitation may have a downside when the dominating agency is beaten and then imitates the second agency's past, underperforming technology. In this model, this agency's response is to adopt the underperforming technology, resulting in a lower equilibrium performance path.

Naive Random Punishment

The last extension replaces competition and comparison with a system of random punishment. Random punishment alters the performance with which the agency is credited; this credited performance feeds back into the agency's adaptive process of goal setting and technology search. Neither competition nor imitation is allowed; the only shock to the system is random punishment.

Specifically, I draw a uniform random number and impose random punishment on each agency one-third of the time. If an agency is punished, it receives a 10 percent reduction in its performance credit. Two-thirds of the time, an agency will not be punished. In this exercise, agencies are never punished simultaneously. Figure 13 shows the performance and goals for two agencies in one simulation.

In this essay, I do not claim that these level increases are general. However, across many simulations the step-level increases in agency performance appear to be general. Again, the principal mechanism is search: once either agency has arrived at an equilibrium performance level, the agency no longer searches for new implementation technology. As figure 14 shows, the propensities to search for an agency are markedly different in this system. Search ebbs and wanes in direct relationship to the incidence of random punishment.

What is the relevant indicator of agency performance: its raw performance level or its search propensity? In each of these models, the baseline agency lacking external shocks fails to search for new technologies in order to enhance its performance once it is in equilibrium. Three basic means of external shocks are proposed: punishments based on simple competition; the imitation of known, winning technologies; and random punishments.

Each produces more complex behavior by this "model" agency; each generates internally consistent agency search for new technology. Naive random punishment produces the greatest amount of search and the most predictable pattern of increasing performance but at the expense of predictability for the agency. And under even random punishment there is significant nonlinear variation in the performances of agencies over time.

Discussion

This essay first provides a baseline model for understanding how agencies search for techniques and tools for bettering their performances. It then nests this baseline model in four institutional frameworks for redirecting agency behavior. The implications of these models are offered as

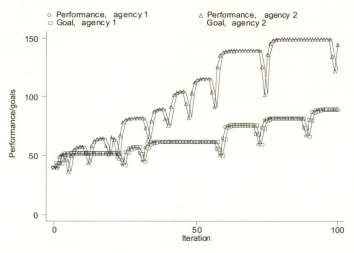

Fig. 13. Random punishment: Performance and goals

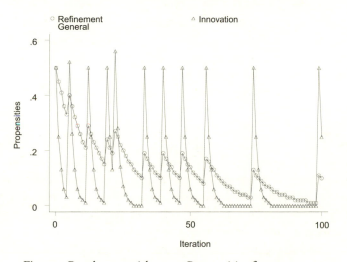

Fig. 14. Random punishment: Propensities for agency 2

exhibitions of how institutional frames alter internal agency processes in nonlinear, adaptive ways. They provide a fertile ground for extending past research on the nature of competition, comparison, imitation, and raw punishment in bureaucratic politics. In each case, the baseline agency is fully consistent with past work on adaptation and incrementalism in bureaucratic politics, public administration, and organizational theory.

Adaptation, competition, and imitation each can lead to radically different agency behaviors over time. Competition and comparison may better the performance of agencies and address concerns about how agencies produce outputs. In fact, the baseline agency may perform better under competition; in this model, there clearly is enhanced search for more productive technologies and procedures.

This achievement comes at two costs, though. First, greater performance may be the enemy of stability. Agencies perform better but with less stability in specific measurements. Specifically, agencies achieving a higher equilibrium level of performance (or long-term stability) may suffer oscillation getting there (or short-term instability). Second, agencies may separate into groups of winners and losers. In this case, a punishment strategy may ensure that one agency is a systematic underperformer.

In contrast, imitation produces a counterintuitive result: agencies that dominate other agencies produce less after being imitated, and agencies that imitate are forced to search. It appears that the amount of diversity in the system (the extent of search for new technologies) is enhanced by imitation but the system's stability is limited. Essentially, agencies rely on imitation, and search at points and thus are more likely to produce high performances. However, relative agency performance is less predictable.

The introduction of random punishment represents a quandary. The model suggests that unpredictable punishment leads to greater search opportunities—and increased performance—than under imitation with competition or even competition alone. It is important to point out that this exercise does not address substantial concerns like the costs of random intervention or the gaming of performance indicators. Yet the fact that naive punishment has this effect on a model agency signals the importance of knowing which system aspect a designer is attempting to control. If the intent is to create diversity of search and technological change, perhaps with the assumption that raw performance will increase, random punishment may be a first-best approach. If the point is predictability and stability, punishment strategies may be less than desirable. Some might even wonder if this is not a more realistic model of political intervention in agencies.

While this model's implications may not hold for thick competition (and current work in computational economics indicates that thick interactions are important for these social settings), thick interaction may not be empirically relevant for many agencies. Indeed, local interaction may be much more significant.

What matters for bureaucratic performance in this model? Clearly, goal setting, search and innovation, and the linkage of performance and search are key to increasing performance levels. Layering such an organization in a competitive process (even thin competition) suggests that while some will do better losers may do worse. Allowing collaboration— or at least imitation—may enhance any agency's learning, but it may also reduce the overall predictability of outcomes at both the system and agency levels. The trade-off is clear: innovation and predictability compete when punishment is present.

Appendix

TABLE A1. Variable Definitions and Initial Conditions

Variable Name	Initial Condition
Environmental variable (a)	0.05
Weight given to performance in changing goals (b_1)	1
Control of rate of change of refinement search propensity (b_2)	1
Control of rate of change of innovation search propensity (b_3)	1
Control of rate of change of general investment propensity (b_4)	1
Relation of variance in refinement to new technology (c_1)	0.01
Reduction of variance in refinement draws with experience (c_2)	0.98
Relation of variance in innovation to new technology (c_3)	0.01
Efficiency of refinement ($E_{r,t}$)	0
Efficiency of innovation ($E_{i,t}$)	0
Goal in current time period (G)	40
Refinement slack investment exponent (h_r)	1.1
Innovation nonslack investment exponent (h_i)	1.1
Innovation investment in current time period (I)	5
Number of refinement draws this period ($K_{r,t}$)	3
Number of innovation draws this period ($K_{i,t}$)	3
Constant for converting to refinement draws (k_r)	0.2
Constant for converting to innovation draws (k_i)	0.2
Performance in the current time period (P)	40
Refinement investment in the current time period (R)	5
Refinement search propensity in the current time period ($S_{r,t}$)	0.5
Innovation search propensity in the current time period ($S_{i,t}$)	0.5
Propensity to invest in this period ($S_{s,t}$)	0.5
Standard deviation of refinement estimation error ($V_{e,r,t}$)	0.5
Standard deviation of innovation estimation error ($V_{e,i,t}$)	0.75
Standard deviation of distribution of refinement opportunities ($V_{r,t}$)	$c_1 T_t$
Standard deviation of distribution of innovation opportunities ($V_{i,t}$)	$c_3 T_t$
Refinement efficiency exponent (w_r)	3.5
Innovation efficiency exponent (w_i)	3.5

Notes

This essay greatly benefited from the comments of George Krause, Ken Meier, Gary Miller, John Sprague, and Dan Wood. An early version of the essay was presented at the 1999 National Public Management Research Conference in College Station, Texas. All errors that remain are my own.

1. The term $b_1 > 1$ makes the target an exponentially weighted moving average of past performance; I assume $b_1 = 1$.

2. A general model would allow technology to change over time (to decay or improve). I assume constant technology in order to isolate the effects of organizational search on agency performance.

3. One way to present simulations is to generate a population of representative agencies, allow the population to evolve, and summarize the results for the population by either summary statistics or plotting the trajectory for the average member (for an example, see Cohen, Roilo, and Axelrod 1999). The figures for the simple adaptive agencies are representative of those obtained from multiple simulations. The figures for the extensions (except where indicated) are also representative. These simulations were written in Gauss.

4. Early work on adaptive systems shows that behavior becomes unpredictable when the number of interacting agents is large or as an agent's environment becomes more complex (Masuch and LaPotin 1989).

5. The use of light punishment has support in Ostrom's work on common pool resources (1990).

Part 3. Empirical Studies

Consensual Rule Making and the Time It Takes to Develop Rules

Steven J. Balla and John R. Wright

Observers of and participants in rule making have long pointed out that the process is often quite slow. Some rules, such as those governing hazardous waste transportation and hydroelectric power licensing, take more than ten years to develop (Kerwin 1999). Two decades ago, a congressional study found that the average amount of time that elapsed between publication of a proposed rule in the *Federal Register* and promulgation of a final rule was 429 days for the Interstate Commerce Commission (U.S. Congress 1977). More recent data on the Environmental Protection Agency (EPA) indicate that this duration is 523 days and that an additional 571 days typically elapse between the initiation of rule making and publication of a proposed rule. EPA rule makings, in other words, average more than 1,000 days in length (Kerwin and Furlong 1992).

There are a variety of outcomes associated with lengthy rule makings. According to the General Accounting Office (GAO), a fifteen-month delay in the promulgation of a Medicaid cost-sharing rule resulted in the loss of $81.2 million in projected budgetary savings (GAO 1977). More broadly, lengthy rule makings postpone the realization of the intended benefits of rules, which in many instances are the prevention of illness and injury and the saving of lives (Kerwin 1999; Kerwin and Furlong 1992; U.S. Congress 1977). Conversely, a delay in rule making has positive consequences in that it protects regulated parties from rules that are arbitrary and capricious and in general provides due process to parties with a stake in agency actions (Kerwin 1999; U.S. Congress 1977). In sum, the time it takes to develop rules has important implications for both the expected beneficiaries and targets of agency policies.

Despite the prevalence of and distributional consequences associated with lengthy rule makings, little is known about the sources of delay. The hypothesized causes include the complexity of issues addressed in rule makings; the legal requirements imposed on agencies by presidents, Congress, and the courts; shortcomings in agency leadership and organization; and conflict between parties affected by rules (Hawkins and Thomas 1989; Kerwin and Furlong 1992). Researchers have not, for the most part, subjected these hypotheses to empirical scrutiny, and much of what is known about delay is the product of anecdotes and case studies (Eisner 1989; U.S. Congress 1977; GAO 1977).

In this research, we examine the time it took to develop 170 major rules issued by federal agencies between March 1996 and June 1999. Our central focus is on the procedural environments that governed these rule makings. Historically, the basic framework for rule making has been provided by the Administrative Procedure Act of 1946, which mandates that agencies give notice of their intention to issue rules and that interested parties be given an opportunity to comment on agency proposals. Although these requirements have been augmented by a variety of executive orders, statutes, and court rulings, the structure of rule making has remained largely the same for more than a half century (Mintz and Miller 1991). In recent years, however, there has been a movement toward consensual rule making, an approach that fundamentally alters the way in which rules are developed, in particular the timing and mechanism of public participation. In consensual rule making, parties with a stake in particular rules collectively participate in the development of agency proposals in a variety of ways, such as serving on advisory committees and taking part in regulatory negotiations. One of the central tenets of consensual rule making is that it speeds the development of rules by providing a forum through which agencies and stakeholders can identify and resolve differences early in the process. Although it is widely argued that consensual rule making diminishes the likelihood of protracted comment periods (Harter 1982; Mintz and Miller 1991; Susskind and McMahon 1985), existing empirical evidence is limited and mixed (Coglianese 1997; Kerwin 1999; Kerwin and Furlong 1992).

Our central objective is to assess the extent to which consensual rule making affects the time it takes to develop rules. Despite its potential expediency, consensual rule making may not, in practice, speed the development of rules. For example, consensual rule making is thought to be most effective under certain conditions, such as when the number of stakeholders is small and when stakeholders share fundamental values and perceive opportunities for mutual gain (Harter 1982; Mintz and Miller 1991; Susskind and McMahon 1985). These conditions must be accounted for when assessing the efficacy of consensual rule making, as a failure to consider the circumstances under which rules are made could obscure the effects of the procedural environment.

This consideration is particularly important given that the use of consensual rule making is not likely random. For example, agencies may use consensual rule making to expedite or delay the issuing of rules and, by extension, to affect the distribution of benefits and costs among stakeholders. With this in mind, it is important to understand the application of consensual rule making, as these decisions have important implications for the relationship between consensus-based procedures and the time it takes to develop rules. In the analysis that follows, we do not endeavor to explicate fully the factors that affect the use of consensual rule making. Rather, we focus on its expediency, taking into account the circumstances that surround its application.

Consensual Rule Making

Consensual rule making is a broad approach that encompasses a variety of structures and processes. Its basic feature is bargaining between parties with a stake in agency actions early in the development of rules (Kerwin 1999). Two statutes provide the institutional foundations of consensual rule making—the Federal Advisory Committee Act of 1972 and the Negotiated Rulemaking Act of 1990. The Federal Advisory Committee Act governs the formation and operation of advisory committees of the federal bureaucracy. Advisory committees can be created by agencies, Congress, and the president and must be composed of representative cross sections of stakeholders. Advisory committee functions vary widely but typically include making recommendations on rule-making priorities, conducting studies on issues relevant to rule makings, and commenting on proposed rules prior to publication. Examples of advisory committees are the Department of Transportation's National Motor Carrier Advisory

Committee, the Department of Health and Human Services' National Advisory Council on Aging, and the Department of Labor's National Advisory Committee on Occupational Safety and Health.

The Negotiated Rulemaking Act codifies the framework for regulatory negotiation, a process in which agencies and stakeholders collectively draft proposed rules. The central institutional arrangement is the negotiated rule-making committee, a type of advisory committee that is distinctive in several respects. Negotiated rule-making committees are established to draft specific rules and are terminated upon promulgation of these rules. They are typically charged with achieving unanimous concurrence among agencies and stakeholders. Once unanimous concurrence is achieved, the recommendations of negotiated rule-making committees are published as agency proposals and are subjected to public comment and other procedural requirements.

In 1983, the Federal Aviation Administration (FAA) became the first agency to implement regulatory negotiation when it used the process to develop a rule governing the maximum flight and duty time of pilots and other air carrier personnel (Eisner 1984). Since then, regulatory negotiation has been applied in areas such as roadway worker protection, direct student loans, and subsidies for public housing. The EPA has conducted more regulatory negotiations than any other agency and accounts for about one-third of all such proceedings (Coglianese 1997). Other agencies are increasingly turning to regulatory negotiation, in part because in 1993 President Clinton issued a memorandum mandating that each agency develop at least one rule through this process. In addition, several agencies, such as the Department of Education and the Nuclear Regulatory Commission, are required by statute to use regulatory negotiation to develop particular rules (Kerwin 1999).

Advantages of Consensual Rule Making

The FAA initiated a regulatory negotiation to develop its flight and duty time rule because it had previously published several proposed rules but, due to substantial stakeholder objections, had been unable to issue a final rule (Eisner 1984). In general, the movement toward consensual rule making is the product of discontent with the traditional approach to developing rules (Eisner 1984; Harter 1982; Kerwin 1999). According to critics of traditional rule making, the fundamental shortcoming of the Administrative Procedure Act is that its proceedings are inherently adversarial. For example, parties that comment on proposed rules frequently stake out extreme positions and focus on pointing out flaws in agency proposals. In addition, participants often do not fully reveal their information or the intensity of their preferences. In general, participation is not oriented toward resolving complex or contentious issues but toward establishing a basis for lawsuits challenging agency actions.

Consensual rule making has the potential to reduce this "malaise" by altering the role of agencies and stakeholders (Harter 1982, 2). Stakeholders participate directly in the development of rules rather than merely commenting on agency actions. Stakeholders also deal directly with one another rather than through agency arbiters. Given their enhanced involvement and interaction, stakeholders have incentives to eschew extreme positions, prioritize their preferences, exchange information, and in general search for common ground that can provide the basis for mutually acceptable rules (Harter 1982; Susskind and McMahon 1985). As a result, rules developed through consensual rule making may be of high quality and may enjoy widespread legitimacy among stakeholders.

Consensual rule making may also reduce the time it takes to develop rules, in particular in the period between publication of the proposed rule and promulgation of the final rule (Harter 1982; Susskind and McMahon 1985). The rationale behind this argument is that because "most of the parties likely to comment have already agreed on the notice of proposed rulemaking, the review period should be uneventful" (Susskind and McMahon 1985, 137; see also Eisner 1984). For example, stakeholders should submit relatively few comments, and comments should be oriented toward fine tuning, rather than overhauling, agency proposals.

When and Why Consensual Rule Making May Not Work

According to advocates of consensual rule making, regulatory negotiation is more effective in reducing delay than other approaches (Harter 1982; Susskind and McMahon 1985). For example, the Occupational Safety and Health Administration (OSHA) failed in its effort to use consensual rule making to develop a rule governing occupational exposure to benzene. One explanation for this failure is that OSHA "merely invited those affected by the rule to develop a version that they could agree upon" (Susskind and McMahon 1985, 137). In other words, OSHA did not convene a negotiated rule-making committee, nor did it participate directly in the bargaining process. Supporters of regulatory negotiation are particularly skeptical about the efficacy of advisory committees, claiming that they often offer "bland recommendations" and succeed only in adding "another layer and more delay to the rulemaking process" (Harter 1982, 66–67). One reason for this skepticism is that the Federal Advisory Committee Act requires proceedings to be open to the public, which may make stakeholders less inclined to divulge their information and preferences and to make concessions to opposing interests.

Advocates also acknowledge that regulatory negotiation may not be expedient in certain situations (Harter 1982; Mintz and Miller 1991; Susskind and McMahon 1985). For example, it is difficult to conduct regulatory negotiations when there are many stakeholders. In addition, stakeholders may refuse to participate if there is a party that can dominate the proceedings and secure a favorable outcome at the expense of others. Issues must also be structured so that stakeholders can reach mutually beneficial agreements. For this reason, advocates argue that disputes over fundamental values are not generally amenable to regulatory negotiation.

Empirical Evidence

Is there any direct evidence that consensual rule making affects the time it takes to develop rules? There has been little research on the expediency of consensual rule making, and this research has focused exclusively on regulatory negotiation. Kerwin and Furlong (1992) studied more than one hundred rules issued by the EPA between 1986 and 1989. Four of these rules were developed through regulatory negotiation, which consumed, on average, 330 fewer days than the typical EPA proceeding. Regulatory negotiation was particularly expedient in the period between publication of the proposed rule and promulgation of the final rule. The average duration of this period was 319 days for regulatory negotiation and 523 days for rule making in general. In contrast, Coglianese (1997) collected data on all regulatory negotiations conducted by the EPA between 1983 and 1996 and found that these proceedings were not, on average, shorter in duration than the typical EPA rule making.

In sum, the evidence that consensual rule making affects the time it takes to develop rules is mixed. It is also limited in two important respects. First, researchers have focused predominantly on the EPA, the agency that has made the most extensive use of consensual rule making. As a result, little is known about the impact of consensual rule making at other agencies. Second, researchers have studied only one type of consensual rule making. Although it is widely argued that regulatory negotiation is more expedient than other approaches, this argument cannot be fully evaluated until more is learned about these approaches. With these limitations in mind, the analysis that follows examines the effect that advisory committees and regulatory negotiation have had on the speed with which rules are developed in dozens of agencies.

The Sample of Rules

Researchers assessing the effects of consensual rule making have used several criteria to decide on which rules to focus. In an analysis of stakeholder evaluations of different approaches to rule making, Langbein and Kerwin (2000) examined fourteen rules, divided nearly equally between regulatory negotiations and conventional proceedings. Although this strategy has important advantages (e.g., it facilitated interviews with participants in both types of rule makings), its major drawback is that it is not clear to what extent Langbein and Kerwin's findings apply to rule making in general. Kerwin and Furlong (1992, 122) focused on a larger set of rules, excluding only those that were "deemed sufficiently routine or inconsequential." This exclusion is reasonable given that agencies are not likely to use consensual rule making to attend to issues in which there is little interest or conflict among stakeholders (Coglianese 1997).

Our sample is similar to that of Kerwin and Furlong (1992), but we do not restrict our focus to EPA rules. We examine 170 major rules issued by nearly forty agencies between March 1996 and June 1999. During this period, agencies issued 204 major rules, 34 of which were promulgated without being preceded by a proposed rule. Several types of rules are exempted from the Administrative Procedure Act's notice and comment requirements, including interpretive rules, rules addressing military or foreign affairs functions, and rules for which the agency finds good cause that the requirements are impracticable, unnecessary, or contrary to the public interest. For example, in 1997 the Animal and Plant Health Inspection Service's rule on Karnal bunt (a fungal disease of wheat) was expedited because without it growers could not adequately plan for the upcoming crop season. Since consensual rule making is thought to be particularly effective in reducing the length of the period between publication of the proposed rule and promulgation of the final rule (Eisner 1984; Susskind and McMahon 1985), we focus on the 170 rules that were subjected to the notice and comment process.

Given that the sample consists of most major rule makings completed in a more than three-year period, the rules address a wide variety of topics, such as respiratory protection in the workplace, drinking water contamination, and meat and poultry inspection. The most active agency was the Federal Communications Commission (FCC), which issued 40 rules. Other active agencies included the EPA, Fish and Wildlife Service, Health Care Financing Administration, and Securities and Exchange Commission (SEC). Agencies used advisory committees and regulatory negotiation in the development of nineteen rules. The EPA made the most extensive use of these approaches, applying them to seven rules. The FCC, OSHA, and Food and Drug Administration also applied consensual rule making to multiple rules.

Although the rules were completed in a particular period, there is no immediate reason to suspect that the sample is unrepresentative of contemporary rule making. For example, between July 1999 and September 2001, agencies issued, on average, about five rules a month, a rate quite similar to that of the period under study. Many of the same agencies were once again the most active issuers of rules. The rule makings in the sample varied substantially in duration; although many proposed rules were published merely weeks before final rules were issued, this stage of the process lasted for many years in some cases. In fact, about one-third of the proposed rules appeared in the *Federal Register* prior to March 1996, and several were published during the Bush administration. This variation in proposal dates holds for both consensual and conventional proceedings. In general, it does not appear that either subset of the sample constitutes a biased representation of its genre of rule making.

Variables and Methods

Measuring the Duration of Rule Making

The dependent variable is the number of days that elapsed between publication of the proposed rule and promulgation of the final rule. We used GAO reports on major rule makings (<http://www.gao.gov>) and the texts of the final rules to determine the dates on which the proposed rules appeared in the *Federal Register.* For most rule makings, identification of the proposed rule was straightforward. In other instances, however, final rules were preceded by more than one preliminary notice, raising the issue of which notice to denote as the proposed rule. For example, prior to issuing its final rule on polychlorinated biphenyl (PCB) disposal, the EPA published two preliminary notices. The first notice outlined the changes in PCB disposal that the EPA was considering (e.g., whether to expand the list of available decontamination procedures), while the second notice contained the agency's full-blown proposal (which indicated its preference for expanding the decontamination list). In this instance, we designated the second notice as the proposed rule. We did not always select the notice that directly preceded the final rule, however. For the EPA's rule on ozone transport, the penultimate notice revised an earlier notice's emissions budget calculations and used newly available information to update its electricity demand forecasts. With this in mind, we identified the earlier notice, in which the EPA first laid out its proposal in comprehensive detail, as the proposed rule.[1]

We focus on the period between publication of the proposed rule and promulgation of the final rule for two reasons. The first reason is that, as noted earlier, advocates assert that consensual rule making likely increases stakeholder satisfaction with proposed rules (Eisner 1984; Susskind and McMahon 1985). If the post–proposed rule period is not shorter than under conventional proceedings, then consensual rule making is not likely to reduce delay, given that the preproposed rule period entails a "preemptive, intense, time consuming negotiated interaction" (Polkington 1995, 28). Second, it is difficult to identify the start of a rule making and, by extension, its overall duration. Kerwin and Furlong (1992) identified the start of EPA rule makings by examining files in the agency's internal regulation development management system. Replicating this process for dozens of agencies would be time consuming and potentially problematic, as it is not immediately clear that agencies other than the EPA maintain the requisite information in a readily accessible format.

The average amount of time that elapsed between publication of the proposed rules and promulgation of the final rules was 433 days. Seventeen rule makings had durations of less than 60 days. All but one of these rules were issued by the Fish and Wildlife Service and established parameters for seasonal migratory bird hunting. The rule making with the longest duration— more than six years—was the Pension Benefit Guaranty Corporation's regulation on payment of premiums. Five EPA rule makings took longer than 1,000 days. These rules addressed issues such as surface water treatment, emission standards for pulp and paper production, and municipal solid waste landfill facilities.

The Use of Advisory Committees and Regulatory Negotiation

We used the text of the final rule to determine whether the agency consulted with an advisory committee or conducted a regulatory negotiation. We searched for a variety of terms that agencies typically use when describing these types of consensual rule making.[2] We then carefully read the relevant sections of the rules that used any of these terms. If the agency mentioned that an advisory committee was active in the rule making, then we considered the agency to have consulted with an advisory committee. Similarly, we identified regulatory negotiations as instances in which the agency mentioned that a negotiated rule-making committee was involved in the development of the rule. Through this process, we concluded that agencies used advisory committees in fifteen instances and conducted four regulatory negotiations.

This approach facilitates the identification of instances in which these types of consensual rule making were important enough to merit mention in the final rule. It does not account for instances in which consensual rule making played an unmentioned, and presumably minor or perfunctory, role.[3] This restriction is reasonable given our interest in assessing the performance of consensual rule making as an instrument of rule development. In other words, it makes sense to analyze the expediency of consensual rule making in instances in which it was a noteworthy part of the process. In addition, other ways of identifying the use of consensual rule making are problematic in important respects. For example, asking agency officials and stakeholders to make this identification would be difficult for a large number of rules, as would relying on agency records other than readily available public notices.

Controlling for Other Determinants of the Duration of Rule Making

The time it takes to develop a rule is plausibly a function of a variety of agency and rule characteristics (Eisner 1989; Hawkins and Thomas 1989; Kerwin and Furlong 1992).[4]

Rule Characteristics

Rules vary in substantive complexity. Some rules, such as the Health Care Financing Administration's rule on Medicare hospital payments, draw heavily on economic, scientific, and technical information. Other rules, such as the FCC's rule requiring hearing aid compatible telephones in locations such as workplaces, hotels, and nursing homes, address relatively uncomplicated issues. The application of economic, scientific, and technical information can slow rule making in two central ways (U.S. Congress 1977). First, if the necessary information does not exist, a substantial amount of time may elapse while it is developed. Second, it may take the agency time to determine how to use information about which there is controversy or disagreement (Eisner 1989). We measure substantive complexity as the number of pages in the proposed rule, on the assumption that there is a positive relationship between length and complexity (Kerwin and Furlong 1992).

Some rule makings revise rules that are already in existence. For example, in 1996 the Nuclear Regulatory Commission amended its schedule of licensing, inspection, and annual fees. It is plausible that it takes less time to revise rules than to establish new requirements and standards (e.g., it was likely less difficult for the commission to adjust its fees than to create the fee schedule in the first place). We assess this possibility through an indicator of whether the rule revised an existing rule.

Some rules address activities that take place in a particular period. In 1996, the National Highway and Traffic Safety Administration (NHTSA) issued a rule setting the corporate average fuel economy standard for model year 1998 light trucks. The Fish and Wildlife Service annually issues a number of rules establishing frameworks for migratory bird hunting seasons. We expect that these types of rules were developed relatively quickly, given the time-specific nature of their provisions.

In some rule makings, stakeholders were given the opportunity to submit comments prior to publication of the proposed rule. For example, the EPA solicited comments on its rule establishing emissions standards for engines used in lawnmowers and garden tractors by circulating an advance notice of the proposed rule making. This type of comment period potentially reduces the time that elapses between publication of the proposed rule and promulgation of the final rule, as it provides stakeholders with a chance to express their preferences and agencies with a chance to incorporate these preferences into their proposals.

Agency Characteristics

Agencies can be divided into several broad categories, such as Cabinet departments, independent agencies, and government corporations (Meier 2000). These distinctions are important in that certain procedural requirements apply to only particular types of agencies. For example, independent regulatory agencies are exempt from the requirement to provide the Office of Management and Budget (OMB) with extensive information about significant rules, including justifications of their need, analyses of their costs and benefits, and assessments of their consistency with presidential priorities. The development of this information, and OMB's review of it, potentially increases the duration of rule making (Kerwin and Furlong 1992; National Academy of Public Administration 1987). We therefore include an indicator of whether the source of the rule was an independent regulatory agency.

The nature of agency rule-making agendas varies over time. For example, after the Safe Drinking Water Act was amended in 1996, the EPA's Office of Ground Water and Drinking Water initially spent much of its time laying out a timetable for developing the requisite rules. As time elapsed, the agency's focus increasingly shifted toward drafting these rules, and in 1998 it issued rules on surface water treatment and disinfectants and disinfection by-products. It is plausible that the period between publication of the proposed rule and promulgation of the final rule is generally longer when agencies are finalizing relatively large numbers of rules, as substantial agency resources are often needed to process comments and address stakeholder discontent with proposals. For example, in 1991 the Health Care Financing Administration received nearly one hundred thousand comments on its proposed schedule of Medicare physician fees and reassigned staff from other projects to expedite the handling of these comments. We examine the importance of the opportunity costs associated with this type of reallocation through the proportion of the agency's rule-making agenda for which the next step is "to publish a final rule or an interim final rule or to take other final action" (Regulatory Information Service Center 1998, 61,205).[5]

Estimation Issues

There are two main issues that affect our approach to estimation. The first is that we are interested in explaining the occurrence of a particular type of event—the promulgation of final rules. As Alt, King, and Signorino (2001) point out, data recording the occurrence of events can be arranged in several ways. For example, duration variables measure the time that elapses before events occur, while count variables measure the number of events that occur in specific periods. Given that the dependent variable measures the number of days that elapsed between publication of the proposed rule and promulgation of the final rule, duration analysis is an appropriate approach to estimation (Allison 1984; Greene 1993). Duration analysis models the likelihood that an event occurs in a given interval, given that it had not occurred prior to that interval.

There are a variety of ways in which duration models can be estimated but "few firm guidelines" for model selection (Bennett and Stam 1996, 244). There are two major issues to consider when selecting a model: whether to use a semiparametric or parametric model, and, if the latter, which parametric model is most appropriate. Semiparametric models, such as the Cox model, make relatively few assumptions about duration dependence, the relationship between the passage of time and the occurrence of events. This feature is useful because misspecification of duration dependence can lead to incorrect substantive inferences. Since we have no prior expectations regarding duration dependence, we have chosen to focus on results generated by the Cox model. However, given that parametric models are preferable to the Cox model if their assumptions accurately characterize the actual pattern of duration dependence, we also ran the analysis using a variety of parametric models, both monotonic and nonmonotonic in their specification. In all cases, the results did not differ meaningfully from those of the Cox model.

The second issue that affects our approach to estimation is endogeneity or selection bias. As discussed earlier, consensual rule making may be applied to proceedings that are distinct in their likely duration. This possibility has significant inferential implications (Achen 1986). If agencies generally use consensual rule making under favorable conditions, then estimates of its effect will exaggerate its expediency. Conversely, if agencies generally use consensual rule making in difficult situations, then estimates of its effect will mask its efficacy. With this in mind, an appropriate approach is to estimate a treatment effects model (Achen 1986; Greene 1993). This model consists of two equations, the first of which addresses the selection process (whether the agency used consensual rule making) and the second of which addresses the outcome (the number of days that elapsed between publication of the proposed rule and promulgation of the final rule). Probit analysis is used to estimate the selection equation.[6] The results of this estimation are used to calculate a variable that accounts for selection bias. This variable is then included in the outcome equation. If the variable is a significant predictor of the duration of rule making, then selection bias is present at a level that warrants concern and the treatment effects model is preferable to estimation that does not take selection bias into account.

The outcome equation is estimated through ordinary least squares (OLS) regression. King (1988) points out that applying OLS to data measuring the occurrence of events produces a variety of problems, such as inefficient estimates and predictions that are less than zero. We thus face a trade-off between accounting for selection bias in the use of consensual rule making and using an estimator that reflects the process underlying the issuing of final rules. With this trade-off in mind, we report the results of both Cox and treatment effects models, in tables 1 and 2, respectively.

Results

Tables 1 and 2 each report the results of three equations, the first of which assesses the efficacy of advisory committees, the second of which assesses the expediency of regulatory negotiation, and the third of which assesses the aggregate effect of these types of consensual rule making. The results of the Cox model indicate that there is a positive relationship between advisory committee use and the number of days that elapsed between publication of the proposed rule and promulgation of the final rule.[7] One interpretation of this finding is that advisory committee use increased the duration of rule making. This interpretation is defensible, as illustrated by OSHA's rule on occupational exposure to methylene chloride. The agency presented its proposed rule to the Advisory Committee on Construction Safety and Health, which established a work group to investigate methylene chloride use and exposure in the construction industry. After several months of research, the advisory com-

mittee provided OSHA with extensive information and numerous recommendations. In response to this input, OSHA convened public hearings and extended the deadline for submitting comments. Consultation
with the advisory committee therefore likely increased the time it took
OSHA to finalize the rule.

Another interpretation is that this result is a function of selection bias.
Agencies may have consulted with advisory committees on rules that
would have taken a relatively long time to develop no matter what the
procedural environment. The results of the treatment effects model,
however, do not support this interpretation. The variable that accounts
for selection bias is not significant, indicating that the likelihood with
which agencies consulted with advisory committees was not related to

TABLE 1.   Cox Model of the Duration of Rule Making

Variable	Parameter Estimate (standard error)		
Whether the agency consulted with an advisory committee	−.57** (.27)		
Whether the agency conducted a regulatory negotiation		−.50 (.75)	
Whether the agency consulted with an advisory committee or conducted a regulatory negotiation			−.67*** (.21)
Number of pages in the proposed rule	−.002 (.002)	−.003 (.002)	−.002 (.002)
Whether the rule revised an existing rule	−.26 (.25)	−.29 (.26)	−.30 (.25)
Whether the rule addressed activities occurring in a particular period	3.41*** (.31)	3.45*** (.29)	3.37*** (.30)
Whether there was a comment period prior to publication of the proposed rule	.34 (.34)	.27 (.35)	.32 (.34)
Whether the agency was an independent regulatory agency	.58*** (.21)	.60*** (.19)	.55*** (.20)
Proportion of the agency's rule-making agenda in the final rule stage	1.17** (.51)	1.14*** (.43)	1.04** (.48)
Log likelihood	−643.32	−645.05	−642.34
Likelihood ratio χ^2	211.88***	186.71***	184.81***
N	170	170	170

Note: The standard errors are robust and adjusted for clustering on agencies.
* indicates statistically significant at $p < .10$, one tailed.
** indicates statistically significant at $p < .05$, one tailed.
*** indicates statistically significant at $p < .01$, one tailed.

the duration of rule makings. In addition, the estimate for the indicator of advisory committee use is positive and significant ($p < .09$). Given the absence of serious selection bias, this result suggests that advisory committee use, if anything, slowed the development of final rules. This interpretation is consistent with the aforementioned skepticism about advisory committees voiced by supporters of regulatory negotiation (Harter 1982).

According to the Cox model, the time it took to finalize rules was not affected by the use of regulatory negotiation. The treatment effects model, however, suggests that this result is a function of selection bias.

TABLE 2.   Treatment Effects Model of the Duration of Rule Making

Variable	Parameter Estimate (standard error)		
Whether the agency consulted with an advisory committee	650.75* (484.63)		
Whether the agency conducted a regulatory negotiation		2,334.23** (1,263.34)	
Whether the agency consulted with an advisory committee or conducted a regulatory negotiation			978.42*** (380.01)
Number of pages in the proposed rule	.63 (.76)	.22 (1.11)	.07 (.87)
Whether the rule revised an existing rule	30.22 (61.30)	73.48 (72.74)	57.82 (64.93)
Whether the rule addressed activities occurring in a particular period	−487.58*** (72.47)	−492.58*** (97.66)	−457.80*** (74.13)
Whether there was a comment period prior to publication of the proposed rule	53.70 (70.59)	49.60 (109.08)	62.54 (78.38)
Whether the agency was an independent regulatory agency	−143.60** (80.41)	−169.97** (91.32)	−96.81 (82.73)
Proportion of the agency's rule-making agenda in the final rule stage	−336.93** (194.03)	−199.93 (257.57)	−196.58 (217.07)
Constant	560.05*** (94.21)	535.60*** (109.11)	459.50*** (104.41)
Selection bias variable	−216.49 (252.66)	−943.01** (550.94)	−387.04** (201.60)
F-statistic	9.26***	10.61***	10.61***
N	170	170	170

* indicates statistically significant at $p < .10$, one tailed.
** indicates statistically significant at $p < .05$, one tailed.
*** indicates statistically significant at $p < .01$, one tailed.

The selection bias variable is negative and significant, indicating that agencies were more likely to apply regulatory negotiation to rule makings of relatively short duration. The estimate for the regulatory negotiation variable demonstrates that, once this selection bias is taken into account, there is a positive relationship between the use of regulatory negotiation and the number of days that elapsed between publication of the proposed rule and promulgation of the final rule. Although this result is consistent with Coglianese (1997), it is striking in that consensual rule making is thought to be most efficacious in the proposed rule-final rule period, as the period preceding the proposed rule is characterized by extensive stakeholder consultation and negotiation (Eisner 1984; Harter 1982; Susskind and McMahon 1985).

Three factors are associated with decreases in the amount of time it took agencies to issue final rules. The first factor is that the rule addressed time-specific activities such as the FCC's rule on the assessment and collection of regulatory fees in fiscal year 1996. Agency type was also related to the duration of rule making in that independent regulatory agencies issued final rules at a faster rate than other agencies. The last factor, which is contrary to our expectation, is the proportion of the agency's rule-making agenda that was in the final rule stage.

In sum, the analysis demonstrates that both agency and rule characteristics affected the number of days that elapsed between publication of the proposed rule and promulgation of the final rule. Most importantly, it provides evidence that advisory committees and regulatory negotiation, if anything, increased the time it took to finalize rules. These results generally hold across the Cox and treatment effects models and therefore are not likely attributable to selection bias or the use of an estimate that does not reflect the process underlying the issuing of final rules.

Discussion

The time it takes to develop rules has been a principal concern of scholars and policymakers for decades. In recent years, consensual rule making has attracted widespread attention as a way to reduce delay in the issuing of rules. In particular, it is widely thought that regulatory negotiation, when used in appropriate circumstances, provides stakeholders and agencies with a forum through which obstacles to rule making can be removed early in the process. Our research demonstrates, to the contrary, that rules to which regulatory negotiation was applied took longer to issue than those developed through conventional proceedings, despite the fact that agencies were more likely to conduct regulatory negotiations in situations that were amenable to relatively rapid resolution. In general, we find no evidence that consensual rule making reduces the time it takes to develop rules.

These findings have important policy implications because a variety of organizations, such as former vice president Gore's much-publicized National Partnership for Reinventing Government, have endorsed consensual rule making as a way to streamline decision making in the federal bureaucracy. The partnership's support for consensual rule making was one element of a broader initiative intended to enhance public trust in government. This initiative rested on the notion that the responsiveness of policymakers, of which expediency is one component, greatly affects citizen satisfaction with government (Almond and Verba 1973). Our results, however, suggest that consensual rule making does not reduce bureaucratic delay and therefore is not likely to foster positive perceptions of government performance.

Regardless of its expediency, consensual rule making affects the benefits received and costs incurred by parties with a stake in agency actions. For this reason, the decision to use consensual rule making has important distributional consequences. Although our analysis, in particular the treatment effects model, accounts for this decision, it does not provide a comprehensive assessment of the factors that affect the use of consensual rule making. In recent years, scholars have improved our understanding of bureaucratic policymaking by viewing the selection of structure and process as a function of the transaction costs associated with alternative institutional arrangements (Huber and Shipan 2002). One logical extension of our research is to analyze more thoroughly the conditions under which policymakers turn to consensual rule making.

Previous research on bureaucratic structure and process may also provide an explanation for our finding that consensual rule making does not reduce the time it takes to develop rules. Positive theorists contend that structural and procedural constraints, such as empowering groups of stakeholders to conduct studies on issues that arise during rule makings and requiring agencies to secure the support of these groups prior to proposing rules, are in part designed to facilitate political control of the bureaucracy (McCubbins, Noll, and Weingast 1987, 1989). These constraints work by increasing agency reliance on stakeholder information and by delaying bureaucratic action. Although costly, delay provides stakeholders with an opportunity to observe agency decision making and protest prospective policies with which they are dissatisfied. Elected officials can then take steps to prevent agencies from issuing policies that are inconsistent with the interests of influential stakeholders. If this account is accurate, then it is unlikely that approaches to rule making that enhance stakeholder involvement and interaction, such as advisory committee and regulatory negotiation, will generally expedite the issuing of rules.

Even if consensual rule making does not speed bureaucratic action, it may be beneficial in other respects. For example, it may reduce the incidence of litigation, as stakeholders play a direct and substantial role in the development of rules and therefore are not likely to object fundamentally to agency policies (Harter 1982; Kerwin 1999; Susskind and McMahon 1985). Coglianese (1997), however, presents evidence that legal challenges were mounted against at least half of the rules that the EPA developed through regulatory negotiation between 1983 and 1996. In roughly the same period, lawsuits were filed against only 31 percent of clean air rules and 43 percent of hazardous waste rules developed through conventional proceedings. Although this evidence suggests that consensual rule making does not reduce the incidence of litigation, additional research is needed to assess this relationship more fully. For example, it is not clear that Coglianese's findings hold for agencies other than the EPA or when factors other than the structure and process of rulemaking, such as agency and rule characteristics, are taken into account. In general, research on the effects of consensual rule making is in its early stages, and researchers should continue to evaluate its performance on a variety of dimensions. This research is important in that it can inform both scholarly debates about bureaucratic structure and process and policymakers' decisions regarding the use of consensual rule making.

Notes

A previous version of this research was presented at the Fifth National Public Management Research Conference, College Station, Texas, December 3–4, 1999. We thank Rory Austin, Jan Box-Steffensmeier, John Brehm, Cary Coglianese, George Krause, Eric Lawrence, Ken Meier, Lee Sigelman, Dave

Spence, Paul Wahlbeck, Andy Whitford, and Dan Wood for advice and comments, Jason MacDonald for research assistance, and George Washington University for financial support.

1. These decisions were aided by the fact that agencies often use terms such as *advance notice of proposed rule making* and *supplementary notice of proposed rule making* to denote notices that precede and follow proposed rules.

2. The terms are *advisory, committee, board, council, group, panel, task force, work group, working group, negotiate, negotiation,* and *regneg* (a commonly used phrase that refers to regulatory negotiation).

3. Nor does this approach identify cases in which consensual rule making failed to bring stakeholders together and the agency neglected to mention this failure in the final rule. Our experience, however, is that agencies generally highlight important procedural milestones, in failure as well as success. For example, the process leading up to the 1994 publication of a proposed rule on Indian self-determination and education assistance was documented thoroughly in the *Federal Register,* even though the proposal was vehemently opposed and ultimately scrapped by the issuing agencies.

4. Unless otherwise noted, the sources for the explanatory variables are GAO reports on major rule makings and the texts of the final rules.

5. The source of this variable is the *Unified Agenda,* a publication in the *Federal Register* in which agencies provide information about their regulatory plans. As part of these reports, agencies list their activities by rule-making stage. We divided the number of actions in the final rule stage by the total number of active rule makings (i.e., long-term actions and rule makings in the prerule, proposed rule, and final rule stages).

6. The probit equation includes all the explanatory variables discussed earlier except the indicator of rules addressing activities that take place in a particular period, as consensual rule making was not applied to any of these rules. It also includes two variables not included in the outcome equation: (1) the number of advisory committees located in the agency and (2) the number of reports issued by the agency's advisory committees. We expect these variables to be positively related to the use of consensual rule making, assuming that agencies with relatively large numbers of advisory committees and advisory committees that are relatively active are more likely than other agencies to use consensual rule making to develop particular rules. This expectation is borne out for second variable but not the first.

7. In table 1, a negative (positive) estimate indicates that increases in the explanatory variable are associated with decreases (increases) in the likelihood of publication of the final rule and thus an increase (decrease) in the duration of rule making.

Why It Matters Whether State Bureaucrats as Opposed to Federal Bureaucrats Administer Federal Programs

Lael R. Keiser

Writing legislation is but the first step in creating public policy. It is through the implementation of policy that legislation is given substance and meaning (Goggin et al. 1990). Most policy implementation in the United States takes place in an intergovernmental context. Because the federal government delegates authority to state elected institutions and street-level bureaucracies, the implementation process provides an opportunity for state governments to exert their influence over public policy by acting strategically (Bardach 1980; Derthick 1972; Stoker 1991). In fact, the structure of intergovernmental programs allows states to manipulate policy to increase benefits for state government (Beamer 1999). State governments manipulate federal programs either through having power to write legislation that carries out federal intent or by controlling the administration of federal programs (Keiser 2001).

Although some empirical research exists that examines how state governments can influence implementation through their legislative powers (see Beamer 1999; and Hill and Weissert 1995), little research has examined whether state governments use their administrative powers to manipulate intergovernmental programs for state advantage. In earlier research, I analyzed the implementation of two federal disability programs to see whether or not state governments use their administrative powers strategically. I found that state street-level bureaucracies implement policy in a way that reflects state government interests; variation in incentives to grant high awards to Supplemental Security Income (SSI) applicants helps to explain variation in eligibility awards across the fifty states. These incentives pertain to the gains and losses that state governments incur through high participation in the SSI program (Keiser 2001). In this essay, I extend this earlier research to explore how the historical relationship between agencies and their state political principals affects the ability of state governments to engage in vertical transfer and how incentives to transfer the needy from other state-sponsored programs to SSI affects eligibility decisions.

State Governments and Policy Implementation

Principal-agent theory suggests that the federal system can be understood as a multitiered hierarchy of principal-agent relationships (Chubb 1985). In one tier, federal elected institutions act as principals and federal agencies act as agents. In the second tier, federal agencies act as principals and state governments act as agents (Chubb 1985). The majority of the research stemming from the principal-agent framework focuses on the relationships in the first tier and to a lesser degree the second. A third tier exists, however, between state elected institutions and state street-level bureaucracies because the federal government often gives state governments administrative powers. Street-level bureaucracies serve as agents simultaneously with federal elected institutions (Congress and the president), federal agencies, and state government elected institutions (governors and state legislatures).[1] Although principal-agent research has neglected the relationship between state elected institutions and street-level bureaucracies (for an exception, see Wood 1992), the bottom-up approach to policy implementation stresses the importance of state governments in the implementation process. According to the bottom-up approach to implementation, public policy is actually formulated during the implementation stage as unresolved conflicts are worked out in administrative agencies (Brodkin 1987; Lowi 1969; Majone and Wildavsky 1984). Since most public policy is carried out at the state and local levels, the implementation stage of the policy process provides an opportunity for state and local policy actors to insert their interests into the process (Bardach 1980; Stoker 1991). The federal government delegates to the states both legislative (the ability to affect the design of programs) and administrative (the ability to apply rules) power to state governments.

Members of state elected institutions have a direct interest in how federal policy is implemented in their states because federal policy has an impact on citizens, businesses, and interest groups in state policy environments. Elected officials can take credit for benefits the government provides to citizens. This gives elected officials an electoral incentive to encourage policy implementation that benefits constituents (Mayhew 1974). The interests of elected officials are embedded in the constitutional principle of federalism. Federalism requires that state and local interests are represented in the policymaking process (Berman 1980; Stoker 1991).

In many policy areas, the federal government mandates that state public agencies carry out federal programs. Although this gives power directly to state agencies, it also gives power to state elected officials. State elected institutions have multiple tools that allow them to shape how street-level bureaucracies use their discretion (Wood 1992). State elected leaders design state agencies' administrative structure, control political bureaucratic appointments, influence hiring practices, and provide funding for state agencies. Since these tools have been effective in controlling the bureaucracy at the federal level (Wood and Waterman 1994), it seems likely that they will be effective at the state level.

Many implementation studies recognize the role that state elected institutions play. Research has revealed that states use their legislative power in the implementation process for their own advantage. Hill and Weissert (1995) find that state governments have an incentive to delay policy implementation, and do so, because the state can wait for more favorable winning coalitions to come to power at the federal level. Chubb (1985) finds that the federal government must adopt monitoring devices or else the states will use federal grant money to further state priorities rather than federal ones. Beamer (1999) finds that state legislators use their legislative powers to influence federal programs in creative ways to benefit their states. Although these studies recognize the importance of the state government in policy implementation, they do not specifically focus on whether state governments benefit from their administrative, as opposed to legislative, powers.

We should expect that states will be able to benefit from their administrative powers because state elected institutions serve as the political principals to state bureaucracies (Keiser 2001). Empirical research provides some support for this contention. The partisanship of state legislatures and governors affects how street-level agencies implement a variety of federal policies (Hedge and Scicchitano 1994; Keiser and Soss 1998; Scholz and Wei 1986; Scholz, Twombly, and Headrick 1991; Wood and Waterman 1994; Wood 1992). This link between the partisanship of state elected officials and the behavior of bureaucracies suggests that federalism creates opportunities for the bureaucracy to serve a representative function for local interests (Scholz, Twombly, and Headrick 1991).

Although this research on partisanship and bureaucratic outputs suggests that state elected institutions influence state bureaucracies, it does not reveal whether elected state actors are able to use their administrative powers to exert their own institutional interests in policymaking. This body of research does reveal that some sort of democratic influence takes place during the implementation process. However, the link between partisanship and bureaucratic outputs may be due to the simultaneous impact of interest groups on elected officials and street-level bureaucrats. Similarly, street-level bureaucrats may share political ideology of elected officials because they all spend their daily lives in the same political environment (Scholz, Twombly, and Headrick 1991).

Other research suggests that the state government will not benefit from its ability to control administration. The power that state elected institutions have over state bureaucracies is not complete. Not only do street-level bureaucracies serve as agents to principals in state elected institutions but they also are influenced by principals in the federal government (Anton 1989; Scholz and Wei 1986; Wood 1992). Furthermore, bureaucracies have their own sources of power arising from clientele groups, agency expertise, information asymmetry, standard operating procedures, and leadership (Kaufman 1960; Krause 1996a; Meier 1993a; Rourke 1984; Ringquist 1995).[2] In recent research, I find that state-run street-level bureaucracies' policy outputs reflect the needs of the state, suggesting that state governments are able to use their administrative powers to insert their interests into the process (Keiser 2001).

The Policy Interests of State Government in the Implementation of Federal Programs

Although state governments have various interests that depend on the particular policy needs of the state, in general state governments are concerned with minimizing taxes while expanding or maintaining services (Beamer 1999; Peterson 1981).[3] Federalism offers state governments an opportunity to minimize their benefit-tax ratios because states may engage in vertical transfer. State officials can lower their benefit-tax ratios by transferring tax burdens from the state to another level of government. Empirical evidence exists that state elected institutions engage in vertical transfer during the legislative process (Beamer 1999). We should expect state elected institutions to use their administrative power in the same way. In other words, state elected actors should seek to influence street-level bureaucrats to engage in vertical transfer and shift the costs of providing benefits to the federal government. The vertical transfer hypothesis argues that states will manipulate intergovernmental programs to reduce their benefit-tax ratios.

All states have the incentive to shift costs to the federal government by manipulating eligibility for social welfare programs. However, influencing bureaucratic organizations is not cost free. States must invest resources into making street-level bureaucracies responsive to state needs. The likelihood of a state using its resources to engage in vertical transfer depends on the pressure state governments feel to raise benefit-tax ratios (Beamer 1999). Research shows that street-level bureaucracies respond to the incentives to engage in vertical transfer in the Supplemental Security Income Program (Keiser 2001).

Supplemental Security Income and the Incentive to Engage in Vertical Transfer

In 1972, Congress created the Supplemental Security Income Program to aid the low-income disabled. In order to qualify for SSI, potential clients must be assessed as unable to work in the same range of jobs as nondisabled people given their age, education, and work experience and meet a means test (Roth 1987). The SSI is a federal program with the federal government setting the medical and income eligibility criteria.[4] Although the federal government provides funding to ensure that all recipients receive the minimum benefit, state governments have the option of supplementing the benefit for their residents. Eligibility for SSI also coincides with eligibility for Medicaid, a health insurance program for the poor in which the federal and state governments share costs (U.S. Social Security Administration 2002).

Despite the large role of the federal government in determining rules and providing funding for the SSI program, state governments have been successful throughout the history of the program in institutionalizing a mechanism for state influence, as principal-agent theory would lead us to expect (Keiser 2001).[5] Despite the dominance of the federal government in funding and setting eligibility requirements (Dolgoff, Feldstein, and Skolnik 1993), the bureaucrats making initial eligibility decisions for the SSI program work in state offices of rehabilitation (referred to as Disability Determination Services or DDS). For a variety of reasons, the federal government has been reluctant to take full responsibility for the eligibility determination process despite the domination of federal financing. (Berkowitz 1987).[6]

The federal government does limit state influence by structuring the program so that federal agencies can monitor and alter the decisions of state disability examiners. Claimants who have been denied can appeal to administrative law judges (ALJs), who work for the federal government. If claimants are still dissatisfied, they can take their cases to the Appeals Council, a centralized administrative office that reviews ALJ decisions. Finally, claimants have appeal rights to federal district court. The Social Security Administration implements a quality assurance program through which federal bureaucrats track the accuracy rate and processing times of the DDS offices by processing a sample of cases (Lewin Group 2001).

Although the federal government tries to control the behavior of disability determiners by creating binding rules, it has difficulty because the people who apply them work for the state (Berkowitz 1987). Caseworkers in DDS seem well aware of the implications of state control of DDS offices. According to a state director of one DDS office, for example, "he would probably be discharged if he follow[ed] a strict interpretation of SSA guidelines" (GAO 1978, cited in Berkowitz 1987, 2). This sentiment has been echoed by disability examiners. In an interview with a representative from the General Accounting Office (GAO), an employee of a DDS office said, "We are state employees; therefore, we don't have to pay attention to what the SSA regional office . . . or any other federal agency says" (GAO 1978, 7–8, cited in Berkowitz 1987, 82)."[7]

State governments have aggressively protected their autonomy over the administration of the program. In the late 1970s, the U.S. Department of Health, Education and Welfare (HEW, now Health and Human Services) requested that the state sign a new contractual agreement giving the federal government more supervisory power over disability examiners. It provided the secretary of HEW with the authority to set educational standards for disability examiners and the right to access state agency premises (Berkowitz 1987). Many states simply refused to sign the contract. The state of Wisconsin went so far as to threaten to terminate its contractual agreement with the federal government and stop making disability determinations (Berkowitz 1987). Rather than confront the states, the federal government backed down and allowed states to continue the administration of the program under the existing rules.

Although the federal government has delegated administrative power to the states, state governments' power to control the program is limited. The federal government has retained all legislative power to determine eligibility in the SSI programs. State legislators cannot influence the number of citizens who gain access to the program by writing legislation.

In order for state elected institutions to use their administrative power, street-level bureaucrats must have discretion in how they implement federal rules and requirements. Discretion exists in the SSI program. High levels of discretion exist in the program because the concept of disability resists precise definition and measurement (Berkowitz 1987; Derthick 1990; Mashaw 1983). Furthermore, determining whether a claimant can work given his or her age, education, and work history has high levels of subjectivity (Stone 1984).

Because of the discretionary aspects of the disability decision, federal policymakers have expressed concern over the role of the states in determining eligibility (Stone 1984). The head of the Social Security Administration from 1936 to 1953, Arthur Altmeyer, stated that "if the determination of disability is left to several different disability boards, the likelihood is that their decision will lack uniformity" (1942, cited in Berkowitz 1987, 81). This concern proved valid. Variation exists in disability determination among the states and within the same state from year to year. In 1993, for example, Louisiana turned down 68 percent of the applications for SSI while Utah rejected only 38 percent.[8]

The SSI program provides incentives for state governments to engage in vertical transfer. This incentive varies, however, across the states. All states have the incentive to shift costs to the federal government by manipulating eligibility for social welfare programs so as to transfer as many people as possible to programs in which the state governments incur the least costs. High SSI participation decreases the need to raise taxes or reduce spending because it reduces pressure on other programs for which state governments incur high costs (e.g., Temporary Aid to Needy Families [TANF], formerly Aid to Families with Dependent Children [AFDC]; see Keiser 2001). It also reduces pressure on the state to provide for a needy population. However, influencing bureaucratic organizations is not cost free. States must invest resources in making street-level bureaucracies responsive to state needs. The likelihood of a state using its resources to engage in vertical transfer depends on the pressure state governments feel to raise benefit-tax ratios (Beamer 1999).

Beamer (1999) finds that states are most likely to engage in vertical transfer when state governments enter a crisis and elected institutions are faced with the choice of raising taxes or reducing services. States that are fiscally stressed should be more likely to use scarce resources to influence bureaucratic decision making since they face the highest pressure to raise taxes or reduce spending. As expected from this hypothesis, states that feel fiscally stressed have higher award rates in SSI (Keiser 2001). Fiscal health was measured by state revenues minus state expenditures as a percentage of total state expenditures.[9] This variable is lagged one year and multiplied by −1 so that high values indicate high fiscal stress (see appendix A at the end of this essay for sources).

State governments should also vary in their incentive to engage in vertical transfer because of variations in their program costs associated with SSL. Some state governments lose in terms of their benefit-tax ratios from high SSI participation because some state governments voluntarily contribute to the SSI benefit (Keiser 2001). Although states governments are not required to contribute to the funding of SSI, the majority of states do provide some sort of supplement to SSI beneficiaries. States vary in the amount of the supplement and the terms of eligibility. The SSI supplement creates variation in the incentives for states to reduce access to the program. Disability determination offices in states that spend more money on the supplement have lower award rates in SSI than states that spend less, all else being equal (Keiser 2001). The impact of the SSI supplement is even greater when a state has a high supplement and is experiencing fiscal stress. States that spend a larger share of their budgets on the SSI supplement and are experiencing fiscal stress (measured by an interaction term between fiscal stress and the SSI supplement) have lower award rates than other states, all else being equal (Keiser 2001). The percentage of state expenditures on the SSI supplement was lagged one year (see appendix A for sources). Lagging the SSI supplement by one year alleviates the specification problem that occurs due to the simultaneous relationship between the SSI award rate and spending on the supplement. Lagged endogenous variables can be considered predetermined variables as long as there is no serial correlation in the model (Pindyck and Rubinfeld 1991, 289).

In addition to the state supplement, state government budgets are influenced by the size of the SSI population due to the connection between SSI and Medicaid. All recipients of SSI are automatically eligible for Medicaid, a program in which state governments incur high costs. In the 1980s and 1990s, the Medicaid program created concern among state governments due to its exploding costs. High medical inflation and increased federal mandates for broader enrollments have led to an enormous growth in costs (U.S. Advisory Commission 1992). Although the federal government shares the cost of the Medicaid program, financial responsibility for it has led to fiscal crises in many states. State governments have been forced to either cut nonhealth expenditures or raise taxes in response to the increased costs of Medicaid (Beamer 1999). In-depth interviews with state legislators across eleven states reveal that representatives believe that Medicaid has been the federal mandate that had imposed the highest costs on states (Beamer 1999). For example, a representative from Colorado states that "Medicaid has been driving the state budget for the last seven or eight years." (quoted in Beamer 1999, 128). States have attempted to use their legislative power to vertically transfer costs to the federal government. In Tennessee, for example, the state government created a hospital tax for Medicaid services, thereby increasing the federal matching grant without increasing state spending (Beamer 1999). Following this line of reasoning we should lead to lower award rates for SSI because eligibility coincides with eligibility for Medicaid (Patel and Rushefsky 1995). In fact, increased enrollment in SSI would increase the pressure to raise benefit-tax ratios because it increases Medicaid enrollment. As expected, high Medicaid spending leads to lower award rates in the SSI program, all else being equal (Keiser 2001). To measure Medicaid stress, the percentage of state expenditures on Medicaid, lagged one year, is included in the model (see appendix A for sources and measures).[10] Medicaid is lagged by one year to alleviate the specification problem that occurs due to the simultaneous relationship between Medicaid and SSI (see Pindyck and Rubinfeld 1991, 289).

In short, past research supports the contention that street-level decisions reflect state interests even when state governments only have administrative, not legislative, power. State governments that lose the most from high SSI participation, for example, states with high SSI supplements and high Medicaid costs, have lower SSI award rates at the DDS level (Keiser 2001). Although past research has shown that DDS decisions reflect state interests to lower SSI award rates when Medicaid spending is high and states provide a substantial SSI supplement, the incentives to engage in vertical transfer created by high demand on state-funded programs not administratively connected to the SSI program were not examined. State governments should be more likely to use their resources to influence administration to engage in vertical transfer when facing high demand on state-funded programs. The ADFC program (now TANF) is one in which state governments incur higher costs than they do for SSI.

The structure of the U.S. welfare system suggests that different welfare programs serve objectively distinct groups because different bureaucratic agencies administer them, street-level personnel apply different eligibility standards, and the programs provide qualitatively different benefits (Schneider and Ingram 1997; Stone 1984). Significant overlap exists, however, in potential applicants to both AFDC (now TANF) and SSI (Soss and Keiser 2001). Many people living in poverty do not fit the neat definitions for eligibility in each social welfare program, and it is up to street-level bureaucracies to take applicants and transform them into clients by identifying and highlighting particular characteristics that make them eligible for particular programs (Prottas 1979). Some AFDC clients may be eligible for SSI. Since both programs are means tested, poor citizens who meet the income requirements for AFDC will also meet the income requirements for SSI because SSI has higher income limits (Dolgoff, Feldstein, and Skolnik 1993). Some AFDC clients have physical and mental conditions that may qualify them for SSI. Recent studies suggest that many AFDC clients have disabilities (Loprest and Acs 1995; Danziger, Kalil, and Anderson 2000; Tolman and Raphael 2000).

All state governments have an incentive to have as many people as possible qualify for SSI so that they do not fall back on AFDC. Because it requires resources to influence administration, however, states should vary in their ability to respond to pressure on their AFDC programs. States with high AFDC caseloads should feel more pressure to increase SSI award rates in order to reduce that pressure. To control for this, the number of AFDC recipients per population is included in the model (see appendix A for sources). State elected officials should be more likely to attempt to directly influence DDS offices when they are faced with high AFDC caseloads.

In sum, the vertical transfer hypothesis states that variation in SSI award rates should be explained by variation in the incentive for states to engage in vertical transfer and that states with high Medicaid costs and SSI supplements will have lower incentives (Keiser 2001) whereas states with high AFDC caseloads and high fiscal stress will have higher incentives. A response to these incentives suggests that state governments can use their administrative power to insert their interests into the policy-making process.

However, a limitation exists in our ability to test whether or not state elected officials influence administrations to insert state government interests into the implementation process. The rejection of the null hypothesis only suggests that state governments use their administrative powers to insert their interests into the implementation process by engaging in vertical transfer. We cannot discern whether responsiveness occurs because street-level bureaucrats have as their own preferences the interests of the state, because elected officials pressure street-level bureaucrats to use their discretion in such a way, or because some other mechanism exists. To date, no data exist on the independent preferences of street-level bureaucrats. The findings reported in Keiser 2001 reveal whether street-level bureaucracies use their discretion to benefit the state. The findings do not, however, reveal anything about why they do so. Adding a measure of demand on AFDC does not ameliorate this problem.

If state officials directly influence DDS offices, the strength of the relationship between state officials and DDS offices should help to explain variations in award rates. Not all state elected officials will have relationships with DDS offices that allow them to influence bureaucrats behavior. Variation in vertical transfer in the SSI program should be related to the ability of state elected officials to influence program administration. Government officials in some states may have closer ties to DDS offices than in others. Personal interaction between state officials and street-level bureaucrats makes it more likely that street-level bureaucrats will reflect state government values (Hedge, Menzel, and Krause 1989). The strength of the linkage between elected officials and DDS offices should determine whether state elected officials successfully act as political principals to DDS offices. In order for elected officials to influence

street-level bureaucrats, they first have to interact with them. This interaction may lead to greater policy congruence between the two, but it
does not necessarily need to in order for bureaucrats to respond because
state officials can affect DDS working conditions. Insofar as bureaucrats
are budget maximizers (Niskanen 1971), DDS office workers should be
open to direct influence from state officials because state governments
control administrative decisions such as hiring practices, size of work
force, pay scales, vacation policy, office location, and the condition of
office space and equipment. In a few states, the DDS director is a political appointee. Unfortunately, no quantitative data exist on the levels of
interaction between DDS offices and state elected officials.

To create a proxy measure of interaction between state elected officials
and DDS offices, an examination of the historical record is needed to
create a variable that measures the amount of interaction. The controversy over the use of continuing disability reviews in the Social Security
Disability Program provides a way to quantify, albeit roughly, the DDS
and state official relationship. In 1980, Congress required the Social Security Administration to conduct continuing reviews of disability recipients (Public Law 96–265). The secretary of health and human services
ordered DDS offices to determine whether or not current recipients met
the medical requirements for the program regardless of whether their
condition had changed since the time the agency awarded them benefits.
Many people lost their benefits as a result of these continuing disability
reviews, and many appealed to federal court and/or complained to Congress (Derthick 1990; Mezey 1986). Although the federal courts overturned most of these cases and eventually ruled that the Social Security
Administration had to show that a recipient's medical condition had improved since the initial determination granting them benefits, the administration initially refused to apply these court cases beyond the liti-
gant's claim (Mezey 1986). In response to this situation, many state
elected officials (mostly governors) intervened and ordered DDS offices
in their states to either place a moratorium on continuing disability reviews or find that a claimant's condition improved before terminating
benefits. State DDS offices followed the orders of state officials (U.S.
Congress 1984).

States in which such an interaction took place during the early 1980s
should be more likely to have close relationships between state elected
officials and DDS currently. A dummy variable valued at one for states

in which a state elected official intervened in DDS processing of the continual disability reviews and valued at zero for states in which no intervention occurred is used as a proxy for the amount of interaction between state elected officials and DDS offices. DDS offices under the Ninth Circuit Court were ordered by the court to use a medical improvement standard. Because it is impossible to tell whether these states changed their behavior for the continuing disability reviews due to pressure from state elected officials or the court, states under specific court orders were removed from the analysis (see appendix A for sources).

As a proxy, this variable is not without limitations and is a blunt instrument used to capture the likelihood that state elected officials will intervene with DDS offices. The actions of state elected officials during the 1980s crises may be more a result of the politics of the state elected officials than of the linkages between state officials and DDS offices, and linkages in the past might not translate into linkages today. However, insofar as the interventions of the 1980s set a precedent for state involvement in the disability determination process and helped to create the understanding in DDS offices that DDS examiners are ultimately responsible to the state, states where elected officials have been involved in the past should be more open to state-level influence today. Although all states have the incentive to push as many people as possible onto the SSI program, states with historical linkages between elected officials and DDS offices should be more likely to be successful in their efforts to engage in vertical transfer and therefore should have higher SSI award rates.[11]

In sum, all states have a general interest in having high award rates that are as high as possible in SSI because SSI provides benefits to state citizens at low costs to state governments relative to other antipoverty programs. However, influencing program administration takes resources, and we should expect states that have the highest incentives to engage in vertical transfer will do so at a higher rate than other states do. State governments vary in how much they benefit from high SSI participation. We should expect that states with lower incentives will have lower allowance rates (states with high SSI supplements and Medicaid costs) and states with high incentives (states with high fiscal stress and large AFDC caseloads) will have higher award rates. In addition to variation in incentives to engage in vertical transfer, state officials should also vary in their ability to affect administration. States with a link between DDS offices and state officials (measured by a history of gubernatorial intervention in

DDS policy) should have higher award rates than other states, all else being equal.

Control Variables

We must control for other variables that should affect SSI award rates in order to test the preceding hypotheses. Several control variables were used in this study (for a more detailed discussion of each, see Keiser 2001). The political environment affects how street-level bureaucracies implement policy, and the partisanship of state elected institutions is an important part of that environment (see Wood and Waterman 1994). Social Security disability is fairly partisan (Berkowitz 1987; Stone 1984). Ever since its inception, Democrats have been more supportive of the program, while Republicans have been more concerned with reducing the rolls and federal involvement. Past research indicates that more Social Security disability recipients live in states controlled by Democrats than in states controlled by Republicans (Keiser 1999). We should expect this relationship to be even stronger for eligibility decisions by street-level bureaucrats. To control for political pressure, a dummy variable was created. All states with a Democratic governor were coded one and all states with a Republican or independent governor were coded zero (see appendix A for sources).[12]

In addition to the partisanship of the governor, street-level bureaucracies may also be influenced by the overall political culture in the state. The behavior of street-level bureaucracies is influenced by how much legitimacy their functions have among people outside the bureaucracy (Thompson 1967). This is especially important in human services bureaucracies, like DDS, because the bureaucracy places values on citizens by labeling clients as deserving or undeserving of government assistance (Hasenfeld 1992). Due to variations in historical immigration and migration patterns, the states vary in the level of legitimacy members of political institutions, and the public in general, hold for government assistance to aid the needy. Elazar (1984) argues that historical migration and immigration patterns created some state political cultures that are more conducive to an active government presence and social welfare policies than other state political cultures. He identified states with this culture as moralistic. State political culture should influence how bureaucracies implement policy in two ways. First, it will affect the culture of administrative organizations in the state. Historical immigration and migration patterns provide the context in which state administrative organizations were created. The creation period of an administrative organization is very important in determining the culture, and more specifically the mission, of bureaucracies (Wilson 1989). This culture is perpetuated across time through standard operating procedures and socialization of members (Simon 1957). In addition to influencing bureaucratic culture, state political culture will have a contemporary influence on bureaucratic behavior by influencing the legitimacy of the bureaucracy's task. Bureaucracies that have high award rates in the SSI program will have more legitimacy in moralistic states than in nonmoralistic ones. Administrative organizations created in the context of a moralistic political culture award disability benefits at a higher rate than administrative organizations developed in a nonmoralistic culture (Keiser 2001). To control for political culture, a dummy variable coded one for states with a moralistic culture and zero otherwise was included in the model (see appendix A for sources and measures).

In addition to the political environment, implementation should be influenced by the task environment. The nature of the bureaucracy's task plays a role in influencing bureaucratic behavior (Wilson 1989). The task environment refers to the materials with which the bureaucracy works (Thompson 1967). For human service bureaucracies, the bureaucracy's caseload is a major part of its task environment. Characteristics of the bureaucracy's caseload should therefore explain variation in award rates. If street-level bureaucrats follow their official mandates, higher levels of disability in each state should translate into higher award rates. To measure the level of disability, several variables that measure health and injury risk for residents were included in the model. These are the percentage of jobs found in the manufacturing sector, the percentage of the state population between the ages of fifty-four and sixty-five, and the AIDS rate. Past research demonstrates that these variables coincide with the medical need for benefits (Rice and Feldman 1983; U.S. Department of Labor 1991).[13]

In addition to medical need, award rates should be related to economic need. When unemployment is high, more citizens with marginal medical conditions apply than do so during times of economic prosperity because people with medical problems have an easier time finding work under conditions of low unemployment (Soss and Keiser 1999). To control for unemployment, the civilian labor force participation rate was included.[14]

In addition to levels of need, prior research on Social Security disability has revealed that race is an important variable for understanding award rates. Although minorities tend to have more health problems and less access to health care than whites (Patel and Rushefsky 1995, 121–25), at the individual level DDS examiners deny benefits to black applicants at a higher rate than white applicants in the SSI program because blacks apply for benefits with less severe disabilities and at younger ages than do whites (GAO 1992). This patterns holds at the aggregate level (Keiser 2001). To control for the impact of race, the percentage of the state population that is African-American is included in the model (see appendix A for sources and measures).[15]

In addition to measures of medical and economic need, street-level bureaucracies should also respond to levels of demand. Organizations respond to and try to influence the level of demand for their resources (Thompson 1967). The reaction to levels of demand by street-level bureaucracies is mitigated, however, by the resources of the agency. Bureaucracies with resource shortages should actually limit access to programs when faced with high demand to conserve resources (Lipsky 1980). Although DDS offices do not face resource shortages in terms of how many benefits they can provide, they do have resource shortages in terms of processing cases (Mashaw 1983). Many claimants are denied disability because DDS examiners make decisions on cases prior to collecting all the relevant information. Examiners can request additional information from the claimant or collect additional information themselves but are unlikely to do so when faced with large numbers of caseloads (Mashaw 1983). State agencies with large numbers of caseloads have lower award rates than state agencies with fewer caseloads in the SSI program. To measure demand, the number of applications per ten thousand residents is included in the model (see appendix A for sources).

Research Methods

The hypotheses were tested using pooled cross-sectional analysis of award rates in the thirty-eight states for the years 1991 to 1993.[16] The percentage of SSI applications that DDS offices awarded serves as the dependent variable. Dummy variables for the years 1991 and 1992 were included to reduce potential problems with autocorrelation. The analysis is based on an ordinary least squares (OLS) regression model. Three-stage least squares were performed on the model to test for any reciprocal relationships between the SSI supplement and SSI award rates and Medicaid and SSI award rates.[17]

Findings

Similar to earlier research (Keiser 2001), the findings show that state DDS offices are responsive to the benefits or losses that state governments incur through participation in the SSI program. States that incur higher financial costs through the Medicaid program and the SSI supplement reduce access to the SSI program. Disability determination offices in states with higher SSI supplements provide less access to the SSI program than do DDS offices in states with lower SSI supplements. Similarly, DDS offices in states with high Medicaid costs provide less access to SSI than do those in other states[18] The results of the three-stage least squares model do not lead to different inferences regarding the direction of the causal relationship between the SSI award rate and the SSI supplement as well as between the SSI award rate and Medicaid spending (see table 1; also see appendix B at the end of this essay for results). In addition to being responsive to the SSI supplement and Medicaid spending, DDS offices in states that are under fiscal stress have higher SSI award rates. These findings suggest that state governments are able to use the implementation process to insert their interests into policy even when they yield administrative but not legislative power (Keiser 2001).

The SSI supplement and Medicaid are both variables that directly relate to SSI access. Because potential clients from different social welfare programs overlap, high demand on the AFDC (now TANF) also creates incentives for state governments to increase access to the SSI program. The findings failed, however, to support the hypothesis that states with high AFDC caseloads will have higher SSI award rates. Caseload size does not have a statistically significant relationship with SSI award rates. State governments do not seem to respond to high AFDC caseloads by providing more access to SSI.

In addition to incentives to engage in vertical transfer, the ability to influence bureaucratic offices should also affect whether street-level bureaucracies respond to state government officials. It was hypothesized that states with evidence of direct intervention by governors would have higher award rates for SSI than other states. This hypothesis was not supported. In states with a history of gubernatorial interventions, DDS offices do not have higher allowance rates than other states.

The lack of a connection between historical linkages between state elected officials and DDS offices and SSI award rates has several different interpretations. First, the lack of support for the hypothesis may be due to the quality of the relationship measure. The proxy measure of intervention between state officials and DDS offices may not capture current relationships. We can only conclude from this finding that historical interventions do not make DDS decisions more reflective of state interests currently. However, it is possible that a more current measure of the relationship will yield significant results. Second, state governments may not directly influence eligibility decisions. Instead, state governments may affect the quality of applications. Anecdotal evidence suggests that many states require intake workers for AFDC to investigate whether

TABLE 1. Award Rates in the Social Security Income Program, 1991–93

Variables	SSI	Standard Error
Constant	70.71**	20.59
Incentives to Engage in Vertical Transfer		
SSI Supplement$_{t-1}$	−8.35**	3.25
Medicaid Spending$_{t-1}$	−0.73*	0.43
Fiscal Stress$_{t-1}$	0.411**	0.15
Fiscal Stress × SSI Supplement$_{t-1}$	−0.81**	0.30
AFDC Caseload	−0.04	0.05
Ability to Engage in Vertical Transfer		
State–DDS Relationship	0.99	1.03
Political Environment		
Moralistic culture	5.97**	1.56
Democratic governor	−0.23	1.14
Task Environment		
Demand (application rate)	−0.08**	0.04
Employment Rate	−0.14	0.23
Aged population	−3.18**	0.99
AIDS rate	0.20**	0.05
Manufacturing Employment	0.45**	0.10
Black Population	−0.25*	0.09
Adjusted R^2	.61	
F-score	11.93**	
White's test	$11.4_{df=17}$	$p > .10$
Lagrange multiplier	$1.68_{df=1}$	$p > .10$

$N = 114$, dummy variables not included in table.
* indicates $p \geq .10$. ** indicates $p \geq .05$.

claimants may be eligible for SSI and to help them with their applications. Other states and local governments provide funding to organizations that assist with SSI claims in the hope of reducing demand for state and locally funded programs (Kritzer 1998). In the Social Security system, many claims are ultimately overturned by administrative law judges, often because of more complete medical information in the application at the ALJ stage of the process (Cofer 1985). States that provide a lot of assistance with applications at the initial stage could have an impact on SSI award rates at the DDS level by influencing the quality and quantity of information in SSI applications. Unfortunately, no quantifiable data exist on these programs across the U.S. states. The failure of the AFDC caseload to influence SSI allowance rates does not support this explanation, but the likelihood that states have such assistance programs may be due to other factors besides the size of the AFDC caseload. The creation of a better measure of client assistance with SSI claims is needed if we are to explore this possible explanation.

The findings concerning the control variables are all as expected given earlier research. Overall, the findings reveal that DDS offices are responsive to their professional mandates. Their decisions are reflective of the level of medical need that exists in the state as well as measures that relate to the severity of disability in the caseload. The size of the minority population and high application rates should both lead to a higher proportion of less severe claims (Keiser 2001). Not surprisingly, these variables reduce allowance rates. Although DDS decisions do not seem open to the partisanship of the governor, the political culture of the state affects award rates. Disability offices in states with a moralistic culture have a higher SSI award rate than other states do. For a more detailed discussion of the findings for the control variables, see Keiser 2001.

Need for Qualitative Research

Because the statistical analysis failed to meet expectations concerning the state official interaction variable, personal in-depth interviews with DDS directors were conducted in three states to gain a better understanding of the relationship between DDS and the states. The states are not named so to as protect the confidentiality of the interviewees. Directors were asked to describe their interactions with state officials and whether state officials attempted to influence eligibility decisions. The interviews suggest that states vary in how close the DDS offices are to state elected officials.

Of the three DDS directors who were interviewed, two state directors had little interaction with state officials concerning nonpersonnel issues and one state director had a high level of interaction. In these two low-interaction states, the directors communicated that the interactions they had dealt with were hiring decisions and procurement. Neither director felt that state officials cared about eligibility rates. Both directors discussed how they were obligated to follow the federal rules to protect the Social Security System and U.S. taxpayers. They indicated that they gauged the performance of their offices from the Social Security Administration's calculation of their accuracy rates. One director felt it was her duty to protect U.S. taxpayers and was distressed that administrative law judges reversed so many decisions. Both of these state directors were merit employees.

The third director, a political appointee, had a high level of interaction with state officials through attending the governor's town meetings, answering state legislators' inquiries about cases, and testifying before legislative committees regarding disability fraud scandals. However, she claimed that state elected officials did not pay attention to overall allowance rates or try to influence them in any way. Interestingly, she believed that her state's allowance rates were too low and had taken steps to raise them because she did not think it was fair that citizens in her state had less access to the program than did citizens in other states. She believed that examiners in her state did not apply new Social Security regulations that make it easier to allow cases. She tracked whether examiners used all possible rules to allow cases and used this information to evaluate performance. She was less concerned with whether examiners' decisions were sent back due to errors following review in the Social Security's Quality Assurance Program. This director was also concerned about the fraud in the program and the high reversal rate of the ALJs.

Though preliminary, the results of the interviews suggest that interaction between the DDS offices and state officials may affect allowance rates because it may change bureaucratic culture. Disability offices have two constituencies—U.S. taxpayers and state citizens applying for benefits. Although directors in all three states expressed concern with both of these constituencies, the two states with little interaction between elected officials and DDS offices were less focused on providing access to state residents and more focused on meeting the Social Security Administration's performance standards than was the director in the state with high inter-action. Because of the small number of states included, however, these re-sults are only suggestive and may be due to idiosyncratic factors.

Clearly, more interviews are needed if we are to look inside the black box and understand how the links between state elected officials and DDS offices shape eligibility determinations. The statistical analysis sug-gests that DDS decisions do reflect the needs of the state in the form of the SSI supplement and Medicaid costs. In future research, I will explore three possible mechanisms that may link street-level decisions with state government needs. Assistance with clients' SSI applications, the creation of a bureaucratic culture that focuses on state applicants, and direct in-tervention in policy by elected officials are all possible mechanisms.

Appendix A

Supplemental Security Income Award Rate, 1991–93. Source: unpublished data from the Social Security Administration.

State–DDS Relationship: dummy variable coded one if the governor or other state official ordered DDS to either suspend continuing disability reviews or use a medical improvement standard in evaluating cases in response to the 1980–85 controversy over continuing disability reviews, zero otherwise. Source: U.S. Congress 1984.

Fiscal Stress: state revenues minus state expenditures as a percentage of total state expenditures multiplied by −1, lagged one year, 1990–93. This variable was broken down into three categories. Values below one standard deviation of the mean were coded as zero. Values above one standard deviation of the mean were coded as two, and all other values were coded as one. This variable was broken into categories to reduce collinearity between Fiscal Stress and the interaction between Fiscal Stress and the SSI Supplement. Source: *United States Statistical Abstract, United States Bureau of the Census.*

Medicaid Spending: percentage of expenditures on Medicaid minus the federal contribution, lagged one year. Source: *United States Statistical Abstract, United States Bureau of the Census.*

SSI Supplement: percentage of total state expenditures on the SSI supplement, lagged one year, 1990–92. Source: *U.S. Statistical Abstract, United States Bureau of the Census;* and *Statistical Summary of the Social Security Bulletin.*

Interaction effect for fiscal stress and SSI Supplement: state revenues minus state expenditures as a percentage of total state expenditures multiplied by -1, lagged one year, multiplied by percentage of total state expenditures on the SSI supplement, lagged one year.

AFDC Caseload: number of AFDC recipients per one thousand in population. Source: *United States Statistical Abstract. United States Bureau of the Census.*

Partisanship: dummy variable coded one if Democrats controlled the governorship, zero otherwise, 1991–93. Source: *United States Statistical Abstract, United States Bureau of the Census.*

Political Culture: dummy variable coded one if the state was identified as moralistic, moralistic-individualistic, or individualistic-moralistic, zero otherwise. Source: Elazar 1984, 135.

Employment Rate: civilian labor force participation, 1991–93. Source: *United States Statistical Abstract, United States Bureau of the Census.*

AIDS Cases: number of AIDS cases reported per one hundred thousand in population, 1991–93. Source: United States Centers for Disease Control, <ftp://ftp.cdc.gov/pub/Health_Statistics/NCHS/Datasets/Healthy_People _2000/Health_Status_Indicators/>.

Black Population: percentage of state population that is African American. Source: *United States Statistical Abstract, United States Bureau of the Census.*

Manufacturing Employment: percentage of total employment in manufacturing jobs. Source: *Handbook of Labor Statistics, United States Dept. of Labor.*

Demand: number of applications per one hundred thousand in population for Social Security Disability Insurance and SSI. Source: unpublished data from the Social Security Administration.

Appendix B

TABLE B1. Three-Stage Least Squares Model for SSI
Supplement

Variables	Coefficient	Standard Error
Dependent = SSI Award Rate		
SSI Supplement	−19.83	4.10*
Constant	18.44	21.03
χ^2	29.17*	
Dependent = SSI Supplement$_{t-1}$		
SSI Award Rate	−0.05	0.01*
Constant	0.93	1.09
χ^2	15.82*	

Note: Coefficients for dummy variables for 1991 and 1992 are not included. Instrumental variables = Dollars spent on public education per population, Manufacturing Employment, SSI application rate, and AFDC Caseload per population.
*$p > .05$.

TABLE B2. Three-Stage Least Squares for Medicaid Spending

Variable	Coefficient	Standard Error
Dependent Variable = SSI Award Rate		
Medicaid Spending$_{t-1}$	−1.70*	0.27
Constant	23.35	39.45
χ^2	43.58*	
Dependent Variable = Medicaid Spending$_{t-1}$		
SSI Award Rate	−0.59*	0.11
Constant	13.7	23.23
χ^2	25.03*	

Note: Dummy variables for 1991 and 1992 are not included. Instrumental variables = Total expenditures on nursing homes per capita, Manufacturing Employment, SSI application rate, and AFDC Caseload.
*$p > .05$.

Notes

I would like to thank George Krause and Charles Shipan for their helpful comments. A grant from the University of Missouri Research Board funded this project.

1. The problem of multiple principals becomes even more complicated when we consider that the public is a principal of street-level bureaucrats acting through either federal and state elected officials or direct interactions with street-level bureaucrats.

2. For a similar discussion of the role of state governments in policy implementation, see Keiser 2001.

3. Through the use of case studies of eleven state legislatures, Beamer (1999) found that the collective decisions of state legislatures reflect a desire to minimize constituents' benefit-tax ratios. This relationship held across three different policy areas.

4. Claimants must have an income below $512 per month to be eligible.

5. Disability examiners in DDS offices also process applications for Social Security Disability Insurance (DI). Although DI and SSI differ in income requirements (DI is a social insurance program whereas SSI is a means tested one), the medical criteria for eligibility in both programs is the same. This essay focuses only on SSI because it provides a better test of the hypotheses. See Keiser 2001, however, for an analysis of DI.

6. Current reformers who wish to centralize the determination process face opposition from policy actors hesitant to increase the size of the federal bureaucracy. Hiring federal bureaucrats as disability examiners would also displace current state employees and may increase the cost of the program because federal pay scales are, for the most part, higher than state pay scales (Berkowitz 1987).

7. These comments pertain to the processing of both DI and SSI claims.

8. For a similar general description of the role of the states in the implementation of SSI, see Keiser 1999.

9. This measure has been used in the policy adoption literature to measure state fiscal health (see Berry and Berry 1990; and Stream 1999).

10. Medicaid stress and fiscal stress are obviously closely related. Because Medicaid stress occurs due to increasing mandates from the federal government, it may provide greater incentives for vertical transfer than simple fiscal stress. In addition, states may feel burdened by Medicaid and therefore engage in vertical transfer even when state revenue has kept pace with state spending. Though related, therefore, the two concepts are different.

11. The ability to engage in vertical transfer should interact with the incentives to do so. Therefore, an interaction term of the SSI supplement and the state government involvement variable was included in an earlier version of the model. Although the variance influence factor fell below ten, the sign of the coefficient measuring state influence changed direction, suggesting that collinearity may be a problem. Although the interaction term was statistically significant, it was in the opposite direction (positive), as predicted by theory. Consequently, it was removed from the analysis.

12. The partisanship of the governorship was used instead of the state legislature because the governor has the most direct power over street-level bureaucracies in the state through the power of appointment. The legislative branch also has power over the bureaucracy, however, because it controls its funding. Including the partisanship of the state legislature did not make any difference in the findings. Consequently, it was excluded from the final model to preserve degrees of freedom.

13. In addition to the variables in the model, the infant mortality rate was included in the analysis to further control for the overall health of the state. This variable failed to reach statistical significance, and removing it did not substantively change the results of the model. Because it was highly collinear with Black Population, it was removed from the final analysis.

14. The unemployment rate is also a measure of economic stress. The unemployment rate is not, however, a pure measure of fiscal stress on the states since street-level bureaucrats may take into account the availability of jobs when using their norms to award disability to the most needy. Consequently, I do not consider the unemployment rate as a measure of fiscal stress.

15. In addition to the size of the African American population, the size of the Hispanic population may have an impact on award rates because Hispanics disproportionately suffer from the problems of poverty and poor health. Including Hispanic population in the measure did not effect the results of the analysis. To preserve degrees of freedom, it was removed from the final analysis.

16. Alaska, Arizona, California, Hawaii, Minnesota, Montana, Nevada, Oregon, Washington, and Wisconsin were removed because they were under federal court order during the continuing disability review controversy and therefore have missing data for the DDS and state official relationship variable. Iowa and Ohio were removed from the analysis because of missing data in the Medicaid variable.

17. Regression diagnostics were performed on both models to assess any problems arising from outliers, multicollinearity, autocorrelation, and heteroskedasticity. Studentized residuals and Cook's D indicated that no observations were distorting the regression line. The Lagrange multiplier test for autocorrelation (Maddala 1992, 120–21) revealed no autocorrelation. The variance inflation factor indicated that the model does not have problems with collinearity (Kleinbaum, Kupper, and Muller 1988). White's test for heteroskedasticity (Pindyck and Rubinfeld 1991, 137) indicated no violation of the homoskedasticity assumption.

18. Three-stage least squares reveal that the SSI supplement and Medicaid costs affect award rates, although some reciprocal influence exists. Education spending per population, the SSI application rate, the AFDC caseload, and the

manufacturing employment rate were used as instrumental variables for the SSI supplement model. Nursing home expenditures, the SSI application rate, the manufacturing employment rate, and the AFDC caseload were used as instrumental variables for the Medicaid model.

Structural Choice and Political Control of Bureaucracy: Updating Federal Credit Programs

Kevin Corder

A fundamental problem in democratic politics is control of bureaucracy. Elected officials, handicapped by limited information and uncertainty about policy outcomes, face obstacles to the effective oversight and control of public sector agencies. Agency decision makers have the incentive and the capacity to exacerbate or exploit an often substantial informational advantage over legislative or executive monitors. Considerable attention has been given to the scope of this problem, and a substantial empirical literature has emerged that attempts to identify and measure the effects of various types of political control mechanisms—the role of agency structure, administrative procedures, appointments, budgets, reorganization, and passive forms of political control.

Much of the empirical work that is the basis for evaluation of the instruments of political control, especially the work informed by statistical modeling, is based on the observation of regulatory agencies: the Federal Trade Commission, the Securities and Exchange Commission, the Environmental Protection Agency, and the Nuclear Regulatory Commission. Work that suggests that political control problems are not problematic, particularly the congressional dominance literature pioneered by Weingast and Moran (1983), is almost entirely grounded in the performance of regulatory agencies. This narrow empirical focus may miss important features of the large number of agencies that do not engage in regulation and instead deliver transfer payments, provide services, or intervene in capital markets.

As an alternative to regulatory agencies, the growing and diverse federal credit programs would seem to offer an ideal set of programs with which to test expectations for and experience with political control of bureaucracy. The federal credit programs are somewhat exceptional since program outputs are directly comparable: agency activity is measured by the volume of lending and guarantee activity. The large number of programs permits direct comparison of the outputs of programs operating in a variety of structural contexts and serving different types of constituencies. Using direct lending and loan guarantee and insurance activity from fifteen federal credit programs, I investigate how variation in program structure affects responses to instruments of political control.

The essay proceeds in three parts. First, I locate this project in a broader literature on political control of the bureaucracy with a particular focus on ex ante *structure and process* controls. Second, I describe the federal credit programs and the agencies that are the subject of the essay. Finally, I estimate and discuss five models of federal credit activity: time-series cross-sectional models of direct and loan guarantee activity at the program level for a sample of Cabinet departments, independent agencies, and government-sponsored enterprises. The credit programs overall reveal a much more active and interested Congress than the extant literature on political control suggests. In contrast to the regulatory agencies that have informed much of the empirical work on political control of bureaucracy, the credit programs are routinely reorganized, relocated, and updated to reflect current needs and demands. Specific and highly tailored legislative instructions, either amendments to statutes or indirect instructions embedded in larger legislation, are effective and expedient instruments of political control. Canonical correlates of agency behavior—party control of the White House and changes in the budget, for instance—affect program outputs (especially direct lending) less than the reform and reorganization activities that originate in Congress.

The Problem of Political Control

A substantial empirical and theoretical literature informs our understanding of political control of bureaucracy. No observer could make the case, however, that there is any consensus in this literature about either the general effectiveness of efforts at political control or the effect of particular instruments of control. At one level, is it not even clear if elected officials manage to exercise any control whatsoever. Wilson (1989) and other students of agency behavior note that elected officials face obstacles to the exercise of political control. Agency professional norms or culture, the ambitions and preferences of agency leaders, and the tremendous advantages of agencies in controlling information flow to elected officials all conspire to blunt efforts of elected officials to influence agency policy choices. In contrast, Calvert, McCubbins, and Weingast (1989) and other students of the American Congress claim that agency policy choices can ultimately be traced back to the preferences of elected officials. Despite substantial uncertainty at a number of critical decision points, elected officials monopolize the few resources (money and statutory authority) that can decisively influence or constrain the policy choices of agency leaders. As a consequence, agency leaders respond to changing preferences in the Congress or the White House in an effort to avoid budgetary sanctions or statutory penalties. Elected officials thus exercise an important but often overlooked passive form of control over agencies and have recourse to active control alternatives on the rare occasions when they are required. Given that both perspectives emphasize the absence of overt efforts to control agency behavior, it has been challenging to determine which perspective is a more accurate description of Congress-bureau relationships.

Proponents of both perspectives emphasize the distinction between ex ante and ex post efforts to exert control over policy outcomes. Ex post control describes the instruments of control that contemporary political actors can bring to bear upon agencies that are resistant to change: appointments, statutory change, and budget sanctions and incentives. Ex post controls exploit a fairly well developed monitoring system in the Congress that, while not necessarily generating optimal outcomes, creates opportunities for elected officials to advocate particular policy choices (Aberbach 1990). Skeptics note that responses of members of Congress to agency failures are somewhat constrained by existing agency structures, since legislative updates to structure are costly and time consuming (see Moe 1984). Empirical work investigating the utility of ex post control has generated mixed results. Wood and Waterman (1994) observe agency behavior in a variety of contexts responding to instruments of active political control—the shared appointment and budget choices of Congress and the White House. But Eisner and Meier (1990) reveal how long-term changes in the organization of bureau activity, and not ex post executive or congressional control, drove changes in the Antitrust Division of the Department of Justice during the Reagan administration.

Ex ante control describes choices about agency structure and procedures made at the creation of the agency—choices that place constraints upon contemporary actors and preserve the choices of the legislative majority responsible for creating the agency. Ex ante controls include structural choices such as the length and frequency of appointments or administrative procedures that privilege particular constituents. Ineffective ex post controls could be the function of effective ex ante design (see Horn and Shepsle 1989). Agencies may be "hardwired" to pursue a particular set of goals or respond to a particular set of interests. Moe (1989) claims that past choices about the structure of agencies determines, in some ways, contemporary policy choices. Macey (1992) describes how agency structure affects the influence of groups over agency choices as well as the types of experts that influence agency choices. McCubbins, Noll, and Weingast (1987) identify the central role of procedural constraints on outcomes of agency policy choices. Despite the promise of procedural controls, ex ante control has been difficult to demonstrate empirically. Balla (1998) finds that ex ante controls (implemented through strict control of the notification and comment process) failed to privilege target groups. Spence (1999b) does identify important effects of procedural (and structural) controls in the decisions of the Federal Energy Regulatory Commission but notes that it is unclear whether these effects were the consequence of intentional forward-looking choices made by legislative actors.

Overall, the empirical work investigating ex ante controls has focused on procedural at the expense of structural choices. Some basic questions are ripe for investigation. What are the effects of agency structure on agency performance? How is agency structure updated or contested? Although we presume that, by design, government-sponsored enterprise are somewhat insulated from the demands of elected officials, precious little empirical work has investigated even these basic expectations about how structural choices affect agency responsiveness. This essay is an effort to add to our understanding of how agency structure (distinguished from agency procedure) can affect agency activity over time and, further, how changes in this structure can be an instrument of political control.

The Federal Credit Programs

The federal credit programs directly or indirectly influence the allocation of capital to targeted groups of borrowers. Indirect mechanisms may take the form of guarantee or insurance of new loans or mortgages or secondary market purchases of existing loans or mortgages. Direct lending takes the form of conventional loans or mortgages with the government as primary lender. Some agencies include lending as a one of a number of tools to provide support for some constituency; other programs are the exclusive focus of an agency. These various federal credit programs are implemented through a variety of administrative and fiscal arrangements. Some agencies are small components of Cabinet-level departments, some are independent agencies, and others are privately held government-sponsored enterprise (GSEs).

Members of Congress actively monitor the activities of the federal credit programs, make frequent minor changes to program authority and scope, and occasionally subject programs to broad reorganization. Farm credit programs were restructured financially and organizationally in 1987. Musolf (1991) uses the reorganization of the Farm Credit System to illustrate how reform of GSEs has largely ignored broader administrative and fiscal implications of GSEs and instead focused on the particular needs of borrowers in affected sectors. The veteran's housing program and rural electrification program were moved from independent agencies to existing or new Cabinet departments. The Federal Home Loan Bank Board was abolished in 1989. One of the primary financing mechanisms for a majority of the federal credit programs, the Federal Financing Bank (FFB), was created in 1973 and abolished in 1986. The federal student loan program was started in a Cabinet agency, expanded via a government-sponsored enterprise in 1972, and will be completely privatized by 2008. The reorganization of these diverse programs makes the general point: members of Congress routinely review and reform the federal credit programs.

Despite the large size and continuing activity of the federal credit programs, a relatively small literature investigates their development and impact. Bosworth, Carron, and Rhyne (1987) describe the origins and performance of a number of federal credit programs with the particular objective of highlighting the real role of subsidies in a few of the programs. Ippolito (1984) describes the special accounting and control problems introduced by the credit programs. Meier, Polinard, and Wrinkle (1999) find that farm credit programs are linked to objective economic conditions (farm debt and farm income) but that ongoing systematic influence of program outcomes by presidents and members of Congress is limited. The major exceptions are direct statutory changes to existing programs. Lowi singles out the various cooperative-based federal credit programs that aid agriculture as an overt "private expropriation of public authority" (1969, 68).

Total outstanding loans of the federal credit programs are reported quarterly in the *Treasury Bulletin.* For the analysis that follows, a sample of fifteen programs was selected from more than one hundred programs represented in the quarterly reports. The sample programs include the largest subsidy programs to the household, corporate, and farm sectors of the economy. Total outstanding loans for the entire federal government and each program in the sample are reported in table 1.

The focus of the essay is the change over time in these outstanding loans. If outstanding loans increase, then the program is increasing the level of capital for the target sectors (through the creation of new loans directly or through the subsidy of new private loans). If outstanding loans decline, then the program is decreasing the level of capital for the target sector. This decrease may be caused either by selling existing loans on the private market (each sale diminishes available private capital) or decreasing the volume of new loan activity (new loans fail to keep pace with the maturity of existing loans). The empirical challenge appears to be straightforward. What influences the aggregate lending activity of the programs that we observe? How and to what extent do elected officials exercise meaningful control, through structural choice or other influences, over these programs?

Explaining Lending Activity over Time

Overview

A number of different factors influence the growth of the federal credit programs: structural characteristics of the agencies, features of the financial markets, changes in the broader economy, and variable characteristics of the political process outside of the agency (election calendar, budget allocation, party of the president). The expected effects of each set of characteristics—and measures for each—are described in turn. The structural features are given primary attention since these features are both established ex ante and updated ex post through acts of Congress.

Structural Characteristics of the Programs

The structural features of federal credit programs vary greatly. The most important structural choice is certainly the status of the program as part of an independent agency, a Cabinet department, or a GSE. In addition to agency status, at least three other structural choices are important for credit programs: authority to borrow directly from the public, authority to lend funds directly to the public, and the presence of ceilings on lending authority. These features are specified at the initiation of the

TABLE 1.   Size of the Federal Credit Programs (total and sample),
Total Outstanding Direct Loans, and Loans Guaranteed or Insured, 1991
(in thousands of dollars)

Type of Subsidy	Direct	Guarantee or Insurance
Total	484,927,421	989,349,308
Department of Agriculture		
Agricultural Credit Insurance Fund	17,906,040	4,383,448
Rural Housing Insurance Fund	29,246,446	26,965
Rural Electrification and Telephone	37,276,965	782,914
Department of Housing and Urban Development		
FHA Loan Guaranty Fund	9,315,920	378,450,558
Low-rent public housing	84,826	5,253,477
Department of Veteran's Affairs		
Veteran's Housing Insurance Program	3,637,395	53,817,725
Small Business Administration		
Business and investment loans	3,402,436	12,603,641
Export-Import Bank of the United States	8,923,559	5,391,027
Student Loan Marketing Association (Sallie Mae)	9,733,545	21,557,480
Federal National Mortgage Association (Fannie Mae)	124,954,000	—
Farm Credit System		
Banks for cooperatives	10,782,501	—
Farm credit banks (formerly federal land banks and federal intermediate credit banks)	39,811,774	—
Federal Housing Finance Board (formerly Federal Home Loan Bank Board)		
Advances to member banks	83,945,632	—
Federal Home Loan Mortgage Corporation (Freddie Mac)	23,523,889	—

Source: Treasury Bulletin (figures for quarter ending September 1991).

program, and in nearly all cases they are updated over time. Agency structure is not an exclusively ex ante instrument of political control since structural changes are not uncommon. But since costs of change are not trivial, structural choices—especially status as an independent or Cabinet agency—can be persistent.

Type of Agency

Three basic types of agencies implement federal credit programs—Cabinet departments, independent agencies, and government corporations. These agencies vary in the extent to which they are expected to respond to different types of political direction. The newest type of agency, the government-sponsored enterprise, is expected to be relatively unresponsive to efforts at political control. The instruments of political control are weak or nonexistent: appointments are typically restricted to a few members of a larger board, and the corporations are partially or entirely self-funded. Private stakeholders (investors and corporation management) place important and immediate constraints on agency practice. Expectations about the independent agencies and Cabinet departments are less clear. Kaufman (1976) expects the Cabinet departments to be fairly responsive to direction from the White House. Independent agencies require a more direct investment of White House monitoring and suasion to produce compliance with administration demands. For Kaufman, the principal mechanisms of ex post political control—appointments and appropriations—are more effective in influencing traditional Cabinet departments. Rourke (1978) instead expects that independent agencies will be more accommodating of administration demands. Cabinet departments serve a strong and well-organized constituency and pursue a well-institutionalized set of policy goals. Rourke describes how Roosevelt specifically set up the Rural Electrification Administration to bypass the internal politics of the Department of Agriculture. It was anticipated that the agency could be incorporated into the Cabinet department after agency leaders acquired administrative experience and cultivated a supportive constituency.

Since programs in each type of agency are expected to manage political cues in somewhat different ways, separate models of lending activity are estimated in this analysis—models for programs in Cabinet departments, models for programs administered in independent agencies, and a model for programs administered by a GSE. Comparing the effects of instruments of political control across agency type directly tests for differences in responsiveness. The only clear empirical implication of agency structural choice is that government-sponsored enterprises should be less responsive to political direction, in all forms, than either Cabinet department or independent agencies.

Sources of Funds

Federal credit programs have used three sources to raise capital: traditional appropriations, an exclusive federal intermediary that taps private capital (the Federal Financing Bank), and private investors. The government-sponsored enterprises have unique authority to directly issue debt to private investors. Programs in other agencies are dependent on budget appropriations to lend funds or (prior to 1986) financing through the Federal Financing Bank. Access to the FFB should increase lending and guarantee activity within the independent agencies and Cabinet departments. The abolition of the FFB in 1986 forced managers of independent agency and Cabinet programs to rely on conventional budget appropriations for financing but permitted government-sponsored enterprises to focus on private markets for continued funding.

Direct Lending or Guarantee

Direct lending requires substantial program funding. Lending requires the expenditure of agency resources in exchange for a (tenuous) flow of income in the future. For programs that have a large explicit subsidy, direct lending is the only way to provide capital to targeted borrowers. Programs that do not require very large subsidies can rely on insurance or guarantees. The insurance and guarantees make a somewhat risky loan or mortgage marginally attractive to private lenders. The guarantor agency is not compelled to spend agency resources in the short run and passes costs into the future (costs are contingent on future loan performance). Since direct lending requires resources, direct lending programs should respond immediately to changes in the federal budget. New guarantees, on the other hand, can be extended without fiscal consequences. Further, costs related to past guarantees can be represented as a fait accompli to new political leaders intent on rapidly scaling back agency spending. Decisions about how lending programs are structured—direct or guarantee—should influence the extent of political control through the budget.

Ceilings on Lending Authority

Most federal credit programs have indefinite authorizations (e.g., veteran's mortgage insurance programs are treated as entitlements rather than discretionary spending). Changes in budget allocations are likely to have a small effect on these programs, especially if there is no enforceable ceiling on lending activity. Ripley and Franklin (1980) identify ceilings as important constraints on the lending and guarantee activity of the Export-Import Bank in particular. Review and adjustment of ceilings on lending authority permits members of Congress to monitor the investment decisions of the bank. The initial choice of whether or not programs will be subject to lending ceilings affects the discretion of agency leaders in the future, making it more difficult to expand the program.

Each of these structural features—the existence of a guarantee program, the use of ceilings, and access to the Federal Financing Bank—are used by Congress to direct the expansion or contraction of the federal credit programs. Program management, while permitted substantial discretion over the timing and distribution of credit, faces important structural restraints upon the discretionary expansion of the programs it operates.

Variable Features of the External Political Environment

The incentives and capacity for political control of agency policy choices vary across agencies and over time. As was earlier suggested, the literature on political control focuses particularly on the effectiveness of appointments and budgets—the shared powers of Congress and the president. Four measures related to political control of agencies are included in the program-level models that follow.

Changing Preferences at the White House: The Appointment Mechanism

Wood and Waterman (1994) link the appointment of new agency leaders to changes in agency behavior. This strategy—measuring the impact of a new appointee—is effective for distinguishing between the effects of specific leadership changes and other changes in the political environment (control of key committees in Congress or formal statutory changes). Harris and Milkis (1996) identify appointments made by Reagan (Anne Burford at the Environmental Protection Agency and James

Miller III at the Federal Trade Commission) as key components of the effort to roll back regulation. For the federal credit programs, new appointees are expected to influence program activity and the preferences of appointees are likely to reflect the ideological positions of the appointing presidents. Republican presidents support less federal intervention in financial markets; Democratic presidents support more intervention. This ideological difference especially distinguishes the single Democratic president in the sample, Jimmy Carter, from his successor. Presidential appointees can change the balance between fiscal restraint and promotion of lending and guarantees programs. For Cabinet departments, this presidential influence is measured with the simple change in party control of the White House. For independent agencies and GSEs, presidential influence is measured with the appointment of a new administrator or board member after a change in party control of the White House.

A change in party control could lead to a host of other changes that represent attempts to exert political control. Harris and Milkis (1996) describe Reagan administration budget reallocations and innovative use of the Office of Management and Budget to control social regulatory agencies. But the instrument over which the president exerts the most direct control would certainly seem to be appointments. A simple indicator of the party of the president as a measure of program-level change fails to distinguish between passive adaptation of agency practice, the simple appointment mechanism, and other indirect White House tools. This indicator nevertheless permits an assessment of the relative importance of ex ante and ex post political control of agencies.

Congress and the Budget

One powerful if unwieldy instrument of political control is control of the purse. It is possible to obtain the direct funding of particular federal credit programs (or the ceilings for outstanding loans and guarantees in each program) to determine how members of Congress support each program, but these indicators are problematic. Current expenditures are a function of past lending decisions, and expenditures are therefore a reflection of a series of political choices in the past. Authorizations are similarly uninformative since most programs have an indefinite authorization—in the fifteen-agency sample only the Export-Import Bank of the United States and the Rural Electrification Program have ceilings on lending authority in 1991. Instead of attempting to capture exactly what members of Congress were attempting to direct to particular programs, each program is placed in a broader budget function. If the size of the allocation to farm income security declines, for instance, it is likely that the lending and guarantee activities of the Department of Agriculture credit programs will also decline. If more money is allocated for the advancement of commerce, lending and guarantee activities of the Export-Import Bank and the Small Business Administration should increase.

Budget changes are measured with the fiscal year to fiscal year difference in the amount of money authorized for the relevant budget subfunction.[1] It is expected that agency activity will vary directly with the budget allocation. This relationship should be much stronger for the direct loan programs than for the guarantee programs, as direct lending requires funding in the current fiscal year while guarantee programs pass costs (contingent upon loan performance) into the future.

Congressional Oversight and Action

In addition to budget choices, members of Congress have regular opportunities to monitor and occasional opportunities to reorganize federal credit programs. Credit programs may be addressed and reorganized in the course of broader hearings on agricultural policy, higher education, or veteran's benefits. Since hearings in these subject areas are frequent, it is difficult to use some subset of hearings as a measure of direct interest in or attention to the credit programs. Instead of using hearings, I examine specific instances of legislative action to measure the particular but nonbudget impact of Congress on agency outputs. Basic changes in agency structure or the scope of permissible financial market activity, initiated at the discretion of Congress, influence agency lending and guarantee activity.

Four actions by Congress directly target lending activity of sample agencies: the Agricultural Credit Act of 1987, the Omnibus Budget Reconciliation Acts of 1981 and 1986, and the Financial Institutions Reform, Recovery, and Enforcement Act of 1989 (FIRREA). Each piece of legislation either permitted the addition of new types of loans or debt instruments to the agency portfolio or required the sale of loans in the existing agency portfolio. The Farm Credit System was reorganized under the Agricultural Credit Act of 1987. The 1987 act increased the lending activity of credit banks and cooperatives and reduced the outstanding loans of the land banks to zero. In the 1981 Budget Reconciliation Act, Sallie Mae was given additional authority to consolidate loans and advance funds to state loan agencies. This extension of authority was soon followed by permission to borrow directly from private investors (instead of acquiring funds from the Federal Financing Bank). Both developments contributed to a rapid expansion of Sallie Mae. Language in the Budget Reconciliation Act in 1986 required the credit programs of the Farmers Home Administration to raise capital by selling loans from the agency portfolio. The same act permitted borrowers to prepay direct loans from the REA if those loans were paid for with private capital guaranteed by the REA.

The total volume of legislation affecting the operation and management of the federal credit programs is large and certainly not fully covered by the major changes just described. In the 1970s, legislation affecting the federal credit programs was summarized annually in a special analysis that accompanied the budget of the U.S. government.[2] More than ten pieces of legislation were reported each year in the early 1970s, and by the end of the decade twenty to thirty bills had been included in the summary. In the early Reagan administration, omnibus budget reconciliation bills were important tools for updating the credit programs. The four acts of Congress identified earlier as major reorganizations affecting sample programs were specifically designed to significantly broaden or reduce outstanding loans of particular federal credit programs. Bills that directly mentioned sample agencies but simply increased existing ceilings on guarantee and insurance activity were excluded. No significant legislation affecting the Export-Import Bank, the Small Business Administration Business Lending Program, or the Veteran's Administration (excepting elevation to Cabinet status) was observed in the sample period. (Both the Export-Import Bank and the Small Business Administration were granted new and broader authority in the 1970s, prior to the collection of quarterly data on outstanding loans and guarantees.)

Indirect Congressional Influence

A number of works on regulatory agencies have concluded that agencies passively adapt to changing preferences of members of Congress (notably Weingast and Moran 1983). A measure of congressional preferences—the median first-dimension coordinate of the D-NOMINATE scores for the Senate (described in Poole and Rosenthal 1997)—is included to distinguish the effects of structural choices from the passive updates to agency lending activity that could follow changes in the composition of Congress. There are a number of alternative measures (e.g., the chamber median for the House of Representatives or the median score for the committees that oversee the agencies charged with implementing the credit programs). In practice, all of these measures are highly correlated and the choice of measure does substantively affect model results. Ultimately, the Senate measure was selected since party control of the Senate changed over the sample period. The chamber median was used since jurisdiction over the credit programs is often unclear and occasionally contested; this is particularly the case for the Farm Credit System, which is monitored by both the Banking and Agriculture committees in the Senate and the various housing programs, which are monitored and updated by the Agriculture and Veteran's Affairs and Banking committees in the Senate. Overall, a more conservative Senate is expected to restrict the growth of credit programs of all types.

Elections

Elections create special incentives for politicians, for delivery of benefits to constituents during election years can shape subjective perceptions of the competence of an incumbent. The simple intuition that politicians have incentives to time benefits to correspond to elections motivates investigations of the so-called political business cycle (Nordhaus 1975), as well as other program-level cycles in benefits and subsidies. Keech and Pak (1989) identify effects from the election calendar on veterans' benefits prior to 1978. Corder (1998) finds substantial election year increases in the lending activity of the Small Business Administration. To control for the effects of elections on the guarantee and lending activity of the federal credit programs, I include a dummy variable for presidential election years and a dummy variable for midterm congressional election years. The magnitude of the election effect should be smallest for the government-sponsored enterprises, privately owned corporations with only weak formal links to the White House.

Economic and Financial Market Conditions

Prime Rate

The interest rate charged to borrowers is one of the most important financial market conditions that affect agency choices about lending as well as the demand for federal guarantees and insurance. The real prime rate (prime rate less inflation) is an excellent proxy for these borrowing costs. The expected direction of the effect of the prime rate is clear for direct lending and somewhat less clear for guarantee activity. For direct lending, an increase in the prime rate should result in growth in the amount of outstanding loans. For guarantee activity, the federal credit programs are dependent upon private lenders and borrowers applying for guarantee. If the prime rate moves upward, private borrowers may be reluctant to take out new loans. The prime rate should be positively related to direct lending but may be negatively related to guarantee and insurance activity.

Capital Flows

Capital flows into and out of various sectors of the economy should trigger changes in the level of lending and guarantees through the credit programs. Since federal credit programs attempt to divert credit from one sector to another (or at least to increase the level of capital flowing to particular sectors), variation in the flow of capital should be an important consideration for agency managers. If the flow of capital to the household sector, the financial sector, or the farm sector declines, that decline should trigger increased direct lending activity to that sector in the following year.[3]

Income

A final component of agency considerations should be the economic performance of the sector served by the program. Declining real income to particular sectors of the economy—farm income, household income, corporate profits—should lead to increased subsidy activity. Table 2 summarizes the target sectors (and budget subfunction) of each of the sample programs.

One-Time Shocks and Distributed Lags

It is unlikely that the changes in political or economic conditions just described would have an immediate and one-time impact on agency activities. Since the process of loan application and approval is lengthy, agency activities are somewhat persistent in the face of shocks or changes. For that reason, a lag of changes in loans and guarantees outstanding is included in the model. Gujarati (1995) describes this as a partial adjustment model. The substantive intuition is that there is some long-run equilibrium level of outstanding direct and guaranteed loans in the agency portfolio *given* current economic and political conditions. Changes in the composition of the Congress, budget, prime rate, or economy depress or inflate the desired or optimal level for outstanding loans or guarantees, but the adjustment to the new optimal level is partial in any one year. The observed change in outstanding loans or guarantees is a product of current and past shocks. Interpretation of the coefficients in the partial adjustment model is not substantively different from interpretation in the less general model.

TABLE 2.   Sample Program Characteristics

Agency	Budget Subfunction	Sector
Department of Agriculture		
Agricultural Credit Insurance Fund	Farm income	Farm
Rural Housing Insurance Fund	Mortgage credit	Household
Rural Electrification and Telephone	Farm income	Farm
Department of Housing and Urban Development		
FHA Loan Guaranty Fund	Mortgage credit	Household
Low-rent public housing	Housing assistance	Household
Department of Veteran's Affairs		
Veteran's Housing Insurance Program	Veteran's affairs	Household
Small Business Administration		
Business and investment loans	Other advancement of commerce	Corporate
Export-Import Bank of the United States	Other advancement of commerce	Corporate
Student Loan Marketing Association (Sallie Mae)	Higher education	Financial
Federal National Mortgage Association (Fannie Mae)	Mortgage credit	Financial
Farm Credit System		
Banks for cooperatives	Farm income	Farm
Farm credit banks (formerly federal land banks and federal intermediate credit banks)	Farm income	Farm
Federal Housing Finance Board (formerly Federal Home Loan Bank Board)		
Advances to member banks	Mortgage credit	Financial
Federal Home Loan Mortgage Corporation (Freddie Mac)	Mortgage credit	Financial

Source: Guide to the Flow of Funds, Board of Governors, Federal Reserve System; Policy Agendas Project, U.S. Budget Authority Data Set (1947–95).

Models and Estimates

Estimation Strategy

Direct lending and guarantee activity for fifteen programs are used to estimate the responses of program management to changing economic and political conditions. Five panel models are estimated—guarantee activity and direct lending activity for the Cabinet departments and the independent agencies and direct lending of government-sponsored enterprises.[4] The dependent variable in each instance is the standardized level of real loans outstanding for each program.[5] Each series begins in 1975, after the initial establishment and early growth of the GSEs, and ends in 1991, the final year in which quarterly lending activity is reported in the *Treasury Bulletin*.

The modeling approach adopted is fairly conventional: program outputs are treated as a linear function of a subset of variables expected to influence agency policy choices. Two methodological issues merit particular attention: estimation with panel data and simultaneity. The panel structure of the program data offers more information than a single series or a single cross-sectional sample, but it also presents a methodological challenge. Both heterskedasticity and serial correlation complicate the estimation of model parameters. There are a number of alternative estimation strategies that could be used to recover the parameters of the model. Beck and Katz (1995, 1996) compare the performance of ordinary least squares (OLS) with panel-corrected standard errors and feasible generalized least squares (GLS). Hsiao (1986) describes less general fixed effect approaches (OLS with dummy variables). Ordinary least squares with panel-corrected standard errors accounts for the correlation of error both within and across panel units and appears to offer a substantial improvement over alternative methods. However, introduction of a lagged dependent variable creates new complications in this context. Estimates of coefficients in the panel model are inconsistent since the lagged dependent variable may be correlated with the error term. This correlation can stem from both serial correlation and the unit effects that are incorporated in the error term (especially in panels with many cross sections and few time periods). The credit program panel is marginally time dominated, so unit effects are not highly problematic, but inconsistency could be introduced by means of serial correlation. Using conventions described in Greene (2000), a Lagrange multiplier test for serial correlation is reported for each of the models. Serial correlation is only problematic in the annual models of programs in Cabinet departments, so it is appropriate in most cases to use the simple OLS estimator with panel-corrected standard errors.

The remaining methodological consideration, the problem of simultaneity, can be particularly problematic when ultimate outcomes of agency policy choices are selected as the dependent variable. If ultimate outcomes are modeled as a function of congressional actions *and* congressional actions are responses to these same outcomes, then independent OLS estimates of either relationship would be biased and inconsistent. The dependent variable in the models is not the ultimate outcome—the volume and price of capital for particular borrowers—but an intermediate policy instrument (lending and guarantee activity). It is likely that structural changes to the credit programs are a function of ultimate outcomes—high interest rates, declining capital, or declining sector income. These real and visible credit market problems both affect agency decisions about the volume of lending and motivate Congress to broaden agency lending powers. This suggests that structural changes and measures of financial market performance could be collinear but that the simultaneity will not frustrate the use of a single-equation OLS approach to estimating the impact of structural choices on agency lending activity.

Estimates

Independent Agencies

Table 3 reports model estimates for programs administered by independent agencies. The structural features of the agency—access to the federal financing bank and ceilings on lending activity—have the expected effects. The effects of ceilings described by Ripley and Franklin (1980) are higher for the direct lending programs than for the guarantee programs in similar agencies. Access to the FFB permitted higher levels of lending and guarantee activity—the average liability of an independent agency direct lending program was $11.0 billion higher before the termination of the FFB. Critics of FFB financing feared that agencies could use the bank as an alternative funding source outside the direct control of Congress. The independent agencies were able to expand the pool of loans and guarantees more rapidly when FFB financing was an alternative.

Contrary to expectations derived from the work of Kaufman (1976), election cues and other measures of political influence affected independent agencies to a greater extent than it affected Cabinet departments (or the GSEs). Direct lending activity increases during presidential election years. Guarantees expand during both presidential and midterm election years. Major legislative initiatives also expanded secondary market intervention of the GSE Sallie Mae and direct lending to agriculture during midterm election years (1982 and 1986). The link between the preferences of elected officials and agency guarantee activity extends to more direct measures of political influence. The levels of outstanding

TABLE 3.   Capital Market Intervention: Independent Agencies

	Dependent variable: Standardized real agency loans outstanding	
Explanatory Variables	Direct Loans	Guarantees
Act of Congress (legislation)	n/a[a]	n/a[a]
Financed through Federal Financing Bank	1.37**	1.12**
	(0.48)	(0.42)
Ceilings on lending authority	−0.750**	−0.970**
	(0.37)	(0.35)
Cost of capital (real prime rate)	0.016	0.105**
	(0.06)	(0.04)
Sector income (lagged net income)	−0.288*	0.142
	(0.15)	(0.14)
Capital flow into sector (lagged net liabilities)	0.156	0.173
	(0.13)	(0.11)
Presidential election year	0.577**	0.468**
	(0.23)	(0.19)
Midterm election year	−0.113	0.547**
	(0.23)	(0.18)
Party of president (Republican)	−0.290	−0.513**
	(0.25)	(0.19)
Congressional ideology	−0.741	−4.38**
	(2.99)	(2.22)
Budget subfunction allocation (annual first difference)	0.032	−0.320**
	(0.12)	(0.13)
Lagged dependent variable	0.296	0.420**
	(0.18)	(0.10)
Constant	−0.244	−0.780**
	(0.51)	(0.37)
R^2	.48	.58
Lagrange multiplier test for first-order serial correlation	1.24	0.04

Note: Panel-corrected standard errors are in parentheses.
*$p < .10$ **$p < .05$
[a]No major legislation.

loans and guarantees are much lower under Republican presidents. Guarantee program activity is also linked to changes in the ideological composition of the Senate (a proxy for broader changes in congressional preferences). Outstanding guaranteed loans decline as the Senate becomes more conservative. The magnitude of the effect of congressional preferences is marginally smaller than the effect of presidential influence. Average outstanding liabilities contract by $15 billion under a Republican president and by $11 billion when congressional ideology shifts consistently with the changes in the Senate in 1981 (when the chamber majority shifted from Democratic to Republican). No corresponding effect is observed in the direct lending activity of the independent agencies.

Federal budget priorities are strongly and inversely related to guarantee activity. Agency managers expand guarantee activity when Congress reduces the allocation to the relevant budget subfunction. The program thus incurs few current costs but transfers the contingent liability for the guaranteed lending to the future. The impact of the budget implied by the estimates is not that the budget signals to program managers to expand or contract subsidy activity but that program managers simply use loan guarantee programs (rather than direct loans) to influence capital flows when budget resources are scarce.

The link between economic conditions and program outputs is consistent with expectations. Aggregate lending activity is countercyclical. Guarantee activity increases when the cost of capital increases, and direct lending activity expands as sector income declines. But neither direct nor guarantee programs respond as expected to changes in the flow of capital. As outstanding liabilities (borrowing) contract, the independent agencies do not act to increase the flow of capital to affected sectors. Despite the failure of some of economic controls to predict lending activity as expected, each of the models summarized in tables 3, 4, and 5 explains a substantial part of the variation in program lending activity.

Cabinet Departments

Results for Cabinet department programs are displayed in table 4. The residuals from the models are highly serially correlated, so the OLS estimator is inconsistent and inference is problematic. Overall, the selected controls and structural characteristics explain very little of the volume of lending activity of these programs. Ex ante structural features of the program only marginally affect program outputs. Only a single structural feature—access to the Federal Financing Bank—is statistically significant. This result is consistent with the estimates reported for independent agencies and suggests that restricting access to capital, accomplished with the termination of the FFB, reduced the growth rates of the federal credit programs in Cabinet departments and independent agencies. Ceilings did not curtail lending and guarantee activity. Major changes in lending and guarantee activity are instead a direct consequence of a limited number of statutory changes (particularly changes in the agricultural credit programs). The guarantee programs in the

TABLE 4.   Capital Market Intervention: Cabinet Departments

	Dependent variable: Standardized real agency loans outstanding	
Explanatory Variables	Direct Loans	Guarantees
Act of Congress (legislation)	1.05**	0.826**
	(0.21)	(0.20)
Financed through Federal Financing Bank	−0.345	0.442**
	(0.27)	(0.14)
Ceilings on lending authority	−0.146	0.146
	(0.12)	(0.13)
Cost of capital (real prime rate)	−0.049	0.069**
	(0.03)	(0.02)
Sector income (lagged net income)	0.027	−0.151**
	(0.06)	(0.05)
Capital flow into sector (lagged net liabilities)	0.115*	0.035
	(0.07)	(0.05)
Presidential election year	−0.067	0.066
	(0.13)	(0.09)
Midterm election year	−0.086	0.117
	(0.13)	(0.09)
Party of president (Republican)	0.285	0.246**
	(0.20)	(0.129)
Congressional ideology	1.12	−3.17**
	(1.95)	(1.22)
Budget subfunction allocation (annual first difference)	−0.065	0.036
	(0.07)	(0.06)
Lagged dependent variable	0.412**	0.640**
	(0.13)	(0.057)
Constant	0.237	−0.958**
	(0.457)	(0.28)
R^2	.66	.82
Lagrange multiplier test for first-order serial correlation	17.35**	8.76**

Note: Panel-corrected standard errors are in parentheses.
*$p < 10$ **$p < .05$

Cabinet are, like independent agency lending activity, countercyclical. Guarantees are expanded as the cost of capital increases and sector income declines.

Tables 3 and 4 highlight likely consequences of moving a program from an independent agency to a Cabinet department. Cabinet departments are more likely than independent agencies to be the target of direct congressional actions intended to update program activity. The Cabinet department programs are given more specific direction to accommodate new classes of borrowers or to transfer funds across loan programs. Cabinet programs are less responsive than independent agencies to electoral politics but, like programs in independent agencies, lending volume decreases as more Republicans enter the Senate. The effect of a Republican appointee on Cabinet guarantee programs is unexpected: a Republican White House is associated with modestly higher levels of guarantee activity in the Cabinet department programs. Congress faces a trade-off with elevation to cabinet status: more opportunities for direct control but lower levels of response to both economic and political changes that would be expected to stimulate lending activity.

The Cabinet agency models indicate that congressional action in the form of legislation is a key tool for affecting program outputs. This is somewhat unsurprising given the history of reform and reorganization of federal credit institutions. But this source of congressional control has been neglected in the literature on political control of the bureaucracy. This neglect is either by assumption (legislation is too costly) or reflected in empirical tests (where effects of congressional ideology rather than congressional action are examined). Program outputs of the direct lending programs do not reflect passive adaptation by agencies to a changing Congress. Instead, members of Congress do, in practice, overcome problems of scarce resources and collective action to pass legislation that directly affects outputs of the credit programs.

Government-Sponsored Enterprises

Table 5 reports estimates for the government-sponsored enterprises. The direct lending component of the enterprises responds in expected ways to the costs of capital, but, like the direct lending activity of the Cabinet department programs, it reinforces changing levels of borrowing (rather than counteracting declines in available capital). The estimates reveal one important difference between the GSEs and the credit programs located in the Cabinet and independent agencies. The effects of an important structural change are quite different. When Congress abolished the Federal Financing Bank as a source of capital, rules for the use and acquisition of private capital were liberalized for the GSEs. After these rules for access to private capital were relaxed, the GSE programs expanded. Elimination of the FFB set the stage for the expansion of the GSEs relative to programs in the Cabinet and independent agencies.

Like the independent agencies, the GSEs expand lending activity during election years. This result is inconsistent with the expectation of minimal opportunities for political control over these quasi-public agencies.

TABLE 5.   Capital Market Intervention: Government-Sponsored Enterprise

Dependent variable: Standardized real agency loans outstanding	
Explanatory Variables	Direct Loans
Act of Congress (legislation)	0.345**
	(0.09)
Financed through Federal Financing Bank	−0.229**
	(0.12)
Ceilings on lending authority	n/a
Cost of capital (real prime rate)	0.052**
	(0.02)
Sector income (lagged net income)	0.094*
	(0.05)
Capital flow into sector (lagged net liabilities)	0.229**
	(0.04)
Presidential election year	0.260**
	(0.10)
Midterm election year	0.007
	(0.10)
Party of president (Republican)	−0.051
	(0.13)
Congressional ideology	−0.438
	(1.02)
Budget subfunction allocation (annual first difference)	−0.047
	(0.04)
Lagged dependent variable	0.676**
	(0.06)
Constant	−0.246
	(0.20)
R^2	.83
Lagrange multiplier test for first-order serial correlation	.24

Note: Panel-corrected standard errors are in parentheses.
$*p < .10$ $**p < .05$

The expected increase in net secondary market purchases during an election year would be in excess of $10 billion. But the restriction of GSE activity to transactions in direct, private loans that are without guarantees has important consequences for the extent of political control over agency activity. With the exception of Sallie Mae, the GSEs purchase or advance only nonguaranteed loans. Model estimates for lending activity of independent agencies and Cabinet departments reveal that political influence is most visible for the guarantee rather than the direct lending programs. This result extends to the GSEs, for GSE advances or purchases of loans do not vary as either the partisanship of appointees or the ideological composition of the Congress changes. Like the independent agencies and the Cabinet department direct lending programs, only structural choices by Congress and elections affect the volume of lending activity by these private corporations. This result suggests that decisions about how lending is to be subsidized, directly or through guarantees or insurance, are more important than decisions about the type of agency that will ultimately administer the program.

Conclusion

What do the federal credit programs collectively tell us about political control? First, program structure matters. The presence of some very basic structural effects is a clear indicator that ex ante instruments of political control can operate as expected: ceilings and funding sources have substantial effects on program growth. Second, congressional decisions both to reorganize existing programs (under FIRREA or the Agricultural Credit Act) and to terminate the FFB reveal that structural choices are not permanent. Members of Congress act to update the structure of the credit programs. Six decisions by Congress—four legislative updates to the lending practices of credit programs, termination of the Federal Financing Bank, and the creation of the Department of Veteran's Affairs—account for the major structural changes observed for these fifteen programs over a sixteen-year period. Finally, the choice of policy instrument, direct loans or loan guarantees or insurance, also matters. Loan guarantee programs are more responsive to measures of political influence and appear to be more amenable to political control by elected officials.

The federal credit programs, located in a variety of agencies, offer a distinctive avenue for investigating the effects of structural choices. Federal credit programs are updated and reorganized frequently. Legislation affects the terms of loans, eligible borrowers, and the allocation of agency resources across guarantee, insurance, and direct lending programs. In the case of federal credit programs, structural controls complement shared powers of appointment and budgets. This general feature of credit programs—structure is altered by contemporary actors—suggests that variation in agency structure needs to be more broadly incorporated into the political control literature. The observed structural changes challenge some presumptions of the extant political control literature. Reorganization is patently inconsistent with any description of members of Congress as disinterested or passive. Reorganization also compels us to question the existence of high and unmanageable costs of statutory change. Members of Congress dissatisfied with the capital market outcomes can reform the program to address contemporary needs.

These types of change in program structure blur the distinction, in practice, between ex post and ex ante instruments of political control. Agency structure is conventionally identified as an instrument of ex ante control. Structure is fixed at agency creation and difficult to manipulate. Instead, the federal credit programs indicate that the Congress updates structural features. Agency structure is updated ex post. The federal credit programs instruct us that this type of ambitious and expensive rehabilitation of agencies is not uncommon. Reorganization and direct instructions, like appointments and budgets, are credible instruments of political control that are used in the American context with surprising frequency.

Notes

1. Budget data are extracted from the Policy Agendas Project, U.S. Budget Authority Data Set (1947–95). The data used here were originally collected by Frank R. Baumgartner and Bryan D. Jones with the support of National Science Foundation and are distributed through the Center for American Politics and Public Policy at the University of Washington. Neither the foundation nor the original collectors of the data bear any responsibility for the analysis reported here.

2. "Special Analysis F, federal credit programs," Budget of the U.S. government, various fiscal years.

3. All data on sector income and capital flows are extracted from the quarterly *Guide to the Flow of Federal Funds* published by the Board of Governors of the Federal Reserve System. Capital flows are lagged one period in order to avoid problems of simultaneity. The prime rate series is available from the Federal Reserve Economic Database, Federal Reserve Bank of St. Louis.

4. Only a single government-sponsored enterprise, Sallie Mae, conducts secondary market operations with guaranteed loans. There are insufficient degrees of freedom to estimate the model with the limited annual data.

5. Each program series is standardized to have a mean of zero and a standard deviation of one. This permits comparison across programs of different size. With the exception of Sallie Mae, the standardized series are trend stationary.

Administrative Structure and Social Democratic Results: The Case of Education

Kevin B. Smith

The fundamental administrative challenge of any purposive organization is to specify and prioritize those purposes (Simon 1997, 1). Public bureaucracies find this challenge difficult because they are routinely charged with vague, multiple, and often contradictory missions (Wilson 1989; Meier 1997; Downs and Larkey 1986). Scholars have long recognized that this lack of clarity about ends elevates the importance of means. Administrative structure, the organizational characteristics that shape decision-making processes, exerts a powerful influence on the objectives public agencies pursue (Wilson 1989, 33–38; Simon 1997; Barnard 1968).

The importance of administrative structure thus has an important, and understudied, implication for public sector reform: altering the organizational characteristics that frame decision-making processes may change how public agencies prioritize their missions. Using public education as an exploratory case, I explore this possibility by examining variation between school goals and two elements of administrative structure: (1) whether a school is organized as a public bureaucracy or a private entrepreneurial institution and (2) the degree of discretionary-authority vested in operative employees (teachers). In a multivariate analysis, I find that these variables predict variation for some school goals, supporting the inference that administrative structure can determine organizational mission priorities. The findings imply that popular proposals for public sector reform may change the goals public agencies pursue, not just the means used to achieve those goals.

Agency Goals and Administrative Structure

The importance of administrative structure to agency goals is reflected in the two dominant theoretical perspectives on public sector organization. The Wilsonian/Weberian orthodoxy of public administration scholarship advocates public service provision through bureaucracies in centralized jurisdictions. Decision-making authority (at least formally) is concentrated at the top of such organizations, and the behavior of operative employees is constrained by rules and regulations (Lowery 1982; Weber 1922). In contrast, the public choice challenge to this orthodoxy argues for a competitive market for public services in which producers have no guaranteed clientele and decision-making authority is pushed downward to operative employees (Osborne and Gaebler 1993; Lowery 1982). These theoretical differences reflect underlying differences over the appropriate goals of public agencies. Administrative orthodoxy orients public agencies toward accountability, representativeness, equality, and welfare, while public choice orients public service providers toward the market norms of utility, efficiency, productivity, and profitability (Haque 1996). This implies that shifting to more marketlike structural arrangements will institutionalize market norms in the administrative process and in doing so reorder their mission priorities.

As an example, consider the potential sources of public agency goals and the criteria for successfully achieving them. Moe and Gilmour (1995) argue that public agencies traditionally derived their missions from public law, a practice reinforced by top-down bureaucracies with strong ties to representative institutions. Market-based organizations are bottom up; they deliberately loosen this connection to democratic institutions and force public agencies to derive their missions from the demands of their clienteles. This offers one explanation for why agency goals shift with organizational changes: different institutional arrangements result in agencies using different sources to create mission priorities. These differences also create different criteria for evaluating goal accomplishment. The orthodox approach will use process-oriented criteria such as due process, equity of treatment, and adherence to rules, with the public choice perspective stressing efficiency in the production of outcomes (McCabe and Vinzant 1999).

Despite these differences, there is a common hypothesis: priorities and goals follow the organizational characteristics that shape decision-making processes. Of course, there is considerable disagreement on what priorities will change in any given instance and whether these changes will promote a desirable evolution of public bureaucracy. Public choice advocates argue that their prescriptions will lead to mission clarity. A public service market will send clear signals on clientele preference, and competitive organizations with greater decision-making authority vested in operative employees will be able to identify and quickly respond to those preferences [Tiebout 1956; Osborne and Gaebler 1993). Backers of administrative orthodoxy argue there is no particular reason to believe homogenous sub-groups of citizens will produce agency goals that are representative of the public interest, and may directly contradict the preferences produced by the democratic process, or even the egalitarian mandates of the constitution. The clear mission, in other words, may not be particularly compatible with the progressive underpinnings of administrative orthodoxy (Lowery 1982; McCabe and Vinzant 1999).[1]

Arguments on both sides can be powerful in a normative sense, but none can draw on much systematic empirical work for support. Advocates of reform often take mission priorities as givens or as universally beneficial outcomes of the reorganization process (Osborne and Gaebler 1993; Osborne and Plastrik 1998). Likewise, those with orthodox sympathies tend to assume that the top-down arrangement provides clear enough guidelines and boundaries to connect the behavior of street-level bureaucrats with the often vague laws that purportedly define agency missions (Lipsky 1980). Whether the orthodox arrangements actually are responsible for divining specific public interest missions from this top-down source and whether public choice arrangements can preserve them in its absence are open questions (Meier 1997; Osborne and Plastrik 1998; Goodsell 1994).

Given that they have been a particular target of efforts to replace the institutional arrangements favored by administrative orthodoxy with those favored by public choice, schools make a good choice to test the underlying question of whether variation in administrative structure determines agency goals.

Organizational Structure and School Goals

There are two dominant views on how organizational structure can determine the specific objectives pursued by schools. These mirror the orthodoxy/public choice divide in the public administration literature.

One argues that schools are agents of the state and should be organized so that decision making is guided by the preferences of representative institutions and the law. A top-down, hierarchical arrangement orients teachers (operative employees) toward these preferences through rules such as curriculum requirements. In purposive specifics, the goals pursued by schools are products of the democratic processes and are externally imposed by representative institutions and their bureaucratic management mechanisms. This assumes that top-down, external controls effectively shape behavior at the classroom level (see Smith and Meier 1995, 93–106).

The second perspective argues that top-down, external controls are of limited use in shaping the mission of public education agencies. Democratic processes and institutions rarely formulate clear goals, in practice giving state and local administrative agents the autonomy to determine mission priorities. This means that self-interested bureaucracies, not the democratic process or laudable, but highly abstract, constitutional principles, will determine what schools do. Even if clear missions were thrown up by the democratic process, it is unclear that they could be achieved because each layer in the educational hierarchy has a limited ability to control the actions of the layer below it, a situation that diffuses responsibility and invites shirking (Chubb and Moe 1990). This perspective favors transferring the power to shape school missions to those who are on the receiving end of educational objectives—students and parents—and giving teachers and local school officials the discretionary authority to pursue those missions. The expected results are clarified school goals, operative employees with the decision-making latitude to achieve them, and, with the exit option available, immediate accountability for failing to achieve them (see Hirschman 1970).

Chubb and Moe (1988, 1990) articulated the best-known theoretical treatment of this argument. Chubb and Moe noted that public schools operate in complex environments, with large and heterogeneous constituencies stretching far beyond parents and students. Organized interests ranging from teachers' unions to textbook publishers vie with each other to get the democratic institutions controlling educational policy to respond to their preferences. This complexity manifests itself in numerous regulations, standards, methods and mandates. The result is broad, vague, and even contradictory goals, reflecting the compromises inherent in democratic policy-making. Given the nature of school organization, this environment directs purposive action toward enforcing rules and regulations, a form of goal substitution in which bureaucratic means become organizational ends.

Chubb and Moe claim that this complicated external environment and the bureaucratic decision-making framework it promotes are common to virtually all public schools and so is the consequence of concentrating goal-making power in nonelected bureaucracies. Accordingly, in order to assess the impact of structure on organizational mission public schools should be compared to private schools. Private schools have less complex environments: small, homogeneous constituencies with an exit option. In theory, the exit option translates into immediate and clear signals on organizational mission and performance. If schools do not respond to clientele preference, the clientele votes with its feet and goes elsewhere. This simpler environment and more direct feedback loop means a more focused administrative structure. Private schools have few external controls and are internally regulated by the demands of their clienteles, characteristics that make decision making easier: goals are clarified, and the exit option provides clear signals on what decisions help deliver on those organizational goals. Chubb and Moe's theory, then, supports the hypothesis that administrative structure will produce different mission priorities in public and private schools.

Simply by their existence, private schools demonstrate that they are better than public schools at achieving some goals for some people. Of course, this does not answer the questions of what goals they are pursuing and how they are different from the goals of public schools. The general assumption is that a shift toward market-based institutional forms will promote the goal of academic excellence, which is presented as a universally desirable goal (Chubb and Moe 1990, 82). In contrast, public schools will be oriented toward the lowest common denominator because they are controlled by a process dealing with ambiguity and internal inconsistency and aimed toward compromise. As a result, they will "ordinarily find it politically and organizationally difficult to place high priority on academic excellence" (Chubb and Moe 1988, 1080). Schools freed from external regulatory control will have clearer goals and can provide teachers with greater discretional authority to take the actions necessary to achieve those goals.

Critics of this perspective argue that the assumption that market-based reforms will force schools to prioritize academic excellence is largely untested. Both sides expect priorities to change with institutional reform, though whether these will shift toward academic excellence, more constitutionally dubious missions such as racial segregation or religious indoctrination, or some other unforeseen mix of objectives is unknown. Yet, if school goals can actually be measured, the debate over how structure impacts educational mission priorities is an empirical question.

School Goals

Defining the goals of education is a controversial normative undertaking (Tyack and Cuban 1995, 43). Yet it is possible to empirically establish what school mission priorities *are,* even if philosophical agreement on what they *should be* is impossible: whatever goals schools seek to achieve, they are ultimately dependent upon teachers adopting and actually pursuing them (Tyack and Cuban 1995; Nuthall 1999). Whether they enforce externally imposed mandates or respond to internal student/parent demands, teachers play the key implementation role in achieving school objectives. Whatever schools do in theory, in practice the goals are decided by teachers when the classroom door is closed (Hess 1999, 37).

If the arguments characterizing the administrative orthodoxy/public choice debate are valid, the goals teachers pursue should thus vary in a predictable fashion with organizational characteristics that shape decision making. For example, inculcation of religious and moral codes is likely to have a higher priority in private schools. Public schools are prohibited de jure from religious indoctrination, and the machinery of external democratic control (including the courts charged with interpreting the laws of democratic institutions) goes to some lengths to enforce this ban. Freed from this external control, parochial systems are able to make some form of religious indoctrination a specific educational objective and teachers have the legal freedom to take action to achieve this goal.

Both perspectives predict that public schools will pursue a broader set of objectives than private schools do. This reflects the difference between responding to the complex and conflicting priorities thrown up by the democratic process and responding to a more homogeneous set of preferences expressed by a particular group of consumers. Freed from the distractions of multiple interests imposed by external control, public choice predicts that a higher priority will be placed on academic excellence in private schools. Administrative orthodoxy predicts that private sector priorities will sometimes prioritize goals—such as religious indoctrination—

that for various reasons have been found incompatible with the broad re-publican mission of public education.

Tables 1 and 2 provide mixed confirmation of these expectations. The data are from a national survey conducted by the National Center for Education Statistics (1998) that asked teachers what they considered the most important educational goals. Table 1 breaks down the goals respondents indicated were most important by public and private sector. Table 2 breaks down these goals based on the level of discretionary authority teachers have over pedagogical matters such as classroom topics, teaching methods, and the like. These tables do show some interesting differences in mission priorities between public and private schools. Instilling moral

TABLE 1.   Primary Teaching/Educational Goal by Type of School

Goal	Public School	Private School
Encouraging academic excellence	10.8	12.1
Promoting occupational or vocational/ technical skills	2.6	.3
Promoting good work habits	13.7	9.5
Promoting personal growth	19.7	19.4
Promoting human relations skills	2.2	1.3
Promoting specific moral values or foster- ing religious/spiritual development	1.3	24.6
Building basic literacy skills	49.7	32.9

Note: The figures reflect the percentage of teachers considering the goal most important. See the appendix for data sources.

TABLE 2.   Primary Teaching/Educational Goal by Degree of Teacher Autonomy

Goal	High Autonomy	Low Autonomy
Encouraging academic excellence	12	10
Promoting occupational or vocational/ technical skills	2	1.8
Promoting good work habits	11.7	13.5
Promoting personal growth	20.6	18.2
Promoting human relations skills	2.1	1.7
Promoting specific moral values or foster- ing religious/spiritual development	8.7	7.3
Building basic literacy skills	42.9	47.6

Note: The figures reflect the percentage of teachers considering the goal most important. High autonomy is defined as teachers indicating that they had complete control over selecting instructional materials, classroom content, teaching techniques, grading, and enforcing discipline. Low autonomy is defined as teachers indicating that they had no control over these items. See the appendix for data sources.

or religious codes, as expected, is a much higher mission priority in private schools, with 24.6 percent of private school teachers listing this as their primary educational objective, versus 1.3 percent of public school teachers. Instilling basic literacy is the most common objective for public and private schools, but public schools give it considerably more emphasis, with nearly 50 percent of public school teachers ranking it as their most important goal compared to about 33 percent of private school teachers.[2] The other five goals listed in the survey, however, are more evenly ranked, and here the differences between public and private schools are relatively trivial. Importantly, academic excellence is roughly evenly balanced, with about 11 percent of public school teachers and 12 percent of private school teachers ranking it as their most important goal. The other goals listed in the survey, promoting vocational/technical skills, personal growth (student self-esteem and self-knowledge), good work habits, and human relations skills, are also roughly evenly matched (see the appendix at the end of this essay for complete variable descriptions). There is less variation in table 2, though teachers with higher levels of discretionary authority do seem to place slightly less emphasis on basic literacy. Generally speaking, though, the degree of teacher autonomy seems to have only a trivial impact on the setting of mission priorities.

Table 1 thus presents a picture that is only somewhat consistent with the basic theoretical expectations of how structure impacts school goals. Private schools have a greater focus on academic excellence and also accord instilling religious codes a higher priority. But these differences are in degree rather than kind. If these percentages are used to rank goals, schools tend to look more alike than different. Public schools rank, in order, basic literacy, personal growth, and instilling good work habits as their three primary goals. Private schools rank, in order, basic literacy, instilling moral or religious codes, and personal growth. Academic excellence is ranked fourth for both public and private schools. Table 2 raises questions even about degree—the level of teacher autonomy has no impact on the ranking of goals: basic literacy, personal growth, and instilling good work habits rank one, two, and three and are within a few percentage points of each other in both columns.

Still, these tables present a fairly unsophisticated picture of the variation among educational objectives and say nothing at all about how organizational type and discretionary authority might create differing mission priorities. To shed more definitive light on the theoretical expectations, a multivariate analysis is required.

A Multivariate Model of the Determinants
of Educational Objectives

The primary goal of the multivariate analysis is to isolate the correlates of goal selection among teachers. The dependent variables are the seven goals listed in table 1, coded to reflect which of these goals a respondent considers his or her primary educational objective. The key predictor variables are a dummy variable indicating whether the respondent is at a private or a public school, and two variables that seek to tap the discretionary authority of teachers. The latter two are additive indexes constructed from six response items related to pedagogical influence (teacher influence in selecting instructional materials, classroom content, teaching techniques, grading, discipline enforcement, and homework assignments) and school policy influence (teacher influence in setting curriculum requirements, discipline policy, topics for teacher training, and student assignment mechanisms). To account for the potential unique impacts of private schools that grant high degrees of autonomy to teachers, I also use interaction terms between the public/private and discretionary authority variables. Together these provide the base test of whether administrative structure determines which educational goals teachers pursue.[3]

There are other potential determinants of what goals teachers decide to prioritize. Student and parent characteristics are a logical determinant of educational objectives. A teacher at an elite prep school has a different set of possibilities in terms of educational goals than a special education teacher in an inner city school. Student attributes such as apathy/enthusiasm, academic background, or demonstrated cognitive capacity obviously may play an important role in determining the objectives a teacher will choose to pursue. Objectives may be further constrained by the socioeconomic backgrounds of the students. Affluent background and parents committed to education are characteristics long known to set the boundaries of educational opportunities and goals (Alexander 1998; Rebell 1998). While the survey contained no objective data, teachers were asked for their assessments of these characteristics. Accordingly I include three measures of whether respondents indicated that cutting class, dropping out, and lack of parental involve-ment were problems at their schools. In all four category response items, high numbers indicated less of a problem. There was also a broad set of questions seeking to assess socioeconomic stress and behavioral prob-lems such as student violence and drug and alcohol abuse. Using factor analysis, I collapsed the responses into three indexes of these dimensions (for complete variable descriptions, see the appendix).

The individual characteristics of teachers are also likely to play an important role in determining the objectives they pursue in the class-room. It seems reasonable to suggest that teachers may construct their own ideology of education, and there is a substantial research literature indicating that teachers play a determining role in shaping classroom environment and direction (e.g., Nuthall 1999). Such individual im-pacts should be considered as being potentially independent of institu-tional constraints and student characteristics. While the data do not support the construction of ideological indexes, I include basic demo-graphic characteristics (age, sex, and race) in an attempt to control for individual determinants of goal selection. All data are taken from the second Teacher Followup Survey (National Center for Education Sta-tistics 1998).

The central methodological problem in operationalizing this model is the dependent variable, which is nominal but not dichotomous. Accord-ingly, I employ a multinomial logit technique, an approach that can con-ceptually be viewed as a simultaneous estimation of binary logits for all possible comparisons among the dichotomous sets of outcomes (Long 1997; 148–86; Menard 1995, 80–90). In addition to its ability to handle multiple nominal outcomes, this approach also has the advantage of re-taining a straightforward interpretation by generating parameter esti-mates in comparison with a designated reference category in the de-pendent variable (see the appendix for a more detailed description of the methodology). The methodological approach requires assigning one of the goals to a reference category, and I accordingly used instilling basic literacy. If there is anything that can be viewed as a universal priority of schools, it is to instill basic literacy skills (more teachers select this than any other choice), and anything that prioritizes other goals over this one is likely to reflect core differences in mission. The model estimates are thus interpreted in reference to teachers whose primary educational goal is to instill basic literacy skills.

Results and Discussion

Table 3 presents the log odds ratios for the model. The latter are used because they are easier to interpret than unstandardized logit coefficients. The figures reflect the shift in odds for each educational goal listed in the column over basic literacy that is associated with a one unit of change for the variable listed in the row. For example, the first-column, first-row entry indicates that being at a private school increases the odds of favoring academic excellence over basic literacy by a factor of 1.96. The first-row, second-column entry indicates that being a private school teacher shifts the odds of favoring vocational-technical skills over basic literacy as the primary educational goal by a factor of .12. The coefficients are multiplicative—a coefficient greater than one indicates a positive impact and less than one a negative impact on the odds (Long 1997, 82).[4]

The results presented in table 3 strongly suggest a systematic difference in goal selection between private and public school teachers. All else being equal, private school teachers are roughly twice as likely to select academic excellence over basic literacy as their primary goal. The big

TABLE 3.   Determinants of Primary Educational Goals Chosen by Teachers

Variable	Academic Excellence	Vocational/ Technical	Good Work Habits	Personal Growth	Human Relations Skills	Moral/ Religious Codes
Private School	1.96*	.12*	1.4*	1.6*	2.7*	22.02*
Pedagogical Authority	1.07*	1.05	1.0	1.05*	1.1*	.86*
Policy Authority	1.1*	1.24*	.944	1.15*	1.1	1.27
Private Policy Authority	.894*	.58*	1.06*	.87*	1.2*	.86*
Private Pedagogical Authority	.977*	1.32*	.95*	.98*	.68*	1.15*
Age	1.07*	1.1	1.02	.86*	.87	1.03
Race	.71*	.90	1.04	.71*	.70	.62*
Sex	1.48*	2.2*	1.46*	.78*	1.62*	1.47*
Students Cutting Class	88	1.1	1.0	1.08	1.25	1.1
Dropouts	1.03	.8	1.0	1.19*	.98	.88
Parental Involvement	1.1*	.81	.96	1.0	1.1	.81*
Student Violence	1.1*	.77*	.87*	1.0	.83	.91
Student Drug/Alcohol Abuse	.73*	.78*	.87*	.88*	.95	1.2*
Socioeconomic Stress	1.07	1.25*	1.0	.88*	.78*	1.2

Note: Exp (B) coefficients are reported.
Pseudo R^2 = .20 N = 6,733   IIA test (Hausman) = 1.12
*$p < .05$.

shift in mission priorities between the public and private sectors, however, is not in academic excellence but in instilling moral/religious codes. Private school teachers are a whopping twenty-two times more likely to prioritize this goal compared to basic literacy.

The variables used to tap the levels of discretionary authority held by teachers also indicate some impact on goal selection, though the effects tend to be comparatively mild. Compared to instilling basic skills, greater levels of authority over pedagogical matters tend to result in a slightly greater likelihood of adopting academic excellence and a somewhat lesser likelihood of adopting instilling moral/religious codes. Greater levels of policy authority again result in a modestly greater likelihood of adopting academic excellence, but they also increase the likelihood of adopting vocational/technical goals. Both variables are associated with an increased likelihood of choosing promoting personal growth over instilling basic literacy as the primary educational objective. The interaction terms were, with only one exception, statistically insignificant. This suggests that there is nothing unique about how discretionary authority is deployed in private schools, at least in terms of goal selection.

Among the control variables, the most interesting finding is that the individual characteristics of the teachers, rather than the perceived characteristics of the students, seem to be more important. Most notably, there is a persistent gender difference in goal selection. Male teachers are more likely to emphasize all school goals except human relations skills over basic literacy. This pattern was not expected. One possible explanation is gender-based patterns in discipline and grade level. If male teachers tend to be concentrated in upper grades and outside basic math and English classes, this pattern makes sense.

Overall, the multivariate analysis supports the basic picture presented in tables 1 and 2 but adds valuable information. As organizational characteristics vary, so do the decisions on which educational objectives are prioritized. The positive coefficient indicating that private school teachers are more likely to favor academic excellence over basic literacy backs the arguments of public choice advocates (Chubb and Moe 1988, 1990). However, the much larger coefficient for instilling moral/religious codes supports the concerns raised in the orthodox camp. Freed from the external controls of democratic institutions, private schools do tend to respond to demands for academic excellence, but this is a secondary response. The real demand they respond to is for moral and religious indoctrination, a divisive issue that is tightly regulated in the public sector. Giving teachers greater discretionary authority over pedagogy may constrain the response to this demand, but this constraint is small compared to the institutional difference. It is also worth noting that vesting more discretionary authority in teachers does little to promote academic excellence compared to basic literacy. The mean score on the pedagogical authority variable was 2.9, and the mean score on the policy authority variable was .59. For these representative scores, the model thus estimates, respectively, 21 and 3 percent increases in the likelihood of prioritizing academic excellence over basic literacy.

This suggests that making schools more marketlike will shift educational goals. If academic excellence is a universally desirable goal (a debatable proposition), this shift may be viewed positively. If it results in responding to demands that are unlikely to be appeased by the outcomes of democratic processes—such as the demand for religious indoctrination—it raises questions about how public education relates to its legal authorization (the egalitarian justifications in state constitutions) and its designated agents of governance (state legislatures and, by extension, local school boards).

Conclusion

The primary purpose of this essay was to use the case of education to examine whether changes in administrative structure could change the goals pursued by public agencies. The analysis presented here suggests that changes in administrative structure, those organizational characteristics that shape decision-making processes such as those that determine primary educational objectives, could conceivably pull public education away from its broad democratic foundations. The broader implication is that reforms designed to persuade public agencies to take decision cues from homogeneous clientele groups could result in less representative mission priorities.

At a minimum, the findings here suggest that swapping administrative orthodoxy and its bureaucratic center for the looser arrangements of public choice is likely to shift the ethos of public education. Education's "public" mission will be reoriented away from the communal preferences represented by representative bodies and public law and toward the niche preferences of a more homogeneous clientele. In a normative sense, whether this is good or bad for the democratic purposes of schooling is open to debate. Religion and moral codes are certainly not incompatible with a good education, and Catholic schools provide ample evidence that they need not be incompatible with a broad set of liberal democratic values. Still, such a development clearly seems to be at odds with the arguments of philosophers of education such as Gutmann (1987), Dewey (1929), and Callan (1997). As scholars such as Barber (1992) have argued, the traditional purpose of public education has a strong emphasis on *public;* its job is to produce citizens who can effectively participate in the communal life of a democracy. Using schools to promote sectarian doctrines clearly raises some problems for this goal. If educational priorities shift with institutional arrangements in the fashion seen here, those institutional arrangements essentially shrink, if not eliminate, the central liberal democratic justifications articulated by such for a mass system of public education. The results of such reforms may effect not just school outcomes but the core mission of education as well.

While the analysis and inferences presented here are provocative in the context of education, they also raise a broader question. Does this analysis represent a basic pattern that can be extrapolated to other areas of the public sector? There is no general answer to the question, but the empirical findings for education fit quite well with broader theoretical arguments on market-based reform's potential to add to the problems inherent in democratic governance by significantly changing the mission orientation of public bureaucracies. The "flaws" of public education identified by critics such as Chubb and Moe (1990)—bureaucratic organizations tied to the messy machinations of democratic politics—also seem to result in missions that, however vaguely defined, are broadly oriented toward the polity, a situation that can be generalized to many other public agencies. Take those institutional characteristics away, as they are in the private sector, and you get something more narrowly focused that may well be less compatible with a broad public mission. In short, the normative values embedded in administrative orthodoxy that are generally seen as having a positive influence on public sector mission priorities cannot be taken as givens. They are at least partially institutionalized through organizational structure. If that structure changes, there is the potential that public agency mission objectives will be shaped by a considerably different set of influences.

Appendix: Data, Variables, and Methodology

All data used in this analysis were drawn from the second Teacher Followup Survey (National Center for Education Statistics 1998). As part of this survey, both private and public school teachers were asked to select their most important educational goals from an eight-response survey item. These items were identical except that the final response was "promoting multicultural awareness" for public school teachers and "fostering religious/spiritual development" for private school teachers. The latter goal is essentially barred de jure for public sector educators. To merge these two survey items into a single index for the dependent variable, I collapsed "promoting specific moral values" and "fostering religious/spiritual development" into a single category, reasoning that they were clearly related items and that the former makes the most likely substitute for the latter in the public sector. I also collapsed "promoting multicultural awareness" into "promoting human relations skills" for public school teachers (the former was chosen by less than .5 percent of the public school teachers surveyed). The result was the seven-category list of goals, presented in table 1, that applied to both the public and private sectors. Specific variables used in the analysis are as follows.

Private School: A dummy variable where 1 = private school, 0 = public school.

Pedagogical Authority: An additive index constructed from six questions relating to teacher influence over pedagogical matters (for replication purposes, the questions are identified as TSC248 through TSC253 in the survey). A score of six indicates that teachers have complete control over selecting instructional materials, educational content, teaching techniques, grading, enforcing discipline, and assigning homework.

Policy Authority: An additive index constructed from four questions relating to teacher influence over school policy (for replication purposes, the questions are identified as TSC244 through TSC247 in the survey). A score of four indicates that teachers have a high degree of influence in determining disciplinary policy, the content of in-service programs, student assignments, and curriculum.

Age: A four-category indicator where 1 = <29, 2 = 30–39, 3 = 40–49, 4 = >50

Race: A dummy variable where 1 = white, 0 = nonwhite.

Sex: A dummy variable where 1 = male, 0 = female.

Students Cutting Class: A four-category variable where 1 = not a problem, 4 = a serious problem.

Dropouts: A four-category variable where 1 = not a problem, 4 = a serious problem.

Parental Involvement: A four-category variable where 1 = lack of parental involvement not a problem, 4 = a serious problem.

Student Violence, Drug/Alcohol Abuse, and Socioeconomic Stress Indexes: These variables were generated by first doing an exploratory factor analysis to examine the underlying structure in response to items relating to student/parent attitudes and characteristics. On the basis of these results, separate sets of questions were factor analyzed to generate the indexes. These resulted in maximum extraction of variance—all the indexes used in the analysis represent more than 50 percent of variance in the underlying response items briefly described in the text and are the only factors produced with an Eigenvalue greater than 1. For replication purposes, the code numbers of the questions in each factor analysis are as follows.

Student Violence: TSC257, TSC258, TSC259, TSC260, TSC264, TSC265 (Eigenvalue 3.3, 55 percent of variance).

Student Drug/Alcohol Abuse: TSC261, TSC262, TSC263 (Eigenvalue 2.5, 84 percent of variance).

Socioeconomic Stress: TSC272, TSC273, TSC274, TSC275 (Eigenvalue 2.65, 65.8 percent of variance).

Methodology

Multinomial logistic regression is essentially a straightforward extension of logistic models of binary outcomes, and such binary models could be employed to analyze each of the goal categories analyzed here. The problem with such an approach is the number of comparisons required to make sense of the analysis (e.g., with four outcomes, four binary regressions would entail comparing outcomes 1 to 2, 1 to 3, 1 to 4, 2 to 3, 2 to 4, and 3 to 4). A multinomial logistic regression simplifies this by running a single model in which the nominal outcomes of the dependent variable are contrasted with an excluded reference category (in the text, this was basic literacy). The results then retain the easy interpretation of binary logistic regression in the context of the reference category.

Although the multinomial approach has the advantage of simplicity in presenting results, its use is subject to an important constraint: the independence of irrelevant alternatives (IIA) assumption. Calculating multinomial equations without reference to other potential alternatives to the outcomes included in the dependent variable can have a severe effect on how odds are calculated, and the general rule of thumb is that the IIA assumption is only secure when the outcome categories are really independent in the eyes of those who are making the choices. A Hausman-McFadden test statistic has been proposed to test this assumption, essentially a Hausman-type approach in which the test statistic is a chi-square and significant values indicate that the IIA assumption has been violated. This is the IIA test statistic reported in table 3, and the insignificance of this test score ($p = 1$) indicates the null hypothesis that there is no systematic difference in estimates when some outcome category of the dependent variable is arbitrarily excluded from the analysis.

For a more formal, but accessible introduction to multinomial logistic regression and the issues surrounding the IIA assumption, see Long 1997 (151–60, 182–84).

Notes

1. Education provides an instructive example. The first systematic efforts to establish school choice were made by southern whites seeking to establish a quasi market for education because the hierarchical public system became resistant to demands for racial segregation in the wake of *Brown v Board of Education* (Henig 1994, 102–15).

2. The survey defined this goal as: "Building basic literacy skills (reading, math, writing, speaking)." This should convey a reasonably uniform definition and limit potential measurement error due to differing respondent conceptions of "basic literacy."

3. Thus, the causal path assumed by this argument is that organizational characteristics determine individual goal selection. It is also possible that individual goals determine certain organizational characteristics and goal priorities. The causal path adopted here is backed by a large literature arguing that organizations socialize individuals toward certain goals and into particular patterns of behavior (Merton 1957; Whyte 1956; Porter and Lawler 1965; Shafritz and Ott 1996, 420–29). For discussions of similar issues as they apply to education, see Chubb and Moe 1988; and Schneider et al. 1997).

4. A factor change of 1.70 can thus be interpreted as a 70 percent increase in the odds of favoring a given goal over basic skills as the primary educational goal, while a factor change of .30 represents a decrease of 70 percent in those odds.

Bureaucratic Discretion and Regulatory Success without Enforcement

Michael J. Licari

Discretion, that ability to decide how policies will be implemented, is a key component of bureaucratic power. Since agencies have a great deal of discretion (Rourke 1984), studies of policy effectiveness need to examine what can occur when different implementation choices are made. In order to understand the outputs and outcomes of agency implementation activity, we need to know what happens when policies are vigorously implemented as well as when policies are largely ignored.

Most studies of regulatory effectiveness focus on implementation problems stemming from various enforcement mechanisms. In general, the existing literature on the effectiveness of regulatory policy has found that the strength of government needs to be behind a policy for it to work. This literature has found three rules of thumb. First, command and control regulation works only if enforcement is adequate. For example, highway speed limits are more effective when police are present and enforcing them. Second, information policy works if people pay attention to it, which often requires the government to actively distribute and, if necessary, update the information. Third, incentives work if they are large enough. For maximum effectiveness, this requires the government issuing the incentives to monitor them closely and update them as needed to keep them large enough. Most existing research on regulatory effectiveness thus focuses on the link between government implementation, enforcement, and policy success. The conventional wisdom is that if an agency uses its discretion and decides to implement and enforce a regulation properly it will be more successful.

The problem that remains, of course, is finding out what happens to regulatory policy if the implementing agency decides to ignore it or a policy is adopted without assigning enforcement power to a bureaucracy. Contrary to the conventional wisdom, a choice by an agency to not implement a policy does not automatically mean that the policy will fail. In recognition of the fact that occasionally government coercion is not needed for a successful policy, some research focuses on the regulated individual rather than the regulator. For example, Scholz and Pinney (1995) find that feelings of duty and the subjective fear of getting caught compel people to truthfully report their income and pay taxes to the Internal Revenue Service (IRS). The actual, objective, audit rate often has little to do with tax compliance. This can be adequately explained only by focusing on the attitudes and situations of the taxpayers themselves (see also McGraw and Scholz 1991).

Other research has focused on facilitative models to explain regulatory behavior. Gray and Scholz (1993) and Scholz and Gray (1997) find that coercion by the Occupational Safety and Health Administration (OSHA) can only partially explain drops in worker accident rates. Gray and Scholz show that reaction by management to OSHA inspections, rather than the inspections and penalties themselves, explains increases in worker safety. Scholz and Gray show that inspections initiated by workers rather than OSHA had a greater positive impact, indicating that when OSHA used its discretion to act as a facilitator for cooperation rather than as a coercive agency better results were achieved.

Signaling can also play an important role in compliance decisions. In strategic communications models, one informed actor provides information to another, less-informed actor in an attempt to change that decision maker's behavior (Lupia 1994; Crawford and Sobel 1992; Milgrom and Roberts 1986; Spence 1973). This has important implications for regulatory compliance. The government can attempt to influence compliance decisions by sending signals about the consequences of those decisions.

This essay borrows the frameworks of these studies and applies them to analyzing the effectiveness of a salient command and control regulatory device: state clean indoor air laws aimed at restricting smoking in public buildings and workplaces. Based on the frameworks and the results from the empirical analysis, I find that, contrary to "traditional" expectations of a need for a link between coercion and regulatory effectiveness, clean indoor air laws can be effective in reducing smoking despite an almost total lack of enforcement. State and local law enforcement agencies have simply decided to ignore the implementation of these laws.

This does not mean that public bureaucracies are irrelevant to this policy area. On the contrary, public health and law enforcement agencies could play an important role as signalers and facilitators for cooperation. Scholz and Gray (1997) and Licari and Meier (2000) find that facilitation and signaling can be important in explaining the effectiveness of an agency's activities. In this case, public bureaucracies can use clean indoor air laws to reinforce social norms and send public health signals about smoking. Bureaucracies can use these regulations in noncoercive ways rather than focusing on expensive traditional enforcement methods. Furthermore, this project highlights a key issue for the study of bureaucratic enforcement. It is important to factor in the potential for signals and other heuristics in order to avoid overestimating the impact of regulatory bureaucracies.

The results support the idea that clean indoor air laws compel people to smoke less because of the fear of social disapproval as well as signaled information about the health hazards of smoking. Since strict penalties under the law and high enforcement levels do not exist, these "traditional" indicators of command and control policy success cannot explain why clean indoor air laws are able to reduce levels of smoking. Thus, this essay represents an important extension of the work already done on signaling and duty and fear heuristics. I focus on an element of social regulation. Social regulation in general is often not well received by the public (Eisner 2000). Also, smoking regulation is targeted at a portion of the population that is highly resistant, if only because of the addictive nature of cigarettes. Thus, this study offers a test of signaling and other information heuristics that is very stringent.

The findings in this essay indicate that the link between coercion and successful regulation, while not incorrect, is certainly narrow. When designing regulation and deciding on appropriate enforcement levels, legislators and bureaucrats need to be aware of the existence of policies that are largely "self-enforcing." Also, when policy analysts examine the effectiveness of regulation attention needs to be devoted to the fact that government coercion is only one side of the regulation coin. Social norms (Ostrom 1998; Scholz 1998; Scholz and Lubell 1998) are key to understanding how we can solve the collective action problem of compliance.

Clean Indoor Air Laws and Smoking

The Nature of Clean Indoor Air Laws

Clean indoor air laws were generally not considered by state governments until the 1980s. As research on the harmful effects of secondhand smoke mounted, people began to realize that smoking was not only harmful to smokers themselves but that it also damaged the health of those in the vicinity. This eventually spread to specific objections about smoking in the workplace.

Clean indoor air laws are designed and implemented primarily by state governments, although the federal government has also introduced similar laws of its own, such as smoking bans on domestic airline flights. State laws restricting indoor smoking first appeared mainly in the 1980s. Minnesota was the first to introduce such a law (the Clean Indoor Air Act of 1975), but other states were rather slow to follow. Most states did not introduce their own laws until the late 1980s or early 1990s. Nine states still do not have a clean indoor air law.[1]

In addition to being introduced over a wide spatial and temporal range, clean indoor air laws also vary in scope. Some states have comprehensive laws that completely ban smoking in certain places of work (private or government). Several others have laws restricting smoking to varying degrees across government work sites and private businesses. Other states simply limit indoor smoking to designated areas.

Enforcement of Clean Indoor Air Laws

Command and control regulation typically requires monitoring and penalties for noncompliance. Without monitoring, the government has no way of knowing whether people are complying with the law. Without penalties to accompany the monitoring, there will be little incentive for citizens to comply with the law. These seem like reasonable expectations about how command and control regulation works, and indeed they make up the basic assumptions about how to design and implement a successful command and control policy.

Clean indoor air laws, however, rarely fit this description. Jacobson and Wasserman (1997) find that state clean indoor air laws are "self-enforcing and that they will not be systematically enforced by state or local authorities" (49–50). In other words, citizens voluntarily comply with the laws since government is not willing or able to enforce them with monitoring and penalties. Even in states with strong clean indoor air laws, government enforcement is minimal and relies upon voluntary compliance (Jacobson and Wasserman 1997).[2]

To further underscore the importance of voluntary compliance, the penalties imposed for breaking a clean indoor air law are almost always light. The maximum fine imposed on a smoker in Idaho, for example, is $10 (Downey and Gardiner 1996). More than half of the states do not even have penalties for failing to comply. In these states, there is no mechanism to legally punish a smoker who is reported by another citizen. Thus, even though it may be easy for nonsmoking citizens to detect and report violations, there are still little or no effective legal or enforcement mechanisms preventing people from smoking indoors. With the absence of meaningful penalties, ease of detection becomes irrelevant. There are few or no legal consequences to getting caught, and thus there are no credible threats of enforcement from either the government or nonsmoking citizens. Furthermore, Jacobson and Wasserman (1997); Rigotti et al. (1993); and Rigotti, Stoto, and Schelling (1994) show that oversight by government agencies or citizens (even those actively involved in antitobacco groups) does not meaningfully exist. Nonsmokers do not seem interested in monitoring and reporting smokers. For clean indoor air laws to work and reduce smoking, some other social mechanisms are required.

The lack of enforcement is important because clean indoor air is essentially a collective action or "social dilemma" problem (Ostrom 1998). This occurs when individuals face choices in which maximizing their short-term self-interest yields an outcome that makes everyone worse off. A smoker may choose to maximize his or her short-term self-interest by smoking indoors, thereby polluting the air everyone else in the building is breathing. In this sense, clean indoor air is a public good, or at least a common-pool resource, and compliance is the equivalent of a cooperative solution to the collective action problem (Scholz 1998). Cooperation (not smoking indoors), therefore, leads to Pareto-efficient outcomes. The key problem is achieving this cooperation. One key way it can be attained is through heuristics and social norms as well as rules designed to reinforce those norms (Ostrom 1998). Since voluntary compliance norms are active in these antismoking policies (Jacobson and Wasserman 1997; Rigotti and Pashos 1991; Rigotti et al. 1992, 1993; Rigotti, Stoto, and Schelling 1994), clean indoor air laws can facilitate cooperation.

Clean indoor air laws have a clear goal: they are meant to reduce the amount of secondhand smoke to which nonsmokers are exposed. The facilitative effect is the key to their success. *Simply, if people are influenced by the noncoercive aspects of clean indoor air laws in their state, the amount people smoke should drop.* This is the main test offered in this essay.

Heuristics, Fear, and Signaled Information

Heuristics are cognitive tools that are useful when people face situations in which they need to make a choice based on insufficient information. Scholz and Pinney's (1995) "duty heuristic" claims that a citizen's sense of duty to obey the law provides cues for compliance decisions, and that information is accessed by the citizen when it is relevant and needed. This is akin to voting heuristics, wherein strength of party identification and candidate "likability" play roles in determining vote choice rather than detailed knowledge of the candidate's stance on pertinent issues. Since detailed knowledge is often difficult to obtain, the citizen will rely on cognitive shortcuts to make a choice. Heuristics should be useful for understanding compliance behavior generally as well as in this particular case. When government uses a facilitative mechanism to increase information and reinforce existing norms and heuristics, compliance behavior should increase.

Fear

Fear can influence compliance in an important way. Feelings of fear can influence one's perception of the negative consequences of noncompliance. Furthermore, people who feel a sense of duty to follow the law will estimate the chances of receiving punishment as being great. Those who do not feel an obligation will estimate low chances of getting caught and receiving punishment (see Scholz and Pinney 1995). In this case, fear applies to both the estimations of receiving punishment under the law and "social" punishment. As the popular image of smoking has waned, especially in the last twenty years, smokers may refrain from lighting up out of fear of social embarrassment or as a common courtesy, although it is doubtful that a smoker will quit altogether.

Signaling

Signaling can play a crucial role in the effectiveness of smoking regulations because the government gathers and disseminates information on the health effects of smoking. The federal government officially took on this role in 1964 with the first surgeon general's report on smoking and health. Although the government provides direct information with surgeon general's reports and policies such as warning labels (Fritschler and Hoefler 1995), the government (both state and federal) also sends signals when it is designing and implementing regulations such as clean indoor air laws. Unlike information policy, these signals are less direct since they often are a by-product of the logic for designing and implementing new tobacco regulations.

Signals from clean indoor air laws should exist because the negative health effects of secondhand smoke are not well known or understood. Although the effects of smoking on smokers were well known by the 1980s, secondhand smoke was (and still is) poorly understood.[3] Signals are strongest when the information is new and perhaps unexpected. Thus, clean indoor air laws should send signals precisely because they serve to provide information on an issue that remains confusing to this day.

The government is able to send these signals for a variety of reasons. Media coverage of legislative debates and new laws emphasize health risks and send this signal to citizens along with the specific goals of the new policy. Perhaps most importantly, public health agencies also emphasize the usefulness of tobacco regulation as a public health policy and are involved in signaling this information (see e.g., Department of Health and Human Services 1992, 1994, 1998; and Centers for Disease Control and Prevention 1996). The signals inform smokers that the ultimate goal of the new policy is to reduce the risks of poor health (or even death) from smoking. If the public health signals are received and influence smokers, clean indoor air laws should have an impact on smoking levels. Smokers who act on the signaled information about the public health reasons for the laws have an incentive to cut back on cigarettes. Their choice of whether or not to smoke is influenced by the desire to reduce the risk of smoking-related health problems as well as by the fear of social stigmatization. Clean indoor air acts essentially contribute to a reduction in overall cigarette consumption because the laws and the norms that are fostered by them add to the transaction costs a smoker must absorb.

Signaling and fear, therefore, are both decision aids for smokers. Both should influence smokers to cut back, particularly because the signaled information about the health effects of smoking should create more fear of noncompliance. Although the clean indoor air laws are primarily legislated to protect nonsmokers, the laws signal enough information about public health to make them antismoking policies in their own right.

Since clean indoor air is a collective action problem, the role of government in this case has changed from enforcer to facilitator. Smokers are looking to cooperate, so they use duty and fear combined with signaled information to arrive at the conclusion that smoking indoors is not acceptable. Clean indoor air laws provide these signals, or focal points (Schelling 1960), for equilibrium behavior, which reduces the transaction costs of compliance. This essay thus represents an indirect test of the duty heuristics, insofar as the data on how individual smokers are reacting to clean indoor air laws are not available.

Modeling the Effects of Regulation on Cigarette Consumption

Base Model

Unlike many items that the government seeks to regulate, cigarettes are addictive, perhaps the most addictive commodity known (Department of Health and Human Services 1994). Since the dependent variable is the number of packs of cigarettes consumed per capita per year for each state from 1955 through 1996, my model must explicitly account for this.[4] Addiction implies that current cigarette consumption is greatly affected by past consumption. Quite clearly, the way to model addictive phenomena is via habit persistence, that is, by simply including a lagged value of the dependent variable as an independent variable (Becker and Murphy 1988; Becker, Grossman, and Murphy 1991; Lewit 1989).[5]

Clean Indoor Air Laws

To this base model, I add measures to test the effects of clean indoor air laws on smoking. To measure clean indoor air laws, I first created an "effort" scale for each state, potentially ranging from zero to 6, although the highest any state scored was 4.[6] Zero indicates no clean indoor air law for state government or private work sites. A score of 1 is given to states requiring a designated smoking area in either government or private work sites. States requiring designated smoking areas in both types of work sites are therefore given the score of 2. See table 1 for the rest of the scaling of this measure. Rather than using this continuous scale, I use a series of dummy variables, one for each category 1 through 4 (category zero is omitted). Thus, if a state's effort score is 1 for a particular year, it will be coded 1 in the dummy variable representing that effort category and zero for the three others. Likewise, if a state's effort score is 4, it will be coded 1 in the dummy representing effort category 4 and will be coded zero for categories 1, 2, and 3. All states are scored zero for each year until a law is implemented. This will allow for a demonstration of where the critical "signaling threshold" occurs. Low-end reforms may not have a meaningful effect in a statistical sense, while more stringent policies are expected to have much larger impacts. Using the "effort" measure as a continuous variable would not show these differences.[7]

The logic behind how effort influences cigarette consumption is drawn from the idea of signaling. Increased effort sends stronger public health signals to the smoking population. By sending stronger signals, a state government can expect that cooperation will increase. With more comprehensive clean indoor air laws, the focal point (Schelling 1960) becomes more obvious and the Pareto-efficient outcome should be more easily attainable. The effort dummy variables should therefore be related to reductions in cigarette consumption, although I expect more comprehensive laws to be more effective.

Other Regulation

The tobacco policy area includes other types of regulation as well, namely, information policy and economic disincentives. To measure information policy, I take notice of two key events in government policy. The first effort by the federal government to take action regarding cigarettes was the requirement that all packages contain a warning label (effective January 1, 1966; see Fritschler and Hoefler 1995). The second event was the federal ban of cigarette advertisements on television in 1971. Such a ban is rare and communicates that a product is so danger-

TABLE 1.   Clean Indoor Air Law Effort Scaling

Workplace Type	100% Smoke Free	Designated Area	Designated Area with Ventilation	None
Government	3	2	1	0
Private	3	2	1	0

Note: The Government clean indoor air law score is added to the Private score to form the Effort score. Example: a state requiring a designated area with ventilation for government workplaces and designated smoking areas for private workplaces would receive a score of 3.

ous that producers are prohibited from providing information about it. The variable is coded zero prior to 1966, 1 from 1966 to 1971, and 2 after 1971. This reflects the belief that the warning label represented the start of a negative information policy and that this policy became more forceful after the advertising ban. While I use specific events to code the policy, I am not arguing that these precise events encompass all information policy with regard to cigarettes.[8]

Economic disincentives, that is, excise taxes on cigarettes, are a popular regulatory tool used by both the federal and state governments. Taxes on cigarettes work causally by affecting the price of cigarettes. Because an excise tax is typically passed on to the consumer (see, e.g., Hyman 1996 on the price-distorting effect of excise taxes), I have opted, as have others in this area, to work directly with the real price of cigarettes in cents per pack (1983 = 100).[9] This is then differenced so that the variable measures the change in price.

Some states tax cigarettes much more aggressively than others. These variations must be considered because permeable state boundaries make it more difficult to assess the effectiveness of taxes in reducing cigarette use. Since taxes discourage smoking by increasing the cost, they suffer in performance if there is an opportunity to avoid them and pay lower prices. This avoidance of a high tax by means of purchasing cigarettes in another state with lower taxes (and thus lower prices) is referred to as "bootlegging." To design a proper model of regulatory effectiveness, therefore, the tax levels in the surrounding states and the potential for bootlegging must be taken into account (Baltagi and Levin 1986). Since all cigarette consumption data are actually sales data, failure to do so can result in the apparent effectiveness of a tax increase being exaggerated.

The benefits from bootlegging can be easily measured as the money that would be saved by the individual. Naturally, as the tax in a person's home state increases relative to tax rates in neighboring states, the incentive to bootleg increases. This difference must then be discounted by transaction costs, mostly time and travel (see Manchester 1976; and Wasserman et al. 1991). My measure for the incentive to bootleg is the home state real tax rate (in cents) minus the mean real tax rate for all states that border the home state (for a similar treatment, see Licari and Meier 1997; and Meier and Licari 1997a, 1997b).

Finally, smoking levels are expected to be higher in tobacco states. A variable to control for this is included. It is a simple dummy variable with a value of one if the state is a tobacco state, defined as having grown a tobacco crop that year (Creek, Capehart, and Grise 1994).

As an extension, a variable was tried in order to control for different policy environments. The relevant environmental difference is obviously a state's level of support for the tobacco industry (farming and production). Since state clean indoor air laws require voluntary compliance, it is possible that they will not operate as effectively in tobacco compared to nontobacco states. This was measured by multiplying the tobacco state dummy variable by the continuous effort scale. The interaction was not significant, and the rest of the results were unchanged, so the variable was dropped.

Data Analysis

To analyze the model, I used pooled time-series techniques for the time period of 1955 through 1996 with the states as units of analysis. Serial correlation and heteroskedasticity were tested for using the Lagrange multiplier and the White tests, respectively. Neither posed a problem for my analyses. All nondummy variables are logged, for two reasons. First, it facilitates interpretation. Second, and more importantly, relationships among demand and price and other regulations are not expected to be linear.

Simultaneity is another problem that can plague time-series analyses. Considering that compliance will be due to political and environmental factors, which can also be related to policy adoption, simultaneity is possible. This should not be a problem, however. While I expect clean indoor air laws at time t to influence smoking at time t, smoking at time t can only influence the adoption of smoking regulations at some future time. Lawmakers will only have access to information about smoking rates and attitudes after the fact. Furthermore, legislation or rule making typically takes time, even if there is access to current data. In other words, the statistical model has weak exogeneity, which is sufficient to produce unbiased estimates. As a further check, a Hausman specification test (Davidson and MacKinnon 1993) shows that the estimates do not suffer from simultaneity bias.[10]

Results

The results of the analysis are presented in table 2. Table 3 shows the results of the differenced model as a check on the robustness of the model in table 2. The differenced model, however, also has the advantage on a conceptual level of implicitly controlling for the health consciousness of

TABLE 2. Effects of Clean Indoor Air Laws and Other Regulation on Cigarette Consumption

Dependent variable = Annual per capita cigarette consumption in packs, logged		
Variable	Slope	Standard Error
Lagged consumption	.971	.0046***
Clean indoor air effort 1	−.007	.0022***
Clean indoor air effort 2	−.007	.0022***
Clean indoor air effort 3	−.010	.0028***
Clean indoor air effort 4	−.017	.0055**
Tobacco state	.002	.0009*
Change in price	−.281	.0163***
Bootlegging incentive	−.030	.0038***
Information policy	−.004	.0005***
R^2	.97	
SE	.018	
N	1,986	
Lagrange multiplier	.85	
Prob($df = 5$)	.97	
White test	1.52	
Prob($df = 10$)	.99	

***$p < .001$.   **$p < .01$.   *$p < .05$. All one-tailed tests.

TABLE 3. Effects of Clean Indoor Air Laws and Other Regulation on Cigarette Consumption, Differenced Model

Dependent variable = Change in annual per capita cigarette consumption in packs, logged		
Variable	Slope	Standard Error
Clean indoor air effort 1	−.004	.0022*
Clean indoor air effort 2	−.005	.0023*
Clean indoor air effort 3	−.008	.0028**
Clean indoor air effort 4	−.011	.0055*
Tobacco state	.001	.0009*
Change in price	−.285	.0165***
Bootlegging incentive	−.022	.0035***
Information policy	−.004	.0005***
R^2	.19	
SE	.019	
N	1,986	
Lagrange multiplier	.90	
Prob($df = 5$)	.97	
White test	.99	
Prob($df = 9$)	.99	

***$p < .001$.   **$p < .01$.   *$p < .05$. All one-tailed tests.

a state, which could be seen as a selection bias problem in the model in table 2. However, since the addictiveness of cigarettes is a crucial element of any model of smoking regulation, my discussion will focus on the results in table 2.

The key variables, the clean indoor air law effort dummies, are all associated with lower cigarette consumption. Since these laws depend on voluntary compliance and their primary goal is something other than reduced cigarette consumption, this indicates that noncoercive factors are working. *Without any willingness to voluntarily comply, these laws would not have any effect on cigarette consumption.* Specifically, a state that adopts a clean indoor air law that is relatively weak (i.e., a law that would score a 1 or 2 on the continuous effort scale) sees cigarette consumption drop by .7 percent. A state that adopts a stronger law (e.g., one that would score a 4) has cigarette consumption drop by 1.7 percent. This effect is nearly two and a half times greater than the impact in the first example. Clearly, stronger effort provides much stronger signals, and the two low-end categories provide about equal impact. While these effects may seem to represent insignificant reductions in smoking, these are the first-year impacts only. With the lagged dependent variable in the model, impacts continue into the future at gradually declining rates. The total impact of a shift in a state's clean indoor air law effort is actually quite large.[11]

The other regulations also work to deter smoking. A 1 percent increase in price is associated with a decrease in cigarette consumption of .28 percent. Since this is the first-year impact, even a small price increase will have large long-term effects; the total decrease in per capita consumption from a 1 percent increase is nearly 10 percent. The introduction of warning labels in 1966 is associated with a drop in per capita cigarette use of .4 percent. Since this variable is not reset to zero, this impact occurs each year until 1971, when the television advertising ban was implemented. In each year starting in 1971, the information policy variable is associated with a decrease in per capita cigarette use of .8 percent.

The bootlegging incentives variable indicates that uneven prices across state boundaries influence where people will purchase cigarettes. As the price in the home state increases relative to the surrounding states' prices, smokers will travel to purchase cheaper cigarettes. Conversely, a state with low prices located next to states with higher prices will see an increase in sales. A 1 percent increase in the incentive to bootleg is associated with a decrease in per capita cigarette consumption of .03 percent in the first year.

Conclusions

This essay has presented a test of the idea that command and control regulation can be successful despite its reliance on voluntary compliance. Using an empirical model, I found support for this. With voluntary compliance, state clean indoor air laws work to reduce levels of smoking. Furthermore, there seems to be a signaling threshold. States that implement clean indoor air laws beyond simply requiring designated smoking areas experience declines in smoking that are much more substantial. In general, however, once a clean indoor air law is implemented it appears that annual cigarette consumption declines faster than when no law is passed.

Citizens are taking clean indoor air laws as a strong signal from government that smoking is hazardous to both smokers and nonsmokers. In this way, the introduction of clean indoor air laws may act as a force to further diminish the social acceptance of smoking. Furthermore, these public health signals could be used to a greater degree by public health agencies. Since state and local law enforcement agencies have decided not to make clean indoor air laws coercive regulation, other agencies have the opportunity to use them in other ways, perhaps as facilitative or public health policy.

Duty to follow the law (influenced by fear of noncompliance) apparently has an effect here. Merely having a clean indoor air law will drive down smoking levels. This seems to be a case in which law enforcement agencies have widely used their discretion over implementation to ignore these policies, since vigorously enforcing clean indoor air laws would be expensive and time consuming.

Lack of enforcement or meaningful penalties, however, does not doom these laws to failure. This study shows that agencies can look for noncoercive ways to successfully implement regulatory policy. When there is policy success without enforcement, this may indicate an opportunity to increase the use of signaled information to further increase the successfulness of the policy. This also suggests that other, nonregulatory agencies can play an important role in implementation of regulation. In this analysis, clean indoor air laws provide signals that public health agencies can use to help facilitate compliance.

This study also has ramifications for other studies of bureaucratic enforcement. Some compliance with regulations will occur through signaling and the use of other heuristics. A portion of compliance that is normally attributed to bureaucratic enforcement, therefore, might well have occurred without any actions on the part of bureaucracy. Studies that fail to incorporate these informal, noncoercive elements of enforcement will, as a result, overestimate the impact of regulatory bureaucracies.

Notes

I would like to thank George Krause, Ken Meier, and Mark Lubell for their valuable comments on earlier versions of this essay.

1. For the purposes of this project, the laws under consideration are those that restrict smoking in places of work (both government and private). Laws restricting smoking in other areas (e.g., grocery stores) exist as well but are much less common and have not been included.

2. Some might argue that clean indoor air laws are indeed enforced but by the businesses themselves. If so, then voluntary compliance does not exist because the firm is providing the enforcement and the punishment. However, businesses do not enforce these laws (Rigotti et al. 1992; Rigotti, Stoto, and Schelling 1994) and instead rely on voluntary compliance from both employees and customers.

3. The 1980s and early 1990s saw intense debate among health professionals, government officials, the general population, and the tobacco industry over the effects of secondhand smoke (Department of Health and Human Services 2000).

4. I have data only for states that actually had a cigarette tax or, in the case of Alaska and Hawaii, only for the time since they became states. By 1971, all states had a state cigarette tax. All data are from the Tobacco Institute (1997).

5. Lagging a dependent variable can make spurious results from failure to control for some variables less likely since it will act as a supercontrol variable. However, if such specification results in correlated errors regression coefficients are both inconsistent and biased (Pindyck and Rubinfeld 1991; Greene 1993). Since the degree of bias declines substantially as the number of cases increases relative to the number of parameters estimated, the extent of bias is unlikely to be large in this case. As a final check, I include the results from a model with a differenced, rather than lagged, dependent variable.

6. These data are from the Centers For Disease Control and Prevention (1996).

7. I do not necessarily expect a dynamic effect other than that provided by the lagged dependent variable. Policies in place will have the continuous effect of preventing smoking, and the introduction of new smokers over time does not alter the ways in which the policies will function.

8. Several other efforts are included in information policy, such as pronouncements by public officials, the release of additional studies, and restrictions on the content of nontelevision advertising. The federal government is the main disseminator of this information. The effects of both policies could not be separated due to collinearity problems.

9. Meier and Licari (1997a) demonstrate that state and federal taxes can explain 95 percent of the variation in cigarette prices during the time period under review here. Price (or tax) is not a health signal per se due to the fact that while taxes may indeed carry signals (Licari and Meier 2000) they may also be adopted for reasons completely different from public health (Licari 2001a). They are always economic disincentives, however.

10. The instruments used for the first-stage regression were government ideology scores (Berry et al. 1998) and state fiscal stress, measured as real revenues minus expenditures, divided by expenditures. Both are related to smoking policy adoption but not to smoking (Licari 2001a, 2001b). The suspect variable (clean indoor air effort scale) was regressed on the exogenous variables plus the instruments. The residuals saved from this regression were used as additional regressors in the original model. The coefficient on the first-stage residuals is not significantly different from zero. Therefore, the test fails to reject the hypothesis of consistent OLS estimates.

11. The total impact is $(\beta)/(1-\lambda)$, or the slope divided by one minus the lagged dependent variable coefficent.

Conclusion: An Agenda for the Scientific Study of Bureaucracy

Kenneth J. Meier and George A. Krause

Why the Need for a Scientific Study of Public Bureaucracy?

The literature on how political institutions (i.e., chief executives, legislatures, and the judiciary) attempt to control bureaucratic performance via ex post and ex ante methods is well developed. In the former case, numerous studies have discussed how tools such as budgets, appointments, and oversight, to name a few, can influence bureaucratic performance. In the latter case, the politics of procedural choice has shown theoretical ways to constrain the behavior of administrative agencies through the use of rules. These works have enhanced our theoretical and empirical understanding of the motivation, incentives, and tactics employed by political institutions to mold bureaucracy. They provide a body of systematic inquiry that follows the social scientific enterprise of theory building and empirical testing.

At the same time, however, this work typically ignores or obscures the central role of public bureaucratic organizations and how they behave on institutional and organizational levels. Instead, it treats bureaucratic performance as the result of political bargaining between some combination of the president, Congress, and the courts, yet it fails to reserve a place for the bureaucracy at the table. In doing so, we get a portrait of bureaucracy that is neither bureaucracy centered nor institutionally balanced. In concluding, we provide several suggestions meriting further scientific inquiry. All have a *bureaucentric* focus, as opposed to a political institutions focus, on understanding how the administrative state functions in a democracy.

An Agenda for the Scientific Study of Bureaucracy

Bureaucracy is a growth area in political science. The number of scholars and the quality of skills is at a level unmatched since at least the 1940s. Articles on bureaucracy, while by no means prevalent, are no longer rare. In the last two decades, 110 articles with bureaucracy as a central feature have been published in the four leading general political science journals.[1]

Paralleling the growth in scholarship is the development of institutional apparatuses designed to foster more study of public bureaucracy. The Midwest Public Administration Caucus along with the Public Administration Section of the American Political Science Association (APSA), the development of the *Journal of Public Administration Research and Theory,* and the recently established National Public Management Research Conference data archive and paper posting Web site (<http://bush.tamu.edu/pubman/>) create an infrastructure capable of supporting greater intellectual progress in the area. The Scientific Study of Bureaucracy (S²OB) group met for the first time as part of the Fifth National Public Management Conference in College Station, Texas; those papers became the core of this volume.

At this stage, taking a broad overview of the field and becoming more strategic about developing it seems appropriate. Given our present situation, where are we likely to make the most progress learning more about bureaucracy? Five areas of work are especially promising: getting inside the black box of bureaucracy, taking theory more seriously, exploiting the variance in bureaucracies, making an explicit return to the structural aspects of bureaucracy, and adopting methods that correspond to the data-generating processes of public bureaucracies. The unifying theme for these five areas is a new organizations approach to studying public bureaucracies. By new organizations, we mean a study of public bureaucracy focused on administrative organizations, whether at the macro- (organizational) or microlevel (individual), that generates empirically testable deductive and nondeductive theories of how bureaucratic agencies function to guide research inquiries. In many ways, this new organizational approach can be viewed as the use of rigorous logical, analytical, and statistical methods applied to studying the timeless issues of interest raised by esteemed scholars of public administration such as Max Weber, Herbert Simon, Luther Gulick, James March, Anthony Downs, Francis Rourke, Herbert Kaufman, and James Q. Wilson.

Inside the Black Box

We often treat bureaucracies as black boxes, mysterious entities that respond to environmental pressures. In doing so, we learn a great deal about the interaction between bureaucracy and other political institutions but learn little about how the internal workings of the bureaucracy structure these external activities. Probing inside the black box has classic roots. Barnard's *The Functions of the Executive* (1938) was the first modern scholarship to provide insight into superior and subordinate relationships both within and outside administrative organizations. Simon's first major contribution, *Administrative Behavior* (1947), continued the focus on individual bureaucrats in organizations. His later work moved to the organizational level (Simon, Smithberg, and Thompson 1961) yet retained a behavioral focus that was bureaucentric in nature.

Bureaucracy is not the only field of political science to study a phenomenon as a black box. Virtually all of the quantitative work on the presidency deals with this institution and some other institution or process (e.g., Congress or public opinion) and then studies the presidency in an external fashion. The first priority of bureaucracy scholars should be to understand what bureaucracies do and why they do it. This requires a bureaucentric focus. To illustrate, if compliance in the cases that Brehm and Gates (1997; Brehm, Gates, and Gomez, this volume) study is so difficult (i.e., in hierarchical organizations of a paramilitary nature with a great deal of professionalism), why would we assume that it is so easy in other organizations that we study? Further theoretical and empirical work within organizations on issues of trust, culture, and learning following the lead of Brehm and Gates (1997) and Miller (1992) should reveal a great deal about why organizations respond as they do.

A second illustration is presented by Meier and Bohte (1999; Bohte and Meier 2000), who examine the process of organizational cheating, specifically the ability of school districts to generate higher scores on standardized tests by exempting from the exam the students most likely to fail. The Meier and Bohte studies are only unusual in the sophisticated nature of the cheating, which involves using institutionalized rules and procedures to cloak the activity from public officials. Less sophisticated cheating characterized the Russian bureaucracy, which appeared to simply make up data when reporting results (Barry and Barner-Barry 1991; Conyngham 1982). Similarly, the Philadelphia police department was recently caught submitting false crime data in order to claim a reduction in crime and the U.S. Air Force's recent report that high-altitude bombing destroyed most of the tanks operating around Kosovo was later shown to be grossly inaccurate (Barry and Thomas 2000).

Blatant cheating is likely to be infrequent given the high costs of exposure (although sufficient cases appear to exist). Cheating is far more likely and difficult to counteract when it is imbedded in the rules and standard operating procedures of the organization. Such embedding is common in educational organizations with their emphasis on sorting and classification. The processes of the organization allow them to overassign students to special education and limited English classes and then exclude these students, who are less likely to pass, from state-mandated tests (Meier and Bohte 1999). In short, cheating permits schools to manipulate outputs, and thus political principles, by delivering higher test scores without actually improving performance on the exam. What looks like political responsiveness may in fact be something entirely different.

These illustrations suggest a present imbalance in both our theoretical and empirical models of bureaucracy. Political actors are viewed as having multiple tools at their disposal and also possessing sophisticated knowledge as to how to organize administrative agencies for their own advantage. These actors have access to budgets, personnel decisions, court cases, oversight hearings, and numerous opportunities to signal their preferences (e.g., Moe 1982, 1985; Scholz, Twombly and Headrick, 1991; Weingast and Moran 1983; Wood and Waterman 1994). Bureaucracies, in contrast, are often treated as naïve and unsophisticated, responding to politicians in a stimulus-response pattern.

Furthermore, bureaucratic actors and actions are determined solely by external, formal political constraints that arise out of bargaining between the chief executive and legislature. While such analyses provide an important segment of the administrative portrait, they omit the role bureaucracies play as organizations. Such a perspective runs counter to principal-agent (superior-subordinate) relationships that must be predicated on a zone of acceptable behavior between such parties (Barnard

1938; Simon 1947) that can be thought of as a "two-way street" (Krause 1999). We need models that jointly take into account the utility functions of politicians and bureaucratic agencies without relegating the latter to a constraint on the optimization problem facing the former. One excellent example of a general equilibrium-type approach is the one developed in Brehm and Gates's enhanced principal-agent (EPA) model (1993, 1997).

If parsimony requires simplification, future gains may be greater if we move in a different direction and assume strategic, multiskilled bureaucracies and simple, naive politicians for counterfactual purposes. The implication of information asymmetry is that bureaucrats are more knowledgeable than politicians on policy matters. This might not be limited to technical issues and the supervision of interns; they could be better politicians, too. Altering the assumptions concerning sophistication can provide a complete range of theoretical relationships describing the interaction between politicians and bureaucratic agencies. This will help us know when, why, and under what conditions bureaucracies respond to political actors. Answering these research questions will be easier after scholars get inside the black box of bureaucracy to determine how administrative agencies decide to respond to various environmental stimuli.

One illustration of the benefits of a bureaucracy-centered focus might be a reconsideration of the issue of ex ante political controls over the bureaucracy. McCubbins, Noll, and Weingast (1987, 1989) and others stress the ability of Congress to structure the organization and its processes and thus determine its outputs. To be sure, Congress does at times act to structure a process—the well-known cases of the Consumer Product Safety Commission (Bryner 1987), with its initial bizarre procedures, and the decision to locate the Occupational Safety and Health Administration (OSHA) in the Department of Labor rather than Commerce illustrate such ex ante controls. For ex ante controls to be effective, however, Congress would have to engage in such structuring consciously and we would see evidence of systematic applications of applied organizational theory over time by Congress. Hall and O'Toole (2000) investigate how Congress structured policy programs during two different legislative sessions. Although their purpose was to document the use of networks, they found little evidence that Congress has an organization theory or that it possesses the sophisticated congressional strategy and understanding of organizational relationships necessary to create effective procedural (versus substantive) controls over the bureaucracy. Additional empirical evidence lends credence to this view, showing at best modest support for this proposition in diverse policy areas such as Medicare payments (Balla 1998), state air pollution (Potoski 2000), and federal hydroelectric licensing programs (Spence 1999b). Research on hazardous waste implementation reveals that informal rules are successfully substituted by an agency in place of formal rules when politicians constrain agency decision making by reducing agency discretion (Hamilton and Schroeder 1994; Hamilton 1996).

Recent work has demonstrated empirically what students of bureaucratic politics have long believed: relationships between bureaucracy and political institutions are both dynamic and reciprocal (Krause 1996a, 1999). Bureaucracies by their actions often force political institutions to respond to them or risk ceding control over a policy area to the bureaucracy. For some relatively complex programs, Congress (e.g., credit control programs; see Khademian 1995) or the president (agricultural policy; see Meier, Wrinkle, and Polinard 1995) is quite willing to yield control. In other cases, Congress and the president actively seek to shape the actions of the bureaucracy. The bottom line, however, is that we should not assume that the casual force in the relationship is the political institution. This is especially true if one views principal-agent relationships requiring a basic level of agreement that comprises a zone of acceptable behavior (Barnard 1938; Simon 1947). While the literature on political control over the bureaucracy is well developed, the study of bureaucratic organizations is relatively uncharted territory for political scientists. Change does not require eschewing the analysis of political institutions' incentives, tools, and preferences pertaining to policy administration but rather necessitates a more serious treatment of bureaucratic organizations and their features in models of bureaucratic politics. Failure to do so can only result in scholars drawing biased inferences and misleading conclusions about the functioning of the administrative state.

Taking Theory More Seriously

Principal-agent theory has become the predominant paradigm in the study of bureaucracy over the past few decades. Regrettably, our reading of the literature leads us to conclude that political science scholarship has often, though clearly not always, failed to appropriately apply principal-agent theory in empirical studies.[2] Principal-agent models of political control over the bureaucracy must allow for both a strategic principal and a strategic agent, with each able to behave in a proactive manner in a relationship with inherent goal conflict (Mitnick 1980; Perrow 1986; Ross 1973). Principal-agent theory requires a dynamic, inherently changing set of relationships over time. Perhaps such relationships come to an equilibrium, perhaps not. In the prime area of principal-agent theory, that is, where it originated (e.g., doctor-patient relationship), with voluntary relationships characterized by goal conflict and information asymmetry, many relationships do not evolve to an equilibrium. A large number of relationships between doctors and patients, customers and insurance agents, and homeowners and service personnel are simply terminated. Theories must consider this fact on two dimensions. First, Lewis's study on agency termination in the postwar era (2000b) finds that 62 percent of agencies created since 1946 have been terminated. This impermanence and the nonvoluntary nature of the relationship suggests that the model must be fundamentally changed if it is to be useful. Second, termination is sometimes not feasible because the bureaucracy is a monopoly provider (e.g., national defense) or the transaction costs of termination are massive (e.g., abolishing the Department of Education). Such relationships in realistic terms become mandatory, not voluntary. Both problems illustrate the need for theoretical development that incorporates these institutional aspects of bureaucracy.

Examining the empirical studies reveals few analyses claiming to use agency theory that actually take advantage of the driving features of principal-agent models—goal conflict and information asymmetry (see Waterman and Meier 1998). Principal-agent models assume conflict between the goals of the principal and the agent (Ross 1973). While this may be true for many agencies responsible for implementing regulatory policies, it is a questionable assumption in instances in which politicians and administrative agencies do not have inherently conflicting goals. For instance, distributive policies that yield positive-sum gains for clientele groups, congressional committees, and bureaucratic agencies (Ripley and Franklin 1984) do not fit the depiction of the principal-agent model as it was originally developed in law and financial economics. In these areas, agencies and legislatures will share goals. An appropriate empirical illustration of this symbiotic agency-political relationship can be found in the U.S. Department of Agriculture's (USDA's) farm credit programs (Meier, Polinard, and Wrinkle 1999). The conventional principal-agent hypothesis, that politicians will attempt to control the bureaucracy through monitoring and incentives, is misguided in these types of agency-political relationships. The moral hazard problem endemic in conventional models is not a serious issue when bureaucracies (subordinates) acting in their own best interests take actions consistent with the goals of political institutions (superiors; see Brehm and Gates 1997).

In other ways, our empirical knowledge has far outdistanced this simply theory. As an illustration, Khademian (1995) examined what she called bottom-line agencies, those characterized by goal consensus and substantial information asymmetry. Her conclusion was that infrequent but goal-oriented legislation is the primary method of control. Procedural controls will not be considered. Meier, Polinard, and Wrinkle (1999), examining agricultural debt, corroborated Khademian's finding and demonstrated that other traditional principal-agent variables had little impact. A second, related hypothesis from the literature is that political control is enhanced by, but needed less, when clear, precise statutes are the responsibility of a single agency with sufficient resources (Mazmanian and Sabatier 1989). While this pattern rarely occurs, statutory coherence can be measured, and some evidence suggests that coherence matters (Meier and McFarlane 1996).

Developing theory in this area involves determining which types of bureaucracies respond, and in what ways, to political pressure. From the bureaucratic politics literature, we already know that agencies with support from clientele groups are less likely to respond to demands from political officials (Rourke 1984; Rubin 1985). Meier (1997) speculated that democratic constitutional legitimacy matters; if one defines the legitimacy of political pressure with legislation at one pole and ex parte contact on an adjudication at the other, as one moves toward the legislative pole bureaucracies are more responsive to political demands.

These tidbits of political control could be integrated theoretically. Such a theory would recognize that institutional characteristics generate certain types of interactions with other institutions. The real breakthrough in institutional theory will go to the first person who links the structural characteristics of *both* political and administrative institutions to the ways in which they interact with one another.

Miller (2000) presents another challenge to the principal-agent model. Using theoretical work developed for private sector organizations, he argues that principal-agent models will not produce benefits consistent with the goals of principals. Private sector organizations have solved the moral hazard and adverse selection problems by divorcing ownership (principals) from management (agents) and consciously recruiting managers with goals different from ownership. In these models, goal conflict is a positive good and should not be minimized. Contemporary principal-agent theory, according to Miller, provides the wrong guidance in policy design.

In addition to macrotheories of bureaucracy and its interaction with political institutions, more middle range theories of bureaucratic decision making are also needed. This book provides two illustrations. Daniel P. Carpenter, in his chapter, argues that voting theories are inappropriate because bureaucratic decisions are essentially decisions to stop a process. His stopping processes models can be applied to a wide variety of bureaucratic decisions in which the choice is between action and inaction (Food and Drug Administration drug approvals, issuing rules by regulatory agencies, citing a violation of law, granting a license, etc.). One interesting future theoretical question is how stopping processes are altered when political principals impose a time limit on the processes. Using bureaucratic organizations as the decision unit of analysis, George A. Krause examines agency risk taking in terms of how much discretion agencies wish to obtain in relation to the policy outcome uncertainty that they confront. This allows deriving empirically testable conditions of risk-averse, risk-neutral, and risk-seeking bureaucratic behavior.

Normative theory with regard to bureaucracy has generally been ignored by political scientists, even though theories such as budget maximization have normative implications. David B. Spence in this volume uses rational choice logic to argue that in some cases citizens will prefer decisions made by bureaucrats rather than by elected officials. The degree to which expertise tempers representation processes is the key factor in this decision for citizens. Spence's work is a blueprint for those interested in designing public policy to be responsive to a set of values, be they citizen preferences, overall efficiency, or some other value.

Just as all principal-agent theorists assume that the principal's values should be controlling, an extensive literature in bureaucratic politics supports democratic control over bureaucracy (see Rourke 1984). At the same time, because the process of establishing democratic values through overhead democracy is not especially efficient (i.e., there is a great deal of slippage between the electorate and representatives) and because individual bureaucrats are also citizens and may hold appropriate values, trade-offs between democracy and bureaucracy are possible. A normative theory that started from the premise that democratic values, while important, should not always be controlling (e.g., Meier 1997) would argue for different institutional relationships than would the conventional principal-agent model of political control over the bureaucracy with its key simplifying assumption of principal supremacy.

Exploiting the Variance in Bureaucracies

Bureaucracy scholars overstudy federal regulatory agencies. Early quantitative studies of bureaucracy (Moe 1982; Weingast and Moran 1983; Wood 1988) examined regulatory agencies, and their example provided a template for subsequent studies. Federal regulatory agencies, however, have characteristics distinctly different from those of other bureaucracies, especially in terms of variables related to political control. This overfocus on regulation calls into question how general the findings in the literature are.

At least two solutions to this problem exist. First, most bureaucracies are local. If scholars want a situation in which one can turn some of our variables into constants and get good comparability across agencies, then the best strategy is to select the same type of agencies across states or local jurisdictions (Gordon 2000; Ingraham and Kneedler 1999; Schneider and Jacoby 1996). The most common bureaucracies in both number and employment are schools, yet only recently have schools been used to examine questions of bureaucracy (e.g., Abernathy 2000; Chubb and Moe 1990). Using state or local agencies sometimes increases the difficulty of gathering data since the analyst must contact more than one agency with a survey or a Freedom of Information Act request, but the large number of such agencies means that the response rate does not have to be perfect. A cross-sectional analysis of this sort could also be done cross-nationally, although data-gathering problems would increase significantly. A theoretical effort to do this by Thomas H. Hammond, included in this volume, considers how alternative institutional arrangements produce different types of policy outcomes. Recent cross-national research on the topic of political delegation to the bureaucracy by Huber (2000) and Huber and Shipan (2002, 2000) has begun to make vital theoretical and empirical strides in addressing this issue from an electoral institutions perspective in a manner that builds on American work by Epstein and O'Halloran (1999). What remains unearthed altogether, however, is a concerted theoretical and empirical focus on how public bureaucracies function in a variable manner cross-nationally from an organizational perspective.

Second, we could easily focus on nonregulatory agencies at the federal level. Social service agencies, as another illustration, are differently structured, with different traditions and standard operating procedures (see Goodsell 1983). Similar arguments could be made for redistributive agencies, pork barrel agencies, government corporations, and advisory organizations. If Lowi's (1964) typology of policies is not useful, then perhaps Wilson's (1989) typology of government organizations will be. Recent movements into nonregulatory agencies such as health care (Balla 1998), social welfare (Keiser and Soss 1998), and agriculture (Meier, Wrinkle, and Polinard 1995) are long overdue. Keiser, in this volume, continues her work on social welfare agencies; Smith (this volume) examines bureaucratic values in educational organizations, and Corder (this volume), uses federal credit policies.

Future studies of bureaucracy need to continue these nascent efforts to expand the range of bureaucracies studied. Bureaucracy takes many forms—nonprofits, networks, government corporations—and engages in a wide variety of different relationships with political institutions. Only by increasing the variation in the types of bureaucracy that are studied can we hope to provide general findings about how the bureaucracy functions within a representative democracy.

Explicit Incorporation of Structure

As scholars, we have a great deal to contribute by relying on our strength, the understanding of how structures affect behavior. Two types of structures are relevant. First, standard operating procedures both within and external to the agencies are important. Agriculture agencies, for example, interact with Congress in ways different from, say, the Environmental Protection Agency. Health research agencies have different interactions with appropriations committees than the Equal Employment Opportunities Commission (EEOC) does. A brief reading of congressional hearings can document these differences. Some of these differences in interactions might be a function of mission or it might be something else, but relationships are structured differently across agencies, and this affects policy decisions.

Second, organizational structures need to be incorporated in our work. Structural questions once were central to the study of bureaucracy. The work of Meier and Bohte reintroduces the concept of span of control to the study of bureaucracy. Meier and Bohte (2000a) derived some theoretical expectations and then examined the impact of span of control on agency outputs in educational organizations. A second essay (2000b) claims that wider spans of control provide greater discretion to street-level bureaucrats; they then test this by using the logic of representative bureaucracy, finding that minority teachers have more impact in decentralized systems.

Numerous other internal structures affect organizational performance. Decentralization is a concept that is sometimes addressed by examining local units or regions of federal bureaucracies; it is a concept that needs to be brought to the forefront. Decentralized organizations are dominated by street-level bureaucrats; attempts to generalize the models of Brehm, Gates, and Gomez to other such organizations are likely to have some positive results. Recruitment processes and structures within administrative agencies also clearly matter (Carpenter 2001). The reliance of the USDA on state land grant schools, OSHA's initial preference for industrial hygienists and safety engineers, and the 1960s Federal Trade Commission recruitment from second-rate southern law schools all affected the development of these organizations.

From the public administration literature, the concept of networks is also relevant (Milward and Provan 1998; O'Toole 1997). Policy, in many areas, is no longer implemented by means of a single organization but by a network of organizations that often operate across levels of government. The lack of hierarchical control in networks implies that different leadership styles are needed for effective policy implementation. Theoretical work on networks from sociology can be useful in trying to get a handle on interorganizational networks (e.g., Skvoretz and Fararo 1996; Skvoretz and Willer 1993). For instance, does evidence of strong or weak ties (Granovetter 1973) affect patterns of relationships between superiors and subordinates within an administrative organization, among bureaucratic organizations, and among politicians and agencies? This question has critical implications for key concepts such as control, accountability, and effectiveness. Scholarship on policy networks that focuses on national policy subsystems may be instructive for analyzing how bureaucratic agencies interact with one another as well as with the larger political environment (Carpenter, Esterling, and Lazer 1998; Laumann and Knoke 1987; Heinz, et al. 1993).

Structure is not just an internal variable; it can also be used to sharpen other analyses. Mintzberg's (1983) examination of organizational structures argues for various methods of control within an organization, including oversight, socialization of values, standardizing training, and routinization of procedures. His work is intended to operate within an organization but with little effort could be transformed into an approach to presidential control over the bureaucracy. Presidential tools such as reporting (oversight), socialization of values (orientating political appointees to presidential priorities), recruiting individuals with given values (those who share values with the president), and so on are similar to Mintzberg's internal organizational structures. Mintzberg's theory could both integrate the methods of presidential control and suggest when one set of controls is more likely to be used.

A few hypotheses about how internal structure might affect external relationships also come to mind. Overhead controls will work less well in highly decentralized organizations with strong value socialization like the Forest Service. Agencies that have regional offices but do not rotate their personnel from region to region will develop a heterogeneous set of values that will be difficult to direct centrally. In terms of formal structures, O'Toole's (1997) work on networks suggests that they are far more difficult to control than hierarchies. Relatedly, Milward and Provan's (1998) empirical analysis of mental health networks in four cities finds that the most effective network was controlled by a monopoly provider that dominated both service provision and the terms under which mental health services and funding were provided by other agencies. Taken together, this suggests that networks have considerable difficulty in undertaking concerted action unless authority can be consolidated and exercised in a unified manner.

Considerable merit exists for the thesis that bureaucratic structure is important in understanding how administrative agencies operate and that it is inherently political in nature (Moe 1989, 1990; see also Knott and Miller 1987). Recent research by Lewis (2000a) has shown that some administrative agencies are structured in a manner that makes them more susceptible to political influence than others (see also Wood and Anderson 1992). Analysis of bureaucratic structures can also help us to understand how bureaucratic decisions and outcomes disseminate through the regional field offices found in many federal bureaucracies (Gordon 2000; Schmidt 1995; Whitford 1998). Finally, the structure of bureaucratic organizations also matters in assessing how different types of bureaucratic agents, who are appointed in a differential manner, respond to the "contractual" versus "noncontractual" principals that they must encounter (Krause 1994, 1996b).

Methods

The scientific study of bureaucracy needs to adopt methods that correspond to the data-generating process in bureaucracies. Gill and Meier (2000) make a series of general points about methods and their fit with the types of problems that are relevant to the studies in this book. The correspondence between Bayesian methods and how bureaucracies actually make decisions is self-evident. The essay also suggests greater use of qualitative methods that can reflect values (substantively weighted analytical technique, SWAT), methods that incorporate the autoregressive nature of bureaucracies (time-series), and a skepticism of traditional hypothesis testing. In this volume, two of the essays' main contribution is to push the methodological boundaries of inquiry in the study of public bureaucracy. Brehm, Gates, and Gomez introduce both new graphical and statistical modeling approaches, using compositional data analytic techniques to analyze workers' choices. Whitford's analysis of agency competition, punishment, and imitation applies computational (or computer simulation) methods to analyzing bureaucratic organizations. In addition, recent research has placed considerable emphasis on the timing of bureaucratic decisions (Carpenter 2000b; Whitford 1998) and life expectancies for administrative agencies (initially raised in Downs 1967 and Kaufman 1976) using event history and duration statistical modeling techniques (Carpenter 1999; Lewis 2000b).

Other examples of adjusting methods to problems could be found. A historical example is the way courts and administrative agencies have learned to deal with each other over time. In 1965, Kenneth Culp Davis contended that agencies generally ignored courts, but by 1996 Spriggs (1996) found agencies very responsive to court decisions. The responsiveness of agencies to courts of law varies by agency, but clearly some equilibrium has been reached on the scope of court oversight and the degree of responsiveness by agencies. The conclusion that the relationships between bureaucracy and other institutions will be in long-run equilibrium implies that these relationships should be examined via the methods of cointegration. Similarly, Moe's (1985) argument about the National Labor

Relations Board, whereby labor and management adjust their expectations to the ideology of the board, could also be analyzed in this manner with a long enough time-series.

Conclusion

This volume provides a series of essays that examine public bureaucracy from a bureaucentric perspective. The work has much in common with the "new institutionalism" of the past two decades in terms of an emphasis on systematic inquiry containing logical and/or empirical rigor and the attempt to understand how the administrative state functions in a democracy. This "new organizations" approach, however, departs from new institutionalism with respect to investigating public bureaucracies. The former view maintains that the key to understanding the administrative state is not to focus solely on democratic institutions such as the president, Congress, and the courts in order to explain bureaucratic behavior and decision making, as displayed in new institutionalism scholarship, but to also focus on a thorough analysis of bureaucratic agencies as institutions of governance that contain their own unique incentives, procedures, and preferences for administering public policy. Although administrative agencies can be notably affected by rules and procedures designed by legislatures to control the former's behavior; they do not sit on the sidelines as spectators when chief executives and legislatures bargain and maneuver over their fate (Carpenter 2000; Hammond and Knott 1996; Wilson 1989). The point that administrative agencies play a vital role in shaping how policy is administered cannot be overlooked in the study of the politics of the administrative state.

We concur with a sentiment expressed by Moe (1984, 758) nearly two decades ago when discussing the new economics of organization and its subsequent application to the study of public bureaucracies within political science.

> In all likelihood, the contractual paradigm will continue to dominate economic approaches to organization, owing to its linkages to neoclassicism. But it will also continue to include diverse approaches, some far more concerned than others with the empirical richness. The principal-agent model, ideally suited to the analysis of hierarchical relationships, is understandably the major means of formal modeling at present and should become well-established as an important tool for organizational analysis. Given the counter-

vailing influences, however, and given the broader tasks of organization theory, the current fervor surrounding the principal-agent model will likely give way to a more eclectic methodology within which that model plays a less pronounced but integral role.

Clearly, the application and utility of principal-agent and other contractually based paradigms as important theoretical devices in understanding bureaucratic performance within political science have been demonstrated. At the same time, however, these approaches suffer from inherent limitations that prevent us from acquiring an adequate understanding of many vital issues that we need to address as social scientists concerned with theory building and empirical testing of hypotheses centered on how public bureaucracies function within a democratic system of governance. We believe the time has come for more eclectic approaches in scientifically analyzing public bureaucracy in democratic settings.

The essays contained in this volume attempt to enhance our theoretical and empirical understanding of how bureaucracies operate as distinct organizations as well as in relation to the larger political environment. These works seek a better understanding of how bureaucratic organizations perform by placing primary emphasis on analyzing these entities as opposed to relying on other democratic institutions for answers regarding administrative behavior. Our goal is that future scholarship on public bureaucracy within political science will not eschew the importance of administrative organizations when developing theories and empirical tests concerning the functioning of the administrative state.

Notes

1. These four journals are the *American Political Science Review, American Journal of Political Science, Journal of Politics,* and *British Journal of Political Science,* covering the 1981–2000 period.

2. Our *basic* theoretical understanding of the principal-agent model is well developed in some instances (e.g., see Bendor, Taylor, and Van Gaalen 1985; Perrow 1986; Mitnick 1980; and Moe 1984). The *applied* theoretical work tends to address relatively small, specific problems (e.g., budget maximizing) in order to make the problem tractable. This permits these applied theorists to deal with a relatively sophisticated bureaucracy on the strategy side if not on the goals side.

References

Aberbach, Joel D. 1990. *Keeping a Watchful Eye: The Politics of Congressional Oversight.* Washington, DC: Brookings Institution.

Aberbach, Joel D., Robert D. Putnam, and Bert A. Rockman. 1981. *Bureaucrats and Politicians in Western Democracies.* Cambridge: Harvard University Press.

Aberbach, Joel D., and Bert A. Rockman. 2000. *In the Web of Politics: Three Decades of the U.S. Federal Executive.* Washington, DC: Brookings Institution Press.

Abernathy, Scott F. 2000. "Exit, Voice and Choice: Accountability, Participation and Educational Reform in the United States." Paper presented at the annual meeting of the Midwest Political Science Association. Chicago. April.

Achen, Christopher H. 1986. *The Statistical Analysis of Quasi-Experiments.* Berkeley: University of California Press.

Aitchison, J. 1986. *The Statistical Analysis of Compositional Data.* New York: Wiley.

Aitchison, J., and S. M. Shen. 1980. "Logistic-Normal Distributions: Some Properties and Uses." *Biometrika* 67.

Alchian, Armen, and Harold Demsetz. 1972. "Production, Information Costs, and Economic Organization." *American Economic Review* 62 (December): 777–95.

Alexander, F. King. 1998. "Private Institutions and Public Dollars: An Analysis of the Effects of Federal Direct Student Aid on Public and Private Institutions of Higher Education." *Journal of Education Finance* 23.

Allison, Graham T. 1971. *Essence of Decision: Explaining the Cuban Missile Crisis.* New York: HarperCollins.

Allison, Paul D. 1984. *Event History Analysis: Regression for Longitudinal Event Data.* Newbury Park, CA: Sage.

Almond, Gabriel, and Sidney Verba. 1973. "Expectations of Treatment by Government and the Police." In *Bureaucracy and the Public: A Reader in Official-Client Relations,* ed. Elihu Katz and Brenda Danet. New York: Basic Books.

Alt, James E., Gary King, and Curtis S. Signorino. 2001. "Aggregation among

Binary, Count, and Duration Models: Estimating the Same Quantities from Different Levels of Data." *Political Analysis* 9.

Anton, Thomas J. 1989. *American Federalism and Public Policy: How the System Works.* New York: Random House.

Appleby, Paul H. 1952. *Morality and Administration.* Baton Rouge: Louisiana State University Press.

———. 1949. *Policy and Administration.* Tuscaloosa: University of Alabama Press.

Argyris, Chris. 1972. *The Applicability of Organizational Sociology.* New York: Cambridge University Press.

Arnold, R. Douglas. 1990. *The Logic of Congressional Action.* New Haven: Yale University Press.

———. 1987. "Political Control of Administrative Officials." *Journal of Law, Economics, and Organization* 3.

———. 1979. *Congress and the Bureaucracy: A Theory of Influence.* New Haven: Yale University Press.

Arrow, Kenneth J. 1985. "The Economics of Agency." In *Principals and Agents: The Structure of Business,* ed. John Pratt and Richard J. Zeckhauser. Cambridge: Harvard University Press.

———. 1969. "The Organization of Economic Activity: Issues Pertinent to the Choice of Market versus Nonmarket Allocation." In *The Analysis and Evaluation of Public Expenditure: The PPB System.* Vol. 1, 59–73. U.S. Joint Committee, 91st Cong., 1st sess. Washington, DC: U.S. Government Printing Office.

———. 1951. *Social Choice and Individual Values.* New York: Wiley.

Arthur, Brian. 1989. "Competing Technologies, Increasing Returns, and Lock-in by Historical Events." *Economic Journal* 99 (394).

Ashby, W. Ross. 1957. *An Introduction to Cybernetics.* London: Chapman and Hall.

Axelrod, Robert M. 1997. *The Complexity of Cooperation: Agent-Based Models of Competition and Collaboration.* Princeton: Princeton University Press.

———. 1976. *Structure of Decision: The Cognitive Maps of Political Elites.* Princeton: Princeton University Press.

Balla, Steven J. 1998. "Administrative Procedures and Political Control of the Bureaucracy." *American Political Science Review* 92 (September): 663–73.

Balla, Steven J., and Jack Knight. 2002. "Interest Groups, Advisory Committees, and Political Control of the Bureaucracy." *American Journal of Political Science* 46 (January): 398–425.

Baltagi, Badi, and Dan Levin. 1986. "Estimating Dynamic Demand for Cigarettes Using Panel Data." *Review of Economics and Statistics* 68.

Banks, Jeffrey S., and Barry R. Weingast. 1992. "The Political Control of Bureaucracies under Asymmetric Information." *American Journal of Political Science* 36 (May): 509–24.

Barber, Benjamin. 1992. *An Aristocracy of Everyone.* New York: Oxford University Press.

Bardach, Edward. 1980. *The Implementation Game.* Cambridge: MIT Press.

Barnard, Chester. [1938] 1968. *The Functions of the Executive.* Cambridge: Harvard University Press.

Baron, David P., and John A. Ferejohn. 1989. "Bargaining in Legislatures." *American Political Science Review* 83 (December): 1181–1206.

Barry, Donald D., and Carol Barner-Barry. 1991. *Contemporary Soviet Politics.* Englewood Cliffs, NJ: Prentice-Hall.

Barry, John, and Evan Thomas. 2000. "The Kosovo Cover-Up." *Newsweek* (May 15): 23–26.

Bawn, Kathleen. 1999. "Money and Majorities in the Federal Republic of Germany: Evidence for a Veto Players Model of Government Spending." *American Journal of Political Science* 43.

———. 1995. "Political Control versus Expertise: Congressional Choices about Administrative Procedures." *American Political Science Review* 89 (March): 62–73.

———. 1994. "Bureaucratic Accountability for Regulatory Decisions: Comment on Lupia and McCubbins." *Law and Contemporary Problems* 57 (1).

Beamer, Glenn. 1999. *Creative Politics: Taxes and Public Goods in a Federal System.* Ann Arbor: University of Michigan Press.

Beck, Nathaniel, and Jonathan Katz. 1996. "Nuisance vs. Substance: Specifying and Estimating Time-Series–Cross-Section Models." *Political Aalysis* 6.

———. 1995. "What to Do (and Not to Do) with Time-Series Cross-Section Data." *American Political Science Review* 89 (September): 634–47.

Becker, Gary, Michael Grossman, and Kevin Murphy. 1991. "Rational Addiction and the Effect of Price on Consumption." *American Economic Review* 81.

Becker, Gary, and Kevin Murphy. 1988. "A Theory of Rational Addiction." *Journal of Political Economy* 96.

Bendor, Jonathan. 1995. "A Model of Muddling Through." *American Political Science Review* 89 (4): 819–40.

———. 1985. *Parallel Systems: Redundancy in Government.* Berkeley: University of California Press.

Bendor, Jonathan, and Terry M. Moe. 1986. "Agenda Control, Committee Capture, and the Dynamics of Institutional Politics." *American Political Science Review* 80 (December): 1187–207.

———. 1985. "An Adaptive Model of Bureaucratic Politics." *American Political Science Review* 79 (September): 755–74.

Bendor, Jonathan, Serge Taylor, and Roland Van Gaalen. 1987. "Politicians, Bureaucrats, and Asymmetric Information." *American Journal of Political Science* 31 (November): 796–828.

———. 1985. "Bureaucratic Expertise versus Legislative Authority: A Model of

Deception and Monitoring in Budgeting." *American Political Science Review* 79 (4): 1041–60.

Bennett, D. Scott, and Allan C. Stam III. 1996. "The Duration of Interstate Wars, 1816–1985." *American Political Science Review* 90 (March): 239–57.

Berkowitz, Edward, 1987. *Disabled Policy.* Cambridge: Cambridge University Press.

Berman, P. 1980. "Thinking about Programmed and Adaptive Implementation: Matching Strategies to Situations." In *Why Policies Succeed or Fail,* ed. H. Ingram and S. Mann, 205–27. Beverly Hills: Sage.

Bernstein, Marver H. 1955. *Regulating Business by Independent Commission.* Princeton: Princeton University Press.

Berry, Frances, and William Berry. 1990. "State Lottery Adoptions as Policy Innovations." *American Political Science Review* 84 (June): 395–415.

Berry, William, Evan Ringquist, Richard Fording, and Russell Hanson. 1998. "Measuring Citizen and Government Ideology in the American States, 1960–93." *American Journal of Political Science* 42.

Bianco, William T. 1994. *Trust: Representatives and Constituents.* Ann Arbor: University of Michigan Press.

Bikhchandani, Sushil, David Hirshleifer, and Ivo Welch. 1992. "A Theory of Fads, Fashion, Custom, and Cultural Change as Informational Cascades." *Journal of Political Economy* 100.

Blais, André, and Stéphane Dion, eds. 1991. *The Budget-Maximizing Bureaucrat: Appraisals and Evidence.* Pittsburgh: University of Pittsburgh Press.

Blau, Peter. 1968. "The Hierarchy of Authority in Organizations." *American Journal of Sociology* 73 (January): 453–67.

Bohte, John, and Kenneth J. Meier. 2000. "Goal Displacement: Assessing the Motivation for Organizational Cheating." *Public Administration Review* 60 (March/April): 173–82.

Bosworth, Barry P., Andrew S. Carron, and Elisabeth Rhyne. 1987. *The Economics of Federal Credit Programs.* Washington, DC: Brookings Institution.

Boyne, George A. 1998. "Competitive Tendering in Local Government: A Review of Theory and Evidence." *Public Administration* 76 (winter).

Bozeman, Barry. 1987. *All Organizations Are Public.* San Francisco: Jossey-Bass.

Brehm, John, and Scott Gates. 1999. "The Task Allocation Problem in Public Bureaucracies." Paper presented at the annual meeting of the Midwest Political Science Association.

———. 1997. *Working, Shirking, and Sabotage: Bureaucratic Response to a Democratic Public.* Ann Arbor: University of Michigan Press.

———. 1994. "When Supervision Fails to Induce Compliance." *Journal of Theoretical Politics* 6.

———. 1993. "Donut Shops and Speedtraps: Evaluating Models of Supervision of Police Behavior." *American Journal of Political Science* 37.

Brehm, John, and James Hamilton. 1996. "Noncompliance in Environmental Reporting." *American Journal of Political Science* 40.

Brest, Paul. 1988. "Further beyond the Republican Revival, toward Radical Republicanism." *Yale Law Journal* 97.

Breton, Albert, and Ronald Wintrobe. 1975. "The Equilibrium Size of a Budget-Maximizing Bureau: A Note on Niskanen's Theory of Bureaucracy. *Journal of Political Economy* 83 (1): 195–207.

Brodkin, Evelyn Z. 1987. "If We Can't Govern, Can We Manage?" *Political Science Quarterly* 102 (4).

Bryner, Gary C. 1987. *Bureaucratic Discretion: Law and Policy in Federal Regulatory Agencies.* New York: Pergamon.

Burton, Richard M., and Borge Obel. 1995. *Design Models for Hierarchical Organizations: Computation, Information, and Decentralization.* Boston: Kluwer.

Callan, Eamon. 1997. *Creating Citizens: Political Education and Liberal Democracy.* New York: Oxford University Press.

Calvert, Randall, Mathew D. McCubbins, and Barry R. Weingast. 1989. "A Theory of Political Control and Agency Discretion." *American Journal of Political Science* 33 (August): 588–611.

Calvert, Randall, Mark J. Moran, and Barry R. Weingast. 1987. "Congressional Influence over Policymaking: The Case of the FTC." In *Congress: Structure and Policy,* ed. Mathew D. McCubbins and Terry Sullivan. New York: Cambridge University Press.

Carley, Kathleen M., and Michel J. Prietula, eds. 1994. *Computational Organization Theory.* Hillsdale, NJ: Lawrence Erlbaum Associates.

Carpenter, Daniel P. 2002. "Groups, the Media, Agency Waiting Costs, and FDA Drug Approval." *American Journal of Political Science* 46 (2): 490–505.

———. 2001. *The Forging of Bureaucratic Autonomy: Networks, Reputations, and Policy Innovation in Executive Agencies, 1862–1928.* Princeton: Princeton University Press.

———. 2000b. "State-Building through Reputation-Building: Coalitions of Esteem and Policy Innovation at the Post Office, 1880–1912." *Studies in American Political Development* 14 (2).

———. 2000c. "Protection without Capture: A Model of Product Approval by a Politically Responsive, Bayesian Regulator." Typescript, University of Michigan.

———. 2000d. "The Non-neutrality of Bureaucratic Memory: Optimal Stopping by Teams with Poisson Forgetting." Typescript, University of Michigan.

———. 1999. "Informational Delegation, Administrative Failure, and the Lifetime of Bureaus." Manuscript, University of Michigan.

———. 1997. "Institutional Selection and Corporate Attachment at the U.S. Department of Agriculture, 1880–1920." Typescript, Princeton University.

———. 1996. "Adaptive Signal Processing, Hierarchy, and Budgetary Control in Federal Regulation." *American Political Science Review* 90 (2): 283–302.

Carpenter, Daniel P., Kevin M. Esterling, and David M. J. Lazer. 1998. "Strength of Weak Ties in Lobbying Networks: Evidence from Health-Care Politics in the United States." *Journal of Theoretical Politics* 10 (October): 417–44.

Carpenter, Daniel P., and Michael M. Ting. 2001. "Product Approval with Endogenous Submissions." Typescript, University of Michigan.

Center for Deliberative Polling. 1996. The National Issues Convention, January 1996, Austin, Texas. <http://www.la.utexas.edu/research/delpol/Addendum .html#NIC>.

———. 1994. British Deliberative Poll on Crime, 1994. <http://www.la.utexas .edu/research/delpol/Addendum.html#brit1>.

Centers for Disease Control and Prevention. 1996. *State Tobacco Control Highlights, 1996.* Atlanta: Centers for Disease Control and Prevention.

Chandler, Alfred. 1990. *Scale and Scope: The Dynamics of Industrial Capitalism.* Cambridge: Harvard University Press.

Chubb, John E. 1985. "The Political Economy of Federalism." *American Political Science Review* 79 (4): 994–1015.

Chubb, John E., and Terry M. Moe. 1990. *Politics, Markets, and America's Schools.* Washington, DC: Brookings Institution.

———. 1988. "Politics, Markets, and the Organization of Schools." *American Political Science Review* 82 (December): 1065–87.

Coase, Ronald H. 1937. "The Nature of the Firm." *Economica* 4:386–405.

Cofer, Donna Price. 1985. *Judges, Bureaucrats, and the Question of Independence.* Westport, CT: Greenwood.

Coglianese, Cary. 1997. "Assessing Consensus: The Promise and Performance of Negotiated Rulemaking." *Duke Law Journal* 46: 1255–1349.

———. n.d. "Challenging the Rules: Litigation and Bargaining in the Administrative Process." Manuscript.

Cohen, Michael D. 1984. "Conflict and Complexity: Goal Diversity and Organizational Search Effectiveness." *American Political Science Review* 78 (2).

———. 1981. "The Power of Parallel Thinking." *Journal of Economic Behavior and Organization* 2.

Cohen, Michael D., and Robert M. Axelrod. 1984. "Coping with Complexity: The Adaptive Value of Changing Utilities." *American Economic Review* 74.

Cohen, Michael D., James G. March, and Johan P. Olsen. 1972. "A Garbage Can Model of Organizational Choice." *Administrative Science Quarterly* 17 (1).

Cohen, Michael D., Rick L. Roilo, and Robert M. Axelrod. 1999. "The Emergence of Social Organization in the Prisoner's Dilemma: How Context-Preservation and Other Factors Promote Cooperation." Santa Fe Institute, Working Paper 99–01–002.

Conybeare, John A. C. 1984. "Bureaucracy, Monopoly, and Competition: A Critical Analysis of the Budget-Maximizing Model of Bureaucracy." *American Journal of Political Science* 28 (3).

Conybeare, William J. 1982. *The Modernization of Soviet Industrial Management.* Cambridge: Cambridge University Press.

Corder, J. Kevin. 1998. "Political Control of Federal Credit Subsidy: Small Business Administration 7(a) Loan Guarantees." *American Review of Public Administration* 28.

Crawford, Vincent, and Joel Sobel. 1992. "Strategic Information Transmission." *Econometrica* 50.

Crecine, J. P. 1969. *Governmental Problem-Solving.* Chicago: Rand-McNally.

Creek, Laverne, Tom Capehart, and Verner Grise. 1994. *U.S. Tobacco Statistics, 1935–92.* Washington, DC: Government Printing Office.

Crewson, Philip E. 1995. "A Comparative Analysis of Public and Private Sector Entrant Quality." *American Journal of Political Science* 39 (3).

Crozier, Michel. 1964. *The Bureaucratic Phenomenon.* Chicago: University of Chicago Press.

Cyert, Richard M., and James G. March. 1963. *A Behavioral Theory of the Firm.* Englewood Cliffs, NJ: Prentice-Hall.

Dahl, Robert. 1970. *Preface to Democratic Theory.* Chicago: University of Chicago Press.

Dahl, Robert, and Charles Lindblom. 1953. *Politics, Economics, and Welfare.* New York: Harper and Row.

Danziger, Sandra K., Ariel Kalil, and Nathaniel J. Anderson. 2000. "Human Capital, Physical Health, and Mental Health of Welfare Recipients: Co-occurrences and Correlates." *Journal of Social Issues* 56 (4): 635–54.

David, Paul. 1985. "Clio and the Economics of QWERTY". *American Economic Review* 75 (2).

Davidson, Russell, and James G. MacKinnon. 1993. *Estimation and Inference in Econometrics.* New York: Oxford University Press.

Davis, Kenneth Culp. 1965. *Administrative Law.* St. Paul: West Publishing.

DeGroot, Morris. 1970. *Optimal Statistical Decisions.* New York: McGraw-Hill.

de Haan, Jakob. 1997. "The European Central Bank: Independence, Accountability, and Strategy: A Review." *Public Choice* 93.

Department of Health and Human Services. 2000. *Reducing Tobacco Use: A Report of the Surgeon General.* Atlanta: Department of Health and Human Services.

———. 1998. *Tobacco Use among U.S. Racial/Ethnic Minority Groups: A Report of the Surgeon General.* Atlanta: Department of Health and Human Services.

———. 1994. *Preventing Tobacco Use among Young People: A Report of the Surgeon General.* Atlanta: Department of Health and Human Services.

————. 1992. *Smoking and Health in the Americas: A Report of the Surgeon General.* Atlanta: Department of Health and Human Services.

Derthick, Martha. 1990. *Agency under Stress: The Social Security Administration in American Government.* Washington, DC: Brookings Institution.

————. 1972. *New Towns In-Town.* Washington, DC: Urban Institute Press.

Dewey, John. 1929. *My Pedagogic Creed.* Washington, DC: Progressive Education Association.

DiMasi, Joseph A., Henry G. Grabowski, and John Vernon. 1995. "R&D Costs, Innovative Output, and Firm Size in the Pharmaceutical Industry." *International Journal of the Economics of Business* 2(2).

DiMasi, Joseph A., Ronald W. Hansen, Henry G. Grabowski, and Louis Lasagna. 1991. "The Cost of Innovation in the Pharmaceutical Industry." *Journal of Health Economics* 10.

Dixit, Avinash K. 1993. *The Art of Smooth Pasting.* Chur, Switzerland: Harwood Academic Publishers.

Dixit, Avinash K., and Robert S. Pindyck. 1994. *Investment under Uncertainty.* Princeton: Princeton University Press.

Dolgoff, Ralph, Donald Feldstein, and Louise Skolnik. 1993. *Understanding Social Welfare.* 3d ed. New York: Longman.

Downey, La Vonne, and John Gardiner. 1996. *Reducing Youth Access to Tobacco: A Partial Inventory of State Initiatives.* Chicago: University of Chicago Press.

Downs, Anthony. 1972. "Up and Down with Ecology: The "Issue-Attention Cycle." *Public Interest* 28 (summer).

————. 1967. *Inside Bureaucracy.* Boston: Little, Brown.

————. 1957. *An Economic Theory of Democracy.* New York: Harper.

Downs, George, and Patrick Larkey. 1986. *The Search for Government Efficiency.* Philadelphia: Temple University Press.

Dranove, David, and David Meltzer. 1994. "Do More Important Drugs Reach the Market Sooner?" *RAND Journal of Economics* 25 (3).

Easterbrook, Frank H. 1983. "Statute's Domains." *University of Chicago Law Review* 50.

Edwards, J. Terry, John Nalbandian, and Kenneth R. Wedel. 1981. "Individual Values and Professional Education." *Administration and Society* 13 (2): 123–33.

Eijffinger, Sylvester, and Jakob de Haan. 1996. The Political Economy of Central Bank Independence. Princeton Special Papers in International Economics, no. 19.

Eijffinger, Sylvester, Marco Hoeberichts, and Eric Schaling. 1996. "Central Bank Independence: A Panel Data Approach." *Public Choice* 89.

Eisner, Marc. 2000. *Regulatory Politics in Transition.* 2d ed. Baltimore: Johns Hopkins University Press.

————. 1991. *Antitrust and the Triumph of Economics.* Chapel Hill: University of North Carolina Press.

Eisner, Marc, and Kenneth Meier. 1990. "Presidential Control versus Bureaucratic Power: Explaining the Reagan Revolution in Antitrust." *American Journal of Political Science* 34.

Eisner, Neil R. 1989. "Agency Delay in Informal Rulemaking." *Administrative Law Journal* 3.

————. 1984. "Regulatory Negotiation: A Real World Experience." *Federal Bar News and Journal* 31.

Elazar, Daniel J. 1984. *American Federalism: A View from the States.* 3d ed. New York: Harper and Row.

EPA (Environmental Protection Agency). 1987. *Unfinished Business: A Comparative Assessment of Environmental Problems.* Washington, DC: Environmental Protection Agency.

Epstein, David, and Sharyn O'Halloran. 1999. *Delegating Powers: A Transaction Cost Politics Approach to Policy Making under Separate Powers.* New York: Cambridge University Press.

————. 1996. "Divided Government and the Design of Administrative Procedures: A Formal Model and Empirical Test." *Journal of Politics* 58 (May): 373–97.

————. 1994. "Administrative Procedures, Information, and Agency Discretion." *American Journal of Political Science* 38 (August): 697–722.

Epstein, Steven. 1996. *Impure Science: AIDS, Activism, and the Politics of Knowledge.* Berkeley: University of California Press.

Fayole, Henri. 1949. *General and Industrial Management.* New York: Pitman.

Federalist 10 (Madison). Library of Congress (on-line). <http://memory.loc.gov/const/fed/fed_10.html>.

Federalist 63 (Madison or Hamilton). Library of Congress (on-line). <http://memory.loc.gov/const/fed/fed_63.html>.

Fenno, Richard F., Jr. 1978. *Home Style: House Members in Their Districts.* Glenview, IL: Scott, Foresman.

Ferejohn, John. 1987. "The Structure of Agency Decision Processes." In *Congress: Structure and Policy,* ed. Mathew D. McCubbins and Terry Sullivan. New York: Cambridge University Press.

Finer, Herman. 1941. "Administrative Responsibility in Democratic Government." *Public Administration Review* 1 (summer): 335–50.

Fiorina, Morris P. 1986. "Legislator Uncertainty, Legislative Control, and the Delegation of Legislative Power." *Journal of Law, Economics, and Organization* 2.

————. 1985. "Group Concentration and the Delegation of Legislative Authority." In *Regulatory Policy and the Social Sciences,* ed. Roger G. Noll. Berkeley: University of California Press.

————. 1982. "Legislative Choice of Regulatory Forms: Legal Process or Administrative Process?" *Public Choice* 39.

————. 1981. *Retrospective Voting in American National Elections.* New Haven: Yale University Press.

Fishkin, James S. 1996. "The Televised Deliberative Poll: An Experiment in Democracy." In *The Annals of the American Academy of Political and Social Science.* London: Sage Periodicals Press.

Frederickson, H. George. 1997. *The Spirit of Public Administration.* San Francisco: Jossey-Bass.

Friedman, Daniel. 1991. "Evolutionary Games in Economics." *Econometrica* 59.

Friedrich, Carl J. 1940. "Public Policy and the Nature of Administrative Responsibility." *Public Policy* 1:3–24.

Fritschler, A. Lee, and James Hoefler. 1995. *Smoking and Politics.* Englewood Cliffs, NJ: Prentice-Hall.

GAO (United States General Accounting Office). 1995. "FDA Drug Approval: Review Time Has Decreased in Recent Years." GAO/PMED–96–1, Washington, DC, October.

————. 1992. "Social Security: Racial Differences in Disability Decisions Warrants Further Investigation." Washington, DC: HRD–92–56.

————. 1978. "A Plan for Improving the Federal Disability Determination Process by Bringing It under Complete Federal Management Should Be Developed." Washington, DC: HRD 78–146.

————. 1977. *Fundamental Improvements Needed for Timely Promulgation of Health Program Regulations.* Washington, DC: U.S. General Accounting Office.

Gill, Jeff, and Kenneth J. Meier. 2000. "Public Administration Research and Practice: A Methodological Manifesto." *Journal of Public Administration Research and Theory* 10 (January): 157–200.

Goggin, Malcolm L., Ann O'M. Bowman, James P. Lester, and Laurence J. O'Toole Jr. 1990. *Implementation Theory and Practice: Toward a Third Generation.* Glenview, IL: Foresman and Little, Brown Higher Education.

Goodnow, Frank. 1900. *Politics and Administration: A Study in Government.* New York: Macmillan.

Goodsell, Charles T. 1994. *The Case for Bureaucracy.* 3d ed. Chatham, NJ: Chatham House.

————. 1983. *The Case for Bureaucracy.* Chatham, NJ: Chatham, House.

Gordon, Sanford C. 2000. "Policy Learning and Regulatory Inspection Regimes." Paper presented at the annual meeting of the Midwest Political Science Association. Chicago.

————. 1999. "Managing Fairness." PhD. diss., Department of Politics, Princeton University.

Gormley, William. 1989. *Taming the Bureaucracy: Muscles, Prayers, and Other Strategies.* Princeton: Princeton University Press.

Graham, John D., and Jonathan B. Wiener. 1995. "Confronting Risk Tradeoffs." In *Risk versus Risk: Tradeoffs in Protecting Health and the Environment,* ed. John Graham and Jonathan Wiener. Cambridge: Harvard University Press.

Granovetter, Mark. 1973. "The Strength of Weak Ties." *American Journal of Sociology* 78 (May): 1360–80.

Gray, Wayne, and John Scholz. 1993. "Does Regulatory Enforcement Work? A Panel Analysis of OSHA Enforcement." *Law and Society Review* 27.

Greene, William H. 2000. *Econometric Analysis.* 4th ed. Upper Saddle River, NJ: Prentice-Hall.

———. 1997. *Econometric Analysis.* 3d ed. New York: Prentice-Hall.

———. 1993. *Econometric Analysis.* 2d ed. Englewood Cliffs, NJ: Prentice-Hall.

Grofman, Bernard, and Donald Wittman. 1989. *The Federalist Papers and the New Institutionalism.* New York: Agathon.

Gujarati, Damodar. 1995. *Basic Econometrics.* 3d ed. New York: McGraw-Hill.

Gulick, Luther. 1937. "Notes on the Theory of Organization." In *Papers on the Science of Administration,* ed. Luther Gulick and Lydal Urwick, 191–95. New York: Institute of Public Administration, Columbia University.

Gulick, Luther, and Lydal Urwick, eds. 1937. *Papers on the Science of Administration.* New York: Institute of Public Administration, Columbia University.

Gupta, Rameshwar D., and Donald St. P. Richards. 1987. "Multivariate Liouville Distributions." *Journal of Multivariate Analysis* 23.

Gutmann, Amy. 1987. *Democratic Education.* Princeton: Princeton University Press.

Hall, Thad E., and Laurence J. O'Toole. 2000. "Structures for Policy Implementation: An Analysis of National Legislation." *Administration and Society* 31 (January): 667–86.

Hamilton, James T. 1996. "Going by the (Informal) Book: The EPA's Use of Informal Rules in Enforcing Hazardous Waste Laws." *Advances in the Study of Entrepreneurship, Innovation, and Growth* 7: 109–55.

———. 1994. *Time Series Analysis.* Princeton: Princeton University Press.

———. 1992. *Regression with Graphics.* Pacific Grove, CA: Brooks/Cole.

Hamilton, James T., and Christopher H. Schroeder. 1994. "Strategic Regulators and the Choice of Rulemaking Procedures: The Selection of Formal vs. Informal Rules in Regulating Hazardous Waste." *Law and Contemporary Problems* 57 (spring): 111–60.

Hammond, Thomas H. 1996. "Formal Theory and the Institutions of Governance." *Governance* 9.

———. 1986. "Agenda Control, Organizational Structure, and Bureaucratic Politics." *American Journal of Political Science* 30 (May).

Hammond, Thomas H., and Christopher K. Butler. 2003. "Some Complex Answers to the Simple Question 'Do Institutions Matter?': Policy Choice and Policy Change in Presidential and Parliamentary Systems." *Journal of Theoretical Politics* 15: 145–200.

Hammond, Thomas H., and Jack H. Knott. 2000. "Public Management, Administrative Leadership, and Policy Choice." In *Advancing Public Management: New Developments in Theory, Methods, and Practice,* ed. Jeffrey L. Brudney, Laurence J. O'Toole Jr., and Hal G. Rainey. Washington, DC: Georgetown University Press.

———. 1999. "Political Institutions, Public Management, and Policy Choice." *Journal of Public Administration Research and Theory* 9.

———. 1996. "Who Controls the Bureaucracy? Presidential Power, Congressional Dominance, Legal Constraints, and Bureaucratic Autonomy in a Model of Multi-institutional Policymaking." *Journal of Law, Economics, and Organization* 12 (April): 119–66.

Hammond, Thomas H., and Gary J. Miller. 1987. "The Core of the Constitution." *American Political Science Review* 81 (December): 1155–74.

Haque, M. S. 1996. "The Intellectual Crisis in Public Administration in the Current Epoch of Privatization." *Administration and Society* 27.

Harris, Richard A., and Sidney M. Milkis. 1996. *The Politics of Regulatory Change: A Tale of Two Agencies.* 2d ed. New York: Oxford University Press.

Harrison, Michael. 1985. *Brownian Motion and Stochastic Flow Systems.* New York: Wiley.

Harter, Philip J. 1982. "Negotiated Rulemaking: A Cure for Malaise." *Georgetown Law Journal* 71.

Hasenfeld, Yeheskel, ed. 1992. *Human Services as Complex Organizations.* Newbury Park, CA: Sage.

Hassapis, Christis. 1996. "Are Bureaucrats Efficient? An Application to the Provision of AFDC." *Public Choice* 86.

Hawkins, Keith, and John M. Thomas. 1989. "Rule Making and Discretion: Implications for Designing Regulatory Policy." In *Making Regulatory Policy,* ed. Keith Hawkins and John M. Thomas. Pittsburgh: University of Pittsburgh Press.

Hedge, David M., Donald C. Menzel, and Mark A. Krause. 1989. "The Intergovernmental Milieu and Street-level Implementation." *Social Science Quarterly* 70 (2).

Hedge, David M., and Michael J. Scicchitano. 1994. "Regulating in Space and Time: The Case of Regulatory Federalism." *Journal of Politics* 56 (1): 134–53.

Heimann, C. F. Larry. 1997. *Acceptable Risks: Politics, Policy, and Risky Technologies,* Ann Arbor: University of Michigan Press.

———. 1993. "Understanding the *Challenger* Disaster: Organizational Structure and the Design of Reliable Systems." *American Political Science Review* 87.

Heinz, John P., Edward O. Laumann, Robert L. Nelson, and Robert H. Salisbury. 1993. *The Hollow Core: Private Interests in National Policy Making.* Cambridge: Harvard University Press.

Henig, Jeffrey. 1994. *Rethinking School Choice: Limits of the Market Metaphor.* Princeton: Princeton University Press.

Henry, Nicholas. 1995. *Public Administration and Public Affairs.* 6th ed. Englewood Cliffs, NJ: Prentice-Hall.

Herring, E. Pendleton. 1936. *Public Administration and the Public Interest.* New York: McGraw-Hill.

Hess, Frederick. 1999. *Spinning Wheels: The Politics of Urban School Reform.* Washington, DC: Brookings Institution Press.

Higgins, Richard S., William F. Shughart II, and Robert D. Tollison. 1987. "Dual Enforcement of the Antitrust Laws." In *Public Choice and Regulation,* ed. Robert J. Mackay, James C. Miller III, and Bruce Yandle. Stanford: Hoover Institution Press.

Hill, Jeffrey S., and Carol S. Weissert. 1995. "Implementation and the Irony of Delegation: The Politics of Low-Level Radioactive Waste Disposal." *Journal of Politics* 57 (2).

Hirschman, Albert O. 1970. *Exit, Voice, and Loyalty: Responses to Decline in Firms, Organizations, and States.* Cambridge: Harvard University Press.

Hirshliefer, Jack, and John G. Riley. 1992. *The Analytica of Uncertainty and Information.* New York: Cambridge University Press.

Hirshman, Linda R. 1989. "Kicking over the Traces of Self-Government." *Chicago-Kent Law Review* 64.

Holmström, Bengt. 1982. "Moral Hazard in Teams." *Bell Journal of Economics* 13.

Horn, Murray J. 1995. *The Political Economy of Public Administration: Institutional Choice in the Private Sector.* New York: Cambridge University Press.

Horn, Murray J., and Kenneth A. Shepsle. 1989. "Commentary on 'Administrative Arrangements and the Political Control of Agencies': Administrative Process and Organizational Form as Legislative Responses to Agency Costs." *Virginia Law Review* 75:504–9.

Howards, Irving, Henry P. Brehm, and Saad Z. Nagi. 1980. *Disability: From Social Problem to Federal Program.* New York: Praeger.

Hsiao, Cheng. 1986. *Analysis of Panel Data.* New York: Cambridge University Press.

Huber, John D. 2000. "Delegation to Civil Servants in Parliamentary Democracies." *European Journal of Political Research* 37 (May): 397–413.

Huber, John D., and Charles R. Shipan. 2002. *Deliberate Discretion? The Institutional Foundations of Bureaucratic Autonomy.* New York: Cambridge University Press.

———. 2000. "A Comparative Theory of Statutory Control of Bureaucrats." Typescript, Columbia University.

Humphreys, N. Macartan. 2001. "Core Existence in Multigroup Spatial Games." Paper presented at the annual meeting of the American Political Science Association, San Francisco.

Huntington, Samuel P. 1952. "The Marasmus of the ICC." *Yale Law Journal* 61 (April): 467–509.

Hyman, David. 1996. *Public Finance: A Contemporary Application of Theory to Practice.* 5th ed. Fort Worth: Dryden.

Hyneman, Charles. 1950. *Bureaucracy in a Democracy.* New York: Harper.

Inglehart, Ronald. 1990. *Culture Shift in Advanced Industrial Society.* Princeton: Princeton University Press.

Ingraham, Patricia W., and Amy E. Kneedler. 1999. "Dissecting the Black Box Revisited." Paper presented at the Governance Workshop, University of Arizona. May.

Ippolito, Dennis S. 1984. *Hidden Spending.* Chapel Hill: University of North Carolina Press.

Jacobson, Peter, and Jeffrey Wasserman. 1997. *Tobacco Control Laws.* Santa Monica: Rand.

Jensen, Michael, and William Meckling. 1976. "Theory of the Firm: Managerial Behavior, Agency Costs, and Capital Structure." *Journal of Financial Economics* 3 (October): 305–60.

Johnson, Ronald N., and Gary D. Libecap. 1994. *The Federal Civil Service System and the Problem of Bureaucracy: The Economics and Politics of Institutional Change.* Chicago: University of Chicago Press.

Jones, Bryan D. 2001. *Politics and the Architecture of Choice.* Chicago: University of Chicago Press.

Joskow, Paul. 1974. "Inflation and Environmental Concern: Structural Change in the Process of Public Utility Price Regulation." *Journal of Law and Economics* 17.

Jovanovic, Boyan. 1979. "Job Matching and the Theory of Turnover." *Journal of Political Economy* 87 (5): 972–90.

Kadushin, Alfred. 1992. *Supervision in Social Work.* 3d ed. New York: Columbia University Press.

Kaitin, Kenneth I., and Michael Manocchia. 1997. "The New Drug Approvals of 1993, 1994, and 1995: Trends in Drug Development." *American Journal of Therapeutics* 4.

Kaitin, Kenneth I., Michael Manocchia, Mark Seibring, and Louis Lasagna. 1994. "The New Drug Approvals of 1990, 1991, and 1992: Trends in Drug Development." *Journal of Clinical Pharmacology* 34.

Katz, Jonathan N., and Gary King. 1999. "A Statistical Model of Multiparty Electoral Data." *American Political Science Review* 93.

Katz, Michael B. 1989. *The Undeserving Poor: From the War on Poverty to the War on Welfare.* New York: Patheon.

Kaufman, Herbert. 1991. *Time, Chance, and Organizations.* 2d ed. Chatham, NJ: Chatham House.

———. 1977. *Red Tape, Its Origins, Uses, and Abuses.* Washington, DC: Brookings Institution.

———. 1976. *Are Government Organizations Immortal?* Washington, DC: Brookings Institution.

———. 1973. *Administrative Feedback.* Washington, DC: Brookings Institution.

———. 1960. *The Forest Ranger: A Study in Administrative Behavior.* Baltimore: Johns Hopkins University Press.

Keech, William, and K. Pak. 1989. "Electoral Cycles and Budgetary Growth in Veteran's Benefit Programs." *American Journal of Political Science* 33.

Keiser, Lael R. 2001. "Street-Level Bureaucrats, Administrative Power, and Manipulation of Federal Social Security Disability Programs." *State Politics and Policy Quarterly* 1 (2).

———. 1999. "State Bureaucratic Discretion and the Administration of Social Welfare Programs: The Case of Social Security Disability." *Journal of Public Administration Research and Theory* 9 (1): 87–106.

Keiser, Lael R., and Kenneth J. Meier. 1996. "Policy Design, Bureaucratic Incentives, and Public Management: The Case of Child Support Enforcement." *Journal of Public Administration Research and Theory* 6 (3).

Keiser, Lael R., and Joe Soss. 1998. "With Good Cause: Bureaucratic Discretion and the Politics of Child Support Enforcement." *American Journal of Political Science* 42 (4): 1133–56.

Kerwin, Cornelius M. 1999. *Rulemaking: How Government Agencies Write Law and Make Policy.* 2d ed. Washington, DC: Congressional Quarterly Press.

Kerwin, Cornelius M., and Scott R. Furlong. 1992. "Time and Rulemaking: An Empirical Test of Theory." *Journal of Public Administration Research and Theory* 2.

Kettl, Donald F. 1993. *Sharing Power: Public Governance and Private Markets.* Washington, DC: Brookings Institution.

Key, V. O. 1959. "Legislative Control." In *Elements of Public Administration,* ed. Fritz Morstein Marx, 312–36. Englewood Cliffs, NJ: Prentice-Hall.

Khademian, Anne M. 1995. "Reinventing a Government Corporation: Professional Priorities and a Clear Bottom Line." *Public Administration Review* 55 (January/February): 17–28.

———. 1992. *SEC and Capital Market Regulation.* Pittsburgh: University of Pittsburgh Press.

King, Gary, 1989. *Unifying Political Methodology: The Likelihood Theory of Statistical Inference.* New York: Cambridge University Press.

———. 1988. "Statistical Models for Political Science Event Counts: Bias in Conventional Procedures and Evidence for the Exponential Poisson Regression Model." *American Journal of Political Science* 32.

Kleinbaum, David G., Lawrence L. Kupper, and Keith E. Muller. 1988. *Applied Regression Analysis and Other Multivariable Methods.* Boston: PWS-Kent.

Knight, Kenneth. 1967. "A Descriptive Model of Intra-firm Innovative Process." *Journal of Business* 40.

Knott, Jack H., and Gary J. Miller. 1987. *Reforming Bureaucracy: The Politics of Institutional Choice.* Englewood Cliffs: Prentice-Hall.

Kolko, Gabriel. 1966. *Railroads and Regulations, 1877–1916.* New York: Norton.

Kollman, Ken, John H. Miller, and Scott E. Page. 1992. "Adaptive Parties in Spatial Elections." *American Political Science Review* 86 (4): 929–37.

Krause, George A. 1999. *A Two-Way Street: The Institutional Dynamics of the Modern Administrative State.* Pittsburgh: University of Pittsburgh Press.

———. 1996a. "The Institutional Dynamics of Policy Administration: Bureaucratic Influence over Securities Regulation." *American Journal of Political Science* 40 (4): 1083–121.

———. 1996b. "Agent Heterogeneity and Consensual Decision Making on the Federal Open Market Committee." *Public Choice* 88 (July): 83–101.

———. 1994. "Federal Reserve Policy Decision Making: Political and Bureaucratic Influences." *American Journal of Political Science* 38 (February): 124–44.

Kreps, David. [1984] 1990. "Corporate Culture and Economic Theory." In *Perspectives on Positive Political Economy,* ed. James E. Alt and Kenneth A. Shepsle. New York: Cambridge University Press.

Kritzer, Herbert M. 1998. *Legal Advocacy: Lawyers and Nonlawyers at Work.* Ann Arbor: University of Michigan Press.

Landau, Martin. 1969. "Redundancy, Rationality, and the Problem of Duplication and Overlap." *Public Administration Review* 29 (4).

Langbein, Laura I., and Cornelius M. Kerwin. 2000. "Regulatory Negotiation versus Conventional Rule Making: Claims, Counterclaims, and Empirical Evidence." *Journal of Public Administration Theory and Research* 10.

Laumann, Edward O., and David Knoke. 1987. *The Organizational State: Social Choice in National Policy Domains.* Madison: University of Wisconsin Press.

Levinthal, Daniel, and James G. March. 1981. "A Model of Adaptive Organizational Search." *Journal of Economic Behavior and Organization* 2.

Lewin Group, Inc., and Pugh Ettinger McCarthy Associates, L.L.C. 2001. *Evaluation of SSA's Disability Quality Assurance (QA) Processes and Development of QA Options That Will Support the Long-Term Management of the Disability Program.* Ithaca, NY: The Lewin Group, Cornell University.

Lewis, David E. 2000a. "Political Insulation and the Durability of United States Government Agencies." Paper presented at the annual meeting of the Midwest Political Science Association. Chicago.

———. 2000b. "The Myth of Agency Immortality: The Politics of Agency Termination." Typescript, College of William and Mary.

Lewit, Eugene. 1989. "U.S. Tobacco Taxes: Behavioral Effects and Policy Implications." *British Journal of Addiction* 84.

Licari, Michael. 2001a. "Regulation and Federalism: The Politics of Cigarette Taxation." Paper presented at the Midwest Political Science Association meeting.

———. 2001b. "Smoking and the States: The Politics of State Clean Indoor Air Laws." Paper presented at the American Political Science Association meeting.

Licari, Michael, and Kenneth J. Meier. 2000. "Regulation and Signaling: When a Tax Is Not Just a Tax." *Journal of Politics* 62.

———. 1997. "Regulatory Policy When Behavior Is Addictive." *Political Research Quarterly* 50.

Likert, Rensis. 1967. *The Human Organization.* New York: McGraw-Hill.

Lindblom, Charles E. 1959. "The Science of Muddling Through." *Public Administration Review* 19.

Lipsky, Michael. 1980. *Street-Level Bureaucrats: Dilemmas of the Individual in Public Services.* New York: Russell Sage Foundation.

Long, J. Scott. 1997. *Regression Models for Categorical and Limited Dependent Variables.* Thousand Oaks, CA: Sage.

Long, Norton E. 1952. "Bureaucracy and Constitutionalism." *American Political Science Review* 46 (September): 808–18.

Loprest, Pamela, and Gregory Acs. 1995. *Profile of Disability among Families on AFDC.* Washington, DC: Urban Institute.

Lowery, David. 1982. "Public Choice When Services Are Costs: The Divergent Case of Assessment Administration." *American Journal of Political Science* 26.

Lowi, Theodore J. 1992. "The State of Political Science: How We Are Becoming What We Study." *American Political Science Review* 86.

———. 1979. *The End of Liberalism: the Second Republic of the United States.* 2d ed. New York: Norton.

———. 1969. *The End of Liberalism: Ideology, Policy, and the Crisis of Public Authority.* New York: Norton.

———. 1964. "American Business, Public Policy, Case-Studies, and Political Theory." *World Politics* 16 (July): 677–715.

Lupia, Arthur. 1994. "Shortcuts versus Encyclopedias: Information and Voting Behavior in California Insurance Reform Elections." *American Political Science Review* 88 (March): 63–76.

Lupia, Arthur, and Mathew D. McCubbins. 1998. *The Democratic Dilemma: Can Citizens Learn What They Need to Know?* Cambridge: Cambridge University Press.

———. 1994a. "Designing Bureaucratic Accountability." *Law and Contemporary Problems* 57 (1).

———. 1994b. "Learning from Oversight: Fire Alarms and Police Patrols Reconstructed." *Journal of Law, Economics, and Organization* 10.

Macey, Jonathan. 1992. "Organizational Design and Political Control of Administrative Agencies." *Journal of Law, Economics, and Organization* 8.

Maddala, G. S. 1992. *Introduction to Econometrics.* 2d ed. New York: Macmillan.

Magat, Wesley, Alan Krupnick, and Winston Harrington. 1986. *Rules in the Making: A Statistical Analysis of Regulatory Agency Behavior.* Washington, DC: Resources for the Future.

Majone, G., and Wildavsky, Aaron. 1984. "Implementation as Evolution." In *Implementation,* ed. J. Pressman and Aaron Wildavsky. 3d ed. Berkeley: University of California Press.

Manchester, Paul. 1976. "Interstate Cigarette Smuggling." *Public Finance Quarterly* 4.

March, James G. 1999. *The Pursuit of Organizational Intelligence.* Malden, MA: Blackwell.

March, James G., and Johan P. Olsen. 1976. *Ambiguity and Choice in Organizations.* Bergen, Norway: Universitesforlaget.

March, James G., and Herbert A. Simon. 1958. *Organizations.* New York: Wiley.

Martin, Elizabeth. 1997. "An Informational Theory of the Legislative Veto." *Journal of Law, Economics, and Organization* 13.

Mashaw, Jerry L. 1998. *Greed, Chaos, and Governance: Using Public Choice to Improve Public Law.* New Haven: Yale University Press.

———. 1983. *Bureaucratic Justice: Managing Social Security Disability Claims.* New Haven: Yale University Press.

Masuch, Michael, and Perry J. LaPotin. 1989. "Beyond Garbage Cans: An AI Model of Organizational Choice." *Administrative Science Quarterly* 34 (1): 38–67.

Mayhew, David R. 1974. *Congress: The Electoral Connection.* New Haven: Yale University Press.

Mazmanian, Daniel A., and Paul A. Sabatier. 1989. *Implementation and Public Policy.* Lanham, MD: University Press of America.

McCabe, Barbara Coyle, and Janet Coble Vinzant. 1999. "Governance Lessons: The Case of Charter Schools." *Administration and Society* 31.

McCubbins, Mathew D. 1985. "The Legislative Design of Regulatory Structure." *American Journal of Political Science* 29 (November): 721–48.

McCubbins, Mathew D., Roger G. Noll, and Barry R. Weingast. 1989. "Structure and Process, Politics and Policy: Administrative Arrangements and the Political Control of Agencies." *Virginia Law Review* 75 (March): 431–82.

———. 1987. "Administrative Procedures as Instruments of Political Control." *Journal of Law, Economics, and Organization* 3 (fall): 243–77.

McCubbins, Mathew D., and Talbot Page. 1987. "A Theory of Congressional Delegation." In *Congress: Structure and Policy,* ed. Mathew D. McCubbins and Terry Sullivan. New York: Cambridge University Press.

McCubbins, Mathew D., and Thomas Schwartz. 1984. "Congressional Oversight Overlooked: Police Patrols versus Fire Alarms." *American Journal of Political Science* 28 (February): 165–79.

McFadden, Daniel. 1976. "The Revealed Preferences of a Public Bureaucracy: Evidence." *Bell Journal of Economics* 7.

McGraw, Kathleen, and John Scholz. 1991. "Attention to Self-Interest: Effects on Tax Compliance." *Law and Society Review* 25.

———. 1988. "Norms, Social Commitment, and Citizen Adaptation to New Laws." In *Lawyers on Psychology and Psychologists on Law,* ed. P. J. van Koppen, D. J. Hessing, and G. van den Heuvel. Amsterdam: Swets and Zeitlinger.

McGregor, Douglas. 1960. *The Human Side of Enterprise.* New York: McGraw-Hill.

McGuire, Thomas G., Michael Coiner, and Larry Spancake. 1979. "Budget Maximizing Agencies and Efficiency in Government. *Public Choice* 34 (3–4).

Meier, Kenneth J. 2000. *Politics and the Bureaucracy: Policymaking in the Fourth Branch of Government.* 4th ed. Forth Worth: Harcourt College Publishers.

———. 1997. "Bureaucracy and Democracy: The Case for More Bureaucracy and Less Democracy." *Public Administration Review* 57 (May/June): 193–99.

———. 1993a. *Politics and the Bureaucracy: Policymaking in the Fourth Branch of Government.* 3d ed. Pacific Grove, CA: Brooks/Cole.

———. 1993b. "Representative Bureaucracy: A Theoretical and Empirical Exposition." In *Research in Public Administration,* ed. James Perry. Greenwich, CT: JAI Press.

Meier, Kenneth J., and John Bohte. 2000a. "Ode to Luther Gulick: Span of Control and Organizational Performance." *Administration and Society* 32 (May): 115–37.

———. 2000b. "Structure and Discretion: Missing Links in Representative Bureaucracy." Typescript, Texas A&M University.

———. 1999. "Putting the Bureaucracy Back In: Principals, Agents and Bureaucratic Strategy." Paper presented at the annual meeting of the Midwest Political Science Association.

Meier, Kenneth J., and Michael Licari. 1997a. "Public Policy Design: Combining Policy Instruments." Paper presented at the American Political Science Association annual meeting, Washington, DC, August.

———. 1997b. "The Effect of Cigarette Taxes on Cigarette Consumption, 1955 through 1994." *American Journal of Public Health* 87.

Meier, Kenneth J., and Deborah R. McFarlane. 1996. "Statutory Coherence and Policy Implementation." *Journal of Public Policy* 15 (3): 281–98.

Meier, Kenneth J., and L. G. Nigro. 1976. "Representative Bureaucracy and Policy Preferences: A Study in the Attitudes of Federal Executives." *Public Administration Review* 36:458–69.

Meier, Kenneth, J. L. Polinard, and Robert D. Wrinkle. 1999. "Politics, Bureaucracy, and Farm Credit." *Public Administration Review* 59 (4): 293–302.

Meier, Kenneth, J., Robert D. Wrinkle, and J. L. Polinard. 1995. "Politics, Bureaucracy, and Agricultural Policy: An Alternative View of Political Control." *American Politics Quarterly* 23 (October): 427–60.

Menard, Scott. 1995. *Applied Logistic Regression Analysis.* Thousand Oaks, CA: Sage.

Merton, Robert K. 1957. "Bureaucratic Structure and Personality." In *Social Theory and Social Structure,* ed. Robert K. Merton. New York: Free Press.

Meyer, Marshal. 1968. "Two Authority Structures of Bureaucratic Organizations." *Administrative Science Quarterly* 13 (September): 211–28.

Mezey, Susan Gluck. 1986. "Policymaking by the Federal Judiciary: The Effects of Judicial Review on the Social Security Disability Program." *Policy Studies Journal* 14 (March).

Migue, J. and G. Belanger. 1974. "Toward a General Theory of Managerial Discretion." *Public Choice* 17.

Mikva, Abner J. 1988. "The Theory of Public Choice." *Virginia Law Review* 74:167–77.

Milgrom, Paul, and John Roberts. 1986. "Relying on the Information of Interested Parties." *Rand Journal of Economics* 17.

Miller, Gary J. 2000. "Above Politics: Credible Commitment and Efficiency in the Design of Public Agencies." *Journal of Public Administration Research and Theory* 10 (April): 289–328.

———. 1992. *Managerial Dilemmas: The Political Economy of Hierarchy.* New York: Cambridge University Press.

Miller, Gary J., and Terry M. Moe. 1983. "Bureaucrats, Legislators, and the Size of Government." *American Political Science Review* 77 (June): 297–322.

Milward, H. Brinton, and Keith G. Provan. 1998. "Principles for Controlling Agents: The Political Economy of Network Structure." *Journal of Public Administration Research and Theory* 8 (April): 203–21.

Mintz, Benjamin W., and Nancy G. Miller. 1991. *A Guide to Federal Agency Rulemaking.* 2d ed. Washington, DC: Administrative Conference of the United States.

Mintzberg, Henry. 1983. *Power in and around Organizations.* Englewood Cliffs, NJ: Prentice-Hall.

———. 1979. *The Structuring of Organizations.* Englewood Cliffs, NJ: Prentice-Hall.

Miroschnichenko, T. P. 1963. "Optimal Stopping of an Integral of a Wiener Process." *Theory of Probability and Its Applications* 9 (4) (July): 355–92.

Mitnick, Barry M. 1980. *The Political Economy of Regulation: Creating, Designing, and Removing Regulatory Forms.* New York: Columbia University Press.

Moe, Ronald, and Robert Gilmour. 1995. "Rediscovering Principles of Public Administration: The Neglected Foundation of Public Law." *Public Administration Review.* 55.

Moe, Terry M. 1997. "Political Institutions: The Neglected Side of the Story." *Journal of Law, Economics and Organization* 6.

———. 1990. "The Politics of Structural Choice: Toward a Theory of Public Bureaucracy." In *Organization Theory: From Chester Barnard to Present and Beyond,* ed. Oliver E. Williamson. New York: Oxford University Press.

———. 1989. "The Politics of Bureaucratic Structure." In *Can the Government Govern?* ed. John E. Chubb and Paul E. Peterson. Washington, DC: Brookings Institution.

———. 1987. "An Assessment of the Positive Theory of 'Congressional Dominance'." *Legislative Studies Quarterly* 12 (November): 475–520.

———. 1985. "Control and Feedback in Economic Regulation: The Case of the NLRB." *American Political Science Review* 79 (December): 1094–116.

———. 1984. "The New Economics of Organization." *American Journal of Political Science* 28 (November): 739–77.

———. 1982. "Regulatory Performance and Presidential Administration." *American Journal of Political Science* 26 (May): 197–224.

Mosher, Frederick C. 1968. *Democracy and the Public Service.* New York: Oxford University Press.

Mullainathan, Sendhil. 1998. "A Memory-Based Model of Bounded Rationality." Typescript, Department of Economics, MIT.

Musolf, Lloyd. 1991. "Government-Sponsored Enterprises and Congress." *Public Administration Review* 51.

Nalbandian, John, and J. Terry Edwards. 1983. "The Values of Public Administrators." *Review of Public Personnel Administration* (fall): 114–27.

National Academy of Public Administration. 1999. *Helpful Practices in Improving Government Performance: A Compilation of Papers.* Washington, DC: National Academy of Public Administration.

———. 1987. *Presidential Management of Rulemaking in Regulatory Agencies: A Report.* Washington, DC: National Academy of Public Administration.

National Center for Education Statistics. 1998. *Teacher Followup Survey.* U.S. Department of Education, CD-ROM, NCES 98–312.

Nelson, Richard R., and Sidney G. Winter. 1978. "Forces Generating and Limiting Concentration under Schumpeterian Competition." *Bell Journal of Economics* 9.

Nelson, William E. 1982. *The Roots of American Bureaucracy, 1830–1900.* Cambridge: Harvard University Press.

Newell, Allen, and Herbert A. Simon. 1972. *Human Problem Solving.* Englewood Cliffs, NJ: Prentice-Hall.

Niskanen, William A., Jr. 1971. *Bureaucracy and Representative Government.* Chicago: Aldine Atherton.

———. 1968. "The Peculiar Economics of Bureaucracy." *American Economic Review* 58.

Noll, Roger G. 1985. "Government Regulatory Behavior: A Multidisciplinary Survey and Synthesis." In *Regulatory Policy and Social Sciences,* ed. Roger G. Noll. Berkeley: University of California Press.

Nordhaus, William D. 1975. "The Political Business Cycle." *Review of Economic Studies* 42.

North, Douglass C. 1990. *Institutions, Institutional Change, and Economic Performance.* New York: Cambridge University Press.

Nuthall, Graham. 1999. "Introduction and Background." *International Journal of Educational Research* 31: 141–256.

Ogul, Morris. 1976. *Congress Oversees the Bureaucracy.* Pittsburgh: University of Pittsburgh Press.

Olson, Mancur. 1971. *The Logic of Collective Action: Public Goods and the Theory of Groups.* Cambridge: Harvard University Press.

Olson, Mary. 1997. "Firm Characteristics and the Speed of FDA Drug Approval." *Journal of Economics and Management Strategy* 6 (2).

———. 1996. "Substitution in Regulatory Agencies: FDA Enforcement Alternatives." *Journal of Law, Economics, and Organization* 11.

———. 1995. "Regulatory Agency Discretion among Competing Industries: Inside the FDA." *Journal of Law, Economics, and Organization* 11 (2).

Osborne, David, and Ted Gaebler. 1993. *Reinventing Government: How the Entrepreneurial Spirit Is Transforming the Public Sector.* New York: Plume.

Osborne, David, and Peter Plastrik. 1998. *Banishing Bureaucracy.* Reading, MA: Plume.

Ostrom, Elinor. 1998. "A Behavioral Approach to the Rational Choice Theory of Collective Action." *American Political Science Review* 92 (March): 1–22.

———. 1990. *Governing the Commons: The Evolution of Institutions for Collective Action.* Cambridge: Cambridge University Press.

Ostrom, Elinor, Roger B. Parks, and Gordon Whittaker. 1988. "Police Services Study, Phase II, 1977: Rochester, St. Louis, and St. Petersburg." ICPSR 8605.

O'Toole, Laurence J., Jr. 1997. "Treating Networks Seriously: Practical and Research-Based Agendas in Public Administration." *Public Administration Review* 57 (January/February): 45–52.

Padgett, John F. 1981. "Hierarchy and Ecological Control in Federal Budgetary Decision Making." *American Journal of Sociology* 87.

———. 1980. "Bounded Rationality in Budgetary Research." *American Political Science Review* 74 (June): 354–72.

Patel, Kant, and Mark E. Rushefsky. 1995. *Health Care Politics and Policy in America.* Armonk, NY: M. E. Sharpe.

Peltzman, Sam. 1976. "Toward a More General Theory of Regulation." *Journal of Law and Economics* 19.

———. 1973. "An Evaluation of Consumer Protection Legislation: The 1962 Drug Amendments." *Journal of Political Economy* 81 (5).

Perrow, Charles. 1986. *Complex Organizations: A Critical Essay.* 3d ed. New York: McGraw-Hill.

———. 1972. *Complex Organizations: A Critical Essay.* Glenview, IL: Scott Foresman.

Perry, James L., and Lois R. Wise. 1990. "The Motivation Basis of the Public Service." *Public Administration Review* 50 (July/August): 367–73.

Peterson, Paul. 1981. *City Limits.* Chicago: University of Chicago Press.

Pierson, Paul. 2000. "Increasing Returns, Path Dependence, and the Study of Politics." *American Political Science Review* 94 (June): 251–68.

Pindyck, Robert S., and Daniel L. Rubinfeld. 1991. *Econometric Models and Economic Forecasts.* 3d ed. New York: McGraw-Hill.

Polkington, Brian. 1995. "The Influence of Regulatory Negotiations on the U.S. Environmental Protection Agency as an Institution." Paper presented at the annual meeting of the American Political Science Association, Washington, DC.

Poole, Keith, and Howard Rosenthal. 1997. *Congress: A Political Economic History of Roll Call Voting.* New York: Oxford University Press.

Porter, L. W., and E. E. Lawler III. 1965. "Properties of Organization Structure in Relation to Job Attitudes and Job Behavior." *Psychological Bulletin* 64.

Potoski, Matthew. 2000. "Designing Bureaucratic Performance: Administrative Procedures and the Political Control-Expertise Tradeoff." Typescript, Iowa State University.

———. 1999. "Managing Uncertainty through Bureaucratic Design: Administrative Procedures and State Air Pollution Control Agencies." *Journal of Public Administration and Research Theory* 9 (October): 623–39.

Pressman, Jeffrey L., and Aaron B. Wildavsky. 1973. *Implementation.* Berkeley: University of California Press.

Prottas, Jeffrey Manditch. 1979. *People-Processing: The Street-Level Bureaucrat in Public Service Bureaucracies,* Lexington, MA: Lexington Books.

Quirk, Paul J. 1981. *Industry Influence in Federal Regulatory Agencies.* Princeton: Princeton University Press.

———. 1980. "The Food and Drug Administration." In *The Politics of Regulation,* ed. James Q. Wilson. New York: Basic Books.

Radner, Roy. 1975. "A Behavioral Model of Cost Reduction." *Bell Journal of Economics* 6.

Rainey, Hal G. 1997. *Understanding and Managing Public Organizations.* San Francisco: Jossey-Bass.

Rebell, Michael. 1998. "Fiscal Equity Litigation and the Democratic Imperative." *Journal of Education Finance* 24.

Redford, Emmette S. 1969. *Democracy in the Administrative State.* New York: Oxford University Press.

Regulatory Information Service Center. 1998. "Introduction to the Regulatory Plan and the Unified Agenda of Federal Regulatory and Deregulatory Actions." *Federal Register* 63.

Rice, D., and J. Feldman. 1983. "Living Longer in the United States: Demographic Changes and Health Needs of the Elderly." *Milbank Memorial Fund Quarterly/Health and Society* 61 (3): 362–96.

Rieselbach, Leroy N. 1995. *Congressional Politics: The Evolving Legislative System.* 2d ed. Boulder: Westview.

Rigotti, Nancy, David Bourne, Amy Rosen, John Locke, and Thomas Schelling. 1992. "Workplace Compliance with a No-Smoking Law: A Randomized Community Intervention Trial." *American Journal of Public Health* 82.

Rigotti, Nancy, and Chris Pashos. 1991. "No-Smoking Laws in the United States: An Analysis of State and City Actions to Limit Smoking in Public Places and Workplaces." *Journal of the American Medical Association* 266.

Rigotti, Nancy, Michael Stoto, Michael Bierer, Amy Rosen, and Thomas Schelling. 1993. "Retail Stores' Compliance with a City No-Smoking Law." *American Journal of Public Health* 83.

Rigotti, Nancy, Michael Stoto, and Thomas Schelling. 1994. "Do Businesses Comply with a No-Smoking Law? Assessing the Self-Enforcement Approach." *Preventative Medicine* 23.

Riker, William H. 1982. *Liberalism against Populism: A Confrontation between the Theory of Democracy and the Theory of Social Choice.* Prospect Heights, IL: Waveland.

Ringquist, Evan. 1995. "Political Control and Policy Impact in EPA's Office of Water Quality." *American Journal of Political Science* 39.

Ripley, Randall B., and Grace A. Franklin. 1984. *Congress, the Bureaucracy, and Public Policy.* 3d ed. Homewood, IL: Dorsey.

———. 1980. *Congress, the Bureaucracy, and Public Policy.* Rev. ed. Homewood, IL: Dorsey.

Roethlisberger, F. J., and W. J. Dickson. 1939. *Management and the Worker.* Cambridge: Harvard University Press.

Rohr, John A. 1986. *To Run a Constitution: The Legitimacy of the Administrative State.* Lawrence: University Press of Kansas.

Rosenbloom, David H. 2000. "Retrofitting the Administrative State to the Constitution: Congess and the Judiciary's Twentieth Century Progress." *Public Administration Review* 60 (January/February): 39–46.

Rosenbloom, David H., and Janet C. Featherstonhaugh. 1977. "Passive and Active Representation in the Federal Service." *Social Science Quarterly* 57:873–82.

Ross, Stephen A. 1973. "The Economic Theory of Agency: The Principal's Problem." *American Economic Review* 63 (May): 134–39.

Roth, William. 1987. "Disabilities: Physical." *Encyclopedia of Social Work.* 18th ed. Silver Spring, MD: National Association of Social Work.

Rothenberg, Lawrence. 1994. *Regulation, Organizations, and Politics: Motor Freight Policy at the Interstate Commerce Commission.* Ann Arbor: University of Michigan Press.

Rourke, Francis E. 1984. *Bureaucracy, Politics, and Public Policy.* 3d ed. Boston: Little, Brown.

———. 1978. "Variations in Agency Power." In *Bureaucratic Power in National Politics,* ed. Francis Rourke. Boston: Little, Brown.

Rubin, Edward L. 1991. "Beyond Public Choice: Comprehensive Rationality in the Writing and Reading of Statutes." *New York University Law Review* 66.

Rubin, Irene S. 1985. *Shrinking the Federal Government.* New York: Longman.

Sabatier, Paul A. 1986. "Top Down and Bottom-Up Approaches to Implementation Research: A Critical Analysis and Suggested Synthesis." *Journal of Public Policy* 6 (1).

Saltzstein, Grace Hall. 1979. "Representative Bureaucracy and Bureaucratic Responsibility." *Administration and Society* 10 (February): 465–75.

Schelling, Thomas. 1960. *The Strategy of Conflict.* Cambridge: Harvard University Press.

Scher, Seymour. 1963. "Conditions for Legislative Control." *Journal of Politics* 25 (August): 526–51.

Schmidt, Diane E. 1995. "The Presidential Appointment Process, Task Environment Pressures, and Regional Office Case Processing." *Political Research Quarterly* 48 (June): 381–401.

Schneider, Anne, and Helen Ingram. 1997. *Policy Design for Democracy.* Lawrence: University Press of Kansas.

———. 1993. "Social Construction of Target Populations: Implications for Politics and Policy." *American Political Science Review* 87 (2): 334–47.

Schneider, Mark, Paul Teske, Christine Roch, and Melissa Marschall. 1997. "Networks to Nowhere: Segregation and Stratification in Networks of Information about Schools." *American Journal of Political Science* 41: 1201–23.

Schneider, Saundra K., and William G. Jacoby. 1996. "Influences on Bureaucratic Policy Initiatives in the American States." *Journal of Public Administration Research and Theory* 6 (October): 495–522.

Scholz, John. 1998. "Trust, Taxes, and Compliance." In *Trust and Governance,* ed. Valerie Braithwaite and Margaret Levi. New York: Russell Sage Foundation.

Scholz, John, and Wayne Gray. 1997. "Can Government Facilitate Cooperation? An Informational Model of OSHA Enforcement." *American Journal of Political Science* 41: 693–717.

Scholz, John, and Mark Lubell. 1998. "Adaptive Political Attitudes: Duty, Trust, and Fear as Monitors of Tax Policy." *American Journal of Political Science* 42.

Scholz, John, and Neil Pinney. 1995. "Duty, Fear, and Tax Compliance: The Heuristic Basis of Citizen Behavior." *American Journal of Political Science* 39.

Scholz, John, Jim Twombly, and Barbara Headrick. 1991. "Street-Level Political Controls over Federal Bureaucracy." *American Political Science Review* 85 (September): 829–50.

Scholz, John, and Feng Heng Wei. 1986. "Regulatory Enforcement in a Federalist System." *American Political Science Review* 80 (4): 1249–70.

Schroeder, Christopher H. 1998. "Rational Choice versus Republican Moment Explanations for Environmental Law, 1969–73." *Duke Environmental Law and Policy Forum* 9.

Seidenfeld, Mark. 1992. "A Civic Republican Justification for the Bureaucratic State." *Harvard Law Review* 105.

Selden, Sally Coleman, 1997. *The Promise of Representative Bureaucracy: Diversity and Responsiveness in a Government Agency.* Armonk, NY: M. E. Sharpe.

Shafritz, Jay M., and J. Steven Ott. 1996. *Classics of Organization Theory.* 4th ed. New York: Wadsworth.

Shapiro, Martin. 1988. *Who Guards the Guardians? Judicial Control of Administration.* Athens: University of Georgia Press.

Simon, Herbert A. 1997. *Administrative Behavior.* 4th ed. New York: Free Press.

———. 1976. *Administrative Behavior: A Study of Decision-Making Processes in Administrative Organization.* 3d ed. New York: Free Press.

———. 1957. *Models of Man, Social and Rational: Mathematical Essays on Rational Human Behavior in a Social Setting.* New York: Wiley.

———. 1947. *Administrative Behavior.* New York: Macmillan.

Simon, Herbert A., Donald W. Smithburg, and Victor A. Thompson. 1961. *Public Administration.* New York: Knopf.

Sivazlian, B. D. 1981. "A Class of Multivariate Distributions." *Australian Journal of Statistics* 23 (2).

Skowronek, Stephen. 1982. *Building a New American State.* New York: Cambridge University Press.

Skvoretz, John, and Thomas J. Fararo. 1996. "Status and Participation in Task Groups: A Dynamic Network Model." *American Journal of Sociology* 101 (March): 1366–414.

Skvoretz, John, and David Willer. 1993. "Exclusion and Power: A Test of Four Theories of Power in Exchange Networks." *American Sociological Review* 58 (December): 801–18.

Smith, Kevin B., and Kenneth J. Meier. 1995. *The Case against School Choice.* Armonk, NY: M. E. Sharpe.

Soss, Joe, and Lael R. Keiser. 2001. "The Political Origins of Administrative Ap-

peals: How Program Designs and Political Environments Shape Resistance to
Agency Denials." Paper presented at the annual meetings of the Midwest Political Science Association, Chicago. April.

———. 1999. "Challenged Bureaucracies: Disability Determinations and the
Politics of Administrative Appeals." Paper presented at the Midwest Political
Science Association meeting, Chicago. April.

Spann, Girardeau A. 1995. "Color-Coded Standing." *Cornell Law Review* 80.

Spence, David B. 1999a. "Managing Delegation Ex Ante: Using Law to Steer
Administrative Agencies." *Journal of Legal Studies* 28 (2).

———. 1999b. "Agency Discretion and the Dynamics of Procedural Reform."
Public Administration Review 59 (September/October): 425–42.

———. 1999c. "Imposing Individual Liability as   Legislative Policy Choice:
Holmesian 'Intuitions' and Superfund Reform." *Northwestern University Law
Review* 93.

———. 1997a. "Modeling Away the Delegation Problem." *Journal of Public Administration Research and Theory* 7.

———. 1997b. "Administrative Law and Agency Policymaking: Rethinking the
Positive Theory of Political Control." *Yale Journal on Regulation* 14.

Spence, Michael. 1973. "Job Market Signaling." *Journal of Economics* 87.

Spence, Michael, and Richard Zeckhauser. 1971. "Insurance, Information, and
Individual Action." *American Economic Review* 61 (May): 380–87.

Spiller, Pablo. 1990. "Politicians, Interest Groups, and Regulators: A Multiple-
Principals Agency Theory of Regulation, or Let Them Be Bribed." *Journal of
Law and Economics* 33.

Spriggs, James F. 1996. "The Supreme Court and Federal Administrative Agencies:
A Resource-based Theory and Analysis of Judicial Impact." *American Journal of
Political Science* 40 (November): 1122–51.

State of Vermont. 1991. "Environment 1991: Risk to Vermont and Vermonters,
a Report by the Public Advisory Committee." Strategy for Vermont's Third
Century.

Steinbruner, John D. 1974. *The Cybernetic Theory of Decision: New Dimensions
of Political Analysis.* Princeton: Princeton University Press.

Stene, Edwin O. 1940. "An Approach to the Science of Administration." *American Political Science Review* 34 (December): 1124–37.

Stigler, George J. 1971. "The Theory of Economic Regulation." *Bell Journal of
Economics* 2.

Stinchcombe, Arthur L. 1990. *Information and Organizations.* Berkley: University of California Press.

Stoker, Robert P. 1991. *Reluctant Partners: Implementing Federal Policy.* Pittsburgh: University of Pittsburgh Press.

Stone, Deborah. 1984. *The Disabled State.* Philadelphia: Temple University Press.

Stream, Christopher. 1999. "Health Reform in the States: A Model of State Small Group Health Insurance Market Reforms." *Political Research Quarterly* 52 (3).

Susskind, Lawrence, and Gerard McMahon. 1985. "The Theory and Practice of Negotiated Rulemaking." *Yale Journal on Regulation* 3.

Taylor, Frederick W. 1919. *The Principles of Scientific Management.* New York: Harper.

Thomas, Lacy Glenn. 1990. "Regulation and Firm Size: FDA Impacts on Innovation." *RAND Journal of Economics* 21 (4).

Thompson, James D. 1967. *Organizations in Action: Social Science Bases of Administrative Theory.* New York: McGraw-Hill.

Tiebout, Charles. 1956. "A Pure Theory of Local Expenditures." *Journal of Political Economy* 64.

Tobacco Institute. 1997. *Tax Burden on Tobacco.* Washington, DC: Tobacco Institute.

Tobin, James. 1958. "Liquidity Preference and Behavior towards Risk." *Review of Economic Studies* 25 (66).

Tolman, Richard M., and Jody Raphael. 2000. "A Review of Research on Domestic Violence." *Journal of Social Issues* 56 (4): 655–82.

Tsebelis, George. 1999. "Veto Players and Law Production in Parliamentary Democracies: An Empirical Analysis." *American Political Science Review* 93.

———. 1995. "Decision-Making in Political Systems: Veto Players in Presidentialism, Parliamentarism, Multicameralism, and Multipartyism." *British Journal of Political Science* 25.

Tsebelis, George, and Jeannette Money. 1997. *Bicameralism.* New York: Cambridge University Press.

Tufts Center for the Study of Drug Development (CSDD). 1995. "White Paper on Four Areas of Relevance to New Drug Development and Review in the United States." Tufts University, Boston.

Tullock, Gordon. 1965. *The Politics of Bureaucracy.* Washington, DC: Public Affairs Press.

Tyack, David. 1974. *The One Best System: A History of Urban Education.* Cambridge: Harvard University Press.

Tyack, David, and Larry Cuban. 1995. *Tinkering toward Utopia: A Century of Public School Reform.* Cambridge: Harvard University Press.

U.S. Advisory Commission on Intergovernmental Relations. 1992. *Medicaid: Intergovernmental Trends and Options.* Washington, DC: Advisory Commission on Intergovernment Relations.

U.S. Congress. 1984. House. Select Committee on Aging. *Social Security Disability Reviews: A Costly Constitutional Crises.* 98th Cong., 2d sess., February 28.

U.S. Congress. 1977. Senate. Committee on Governmental Affairs. *Delay in the Regulatory Process.* 95th Cong., 1st sess.

U.S. Department of Labor. Bureau of Labor Statistics. 1991. *Handbook of Labor Statistics.* Washington, DC: U.S. Government Printing Office.

U.S. Social Security Administration. 2002. <http://www.ssa.gov/notices/supplemental-security-income/8/15/02>.

Van Riper, Paul. 1983. "The American Administrative State: Wilson and the Founders—An Unorthodox View." *Public Administration Review* 43 (November/December): 477–90.

Volden, Craig. 2002. "The Politics of Competitive Federalism: A Race to the Bottom in Welfare Benefits?" *American Journal of Political Science* 46 (2): 352–63.

———. 1999. "The Political Economy of Restrictions on Bureaucratic Discretion." Paper presented at the annual meeting of the Public Choice Society, New Orleans. March 10–12.

Waldo, Dwight. 1984. *The Administrative State.* 2d ed. New York: Holmes and Meier.

Wasserman, Jeffrey, Willard Manning, Joseph Newhouse, and John Winkler. 1991. "The Effects of Excise Taxes and Regulations on Cigarette Smoking." *Journal of Health Economics* 10.

Waterman, Richard, and Kenneth J. Meier. 1998. "Principal-Agent Models: An Expansion?" *Journal of Public Administration Research and Theory* 8 (April): 173–202.

Weaver, R. Kent, and Bert A. Rockman, eds. 1993. *Do Institutions Matter?* Washington, DC: Brookings Institution.

Weber, Max. 1947. *The Theory of Social and Economic Organization,* trans. A. M. Henderson and Talcott Parsons. New York: Free Press.

———. [1946] 1922. "Bureaucracy." In *From Max Weber: Essays in Sociology,* ed. H. Gerth and C. W. Mills. Oxford: Oxford University Press.

Weingast, Barry R. 1984. "The Congressional-Bureaucratic System: A Principal-Agent Perspective (with Application to the SEC)." *Public Choice* 44 (2): 147–91.

Weingast, Barry R., and William Marshall. 1988. "The Industrial Organization of Congress, or, Why Legislatures, Like Firms, Are Not Organized as Markets." *Journal of Political Economy* 96.

Weingast, Barry R., and Mark J. Moran. 1983. "Bureaucratic Discretion or Congressional Control? Regulatory Policymaking by the Federal Trade Commission." *Journal of Political Economy* 91 (October): 756–800.

White, Hal. 1980. "A Heteroskedasticity-Consistent Covariance Matrix and a Direct Test for Heteroskedasticity." *Econometrica* 48.

White, Leonard D. 1926. *Introduction to the Study of Administration.* New York: Macmillan.

Whitford, Andrew. 1998. "If I Had a Hammer: Political Control, Prosecution, and Timing." Typescript, Rice University.

Whitford, Andrew, and Eric Helland. Forthcoming. "Pollution Incidence and Political Jurisdiction: Evidence from the TRI." *Journal of Environmental Economics and Management.*

Whyte, William H., Jr. 1956. *The Organization Man.* New York: Simon and Schuster.

Wildavsky, Aaron. [1984] 1964. *The Politics of the Budgetary Process.* 4th ed. Boston: Little, Brown.

Williamson, Oliver E. 1991. "Comparative Economic Organization: The Analysis of Discrete Structural Alternatives." *Administrative Science Quarterly* 36.

———. 1990. "Chester Barnard and the Incipient Science of Organization." In *Organization Theory: From Chester Barnard to the Present and Beyond,* ed. Oliver E. Williamson. New York: Oxford University Press.

———. 1985. *The Economic Institutions of Capitalism.* New York: Free Press.

———. 1975. *Markets and Hierarchies, Analysis and Antitrust Implications.* New York: Free Press.

Wilson, James Q. 1989, *Bureaucracy: What Government Agencies Do and Why They Do It.* New York: Basic Books.

Wilson, Woodrow. 1887. "The Study of Administration." *Political Science Quarterly* 2 (June): 197–222.

Wood, B. Dan. 1992. "Modeling Federal Implementation as a System: The Clean Air Case." *American Journal of Political Science* 36 (1).

———. 1990. "Does Politics Make a Difference at the EEOC?" *American Journal of Political Science* 34 (May): 503–30.

———. 1988. "Principals, Bureaucrats, and Responsiveness in Clean Air Enforcements." *American Political Science Review* 82 (March): 213–34.

Wood, B. Dan, and James Anderson. 1993. "The Politics of U.S. Antitrust Regulation." *American Journal of Political Science* 37.

———. 1992. "Bureaucratic Responsiveness and Administrative Design: The Independent Commission versus the Executive Branch." Paper presented at the annual meetings of the Midwest Political Science Association. Chicago. April.

Wood, B. Dan, and Richard W. Waterman. 1994. *Bureaucratic Dynamics: The Role of Bureaucracy in a Democracy.* Boulder: Westview.

Wood, B. Dan, and Richard Waterman. 1993. "The Dynamics of Political-Bureaucratic Adaption." *American Journal of Political Science* 37 (May): 497–528.

———. 1991. "The Dynamics of Political Control of the Bureaucracy." *American Political Science Review* 85 (September): 801–28.

Woodward, Joan. 1965. *Industrial Organization: Theory and Practice.* London: Oxford University Press.

Woolley, John T. 1993. "Conflict among Regulators and the Hypothesis of Congressional Dominance." *Journal of Politics* 55 (February): 92–114.

Yandle, Bruce. 1988. "Antitrust Actions and the Budgeting Process." *Public Choice* 59 (December): 263–75.

Contributors

Steven J. Balla, George Washington University, Associate Professor, Department of Political Science.

John Brehm, University of Chicago, Professor and Chairman, Department of Political Science.

Daniel P. Carpenter, Harvard University, Professor, Department of Government.

Kevin Corder, Western Michigan University, Associate Professor, Department of Political Science.

Scott Gates, Michigan State University, Associate Professor, Department of Political Science.

Brad Gomez, University of South Carolina, Assistant Professor, Department of Political Science.

Thomas H. Hammond, Michigan State University, Professor, Department of Political Science.

Lael R. Keiser, University of Missouri, Columbia, Assistant Professor, Department of Political Studies.

George A. Krause, University of South Carolina, Associate Professor, Department of Political Science.

Michael J. Licari, University of Northern Iowa, Assistant Professor, Department of Political Science.

Kenneth J. Meier, Texas A&M University, Charles Puryear Professor of Liberal Arts, Department of Political Science, and Sarah H. Lindsey

Chair in Government, George Bush School of Government and Public Service.

Kevin B. Smith, University of Nebraska, Lincoln, Associate Professor, Department of Political Science.

David B. Spence, University of Texas–Austin, Associate Professor, Department of Management Science and Information Systems, Red McCombs School of Business.

Andrew B. Whitford, University of Kansas, Assistant Professor, Department of Government.

John R. Wright, Ohio State University, Professor, Department of Political Science.

Author Index

Aberbach, Joel D., 8, 43, 235
Abernathy, Scott F., 301
Achen, Christopher H., 199–200
Aitchison, J., 144, 146
Alchian, Armen, 11, 133
Alexander, F. King, 267
Allison, Graham T., 199
Almond, Gabriel, 204
Alt, James, 199
Anderson, James, 24, 39, 43, 216, 304
Anton, Thomas J., 210
Appleby, Paul H., 2, 5
Argyris, Chris, 13
Arnold, R. Douglas, 24, 26, 106, 126
Arrow, Kenneth J., 8, 12
Arthur, Brian, 163
Ashby, W. Ross, 162
Axelrod, Robert M., 162, 184

Balla, Steven J., 26, 69, 187, 236, 297, 302
Baltagi, Badi, 285
Banks, Jeffrey S., 9, 25
Barber, Benjamin, 272
Bardach, Edward, 207
Barnard, Chester, 2, 3, 10–11, 44, 48, 134, 259, 294–95, 297
Baron, David P., 101
Bawn, Kathleen, 15, 25, 41, 63, 75, 107, 294, 295, 303

Beamer, Glenn, 207, 209–11, 214–15
Beck, Nathaniel, 249
Becker, Gary, 283
Belanger, G., 163
Bendor, Jonathan, 2, 9, 25, 126, 161, 162, 164
Berkowitz, Edward, 212, 213
Berman, P., 230
Bernstein, Marver H., 24
Berry, William, 230, 291
Bianco, William T., 106, 113
Bikhchandani, Sushil, 159
Blais, André, 163
Blau, Peter, 19
Bohte, John, 15, 294, 295, 303
Bosworth, Barry, 237
Boyne, George A., 163–64
Bozeman, Barry, 13
Brehm, John, 2, 9–10, 15, 25, 65, 133, 135–37, 145, 156, 159, 294, 299
Brest, Paul, 104
Breton, Albert, 9, 164
Brodkin, Evelyn, 208
Bryner, Gary C., 41, 43, 70, 296
Burton, Richard M., 163
Butler, Christopher K., 75, 77

Callan, Eamon, 272
Calvert, Randall, 41, 235
Carley, Kathleen M., 163

343

Carpenter, Daniel P., 9, 14–15, 24–26, 36, 39, 43–44, 65, 303
Chandler, Alfred, 163
Chubb, John E., 208–9, 262–63, 270, 272, 301
Coase, Ronald H., 11
Cofer, Donna P., 225
Coglianese, Cary, 188, 190, 192–93, 203, 205
Cohen, Michael D., 161–62, 166, 184
Conybeare, John A. C., 163
Corder, J. Kevin, 246, 302
Corzier, Michel, 2, 6, 48
Crawford, Vincent, 277
Crecine, J. P., 162
Creek, Laverne, 286
Crewson, Philip E., 164
Cuban, Larry, 264
Cyert, Richard M., 2, 4, 161–62

Dahl, Robert, 5
David, Paul, 163
Davidson, Russell, 286
Davis, Kenneth Culp, 305
DeGroot, Morris, 31
Demsetz, Harold, 11, 133
Derthick, Martha, 207, 213, 218
Dewey, John, 272
Dickson, W. J., 3
Dion, Stéphane, 163
Dixit, Avinash K., 32, 39–40
Dolgoff, Ralph, 212, 216
Downey, La Vonne, 280
Downs, Anthony, 2, 7, 11, 15, 48, 106, 127, 163, 259, 305
Dranove, David, 36, 40

Easterbrook, Frank H., 126
Edwards, J. Terry, 13
Eijffinger, Sylvester, 126
Eisner, Marc, 2, 14, 278

Eisner, Neil R., 188, 190–91, 194–97, 203
Elazar, Daniel J., 220
Epstein, David, 12, 15, 41, 47, 63, 70, 107, 301
Epstein, Steven, 26, 30

Fayole, Henri, 3
Featherstonhaugh, Janet C., 6
Feldman, J., 221
Feldstein, Donald, 212, 216
Fenno, Richard, 106, 113
Ferejohn, John, 101, 126
Finer, Herman, 5
Fiorina, Morris P., 43, 63, 106
Fishkin, James S., 120, 128, 129
Franklin, Grace A., 242, 250, 298
Frederickson, H. George, 5
Friedrich, Carl J., 4–5
Fritschler, A. Lee, 282, 284
Furlong, Scott R., 187–88, 192–93, 195–98

Gaebler, Ted, 260–61
Gardiner, John, 280
Gates, Scott, 2, 9–10, 15, 25, 65, 133, 135–37, 145, 156, 159, 294, 299
Gill, Jeff, 159, 305
Goggin, Malcolm L., 207
Goodnow, Frank, 2, 115
Goodsell, Charles T., 261
Gordon, Sanford C., 26, 28, 301, 304
Gormley, William, 44
Granovetter, Mark, 303
Gray, Wayne, 277
Greene, William H., 199–200, 249, 290
Grofman, Bernard 105
Grossman, Michael, 283
Gujarati, Damodar, 247

Gulick, Luther, 3, 12
Gutmann, Amy, 272

Hall, Thad E., 296
Hamilton, James T., 69, 124, 297
Hammond, Thomas H., 24, 70, 73–75, 77, 100, 306
Haque, M. S., 260
Harrington, Winston, 24
Harris, Richard A., 242–43
Harrison, Michael, 34, 40
Harter, Philip J., 188–92, 202
Hasenfeld, Yeheskel, 220
Hassapis, Christis, 126
Hawkins, Keith, 188, 196
Headrick, Barbara, 9, 15, 25, 210, 295
Hedge, David, 210, 217
Heimann, C. F. Larry, 25, 164
Heinz, John P., 303
Henig, Jeffrey, 275
Henry, Nicholas, 3
Herring, E. Pendleton, 4
Hess, Frederick, 264
Higgins, Richard S., 164
Hill, Jeffrey S., 208, 209
Hirshman, Albert O., 104, 262
Holmström, Bengt, 133
Horn, Murray J., 12
Hsiao, Cheng, 249
Huber, John D., 12, 24, 63, 204, 301
Humphreys, N. Marcartan, 101
Huntington, Samuel P., 19
Hyman, David, 285
Hyneman, Charles, 5

Inglehart, Ronald, 99
Ingraham, Patricia, 301
Ippolito, Dennis, 237

Jacobson, Peter, 279–80
Jensen, Michael, 8, 19

Johnson, Ronald N., 134
Jones, Brian D., 165, 257
Jovanovic, Boyan, 32

Kadushin, Alfred, 133
Kaitin, Kenneth I., 24
Katz, Michael B., 249
Kaufman, Herbert, 12–15, 158, 210, 240, 250, 294, 305
Keech, William, 246
Keiser, Lael R., 13–14, 17, 207–12, 213–17, 220–23, 225, 230, 302
Kerwin, Cornelius M., 187–90, 192–93, 195–98, 205
Kettl, Donald F., 163
Key, V. O., 5
Khademian, Anne M., 2, 14
King, Gary, 144, 159, 199, 200
Kleinbaum, David G., 231
Knight, Kenneth, 26, 165
Knott, Jack H., 11, 19, 304
Kolko, Gabriel, 126
Kollman, Ken, 162
Krause, George A., 9–10, 24, 26, 44, 65, 126, 210, 296–97, 305
Kreps, David, 134
Kritzer, Herbert M., 225
Krupnick, Alan, 24

Landau, Martin, 164
Langbein, Laura I., 193
Levin, Dan, 285
Levinthal, Daniel, 165
Lewis, David E., 14
Lewit, Eugene, 283
Libecap, Gary D., 134
Licari, Michael, 276, 278, 285, 291
Likert, Rensis, 13
Lindblom, Charles, 167
Lipsky, Michael, 125, 222
Long, J. Scott, 5–6

Loprest, Pamela, 216
Lowery, David, 260–61
Lowi, Theodore J., 63, 104, 208, 238, 302
Lupia, Arthur, 108, 159, 217, 277

Macey, Jonathan, 236
Maddala, G. S., 231
Magat, Wesley, 24
Majone, G., 208
Manchester, Paul, 285
Manocchia, Michael, 24
March, James G., 2, 4, 11, 13, 16, 18, 48, 161, 162
Martin, Elizabeth, 41
Mashaw, Jerry L., 106, 112, 125, 209, 213, 222
Masuch, Michael, 184
Mayhew, David R., 106
Mazmanian, Daniel, 299
McCabe, Barbara Coyler, 260–61
McCubbins, Mathew D., 8–9, 15, 19, 25, 41, 43, 63, 107–8, 114, 127–28, 159, 204, 235–36, 296
McFadden, Daniel, 24, 26
McGraw, Kathleen, 277
McGregor, Douglas, 13
McGuire, Thomas G., 164
McMahon, Gerard, 188–89, 191–92, 194–95, 203, 205
Meckling, William, 8, 19
Meier, Kenneth J., 6, 10, 13–14, 44, 198, 297–98, 302
Meltzer, David, 36, 40
Menard, Scott, 268
Merton, Robert K., 275
Meyer, Marshal, 19
Mezey, Susan G., 218
Migue, J., 163
Mikva, Abner J., 104
Milgrom, Paul, 277

Milkis, Sidney M., 242–43
Miller, Gary J., 2, 9, 11, 19, 25, 164, 294, 304
Milward, H. Brinton, 303, 304
Mintz, Benjamin, 188
Mintzberg, Henry, 13, 304
Miroschnichenko, T. P., 32
Mitnick, Barry M., 8, 10, 19, 298, 307
Moe, Terry M., 2, 7–9, 11, 15, 19, 24–26, 39, 43, 126, 162, 164, 235–36, 295, 301, 304, 306–7
Moran, Mark J., 2, 9, 24, 26, 228, 233, 245, 295, 301
Mosher, Frederick C., 2, 13
Mullainathan, Sendhil, 38
Musolf, Lloyd, 237

Nalbandian, John, 13
Nelson, Richard, 165
Nelson, William E., 2, 165
Newell, Allen, 161–62
Nigro, L. G., 6
Niskanen, William A., Jr., 6, 9, 42, 105, 163, 218
Noll, Roger G., 9, 15, 19, 41–42, 63, 107, 114, 128, 204, 236, 296
Nordhaus, William D., 246
North, Douglass C., 11
Nuthall, Graham, 264, 268

Obel, Borge, 163
Ogul, Morris, 8
O'Halloran, Sharyn, 12, 15, 47, 70, 107, 301
Olson, Mancur, 105
Olson, Mary, 24, 26
Osborne, David, 60, 261
Ostrom, Elinor, 184, 278–80
O'Toole, Laurence, Jr., 296, 303–4

Padgett, John F., 25, 36, 162
Pak, K., 246
Patel, Kant, 222
Peltzman, Sam, 106
Perrow, Charles, 8, 10, 12, 19
Perry, James L., 13
Peterson, Paul, 211
Pierson, Paul, 12
Pindyck, Robert S., 32, 215, 231, 290
Pinney, Neil, 277, 281
Polinard, L., 10, 238, 297–99, 302
Polkington, Brian, 195
Poole, Keith, 246
Porter, L. W., 275
Potoski, Matthew, 297
Pressman, Jeffrey L., 42
Prietula, Michel J., 163
Prottas, Jeffrey, 216

Quirk, Paul J., 30, 44

Radner, Roy, 165
Rainey, Hal G., 13
Rebell, Michael, 267
Redford, Emmette S., 5
Rice, D., 221
Rieselbach, Leroy, 44, 63
Rigotti, Nancy, 280, 290
Riker, William H., 106
Ringquist, Evan, 24–26, 210
Ripley, Randall B., 242, 250, 298
Rockman, Bert A., 74–75
Roethlisberger, F. J., 3
Rohr, John A., 5, 105
Rosenbloom, David H., 5–6
Ross, Stephen A., 8, 19, 298
Roth, William, 211
Rothenberg, Lawrence, 9, 24
Rourke, Francis E., 13, 41–45, 50, 60, 65, 210, 276, 299, 300
Rubin, Irene S., 104, 299

Sabatier, Paul A., 299
Saltzstein, Grace H., 6
Schelling, Thomas, 280, 283–84, 290
Scher, Seymour, 8
Schmidt, Diane E., 304
Schneider, Anne, 216
Schneider, Mark, 275
Schneider, Saundra K., 301
Scholz, John, 9, 15, 25, 210, 277–78, 280–81, 295
Schroeder, Christopher H., 118
Schwartz, Thomas, 8, 9, 15, 25
Scicchitano, Michael J., 209
Seidenfeld, Mark, 105
Selden, Sally Coleman, 6
Shafritz, Jay M., 275
Shepsle, Kenneth A., 114, 236
Shipan, Charles A., 12, 24, 63, 204, 301
Signorino, Curtis, 199
Simon, Herbert A., 2–4, 10, 11, 13, 16, 18, 24, 44, 48, 161–62, 221, 259, 294, 296–97
Skolnik, Louise, 212, 216
Skowronek, Stephen, 2
Skvoretz, John, 303
Smith, Kevin B., 18, 262, 294
Sobel, Joel, 277
Soss, Joe, 210, 216, 221, 302
Spann, Girardeau A., 104
Spence, David B., 19, 65, 69, 104, 107, 121, 128, 206, 236, 277, 297, 300
Spence, Michael, 19, 297
Spiller, Pablo, 25
Spriggs, James F., 305
Steinbruner, John D., 135
Stene, Edwin O., 3
Stigler, George J., 105–6
Stinchcombe, Arthur L., 11, 48

Stoker, Robert P., 207–9
Stoto, Michael, 280, 290
Stream, Christopher, 230
Susskind, Lawrence, 188–89, 191–92, 194–95, 203, 205

Taylor, Frederick W., 3, 9, 164
Thomas, Lacy Glenn, 295
Thompson, James D., 12, 48, 64–65, 69, 220–22
Tiebout, Charles, 261
Tobin, James, 71
Tolman, Richard, 216
Tsebelis, George, 75, 202
Tullock, Gordon, 2, 6, 42, 163
Twombly, Jim, 9, 15, 25, 210, 295
Tyack, David, 264

Urwick, Lydal, 3

Van Gaalen, Roland, 9, 163, 164
Van Riper, Paul, 2
Verba, Sidney, 204
Vinzant, Janet C., 260–61
Volden, Craig, 43, 63

Waldo, Dwight, 2, 5
Wasserman, Jeffrey, 279–80, 285
Waterman, Richard, 2, 5, 9–10, 15,

24, 39, 43, 209–10, 220, 235, 242, 295, 298
Weaver, R. Kent, 74–75
Weber, Max, 2, 115, 260
Wei, Feng Heng, 9, 15, 210
Weingast, Barry R., 2, 9, 15, 19, 24–26, 41, 43, 63, 107, 114, 128, 233, 235–36, 245, 295–96, 301
Weissert, Carol S., 207, 209
White, Hal, 206
White, Leonard D., 2
Whitford, Andrew, 16, 26, 28, 160, 206, 304–5
Whyte, William, 275
Wildavsky, Aaron, 14, 42, 208
Williamson, Oliver E., 11, 25
Wilson, James Q., 11, 41, 44–45, 48, 50, 60, 63, 65, 134–35, 221, 235, 259, 302, 306
Wilson, Woodrow, 2
Wise, Lois R., 13
Wittman, Donald, 105
Wood, B. Dan, 2, 5, 9, 15, 24–26, 39, 43, 208–10, 220, 235, 242, 295, 304
Woodward, Joan, 19
Woolley, John T., 9
Wrinkle, Robert D., 10, 238, 297–99, 302

Yandle, Bruce, 25

Subject Index

abortion policy, 127
accountability, 260
administrative orthodoxy, 254, 271
Administrative Procedure Act of
    1946, 188, 190; notice and com-
    ment requirements, 193
administrative procedures, 24, 25, 233.
    See also procedural environments
administrative rule making, 187–88,
    297. *See also* Administrative Proce-
    dure Act; consensual rule making
administrative state, 107, 293
Aid to Families with Dependent
    Children (AFDC), 213, 216, 217,
    223, 224, 225, 232. *See also* Tempo-
    rary Aid to Needy Families
Arrow's theorem, 126

bounded rationality, 25, 160, 162
Brown v Board of Education, 275
budget maximization, 7, 107
Budget Reconciliation Act of 1986,
    245
bureaucratic autonomy, 45, 74, 76,
    77, 78; and discretion, 41, 42, 44,
    60, 65, 104–5, 276. *See also* discre-
    tionary authority, and discre-
    tionary contexts
bureaucratic culture, 221
bureaucratic representation, 5–6, 105;

as active representation, 6; as
    passive representation, 6. *See also*
    bureaucratic autonomy, and
    discretion
bureaucratic structure, 209, 233–37,
    241, 259, 260, 263, 271. *See also*
    political control of bureaucracy
bureaucratic values, 115; and allocative
    efficiency, 163; and efficiency, 163,
    260; and equity, 260 (*see also*
    bureaucratic representation); im-
    portance of mission to, 134; risk
    and, 33, 57, 300

capture theory, 113, 126
clientele, 210, 299. *See also* bureau-
    cratic autonomy; bureaucratic rep-
    resentation
consensual rule making, 188–92, 200,
    204–5. *See also* administrative rule
    making

Department of Agriculture, 73, 240
Department of Education, 190
Department of Health, Education
    and Welfare, 212
Department of Justice, 236
Department of Veteran's Affairs, 256
discretionary authority, 266, 270, 271;
    and discretionary contexts, 46, 50,

349

discretionary authority (*continued*)
55, 56, 57, 71. *See also* bureaucratic
autonomy, and discretion
divided government, 47, 60

electoral connection, 112–14, 209
Environmental Protection Agency,
128, 187, 190, 192, 194, 197, 205,
233; activities of Office of Ground
Water and Drinking Water, 198

farm credit system, 237, 244; and
Farmers Home Administration,
245; and Federal Financing Bank,
237, 241; and Federal Home Loan
Bank Board, 237
Federal Advisory Committee Act of
1972, 189, 192
federalism, 209
Federal Aviation Administration,
190
Federal Communications Commission, 194, 197, 203
Federal Power Act of 1935, 128
federal reserve system, 73
Federal Trade Commission, 233
Fish and Wildlife Service, 194, 195,
197
Food and Drug Administration,
26–29, 116, 194

General Accounting Office, 187, 206,
212
goal conflict, 262, 298. *See also*
political control of bureaucracy;
principal-agent models
government reform movements: Financial Institutions Reform, Recovery, and Enforcement Act of
1989, 244; as Government Performance and Results Act, 160; as National Partnership for Reinventing
Government, 204
government-sponsored enterprises,
237, 240, 251, 255, 256

Hawthorne experiments, 13
Health Care Financing Administration, 194, 198

incremental decision making,
161–62
Internal Revenue Service, 277
Interstate Commerce Commission,
187
issue attention cycle, 118

Kefauver Amendments, 37

Majority Party Unicameral Core, 82,
85, 96
Medicaid, 211, 215, 216

National Advisory Council on Aging,
190
National Highway and Traffic Safety
Administration, 197
National Motor Carrier Advisory
Committee, 189–90
Negotiated Rulemaking Act of 1990,
189, 190. *See also* Administrative
Procedure Act; administrative rule
making
new institutionalism, 306
Nuclear Regulatory Commission,
190, 197, 233

Occupational Safety and Health Administration, 191, 200, 277; and
National Advisory Committee on
Occupational Safety and Health,
190

Office of Management and Budget,
    198
organizational change: as adaptation,
    162–64, 170, 178; due to asymmet-
    ric competition, 176, 177; as a
    function of bargaining, 42; due to
    competition, 163–64, 173–74, 179,
    182; as a result of imitation,
    178–82; the imitative model, 138; as
    organizational learning, 25; process
    of refinement, 170

parliamentary systems, 75–77
Party Coalition Unicameral Core, 87,
    88, 90, 96
Party-Free Bicameral Core, 92, 96
Party-Free Bicameral Executive Veto
    Core, 93, 94, 96
personnel recruitment, 303; and
    selection, 133
policy implementation, 42–46, 125,
    207–9, 221; in policy networks,
    303, 304; in policy subsystems, 303
political control of bureaucracy, 24,
    234, 242–43; through advisory
    committees, 196; Congress-cen-
    tered theories of, 5, 244; using ex
    ante controls, 236, 296; using
    ex post controls, 235–36; through
    hardwiring, 41, 69; use of monitor-
    ing, 8–9, 25, 235, 279; and police
    patrols, 8; procedural controls,
    297, 299 (*see also* Administrative
    Procedure Act). *See also* bureau-
    cratic structure
politics-administration dichotomy, 2
presidential systems, 75
principal-agent models, 7, 8, 9, 10,
    14, 19, 107, 133–36, 208, 211, 295,
    297, 299, 307; and delegation
    problems, 106, 125, 126; and effect
of agency expertise, 210; the en-
    hanced model (EPA), 135; and in-
    formation asymmetry, 4, 74, 210,
    297–98; role of limited informa-
    tion, 233; shirking behavior and,
    134–35
privatization, 13, 164
procedural environments, 188. *See also*
    administrative procedures
Progressive era, 2–3
proverbs of administration, 3
public choice theory, 6, 260, 261, 264,
    271; market-based reforms and,
    263, 272; public schools and, 262–
    64; as public sector reform, 259

regulatory negotiation, 196, 203
rent-seeking behavior, 106
Rivers and Harpers Act of 1899, 128
Rural Electrification Administration,
    240

Safe Drinking Water Act, 198
Sallie Mae, 245, 251, 256
Securities and Exchange Commis-
    sion, 194, 233
separation of powers, 2, 63
signaling, 277–82
Small Business Administration, 244
Social Security Administration, 157,
    218; and Quality Assurance Pro-
    gram, 226; Supplemental Security
    Income, 208, 211
span of control, 303
street-level bureaucracy, 207, 209–13
supervisor role: as coordinator, 138; as
    facilitator, 278; with regard to sub-
    ordinates' preferences, 133

task environment, 221; complexity of,
    47, 62

Temporary Aid to Needy Families,
    213, 216, 223. *See also* Aid to Fami-
    lies with Dependent Children
transaction cost theory, 10–12, 204,
    298

vertical transfer, 211–14, 217
voluntary compliance, 280–88.
    See also political control of
    bureaucracy; principal-agent
    models